Systems Design in the Fourth Generation

OBJECT-BASED DEVELOPMENT USING d®BASE

Wiley Series in Computing and Information Processing

Hugh J. Watson, University of Georgia-Athens, Series Editor

Blissmer. Introducing Computers: Concepts, Systems, and Applications, 1990-1991 Edition
Burch and Grudnitski. Information Systems: Theory and Practice, 5th
FitzGerald. Business Data Processing: Basic Concepts, Security, and Design, 3rd
FitzGerald. and FitzGerald. Fundamental Systems Analysis: Using Structured Analysis and Design Techniques, 3rd
Lehman. Systems Design in the Fourth Generation: Object-Based Programming Using dBASE
Nelson. End-User Computing: Concepts, Issues, and Applications
Panko. End-User Computing: Management, Applications, and Technology
Stern and Stern. Computing with End-User Applications
Stern and Stern. Computing with End-User Applications and BASIC
Vazsonyi. Information Systems for Management
Watson and Blackstone. Computer Simulation, 2nd
Wysocki and Young. Information Systems: Management Practices in Action
Wysocki and Young. Information systems: Management Principles in Action

Systems Design in the Fourth Generation

OBJECT-BASED DEVELOPMENT USING d®BASE

John A. Lehman

UNIVERSITY OF ALASKA

John Wiley & Sons

NEW YORK / CHICHESTER / BRISBANE / TORONTO / SINGAPORE

Acquisitions Editor: Joe Dougherty
Designer: Laura Nicholls
Production Supervisor: Gay Nichols
Digital Production Supervisor: Ann Louise Stevens

Library of Congress Cataloging in Publication Data:

Lehman, John A.
Systems design in the fourth generation using dBASE III and dBASE IV / John A. Lehman

p. cm. —(Wiley series in business computing and information processing)
Includes index.
ISBN 0-471-52752-1
1. System design. 2. dBase III (Computer program) 3. dBase IV (Computer program) I. Title. II. Series.

QA76.9.S88L45 1991
005.75‘65—dc20 90-48154
CIP

Printed in the United States of America

10 9 8 7 6 5 4 3 2 1

ABOUT THE AUTHOR

John Lehman has worked as a user manager, an applications programmer, a systems programmer, and a software project manager. He is the author of the first article on programming languages for personal computers, as well as the first articles on business use of personal computers, and the first personal computer programs for financial analysis and statistical analysis. His doctoral dissertation was the first integrated software system, combining financial analysis, statistics, database management, and presentation graphics. He has consulted and/or taught for IBM, UNISYS (formerly Sperry and Burroughs), Control Data, Honeywell, and several noncomputer Fortune 500 companies. He has taught at the University level since 1973 and beginning in 1983 has taught program design in the American Assembly of Collegiate Schools of Business summer MIS Faculty Development Institute. He is also a Certified Management Accountant (CMA).

ACKNOWLEDGMENTS

I am grateful to many people for their contributions to the development of this book. I owe particular thanks to the following:

At the AACSB MIS Faculty Development Institute, to Gary Dickson and Chuck Hickman for giving me the chance to refine these materials on 350 faculty guinea pigs, and to the guinea pigs themselves.

At the University of Alaska, to Peter Biesiot, and Mike Rice for providing an environment where I could write 50 pages a week, and to my students for a great deal of useful feedback.

At the University of Michigan, to Jim Fry, Tom Schrieber, Dan Teichrow, and especially to Dennis Severance for inflicting me on the academic world.

At the University of Minnesota, to Gordon Davis and Sal March for extensive advice, encouragement, and assistance.

In the Real World, to Tim Fargo at UNISYS, and especially to the two successful MIS practitioners in my family: my sister Lee whose systems from London to San Francisco and from Miami to Valdez come in on time and under budget, and my wife Lisa who is a Real Programmer on Real Computers (mainframes), and only occasionally believes that IBM stands for "In Bleakest Mordor."

And finally to Don Barker, College of Business Administration, Gonzago University, Spokane, Washington; Jennifer L. Wagner, MSIS Program Director, Roosevelt University, Chicago, Illinois; Mark A. Schlesinger, College of Management, University of Massachusetts, Boston, Massachusetts; Hugh Watson, Department of Management, University of Georgia, Athens, Georgia; and Cyrus Azarbod, Computer Science Department, Mankata State University, Mankato, Minnesota for their efforts as reviewers in helping turn a raw manuscript into a much more useful text!

John A. Lehman

PREFACE

This is a book on modern programming practices as they are adapted to fourth generation languages (described in Chapter 4). They are here applied to a specific fourth generation language: dBASE-III+ and IV. This is not a book on DBASE programming. Rather, it is a book on analysis and design in a fourth generation environment using DBASE examples. Although this book may be used as a programming textbook in conjunction with the dBASE manuals, its main contribution is language-independent.

There are two audiences for this book: students of programming (primarily in business schools) and people who do programming and wish to learn more about it.

For students (and their instructors!) the book has several advantages over competing textbooks. First, it teaches modern techniques of systems analysis and program design in the context of fourth generation languages. In so doing, it combines instruction in modern systems analysis and programming practices with instruction in what is probably the most popular fourth generation language, and with instruction in business systems. Additional advantages are the use of a consistent case study (which teaches about business programming), and the testing that the book (and the teaching method that it represents) has undergone. An additional and unique aspect of this book is that it avoids the use of acronyms except where their non-use would be in blatant conflict with industry terminology.

One of the problems encountered in teaching programming is the need for potential managers and programmers to learn three things:

- How Business Information Systems Work,
- How to Design Programs,
- How to Implement Programs.

Most of us do not have the luxury of three separate courses in these areas. However, this text covers all three. The case study, which is integrated with the discussion throughout, teaches about common transaction-driven systems in business—customer orders, purchase orders, inventory management, billing, and so forth. This provides the student with a knowledge of what such information flows are like and practice in creating programs that are of immediate use. Thus, an instructor who wishes to teach programming, program design, and business systems in the same course need use only one text.

A second advantage of this text is that, unlike existing books on program design, this one modifies the use of analysis and design methods to fit in a fourth generation, database-oriented environment. Many of the methodologies developed for COBOL and file-processing environments are irrelevant, or require modification when they are used with higher-level languages. Specifically, this text integrates data modeling techniques from database design and event-driven analysis techniques. The techniques taught in this book have been proved in both personal computer and mainframe programming environments, using a variety of fourth generation languages.

The course on which this book is based has been taught at both large and small schools, at both the graduate and undergraduate level. It has also been taught to programmers and managers at a number of Fortune 500 companies. In addition, for seven years it has been taught to faculty from around North America at the American Assembly of Collegiate Schools of Business (AACSB) MIS Faculty Development Institute in Minneapolis. This text incorporates suggestions from all of these students (thank you all!)

For the other audience, that of people who are not in school but who wish to develop additional skills, probably on a personal computer, the advantages are much the same. The text covers both how to design programs and how to program in dBASE III and dBASE IV. Most of the content of the book will continue to be valid no matter what computer system one uses. In addition, the case study provides a ready-to-use system for much business programming.

John A. Lehman

CONTENTS

Section 1

INTRODUCTION AND BACKGROUND

Chapter 1

INTRODUCTION

HOW THIS BOOK CAME TO BE

This is a book about modern programming practices as applied to a specific fourth generation language—dBASE (versions III and IV). By way of introduction to the need both for modern programming practices and for fourth generation languages, let me explain how I got involved in this field.

Most readers, whether students or practitioners, are familiar with the process of registering students at a university—a somewhat specialized version of the general task of entering customer work orders. Most major universities put this operation onto punched cards in the 1930s or 1940s, and until the late 1960s, registration was generally done in some sort of batch mode.

In 1968, the university in question decided to produce an on-line registration system. Since everything in data processing needs an acronym, let us call this CRISP (Computerized Registration In Spite of Problems). The estimate in 1968 was that the system would take three years to develop, require four programmers, one manager, and cost approximately $300,000. It was also estimated that 20 operators would be required to run the system during registration.

In the early 1970s, my second job out of college was as registration supervisor. CRISP was brought on-line in 1975—four years late. Total cost to this time was around $1,500,000. A major hardware upgrade had been required, and 30 operators were now needed. Under the old batch system, registration had required about an hour. Under the new on-line system, the average wait to register was approximately nine hours. When high-level administrators showed up to see what was happening, students spat on them. The director of registration had a nervous breakdown and spent the rest of the week at a terminal checking registering students for library fines. I took his job. The system development life-cycle for CRISP is illustrated in Figure 1-1. Ironically, within 10 years the data processing department, which had developed CRISP, was using it as an example of a successful system design effort—marred only by a minor database path specification error that had caused problems at first.

- Wild Enthusiasm
- Disillusionment
- Total Confusion
- Search for the guilty
- Punishment of the innocent
- Promotion of the nonparticipants

FIGURE 1-1 Real-world system development lifecycle.

The next year I went back to school to get an MBA and learn what went wrong. At the time, I thought my experience was uniquely terrible. I soon learned it was normal for large computer projects. About the same time, personal computers and fourth generation languages appeared. Hence, this book.

GOALS

This book has two goals:

- To describe modern programming techniques as applied to database-oriented fourth generation languages.
- To describe how to use DBASE III and IV to create successful programs using those techniques.

A major problem in computer use over the years has been that rapid changes in technology make knowledge obsolete. A given piece of hardware becomes obsolete in a few years, and new versions of software mandate significant relearning every year or two. Much of the reason for this problem is that we traditionally learn details rather than principles. A course devoted only to the syntax of a particular programming language becomes obsolete when that language changes. A widespread example of this problem is the large number of applications programmers in industry who have learned COBOL rather than computer programming, and who therefore find that a change to more modern languages would make most of their knowledge obsolete.

This book presents an alternative approach. Although it is intended to help you learn to develop complex systems in dBASE III and IV, 90% of the contents of the book involve principles of program design that are valid for any database-oriented language. Thus, as the dBASE standard changes over time, most of what you learn in this book will continue to be valid. What is important is not the syntax of a particular language but rather the principles of program design which that language instantiates. These are important for several reasons.

PROGRAM DESIGN

Why this different approach to programming? After all, programming textbooks since the 1950s have concentrated on language syntax and have left design issues for advanced courses. The

Year	Nominal Price	Price in 1988 $
1965	$1.50	$5.13
1975	$0.04	$0.085
1985	$0.0001	$0.0001
1987	$0.00009	$0.00009
1990	$0.00007	$0.00007

FIGURE 1-2 Price per byte of memory.

reasons why it is important to concentrate on design rather than syntax arise from both technical and organizational problems.

The first problem (or more correctly, opportunity) is the precipitous drop in computer hardware costs. You have probably seen the advertisements that boast that if cars had evolved like computers, a Rolls Royce would cost a nickle and get two million miles per gallon. Figure 1-2 shows some comparative prices for computer hardware, adjusted for inflation.

This rapid decline in hardware prices has two impacts on program design. First, the goals of programming are changed. Many programming techniques were developed at a time when computer memory and computer speed were far more expensive than they are today. As a result, these techniques save hardware costs at the expense of people costs. As we shall see in the next few paragraphs, this is backwards with current technology.

An additional impact of declining hardware cost comes from increased demand. As an example, in the twelve years between 1961 and 1973, Digital Equipment Corporation produced about 20,000 of their popular PDP-8 minicomputers—the most popular machine of its day [DEC 1973]. In 1987, IBM produced more than 1,000,000 PS/2 personal computers in six months—and this represented less than 40% of the market for personal computers alone during that period [PC Week 1987]. All of these computers being used by more and more people means that the demand for programs is far higher than it used to be, and the demand is growing exponentially each year.

Additionally, these new computers are increasingly powerful. This means that they require more complex software. In 1974, for example, an IBM 370/158 mainframe provided service for over 100 users and was catered to by a staff of more than a dozen professionals. Today, the same computing power sits on my desk.

```
//FORT          EXEC   PGM=IEYFORT,REGION=100K
//SYSPRINT      DD     SYSOUT=A
//SYSPUNCH      DDS    YSOUT=B
//SYSLIN        DD     SNAME=&LOADSET
//              DISP=(MOD,PASS),UNIT=SYSSQ,
//              PACE=(80,(200,100),RLSE),DCB=BLKSIZE=80
//SYSIN         DD     *
```

FIGURE 1-3 IBM 360 JCL (circa 1968)

As hardware costs have fallen, software development costs have increased. This is due to two reasons: the cost of programmers is higher, and programs are far more complex than was true in the past. One of the reasons for this complexity is that as computers become more integrated into everyday work, they must become easier to use. As a result, modern programs devote a very large portion of their code to implementing a more-or-less friendly user interface. Fifteen years ago this would have been considered a waste of time; now even user-group freeware is user friendly. Consider, for example, the difference between the Job Control Language (JCL) required to run a program on an IBM 360 (Figure 1-3) and doing the same task by moving the cursor over the file with the mouse and clinking the mouse button twice on a Macintosh—and consider that the IBM 360 probably served several hundred people, whereas the Macintosh serves one.

Software development costs do not tell the whole story, however. Depending on the organization, between 70% and 90% of software cost is incurred in program maintenance—the modification of existing programs. Some of this maintenance is required because bugs are discovered in the programs, but most is required because user needs change, the business environment changes, or the technical environment changes. To make the problem worse, traditional program development methods produce programs that are

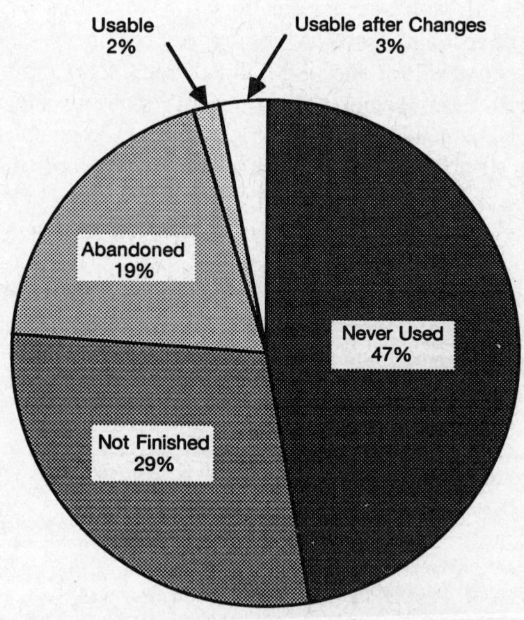

FIGURE 1-4 GAO Software project study.

difficult to maintain. One of the major goals of modern program design, therefore, is to produce programs that are easy to maintain and to modify.

All of these changes in the computer environment are a prelude to the basic problem—software design is not a reliable process. The registration system described earlier is not unique: almost all large software projects are

- Over budget
- Late
- Not what the user expected.

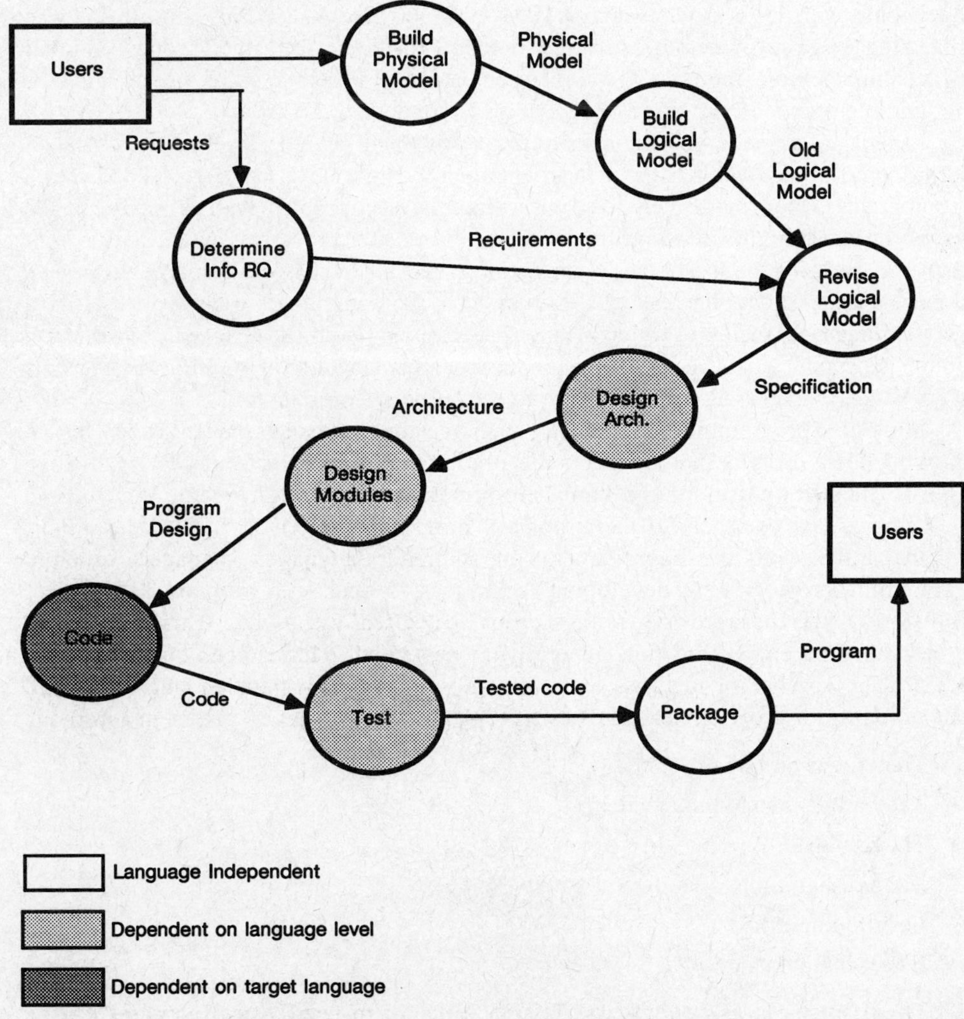

FIGURE 1-5 The systems development life-cycle.

Figure 1-4 shows the results of a GAO study of federal software projects. Note that 95% of them were failures from the user point of view. Large systems that are very late are traditional; there is even a technical term for such commercial products: "vaporware." Contemporary examples include the FAA airspace modernization system [*IEEE Computer* 1987], OS/2, Lotus 123 version 3, and dBASE IV. Modern programming practices have been developed to help deal with these problems.

MODERN PROGRAMMING PRACTICES

Modern programming practices began in the late 1960s in response to a series of major cost and schedule overruns in projects such as IBM's OS-360 [Brooks 1975]. At this time, it was realized that large software projects were somehow different from smaller ones, and that new techniques were required. Two different areas of research gave rise to modern programming practices: language design and system design.

Language design focused originally on the development of higher level languages and on what has come to be known as "structured programming." Higher level languages helped reduce large programs to more moderately sized ones. Since the basic problem with large projects has always been that they grow too large for the human information processing system to deal with (Chapter 2), reducing the size of the system by increasing the level of the language has always had good results. Today, for example, even systems programming is usually done in third generation languages such as C, and application programming is almost universally done in third or fourth generation languages rather than in the assembly language of yore. However, as the level of language increased, the size of the projects increased even more.

Structured programming focused not on increasing the level of the languages, but on improving their design. In retrospect, the improvements involved adapting language design to the weaknesses of the human information processing system. While these developments have been helpful, their impact on programmer productivity has been minor.

In parallel with the improvements in computer languages, managers of large programming projects were developing techniques to deal with program and project complexity. Today these are often referred to as "structured" techniques. "Structured" here is a content-free expression that generally means good. These techniques began as piecemeal approaches or methods and were subsequently put together into integrated methodologies for program design. They have the following characteristics in common:

- They focus on large systems.
- They are language independent.
- They result in

  More design time.

  Less coding time.

  Easier maintenance.

The focus on large systems is primarily a matter of need—small systems can be developed using traditional programming techniques. It is only when systems grow so large that a single programmer cannot understand them that more modern techniques are required. However, even for medium-sized projects, the techniques can be quite helpful. For small projects, the extra overhead generally gets in the way.

At first view, these techniques might appear to be inappropriate for a PC-based language such as dBASE. However, applications requiring several thousand lines of dBASE code are not uncommon. The size of such applications, coupled with the improved design, the greater probability of getting the system right, and the improved maintainability are reasons enough to use modern programming techniques. In addition, skill in using such techniques is transferable to other environments (such as mainframe SQL) because of language independence.

Language independence refers to the fact that most of the program-design stage does not depend on a particular language. Figure 1-5 illustrates the system development life-cycle for a large application; only the coding phase is language specific.

More design time is a feature of the new approaches that is at odds with the traditional approach of starting to program immediately—then figuring out what the system has to do. There is a proverb that "there's never time to do it right, but always time to do it over." Compared with traditional programming, the techniques here call for a great deal of effort to be put into the front end of a project. The payoff is to reduce the actual "programming" or coding time substantially. One result is that the program is more likely to do what it is supposed to do; easier maintenance is another.

Basis for Modern Program Design

A program architecture (Figure 1-5) is the overall design of the program. To quote one of the founders of modern programming techniques, it is: "deciding which components, interconnected in which way will best solve some well-specified problem" [Constantine & Yourdon 1977]. The program architecture is the equivalent of the outline for a book: it specifies what the parts are and how they fit together.

Design of individual modules is what many people consider "program design"—deciding what operations, carried out on what data, will perform a specified function. This is algorithm selection, the sort of task for which tools like flowcharts were developed.

Coding of the modules is what traditionally is considered "programming": the statement of an algorithm in some computer language. If the previous steps have been carried out properly, this is a clerical task.

Design for Fourth Generation Languages in a Database Environment

Modern information systems are designed in an environment where many applications share a single integrated database. On the other hand, most traditional approaches to program design assume that each program works with its own special-purpose file(s); since the program translates between some document and a file used only by that program, the file can be structured to reflect the structure of the document. Figure 1-6 shows the contrast between the old and new approaches. In the old approach, the data in the computer is organized based on the outside documents, and the program structures reflect the document structures.

With a modern approach, the data inside the system is integrated and ordered in a manner usable by all applications, and the programs translate between this internal data

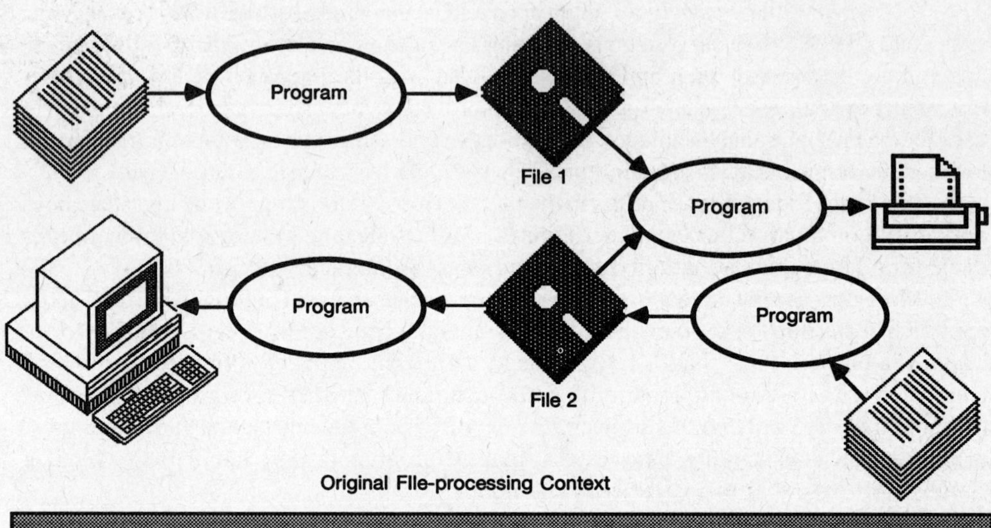

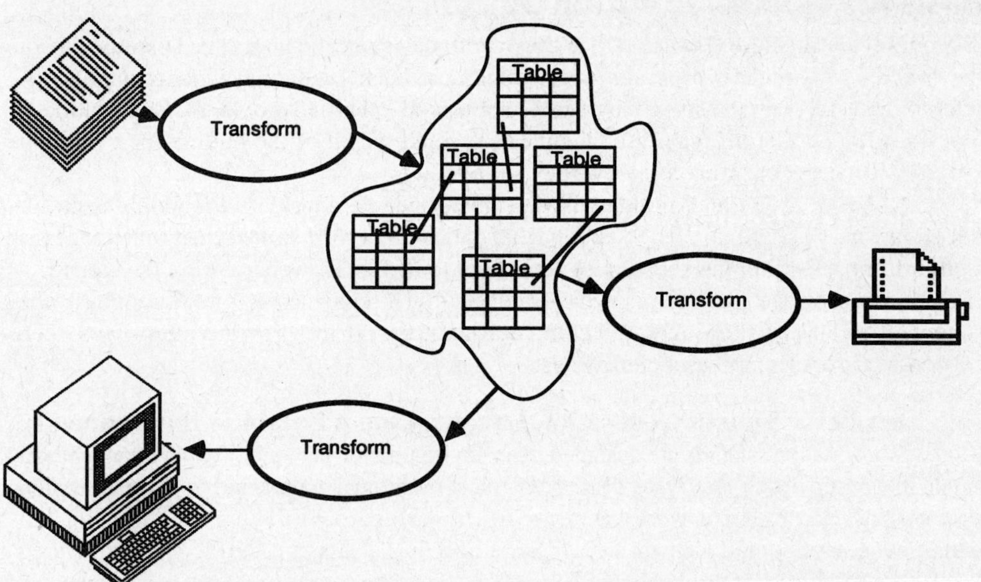

FIGURE 1-6 End-user view of the program design task.

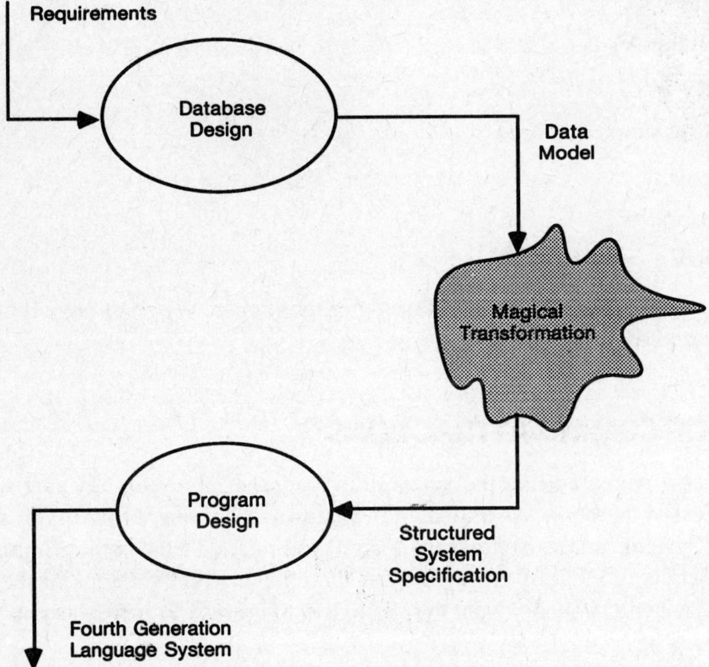

FIGURE 1-7 Missing link in the system development life-cycle.

structure and the structure of the documents outside the system. The internal structure is designed to make the data usable by all programs, and thus that data structure does not reflect the structure of an individual program.

This database approach causes problems for many programmers, who have learned to design programs around special-purpose files. Figure 1-7 shows one of the basic problems with modern program design; we have one set of design techniques for database design and another set for program design, and the two are not compatible. This book shows how to turn the magic of Figure 1-7 into a systematic procedure.

SUMMARY

The modern programming practices described in this book are the result of 20 years of effort in the computer industry to

- Improve the design of computer languages,
- Develop design and management techniques for large programming projects,
- Combine the above into integrated program development methodologies.

The objectives of the techniques are to improve program

- Reliability,
- Maintainability,
- Modifiability,

and to produce systems that are

- Lower cost,
- On time, and
- As ordered.

Such systems can be built in any computer languages. We shall be building them in DBASE III+ and DBASE IV.

PREVIEW OF COMING ATTRACTIONS

The previous few pages outline the system development methodology that we shall be using for the rest of the book. As indicated in Figure 1-5, there are four major steps in the methodology: systems analysis, program design, coding, and final steps. Figures 1-8 to 1-11 show the details of each of these, and list the chapters and sections of the book that discuss them. You will probably want to refer to these figures frequently as you go through

SYSTEMS ANALYSIS (BUILD SYSTEM MODEL)

Identify objects in real-world environment. (Chapter 5)

- Define permanent entities based on objects.
- Build preliminary **entity-relationship diagram.**
- Identify attributes of permanent entities (data elements).
- Document attributes in **data dictionary.**

Identify events and actions in real-world environment. (Chapter 6)

- Define transient entities spawned by each event.
- Updata **entity-relationship diagram.**
- Identify attributes of transient entities (data elements).
- Document attributes in **data dictionary.**

Refine the specification of attributes (Chapter 7)
Produce a physical data dictionary of data elements
Normalize attributes (Chapter 8)
Define views appropriate to end users (Chapter 9)

FIGURE 1-8 Outline of systems analysis steps.

PROGRAM DESIGN (BUILD PROGRAM MODEL)

Determine menu structure from user task description. (Chapter 9)
Define screens and reports appropriate to transactions. (Chapter 9)

Describe menus on **structure chart**. (Chapter 10)
Determine object types from data flow diagram. (Chapter 11)
Complete **structure chart** from object types. (Chapter 11)
Evaluate preliminary design using program measures. (Chapter 12)

For each process on **structure chart**, use **action diagrams** to (Section IV)

- Define windows appropriate to entity.
- Link views to screens or reports.
- Link screens to window.
- Build menus.
- Build higher level logic based on order constraints.

FIGURE 1-9 Outline of program design steps.

CODING (SECTION V)

- Create relations based on permanent entities.
- Create relations based ontransient entities.
- Create screen definitions.
- Create report definitions.
- Create views.
- Create windows.
- Create other program-oriented objects (menus, buttons, scroll bars, etc.).

For each action diagram:

- Translate action diagram into coded modules to manipulate data and objects.

For each coded module:

- Test independently using integration testing. (Chapter 20)

FIGURE 1-10 Outline of coding steps.

FINAL STEPS

- Perform higher order testing. (Chapter 20)
- Package and tune to fit hardware constraints. (Chapter 21)

FIGURE 1-11 Outline of final steps.

the text; they will help you keep track of where you are in the forest when you are lost among the trees.

In each of these figures, items in **boldface** type are types of abstract notations that we will be using for design instead of program code. Chapter 2 explains the reasons for jumping through all of these hoops in terms of how people solve problems. Chapter 3 introduces the problem context for the business systems that we use throughout the text. Chapter 4 introduces dBASE and fourth generation languages.

QUESTIONS AND EXERCISES

1. Why should traditional programming techniques be modernized?
   a. Because software design is totally dependent on the syntax of the programming language used.
   b. Because hardware costs are increasingly more expensive.
   c. Because computer hardware has become much cheaper and more powerful.
   d Because computers have evolved like cars.
2. Modern programming practices result in
   a. More coding time.
   b Less design time.
   c. More dependence on the programming language in use.
   d. More design time and less coding time.
3. The modern database approach to programming is difficult for some because
   a. The database approach is language dependent.
   b. The database approach has set design techniques for database design and another set of design techniques for programs.
   c. The database approach is designed around special purpose-files.
   d. The database approach uses only special-purpose files.
4. Almost all large software projects are
   a. Under budget, early, what the user expected.
   b. Under budget, early, not what the user expected.
   c. Over budget, early, what the user expected.
   d Over budget, late, not what the user expected.
5. The objectives of modern programming techniques are to
   a. Improve program cost.
   b. Improve program modifiability.
   c. Improve program speed.
   d Please the professor.
6. Computer prices have gone _________, while quality and capacity have gone _________.
   a Down, down.
   b. Down, up.

   c. Up, down.
   d. Up, up.
7. Language independence refers to
   a. Choosing among the many computer languages currently available.
   b. A design that doesn't depend on a particular language.
   c. Being able to use many languages in a design.
   d Being able to transfer a program to another machine.
8. The database approach
   a. Designs programs around specific files.
   b. Is easily and joyously used by programmers.
   c. Organizes the data to be used by any application.
   d. Is organized by how it's supposed to look in reports.
9. Vaporware is
   a. Software that is behind schedule.
   b. Hardware so small & quiet, you don't know it's there.
   c. Outdated software.
   d. Outdated hardware.
10. What two factors have caused software development to increase?
   a. The decrease in hardware cost and increase in hardware demand.
   b. The cost of programmers is higher and programs are more complex.
   c. The programming is fairly easy and there are more vendors willing to sell software.
   d. There are more programmers out there and they have unionized.
11. Structured programming is focused on
   a. Increasing the level of the language.
   b. Making the programs more complex to decode.
   c. Improving the design of the language.
   d. Making programs more detailed.
12. For what type of environment is a modern information system designed?
   a. Where many applications share a single database.
   b. Where each application has its own database to use.
   c. Where each terminal has its own database to use.
   d. Where every application is done on paper and then input into the computer.

DISCUSSION QUESTIONS

1. Explain the impact of falling hardware costs on program design.
2. Discuss program design and what helped bring it about.
3. List four major steps in systems development.

REFERENCES

Brooks, F. *The Mythical Man-month*, Addison-Wesley, Reading, MA, 1975.

Constantine, L., and E. Yourdon. *Structured Design*, Prentice-Hall, Englewood Cliffs, NJ, 1979.

IEEE Computer. 20(2) (entire issue).

DEC. *Small Computer Handbook.* Digital Equipment Corp., Maynard, MA, 1973.

PC Week 4,(46), 1.

Chapter 2

DESIGN

CHAPTER GOALS

- Learn the reasons for procedures used later in the book.
- Be able to choose among competing approaches based on their fit with human information processing.

DESIGN AS A HUMAN ACTIVITY

Given that the title of this book is *Systems Design in the Fourth Generation*, it should be obvious that design is an important part of the programmer's toolkit. In fact, most of the modern programming practices discussed in this book are simply adaptations to the programming environment of common human strategies for coping with complexity. In this chapter we look at some of the limits of human information processing, and how several other professions (writing and engineering, to be exact) have dealt with them. The responses in these other professions will be compared with those to be introduced in this book.

Limitations of the Human Information Processing System

Figure 2-1 shows the overall structure of the human information processing system. The parts that are relevant from our point of view are short-term memory and processing. Long-term memory is the repository for all of the information that we accumulate during a lifetime. Short-term memory is used for the actual processing of information. The channel for information transfer between short-term and long-term memory requires a relatively large time, especially when the transfer is from short-term to long-term memory (memorization).

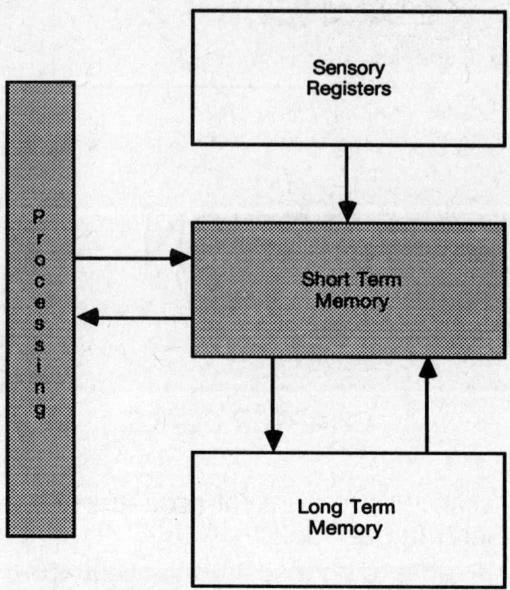

FIGURE 2-1 The human information processing system.

The two aspects of short-term memory which most concern us are speed of transfer and capacity. Transfer between long- and short-term memory is relatively slow—measured in seconds. Transfer between the outside world (via the sensory registers) and short-term memory is quite rapid. Hence, external aids, whether computer based or paper based, can extend the capacity of short-term memory.

This extension is necessary because the capacity of short-term memory is quite limited—five to nine chunks of data with an average of seven. When dealing with interruptions, the capacity goes down to about three chunks. What is a chunk of data? Basically, anything that your mind regards as a whole rather than a group of parts. For example, to me the telephone area code for Alaska is a single chunk: "907." For most people from outside of Alaska, it is probably three chunks: "9," "0," and "7." When you know how to spell a word, it is a single chunk. If you do not know how to spell it, it is a series of chunks, each corresponding to a letter. One of the major things you do when you "learn" is to practice a subject until you can deal with much larger chunks of information than can a novice in the same subject.

One way to do this is to use hierarchy. In fact, hierarchy is the key strategy for dealing with the limitations on the capacity of short-term memory. Hierarchy means that you structure ideas in the form of a tree. Figure 2-2 illustrates the concept, showing some of the hardware components of an IBM-style personal computer. The basic benefit of hierarchy is that when you deal with a topic, you are simultaneously dealing with all of the topics located farther down the tree. Moreover, you can ignore all of the branches of the tree that do not pertain to your problem.

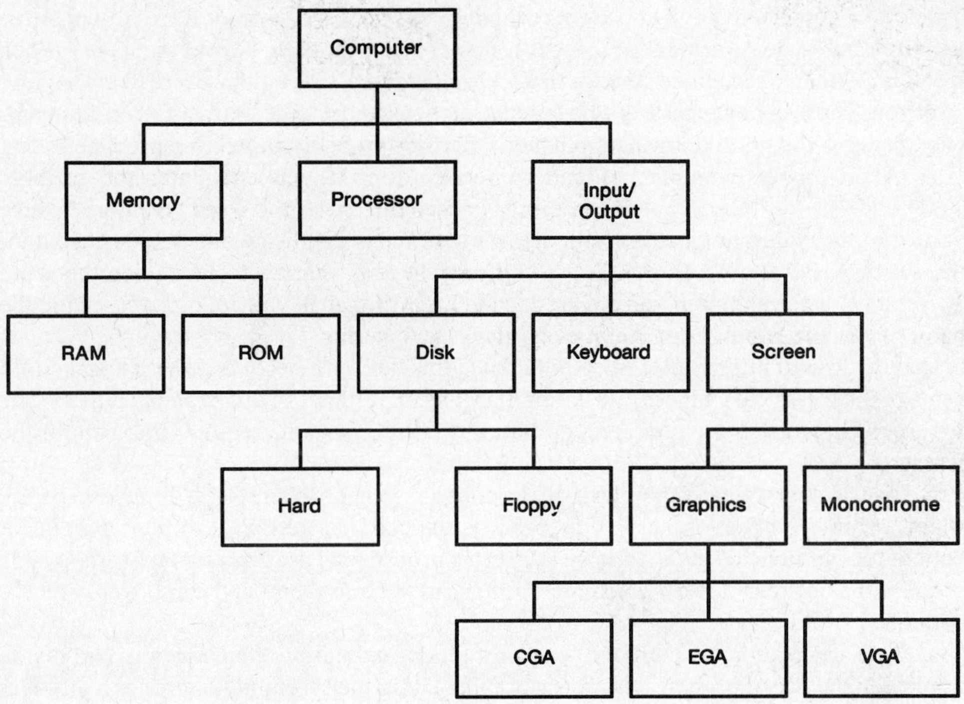

FIGURE 2-2 Example of a hierarchy.

Figure 2-3 illustrates one of the common forms of hierarchy: that of biological classification. The problem here is that there are millions of different species of life on earth. Organizing these life forms into a hierarchy lets us identify a particular example by playing, as it were, 20 questions rather than 20 million questions. Let us walk (literally) through a short example.

Suppose that one August day you are walking through a colorful autumn blueberry patch in the interior of Alaska when you spot a brown object ahead. You wish to identify it. Going through the various species of life on earth sequentially, starting with aardvark, would be rather time consuming. The object moves, and there is no wind—hence, it is an animal. Phylum Chordata, Class Mammalia (since it has brown fur). Order is Carnivora, Family Ursidae. Genus is Ursus. It has a hump at the shoulders and a dished face, so species is Arctos. Since it is in the interior rather than on the coast, subspecies is horribilis. Given that Ursus Arctos horribilis, also known as the grizzly bear, is noted for not taking kindly to sharing its blueberries, perhaps it would be the better part of valor to continue the walk in reverse—slowly.

This example brings us to another characteristic of the human information processing system: the processing part is very good at pattern recognition. Pattern recognition is being able to cut through extraneous details and recognize the underlying essence of something.

The reason people are good at pattern recognition as opposed to other forms of cognitive activity (such as doing arithmetic) probably dates back to the early days of the species when it was important to recognize patterns that were either good to eat or that were likely to think so of you. Those of our ancestors who failed to recognize that large, brown-furred, humped-back patterns did not like to share blueberry patches probably failed to reproduce.

A few more examples of pattern recognition. If you encounter the scribble memory, you can probably recognize it as the word "memory," since you know the underlying pattern both of the letters and of English words. If you encounter the scribble peroratio, it may be a bit harder to recognize the word "peroratio," since although you are used to the Latin alphabet, you are probably not in the habit of reading handwritten Latin every day. Deciphering 食色性也 is probably close to impossible, since both the "alphabet" (Chinese) and the language (4th century B.C. classical Chinese) are unfamiliar. The importance of this example is that while we are innately good at pattern recognition, expertise in an area requires that patterns be learned.

Just as hierarchy is the classical response to our problems with limited-capacity short-term memory, so the use of graphics is the classical response to our strengths at pattern recognition. There is a reason why most professions use charts and diagrams: it is because the user can absorb much more information from them, and can better perceive patterns.

One strategy that is common to almost all design and problem solving, and that is implied in the use of graphics, is abstraction: isolating the essential features of a problem from the irrelevant background. Let us suppose, for example, that you are a bush pilot standing on a gravel bar trying to estimate the height of a spruce tree at the end of the bar. The species of the tree, the size of the gravel, the season of the year, the thickness of the tree, and whether or not there are birds in the tree are all irrelevant; what is relevant is that the tree is one side and the gravel bar is the other side of a right triangle to which the rules of trigonometry apply. You cannot solve this problem if you have never learned the underlying abstract model (trigonometry), nor can you solve the problem if you cannot map the essential features of the real-world situation (the height of the tree and the number of paces on the gravel bar) into the features of the ideal model (lines and angles).

Kingdom
Phylum
Class
Order
Family
Genus
Species
Subspecies

FIGURE 2-3 Hierarchy of biological classification.

All of the discussion above is relevant to program design, rather than simply being entertaining, because programming is an activity that puts a tremendous strain on the abilities of the human information processing system. Large programs are arguably the most complex artifacts with which people have ever dealt. Many of the programming practices recommended in the rest of this book are recommended not because they are fashionable but because they cater to the strengths and avoid the weaknesses of the human information processing system.

An example of a form of activity that caters to our strengths is the practice of putting together a rough-cut first draft or prototype and then refining it. The Great American Novel does not spring whole from the author's head—people do not work that way (or work well that way). But rather than continuing to draw examples at random, let us look at how several other professions deal with this same problem of limited capacity information processing. It turns out that with the notation translated many of the techniques known as modern programming practices have a long history in other professions.

ANALOGS FROM OTHER PROFESSIONS

Compared to other human activities, computer programming is a new profession. This newness is a problem because of the demand for skilled programmers and the complexity of the projects made possible by computer systems. Users are unwilling to tolerate programming's groping toward being as a profession.

Historically, professions have developed in three stages. The first is the art stage, where practitioners develop the skills needed to solve practical problems. At this stage there are wide variations in skill levels. The second stage is *codification* of the skills of the best practitioners. The third stage is *rationalization*, where the codified skills are taught and integrated into a formal curriculum, as in modern professional education. The progression from art to rationalization historically has taken several centuries or more.

Programmers and their managers have looked to other professions, such as mathematics and engineering, in an attempt to short circuit the normal development time for a profession. A more useful analogy is English composition since every college graduate has been exposed to at least one course in it. From an information processing point of view, the problems faced in English composition are very similar to those faced in programming, and the solutions taught for composition since classical times are similar to the major tenants of the structured programming and structured design movements in programming.

Program Design and English Composition

Problem Similarity

The problem faced by both English composition and program design is that, as discussed above, the human information processing system has limited capacities. In both disciplines there is an extremely wide variety of situations that a practitioner must be able to describe and communicate. In both disciplines, the description should correspond to the structure of the problem and must be capable of communicating that problem structure to the target audience (whether human or machine). This situation is dealt with by developing a set of prototype solutions that fit all or most of the problems encountered by the profession. A practitioner learns these prototype solutions, then is faced with the problem of reformulation; fitting the messy real world problem into the learned solution.

English Composition

Problem Decomposition

The first problem writers face is problem decomposition: splitting a topic into its component parts. No reader can memorize every word. A reader can, however, remember an organized group of ideas. The writer's first task, therefore, is to break the situation down into main ideas and then package these ideas to communicate them most effectively.

A reader has difficulty concentrating on more than one idea at a time due to the limitations on the capacity of short-term memory. Writers have found that the most effective way to package ideas is one at a time, each in a separate paragraph. Further guidance to the audience can be furnished if each paragraph is identified with a topic sentence that describes the idea to which the paragraph as a whole is devoted.

Within a paragraph, a writer has guidelines to improve audience communication. These guidelines each serve to avoid overloading short-term memory. The most important of these guidelines are

- To limit the number of points in a paragraph.
- To use an easily understood method of sequencing the sentences in a paragraph,
- To limit the range of sentence structures used in a paragraph.

Limiting the number of points in a paragraph is an obvious way to deal with short-term memory limitations. Since short-term memory can hold seven plus or minus two "chunks" of information at one time, and since this capacity is reduced to three or four chunks when processing is not sequential, it is not surprising that textbooks on composition have long recommended three points as the normal number in a single paragraph, with seven the maximum.

Another approach to limiting the cognitive demands placed on readers is to use an easily understood method of sequencing the sentences in a paragraph. Recommended sequences are temporal or ordered by an obvious facet of problem structure. It is also recommended that sentences be tied together in structure as well as in content through use of such approaches as alliteration and parallelism.

Limiting the range of sentence structures used in a paragraph is characteristic of modern textbooks on English composition. An earlier fashion believed that readers would be most strongly swayed by highly complicated sentences (which they probably would not understand—this approach is not unheard of in modern academic writing). Modern authors recommend that communication will be most effective if a limited number of simple sentence structures are employed.

Limiting sentence structures works in two ways. First, there is use of a limited number of well-recognized sentence types. This contrasts with the elaborate and unusual sentence structures often used by writers in the legal profession, the government, and the social sciences. The advantage to simple sentences is that readers need expend less effort understanding what a sentence means. Second, there is limited use of subordinate clauses. The advantage is that this saves the reader much confusion keeping track of what subordinate clauses go with what other clauses. Subordinate clauses place considerable demands on the human information processing system, because they require nested processing, which reduces the already limited capacity of short-term memory by about half.

Architecture of the Composition

Architecture is used here in the sense of taking the parts and assembling them into a meaningful whole (often called arrangement in composition). Arrangement has three functions:

- To create a discussion of the problem as a whole.
- To emphasize the relationships of the ideas.
- To aid the reader in remembering what is said.

The two major principles employed in creating these structures are the use of *hierarchy* and the use of *standardized organizations.*

Hierarchy is important because it limits the number of chunks that must be held simultaneously in short-term memory. Just as a paragraph is devoted to one idea and made up of a limited number of related sentences, a subsection is devoted to one higher level idea and made up of a limited number of related paragraphs, and so on up the line.

The use of standardized organizations for compositions helps the author to decompose a problem into parts, and helps the reader to know what to expect and at what point to expect it. Several thousand years ago authors and textbook writers identified basic types of compositions and identified subtypes within each. These typologies have continued to this day. For each type, there are rules as to what the major parts should be and how each should be developed and delivered. Once an author has identified the type of composition involved, the division into sections and paragraphs and the recombination into a finished work can be relatively mechanical.

A reader who is familiar with these standard structures likewise derives a good deal of help from them. Knowing what the organization of the composition is likely to be enables a reader to pigeonhole parts of the composition and to keep track of the development of the argument.

Program Design

Program design faces the problem of taking a problem and describing its solution so that a computer can carry out the solution steps. The level at which the computer functions has always been at a lower, more detailed level than that at which people function; hence, problems for computer solution have had to be broken down into subproblems until each subproblem forms a manageable entity. These subprograms then have to be reassembled into complete programs.

Problem Decomposition

Problem decomposition is necessary because programmers suffer the same limitations in the capacity of short-term memory as do all human information processors. Modern programming practice calls for packaging programs into separate modules, each of which deals with one entire problem-related function. Further guidance is furnished if each module is identified by a name describing the function that module performs.

Within a module, a programmer has guidelines to improve comprehensibility and maintainability. These guidelines have in common that they avoid overloading short-term memory. The most important of these guidelines are (1) to limit the number of statements in a module, (2) to use an easily understood method of sequencing those statements, and (3) to limit the range of control structures used in a module.

Limiting the number of statements in a module is an obvious way to deal with short-term memory limitations. The usual recommendation is that a module should contain no more statements than can fit on a screen or on a sheet of paper. The reason for this limitation (rather than the five to nine statements that discussion of short-term memory would lead us to expect) is that statements that are visible are almost as rapidly recalled as those stored in short-term memory. On the other hand, a programmer can still only deal with a limited number of concepts at one time; therefore, it is recommended that the number of subordinate modules (subfunctions) or span of control be limited to the conventional seven plus or minus two.

Using an easily understood method of sequencing the statements in a module is another approach to limiting the cognitive demands placed on programmers. The traditional recommended sequence is temporal or procedural. Newer approaches call for organizing the modules around data structure.

Limiting the range of statement types used in a module is the major recommendation of structured programming. Using GOTO statements, it is possible to create a very large number of alternative approaches to a single problem solution. By limiting oneself to between three and six control structures (such as IF-THEN-ELSE), all problems can be solved in a much more consistent fashion. The advantages of these limitations are (1) a maintenance programmer need not expend a great deal of effort determining what a set of test and branch instructions actually does and (2) one can read a program without keeping track of how one got to the present location. An additional advantage is that all of the allowable control structures have one entry point and one exit. This minimizes the requirements for nested processing and its demands on the human information processing system. This topic is discussed at length in Chapter 14.

Architecture of the Program

Arrangement of the modules in program design involves taking the functions that have been packaged into modules and assembling them into a complete program. This assembly has two functions: (1) to create a solution to the problem as a whole and (2) to help current and future programmers understand how the program works. The two major principles employed in creating these program structures are the use of hierarchy and the use of standardized organizations.

Hierarchy is important for the same reasons that are discussed under English composition. Just as a module is devoted to one function and made up of a limited number of problem-related statements, a subprogram is devoted to one higher level function and is made up of a limited number of related modules, and so on up the line.

The use of standardized organizations for programs aids programmers in decomposing a problem into parts and aids future maintenance programmers in understanding what the program does and how it does it.

Aid in decomposing a program into parts is provided by known algorithms and standard design methodologies that are appropriate for different types of problem structures. Examples of the latter are Yourdon's transaction-based and transform-based design, Jackson's data-structure-based design, and design using standard program skeletons. Once the correct program organization has been identified, decomposition into modules and reassembly into complete programs is more or less mechanical. Section III is devoted to this topic.

Comparison

Both program design and English composition face the problem of pitting a limited-capacity human information processing system against an extremely wide variety of situations that a practitioner must be able to decompose into constituent parts and reassemble into a conventional format. In both disciplines, the description must correspond to the structure of the problem and must be capable of communicating that problem structure to the target audience.

Building blocks for both program design and English composition are conceptually similar. In both areas, the first skill required is that of mastering the use of correct statement types: sentences for English composition and programming language statement types for programmers. This is merely a prerequisite; no one seriously identifies the ability to write a correct sentence in a natural language as skill in writing, although the identification is often made (erroneously) in programming. At the next level in composition are the use of different forms of sentence structures, corresponding to control structures in programming. In English composition, this level of skill has traditionally been considered a required foundation rather than mastery of the subject matter.

The basic building block in English composition above the sentence level is the paragraph, corresponding to the module in programming. Good practice calls for a topic sentence in each paragraph, which corresponds to a module name. In designing a composition, one generally uses an outline to describe the hierarchical relationship of the

English Composition	Programming
Sentence	Statement
Sentence types	Control structures
Paragraph	Module
Topic sentence	Module name
Outline	Structure chart

FIGURE 2-4 English compositional and programming constructs.

paragraphs; a structure chart is used for the same purpose in program design. Figure 2-4 reviews these relationships.

Problem Decomposition

Approaches to problem decomposition between English composition and programming are very similar. Both rely on hierarchy to keep the number of concepts that must be considered at once within the range of the human information processing system. Both limit fanout, the number of subordinate modules that a module can have. Both rely on sequencing to improve comprehension; the sequencing rules in both instances are problem derived. For example, a story may describe events in the order in which they occurred. Both limit the range of control (or sentence) structures, generally aiming for simplicity. For both, this limitation facilitates chunking: fitting a number of elements into one slot in short-term memory. Finally, both disciplines use standard prototypes and associated methodologies of decomposition to simplify the processing load on the designer.

Architecture (Arrangement) of the Solution

Approaches to creating structures for English composition and programming also have many basic similarities. Both aim ultimately at deriving the structure of the solution from that of the problem. Strict problem-derived structures in English composition and the related functional decomposition in programming are considered the most flexible approach. However, they are not teachable in either field except by practice and are associated with a considerable degree of skill. Therefore, both fields make extensive use of standard structures that can be learned by beginners and applied to problems where they fit. Both fields share the related difficulties of having problems forced to fit ill-chosen standard solutions.

Program Design and Engineering

This section examines two additional design concepts that have been borrowed from engineering for use in program design: the use of

- a graphical notation, and
- black boxes and controlled interfaces.

The use of a *graphical design notation* (block diagrams, schematic diagrams, blueprints) for as many design stages as possible takes advantage of the human information processing system's strength at pattern matching. Since people are able to "chunk" pictures more easily than verbal descriptions, the use of diagrams increases the capacity of short-term memory and thus the amount of detail with which an individual can cope.

A *black box* is a part of a system where the inputs and outputs and what is done (the processing) are known, but nothing is known about how the processing is carried out. Controlled interfaces means that there is minimum connection between different parts of the system. The use of black boxes and controlled interfaces is another approach to reducing the complexity of a problem; it allows us to isolate the different parts of the system.

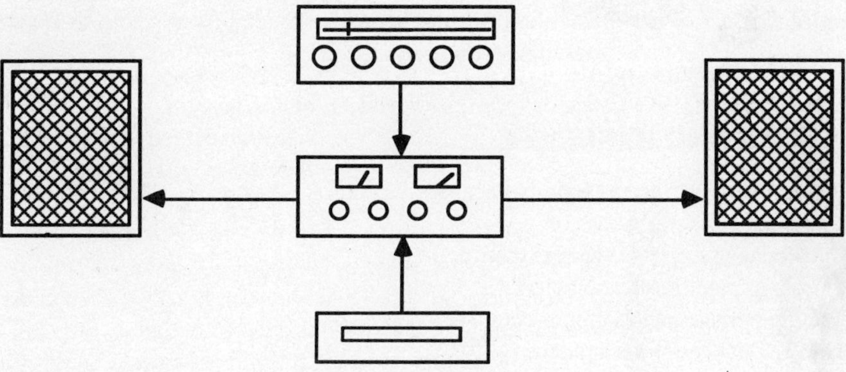

FIGURE 2-5 Modular system.

An example of a black-box–based system is a modular stereo (Figure 2-5). The amplifier, turntable, tuner, speakers, and other components are completely separate. The only thing one box needs to know about others is what sort of connection is required (power, frequency, and impedance). Each box may have a power supply with a different voltage; the different boxes may even use different families of components (e.g., vacuum tubes, bipolar transistors, field effect transistors). If something goes wrong with the system (for example, no sound is coming out of the right speaker), it is a fairly simple task to change the interconnections and isolate the problem. Modification of the system to take advantage of changing needs (such as adding a compact disk player or a tape deck) is trivial.

A non–black-box design would be a boom box. Here, all of the parts of the system are intimately connected; the designer of the amplifier must know a great deal about the other parts of the system, from power supply characteristics to layout details. Isolation of a problem is difficult, and modification of the system to adapt to changing needs is impossible. The same concepts apply to program design. If each module carries out one function and communicates with the rest of the system only insofar as it is necessary to share data, then identification of problem modules and modification of the system to meet new requirements are fairly easy. If the system is bound together into a monolithic ball of spaghetti code, identifying the sources of problems or modifying the program can produce severe heartburn.

SUMMARY

Design is a generalized activity because all problem solving must deal with the strengths and weaknesses of the human information processing system. The major aspects of this system that are of interest to us in programming are the limited capacity of short-term memory and the pattern-matching strengths.

The generalized responses to these characteristics are the use of hierarchy, the use of abstraction, the use of graphical notation, and the use of black boxes. Sections II and III of the book describe how we apply these tools to program design.

QUESTIONS AND EXERCISES

1. Design is a generalized activity because all problem solving must deal with the strengths and weaknesses of
   a. Management information systems.
   b. Large mainframe computers.
   c. The human information processing system.
   d Personal computer systems
2. Hierarchy and graphic notation are two strategies used to deal with the limitations of
   a. Computers.
   b. Paper and pencil.
   c. Human long-term memory.
   d. Human short-term memory.
3. What advantage does using a separate program module for each related function or each specific problem have in program design?
   a It puts all the complexity in one module called the black box.
   b It reduces the cognitive demand of the programmer by reducing one huge complex problem into several smaller more manageable tasks.
   c. It makes one large module and many smaller modules.
   d. It allows the programmer to discover any problem before it would occur.
4. Transfer between long and short-term memory is measured in
   a. Pica-seconds.
   b. Seconds.
   c. Minutes.
   d. Hours.
5. The average capacity of short-term memory is for how many chunks of data?
   a. 5
   b. 7
   c. 9
   d. 11
6. A modular system
   a. Has separate, easily traceable parts.
   b. Is intricately connected to all other parts.
   c. Requires contact among all the individual parts.
   d. Is not a viable option in systems design today.
7. Pattern recognition refers to
   a. Seeing the real essence through extraneous details.
   b. Choosing the best computer language for each job.

c. Finding the maximum amount of hardware the program can run on.
d. Combining several problems together.

8. What parts of the human information processing system should be relevant to you as a programmer?
a. Sensory registration/processing.
b. Long-term memory/sensory registration.
c. Short-term memory/processing.
d. Sensory registration/short-term memory.

9. The key strategy in dealing with limitations on capacity of short-term memory is
a. Studying.
b. Hierarchy.
c. Practice.
d. Flash cards.

10. Historically, what three stages have professions developed in?
a. Developmental, strategic, and historical.
b. Logical, geographical, and time.
c. Art, codification, and rationalization.
d. Ethnical, biological, and organizational.

DISCUSSION QUESTIONS

1. Discuss hierarchy and why it is important to short-term human memory and systems design.
2. In designing a program and in all problem solving, we must deal with the strengths and weaknesses of the human information processing systems. What are the major strengths and weaknesses of interest to us in programming?
3. Briefly explain a black box, and give an example.

Chapter 3

INTRODUCTION TO TRANSACTION PROCESSING SYSTEMS

CHAPTER GOALS

- Understand how order-entry systems work.
- Understand how purchasing systems work.
- Understand how transaction processing systems underlay information systems.

WHAT IS TRANSACTION PROCESSING?

Transactions are the data flows that result from day-to-day business operations. A sale, an order, a receipt—any event that triggers a flow of paper or data is a transaction. Transaction processing systems are the data processing systems, whether manual or computerized, that keep track of the data generated by business transactions.

Most of the effort in preparing accounting statements is the effort of keeping track of transactions, classifying them, and tabulating them. Because of the volume of repetitive paperwork, such systems were among the first business systems to be computerized. They are also among the most important systems in an organization—most firms would grind to a halt in a few weeks if the transaction processing systems failed. Many, such as banks, airlines, and highly automated production facilities, would collapse in a few hours.

When a small business computerizes, transaction processing systems are usually the first to be automated. Transaction processing systems handling millions of transactions are also the reason why corporations and other large entities use expensive, user-hostile mainframe computers with large, costly, dedicated staffs instead of networks of personal computers. The transaction processing needs of many organizations exceed even the capacity of the largest mainframes.

Transaction processing systems are important in their own right, but they are also important as the building blocks for other systems in an organization. Decision support systems, executive information systems, and strategic information systems all depend on the data gathered and organized by transaction processing systems. In fact, most reported examples of information systems used for strategic or competitive advantage, such as airline reservation systems, are common transaction processing systems used with uncommon strategic insight.

In this chapter we examine some of the most common transaction processing systems in organizations. Throughout the rest of the book, program examples will revolve around these systems.

DESCRIPTION OF COMMON TRANSACTION PROCESSING SYSTEMS

Figure 3-1 illustrates some of the common transaction processing systems in organizations; Figure 3-2 illustrates the relationships between them. In Figure 3-2, the arrows indicate the flow of paperwork through the system, and the boxes indicate outside entities who are dealt with (in this case, customers and suppliers). The disk symbols indicate files of data maintained by the system.

To review what is done here, we use the example of an auto repair shop. This example is very much simplified, but should be enough to illustrate what is going on.

The customer work order subsystem keeps track of the data illustrated in Figure 3-3. A customer requests that something be done, and the organization must keep track of the following:

Who requested the work?

When was it requested?

What was done?

How much did it cost?

Customer work order
Customer invoice
Cash receipts
Accounts receivable
Purchasing
Receiving
Inventory
Cash disbursements
Accounts payable

FIGURE 3-1 Common transaction provessing systems in organizations.

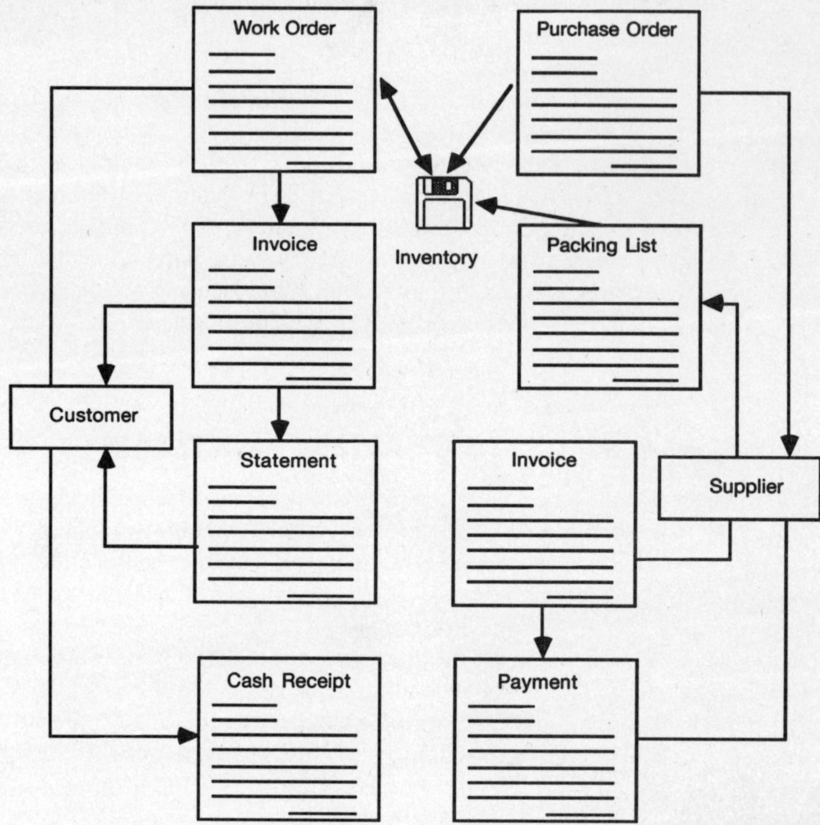

FIGURE 3-2 Relationships of transaction processing systems.

For example, I bring my Toyota Landcruiser into the auto repair shop with a burnt-out starter. The shop keeps track of who I am, along with relevant information such as telephone number, auto make, year, and registration. They also keep track of how much the parts cost (e.g., new starter: $75), how many hours of labor they spend fixing the problem (e.g., install starter: 1 hour), and the date all of this happened in case of later inquiries. Much of this data is gathered so that the shop will know how much to charge me.

The customer invoice subsystem processes the data illustrated in Figure 3-4. The problems here are to keep track of what work is done on what work order and to bill the customer for the correct amount. Especially in businesses where a small number of customers generate many service requests, it is important to keep the work orders straight for billing purposes. It is also helpful to have details on what the bill is for so that customers are less likely to question the charges. For example, the auto repair shop will prepare an invoice for me indicating that parts cost for my starter was $75 and labor cost was one hour at $35. Since there is no sales tax in Alaska, the total bill is $110. The accounting system needs to know about these charges as well,

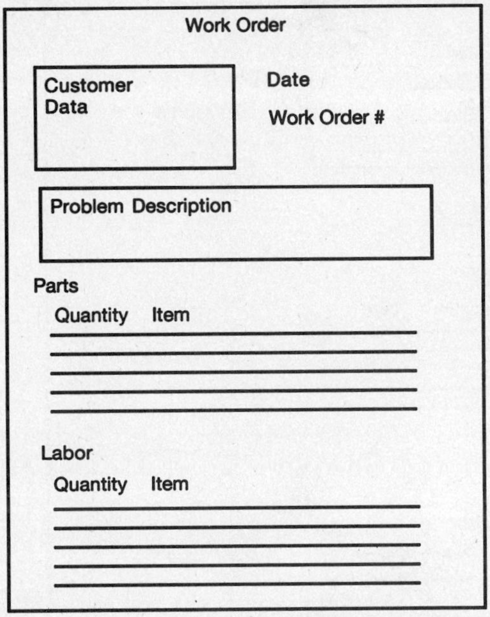

Work Order

Customer Data

Date

Work Order #

Problem Description

Parts

Quantity Item

Labor

Quantity Item

FIGURE 3-3 Customer work order.

since parts sales and service sales must be credited and the appropriate cost of goods sold accounts must be debited.

The cash receipts subsystem keeps track of the data illustrated in Figure 3-5. When the customer gets the invoice, he or she pays it (one hopes!). This usually involves the generation of a receipt for the customer and a notation to the accounting system that the cash was collected (this is often done automatically by the cash register) and what it was collected for. Often, however, some time elapses between the time the invoice is issued and the time the cash is collected. During this time, there is an account receivable outstanding (in English, the customer owes the firm money).

Accounts Receivable

The accounts receivable subsystem keeps track of who owes what. This is simply a notation to the accounting system that a particular customer owes a certain amount on work order such-and-such of such-and-such date. When the customer pays, the accounts receivable are credited as paid, and the cash receipts system records the collection. As part of the output from the accounts receivable system, customers receive a monthly statement (Figure 3-6) that lists all of their work orders that have not yet been paid.

Figure 3-7 shows diagrammatically how all of the forms for the customer-oriented transaction processing systems fit together. Data within similarly shaded boxes is identical. Arrows show the flows of data between different forms, or the relationships of items.

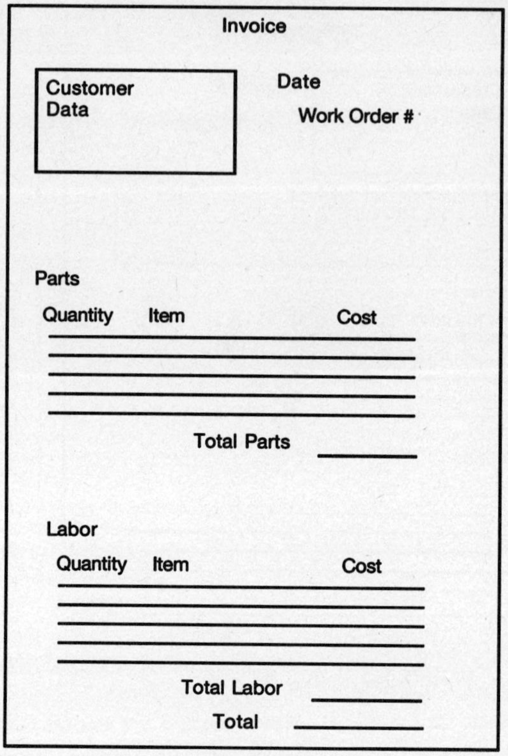

Invoice

Customer Data

Date

Work Order #

Parts

Quantity	Item	Cost

Total Parts ________

Labor

Quantity	Item	Cost

Total Labor ________

Total ________

FIGURE 3-4 Invoice.

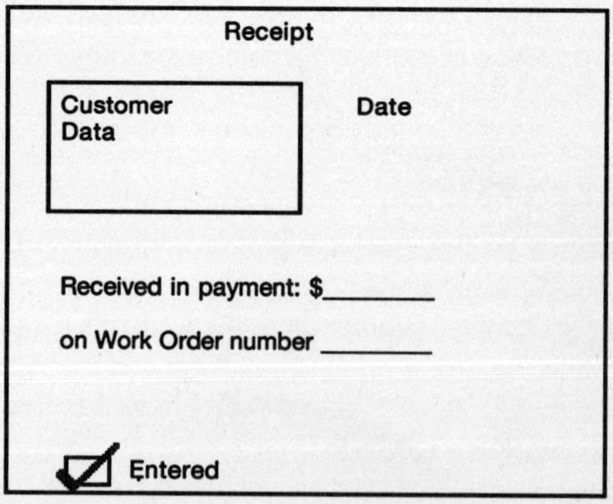

Receipt

Customer Data

Date

Received in payment: $________

on Work Order number ________

☑ Entered

FIGURE 3-5 Cash receipt.

Statement

Customer Data

Date

Work Order	Date	Total
________	—/—/—	—.—
________	—/—/—	—.—
________	—/—/—	—.—
________	—/—/—	—.—
________	—/—/—	—.—
________	—/—/—	—.—

Total ________

Accrued Interest ________

Grand Total ________

All Accounts due 30 days from billing

Amount over 30 days: ________

FIGURE 3-6 Statement.

This flow of data is extremely important, since it constitutes most of what a computer-based automation of the process must do. In a business programming context, the majority of programming effort goes to

- Automate input forms
- Automate output forms or reports
- Keep track of flows of data from input to database to output

All of the systems discussed thus far revolve around relationships with customers. There is yet another set of systems that revolve around relationships with suppliers. After all, one cannot very easily sell parts if no one supplies the parts for sale!

The purchasing subsystem keeps track of the data illustrated in Figure 8. This is basically the ordering system: sending orders to suppliers for parts. It is similar to what you do when you order something by mail: you send an order to the mail order supplier and the company ships you the goods and bills your credit card company. In our auto repair example, the shop has to order a new starter for a Toyota Landcruiser, since they used a starter from inventory to replace mine. They need to keep track of what was ordered when, so that if a part is temporarily out of stock they can determine when it is likely to come in or expedite the shipment if necessary ("You want an engine block via UPS Blue Label???!").

The receiving subsystem keeps track of what has been received. The data are contained in the packing list (Figure 3-9). This way, you know when something ordered through the

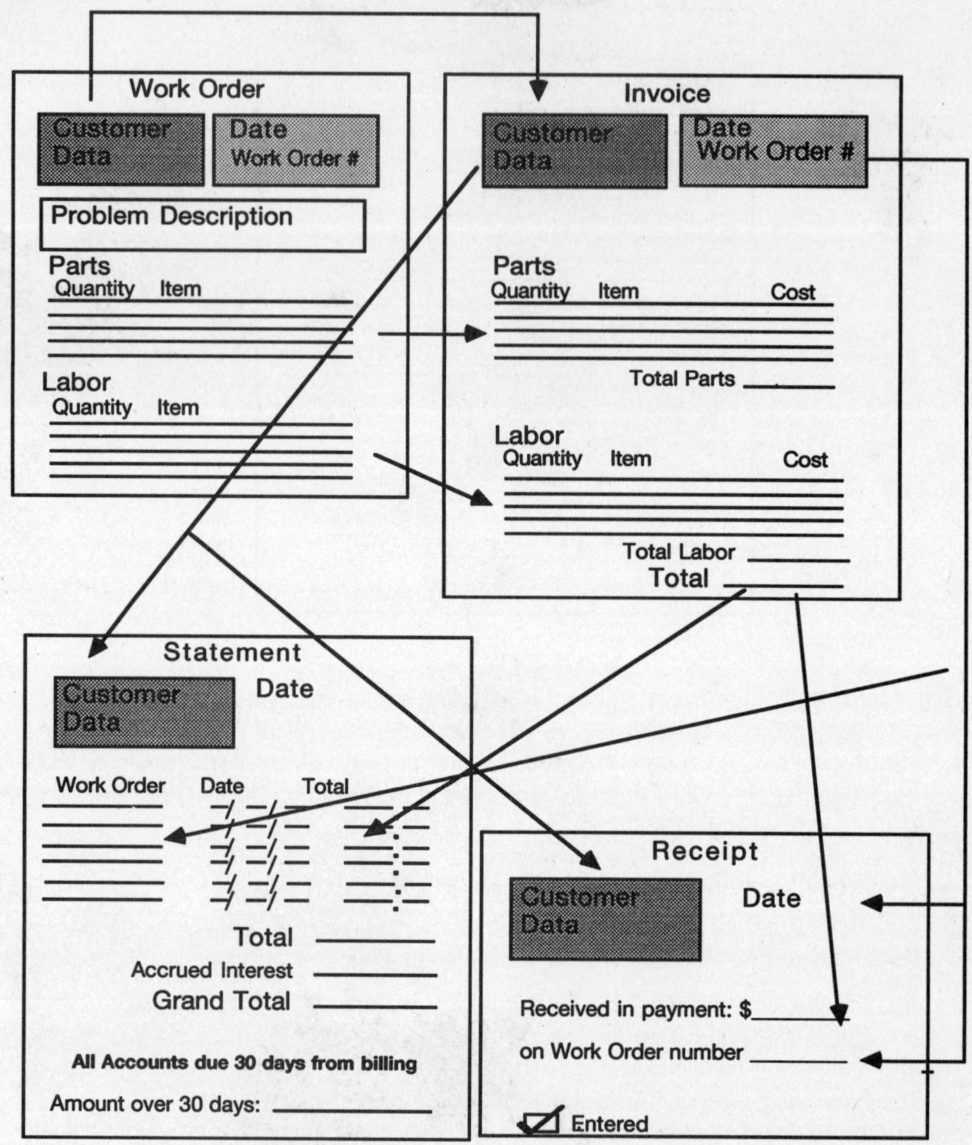

FIGURE 3-7 Customer-oriented transaction.

purchasing system has been received. A company that does not have a good receiving system never knows whether a part that is on order has arrived, which can be rather embarrassing. Note that a receiving system has to be able to deal with backorders and partial orders. From the point of view of the *supplier* company, the packing list that they send to you is a copy of their work order.

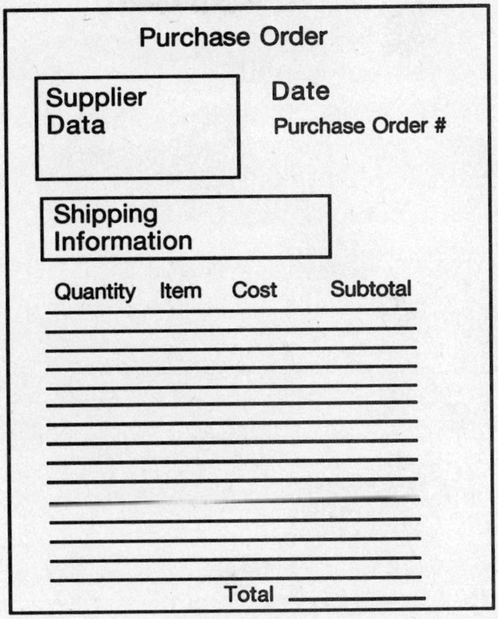

Purchase Order

Supplier Data

Date

Purchase Order #

Shipping Information

Quantity	Item	Cost	Subtotal

Total

FIGURE 3-8 Purchase order.

Packing List

Purchaser Data

Date

Purchase Order #

Shipment #

Quantity Ordered	Quantity Shipped	Item

FIGURE 3-9 Packing List.

Cash Disbursement Memo	Check Number
Date:	
Payee:	
Transaction Type	Purchase order
Transaction number	

FIGURE 3-10 Cash disbursement memo (check stub).

Inventory

Both the purchasing subsystem and the receiving subsystem work together with the inventory subsystem. The inventory system keeps track of what parts are in stock, what parts are on order, what parts are committed to work in progress, and what parts need to be reordered. For example, when I call in the appointment for a new starter, the auto repair shop will probably set aside one of the starters in inventory to make sure that one is available when I drive in (having push-started the car). The inventory system should make sure that if this set-aside starter is the last one, it is not counted in inventory when my neighbor calls in to get the starter in her Toyota fixed and is told that one is in stock.

Accounts Payable

Suppliers expect to be paid, of course, and the accounts payable subsystem keeps track of who is owed how much, when. This is basically a list of amounts owed, to whom they are owed, and when they are due.

Customer work order	Debit work in process	Credit inventory
Customer invoice	Debit cost of goods sold	Credit work in process
Cash receipts	Debit cash	Credit accounts receivable
Accounts receivable	Debit accounts receivable	Credit sales
Accounts payable	Debit inventory	Credit accounts payable
Cash disbursements	Debit accounts payable	Credit cash
Purchasing		
Receiving	No accounting impact	
Inventory		

FIGURE 3-11 Accounting entries.

Eventually one must pay one's accounts payable, hence, the cash disbursements subsystem, the paperwork for which is illustrated in Figure 3-10. This records that a check of such-and-such an amount has been written to a particular supplier in payment of a particular shipment. It enables the company to tell the supplier "your check is in the mail."

For those with an accounting background, Figure 3-11 reviews the accounting entries made in association with each of these subsystems. Note that an actual accounting system would be much more complicated because of the need for detailed journals, general ledger postings, closings, and the like.

SUMMARY

Transaction processing systems are the foundation for organizational information systems. They record all of the day-to-day activities that make up the organization's basic activities. Since they are standardized, repetitious, and require little if any human judgement once they are set up, transaction processing systems have always been prime candidates for computerization.

QUESTIONS AND EXERCISES

1. What is transaction processing?
   a. An event that triggers a flow of paper.
   b. Data processing systems, manual or automated, that keep track of the data generated by business transactions.
   c A sale of goods or services.
   d. Data generated by day-to-day business.
2. Why are transaction processing systems good systems to computerize?
   a. Because they are standardized, repetitious, and require little human judgement.
   b. Because transaction processing systems are different for every business.
   c. Because computerizing the transaction processing systems keeps prices from rising.
   d. Because transaction processing systems requires a great deal of human judgement.
3. Which of the following are only customer-related transactions?
   a. Work orders, invoices, statements, receipts.
   b. Purchase orders, statements, general ledger.
   c. Work orders, purchase orders.
   d. Customer.
4. Most of the effort in preparing accounting statements is the effort of
   a. Keeping track of transactions.
   b. Creating transactions.
   c. Making of the forms.
   d. Make the information presentable.

5. Transaction processing systems handle
   a. Hundreds of transactions.
   b. Thousands of transactions.
   c. Tens of thousands of transactions.
   d. Millions of transactions.
6. When a customer comes in to a garage to have work done to his or her car, what should be the first form generated?
   a. Statement.
   b. Invoice.
   c. Purchase order.
   d. Work order.
7. As part of the output from the accounts receivable system, what is usually sent out to the customer monthly?
   a. Purchase order.
   b. Invoice.
   c. Statement.
   d. Packing list.
8. What subsystem do the purchasing subsystem and the receiving subsystem work with?
   a. Cash subsystem.
   b. Inventory subsystem.
   c Customer subsystem.
   d. Work order subsystem.

DISCUSSION QUESTIONS

1. What are transaction processing systems?
2. Why are transaction processing systems important?
3. What is a transaction?

NORTHSTAR AVIATION

Part 1
Information System Benefits

Northstar Aviation is a general aviation service company located in interior Alaska. The company provides both mechanical and electronics (avionics) repair and maintenance to private and corporate airplane owners (readers from "outside" should realize that Alaska has a very limited road system; most of our state is accessible only by air, so aircraft ownership is very common here). Figure 3-12 shows the organization of the company, which has six employees in addition to the owner and founder.

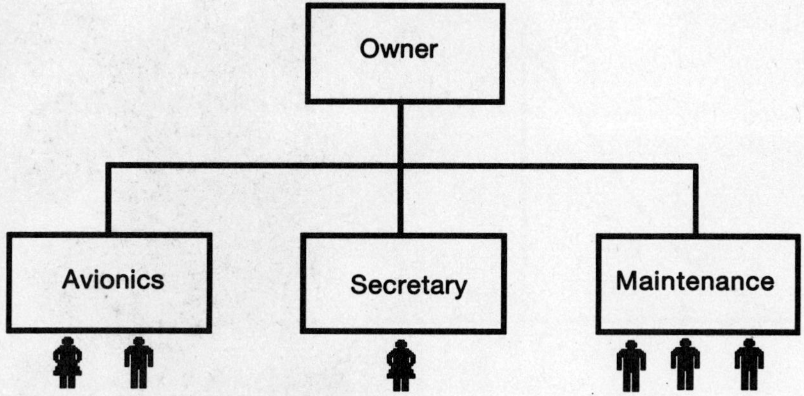

FIGURE 3-12 Northstar Aviation organization chart.

The employees consist of a secretary, who types 100 words a minute, two avionics technicians, and three airframe and powerplant (A & P) mechanics. The owner holds both an A & P certificate and a first-class radiotelephone license; he works on both mechanical and electronics service when he is not working on marketing, customer relations, and paperwork. The secretary is paid $10 per hour for a 40-hour week; the other employees are paid $17.50 per hour, also for a 40-hour week. All employees receive time and a half for any time over 40 hours a week.

Figure 3-13 illustrates the flow of paperwork for the organization. Each customer request generates a work order that lists the parts and labor required.

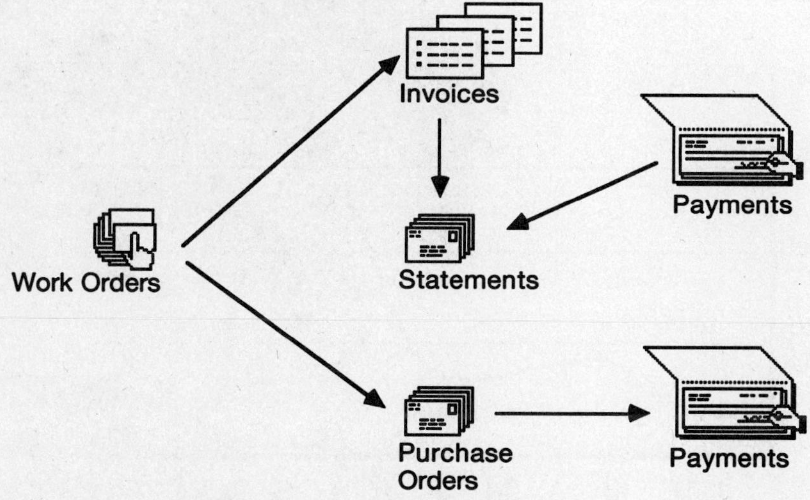

FIGURE 3-13 Northstar paper flow.

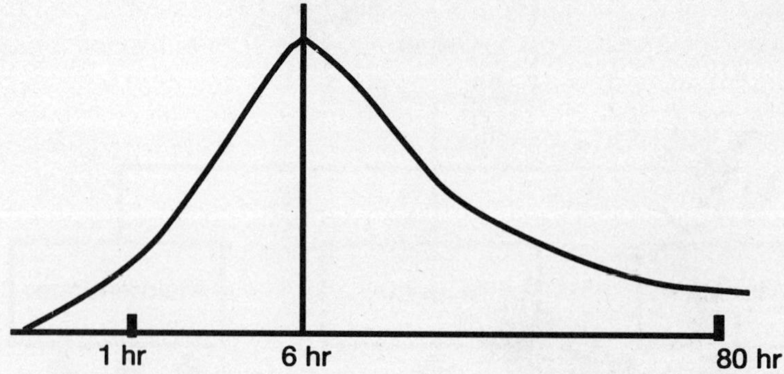

FIGURE 3-14 Time required to fulfill work orders.

When the work is completed, the customer is given an invoice. Once a month, statements are mailed to all customers, showing what they owe on outstanding invoices. Payments are received from customers either when the invoice is issued or later, usually in response to statements. Work orders also generate purchase orders for items that are not in inventory or that are running low. Delivery of these items is accompanied with a bill from the supplier, which has to be paid. All forms are as illustrated in Figures 3-3–3-8 of this chapter.

Figure 3-14 illustrates the distribution of customer service requests in terms of time required. On average, Northstar receives four requests a day for avionics work and six requests a day for mechanical work. Unfortunately, these requests are not evenly distributed throughout the year; Figure 3-15 shows the actual distribution on an annual basis. (Hunting season in Alaska is during the autumn in August and September.

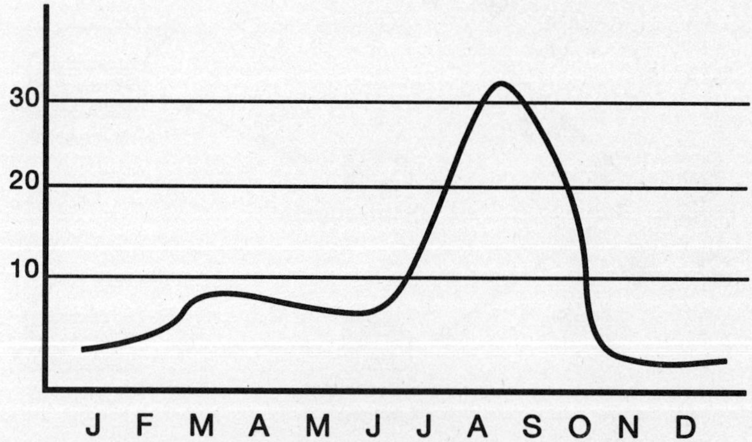

FIGURE 3-15 Cash disbursement memo (check stub).

This results in a great deal of aircraft use and many minor accidents.)

On average, each work order has ten entries and generates four part orders. Part orders result from the discovery that there are not enough parts in inventory or that supplies are running low. These part orders are consolidated into about twenty purchase orders per week. Approximately one half of the work orders are delayed because of parts shortages; three quarters of the purchase orders require shipping by UPS air for that reason. There are about 100 suppliers; information on them is kept in a card file. Invoices from suppliers are paid on receipt.

Northstar has about 1000 customers in total. Two hundred invoices are issued each month (when the associated work order is finished), and about 250 statements are typed and mailed monthly. Accounts receivable average 45 days.

The accounting system at Northstar consists of calling in a CPA once a year to add up the checks, the work orders, the purchase orders, and inventory. The CPA charges $50 per hour and usually takes about 100 hours to prepare the tax returns.

DISCUSSION QUESTIONS

1. Calculate how much time the secretary spends typing up each type of form, and the total for all forms each week assuming a uniform distribution of work (which is admittedly not the case). Given that in instances where she would be required to work more than 60 hours a week the owner helps with the typing (at 50 wpm), what are the approximate time requirements for the actual work distribution?
2. How does the above situation translate into the standard transaction processing situation described in the text? Where are the holes in the system? Are they relevant?
3. What would be the impact on Northstar of a successful automated system in terms of
   - Customer service
   - Capacity
   - Financial impact
4. Assume that Northstar has a choice between two automated systems. Both use the same hardware ($10,000). Customized software would cost an additional $7500, whereas off-the-shelf software would cost an additional $1500. The benefits of the custom software would be:

   Detailed statements listing work order number and date as in Figure 3-6 as opposed to summary statements listing only a total.

   The custom system would duplicate the existing forms and coding scheme, so no changes in work would be required.

   The customized system would provide better ad hoc retrieval and reporting facilities.

   The owner has asked you to recommend which package to buy. Which would you choose, and why?

Chapter 4

INTRODUCTION TO dBASE III+ AND dBASE IV

CHAPTER GOALS

- To define fourth generation languages.
- To discuss how the dBASE languages came to be.
- To provide a roadmap to the dBASE systems,
- To cover the mechanics of using dBASE as a programming language.
- To describe the differences between dBASE III+ and dBASE IV.

This chapter introduces dBASE III+ and dBASE IV in the context of fourth generation languages. In the remainder of this chapter (and throughout the book), "dBASE" refers to both dBASE III+ and dBASE IV. The version number will be specified when it is necessary to distinguish between the two versions.

HISTORY

dBASE III+ and dBASE IV are examples of fourth generation languages (also called Very High Level Languages or VHLL). Basically, a fourth generation language is one where the commands are at a significantly higher level than is true for traditional third generation languages, such as COBOL, BASIC, or PASCAL.

The need for fourth generation languages arises from the economic trends discussed in Chapter 1: the rapid increase in computer numbers and capacity and the decrease in cost, and the fact that programmer productivity has historically increased at a rate of only about 3% a year. Putting these two sets of trends together, we get the forecast that using traditional programming techniques, by the early 1990s about *15% of the entire population of the United States* will be programmers. This includes infants and retirees. Obviously this is demographically impossible [Martin 1984].

The answer to this problem is to change the way in which programming is done. There is ample historical precedent for this. The telephone system is an example. In the early part of this century, the demand for telephone service was growing exponentially. At that time, to "dial" another telephone set, you picked up the receiver, an operator said "Number please?," you gave her the number, and she connected you via a switchboard. The use of "she" and "her" here is not a sexist oversight; at that time the profession of telephone operator was the exclusive domain of unmarried women. Unfortunately, the growth curve for telephone use was such that by the early 1920s, every unmarried woman in the United States would be a telephone operator, at which time growth of telephone service would cease because, barring a population explosion or a diminution of the popularity of marriage, there would be no more unmarried women available to do the job.

As we all know, that is not what happened. Instead, the dial telephone was invented, and we all became telephone operators. Much the same thing has happened to computers: new tools have radically changed the way in which systems are programmed. Fourth generation languages (such as dBASE) are part of that technological revolution.

NATURE OF VHLL

There are two aspects of fourth generation languages that are often misunderstood: the extent to which they are nonprocedural and the audience toward whom they are oriented. The latter problem has historically been particularly acute for the dBASE series of languages. This section of the chapter discusses these issues.

In *procedural language*, the user gives the machine instructions on how to carry out a task. In *nonprocedural language*, the user describes the task (what is to be done), and the language figures out how to do it. Fourth generation languages have often been described as nonprocedural. This is only partially correct.

One confusion is the level of commands available. A single statement in a fourth generation language can carry out as much as a short program in a typical third generation language. This does not, however, make the fourth generation language nonprocedural, since more complicated programs still require specification of how to solve the problem. The same misunderstanding used to be common for third generation languages, which were at one time described as nonprocedural. After all, in a language like BASIC, a programmer could write something like:

```
X=Y+Z
```

whereas in assembly language he or she would have had to specify how the addition was to be done, for example:

```
MOV A,YLOC    ;load the contents of Y into the accumulator
MOV B,ZLOC    ;load the contents of Z into register B
ADD B         ;add the contents of register B to the accumulator
STA XLOC      ;store the contents of the accumulator into X
```

This did not make the third generation language nonprocedural, but simply meant that one could specify the procedure at a higher level. The same is true for fourth generation languages such as dBASE.

A second aspect of fourth generation languages is that they work at a much higher level of abstraction than do earlier languages. This means that they allow many "objects" to be defined and then manipulated as intact objects rather than procedurally. For example, one may define a "screen" of data and thereafter simply tell the program to display or read data from that screen definition without elaborate input and output formatting commands. This object orientation will be discussed at length later in the book.

Fourth generation languages are divided into two groups: those that are *programmer oriented* and those that are *end-user oriented.* This distinction is sometimes obscured by marketing, since the rise in the number of personal computers has meant that the end-user group is much larger—hence they are the target of many of the advertising campaigns.

Programmer-oriented languages are general-purpose programming languages aimed at improving programmer productivity. They are intended as replacements for third generation languages such as COBOL or BASIC. They were not designed for use by end users who do not know how to program, although many of them are now marketed to that group. Examples include dBASE for personal computers, ADF for IBM mainframes, and LINC for UNISYS mainframes.

End-user–oriented languages are intended for people who do not know how to program. They are set up to generate automatically a predefined set of program types based on a fill-in-the-blank approach on the part of the user. Such systems are not often general-purpose programming languages; there are many types of systems that they cannot be used to create. Examples in the personal computer world include DATAEASE and the database portion of ENABLE. Mainframe examples include AS for IBM mainframes and MAPPER for UNISYS mainframes. Many programmer-oriented fourth generation languages such as dBASE have been fitted with user-friendly (or at least non–user-hostile) *shells* and marketed to this group.

These systems also differ in terms of the amount of training required for fluent use (assuming a nonprogramming background). For example, COBOL (the most popular third generation language for business programming) requires about six months of training before a novice is more or less comfortable programming in it. BASIC requires about one or two month's use. A programmer-oriented fourth generation language such as dBASE III+ requires a little less time than a simple third generation language like BASIC, and an end-user–oriented fourth generation language requires only a few days to learn to use fluently. Of course, this is somewhat like pointing out that one can learn to play the bugle in three days, but learning to play the French horn takes years—the latter can do a great deal more!

In all of this discussion, it is helpful to remember that when people say dBASE, they are referring to some combination of

- A fourth generation programming language.
- A database management system (Chapter 7).
- Query facilities for end users.

The distinction is important, because often in product comparisons the term "dBASE III" or "dBASE IV" will be used to refer only to one or two of these. For example, it is commonly pointed out that Oracle is a superior database management system to dBASE IV (which is correct). What is not mentioned is that there is no fourth generation language associated with Oracle, which therefore must be programmed in COBOL, C, or PASCAL (all third generation languages).

ROADMAP TO THE dBASE III+ SYSTEM

In this textbook we treat dBASE III+ as a programming language rather than as a product. However, to program in the language, we need to look at its actual packaging. As distributed by Ashton Tate, dBASE III+ contains

A relational database management system

An interpreter for the dBASE III+ programming language

A menu-driven shell (the Assistant)

A simple utility editor

A simple program generator

A runtime system consisting of

a partial compiler (dBCODE)

a linker for the above (dBLINKER)

a run-time interpreter (dBRUN)

Network management software

This book concentrates on the dBASE III+ programming language and its interfaces with the relational database management system.

Mechanics of Using dBASE III

Having installed the dBASE III+ system according to the manual, you start the program by typing dBASE. By default, this puts you in the Assistant, the menu-driven shell around dBASE III+ intended to make it less user hostile (Figure 4-1). Since we are interested in working at the program level, most of the time in this book we will be working at the "dot-prompt" level. This is the interpreter with the Assistant turned off. It gives no help or suggestions, but puts a period (".") at the beginning of the line and waits for a command (the equivalent of BASIC's "Ok"). You get out of the Assistant by pressing the Escape key ("Esc"). You get back into the Assistant by typing `ASSIST`. Even though we will be pro-

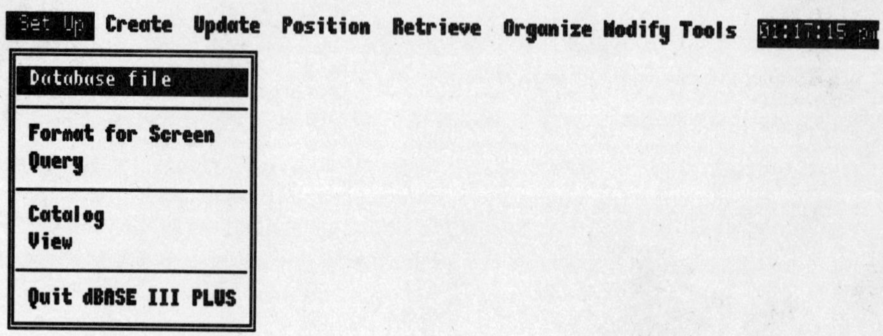

FIGURE 4-1 The Assistant

gramming at the "dot-prompt" level, you may want to use the Assistant for tasks like creating and modifying files and reports. Real Programmers work only at the "dot-prompt" level, but the rest of us will occasionally accept help from the software!

Since dBASE III+ is interpreted, you can enter commands either directly at the "dot-prompt" level or from a file that contains program statements. You create data files (Chapter 7) from within dBASE III+ with the **CREATE** command from the Assistant (Figures 4-2 and 4-3). Program files are created with the `MODIFY COMMAND` instruction (Figure 4-4, which in this example creates or modifies a file called **suppent.prg**).

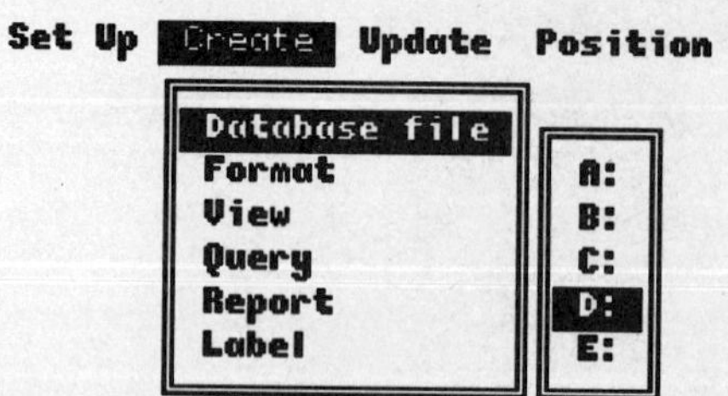

FIGURE 4-2 Use of the Assistant to create a data file, Step 1

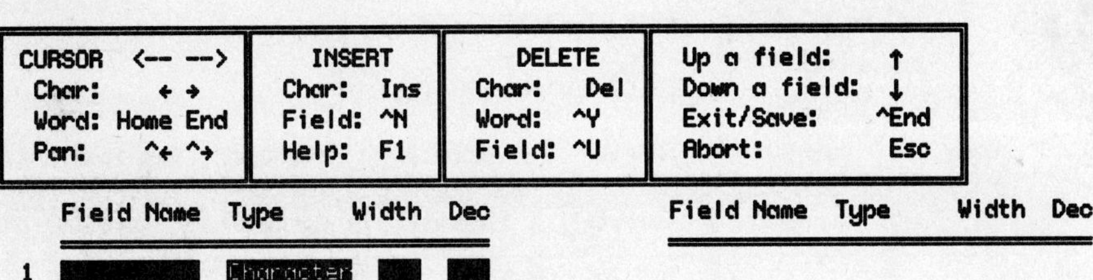

CREATE | D: | TEST | Field: 1/1

Enter the field name.

Field names begin with a letter and may contain letters, digits and underscores

FIGURE 4-3 Use of `MODIFY COMMAND` to create or edit a program file

```
MODIFY COMMAND SUPPENT
```

FIGURE 4-4 Use of `MODIFY COMMAND` to create or edit a program file.

When you are done with dBASE III, you can go back to MSDOS by typing `QUIT` at the "dot-prompt" level or by selecting **`QUIT dBASE III+ PLUS`** from the Assistant menu.

Using dBASE IV

dBASE IV differs from dBASE III+ in the following ways:

- It replaces the Assistant with a new interface called the Control Center (Figure 4-5).
- It contains an improved program editor, a compiler, and a debugger.
- It introduces additional data structures for memory variables (Chapter 7).
- It makes index use and manipulation (Chapter 7) easier.
- It adds a floating point data type (Chapter 7).
- It expands the relational operations, (Chapter 18)
- It adds additional commands and functions (Chapter 18).
- It removes many of the arbitrary limitations left over from dBASE II.

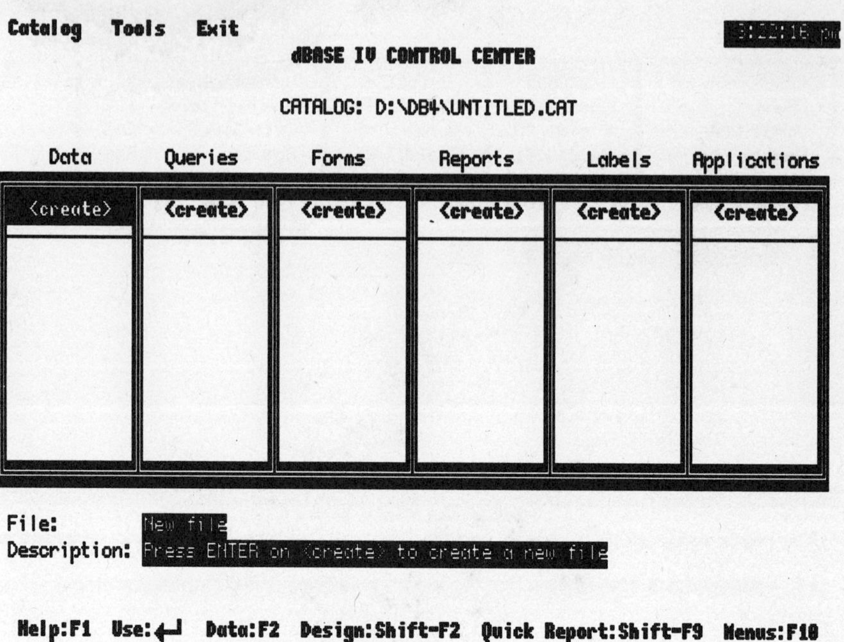

FIGURE 4-5 Control Center.

dBASE IV is really two languages in one. The first is an improved version of the traditional dBASE programming language—improved both in packaging and in language features. The second is a merger of the new dBASE programming language with the industry-standard database manipulation instructions of SQL. We look at both; from a program design standpoint they are very similar.

The next section of the book discusses the basic elements of a program and how these are translated into dBASE.

SUMMARY

dBASE is both a database management system and a fourth generation language. As a fourth generation language, it is oriented toward programmers rather than towards end users. We call it a fourth generation language because it is significantly higher level than third generation languages such as COBOL; on the average, performing a given task requires only 10% to 20% of the code in dBASE as in COBOL. This fourth generation language, which includes many of the best features from modern language design, is what distinguishes dBASE from many competing (and often otherwise superior) products. The language is supported by compilers from several companies other than Ashton-Tate. Versions of the language are also available on Macintosh and UNIX computers.

QUESTIONS AND EXERCISES

1. An example of a Very High Level Language is
   a. C.
   b. COBOL.
   c. dBASE III.
   d. PASCAL.
2. QL is
   a. The set of industry standard database manipulation instructions.
   b. The Standard Queuing Language.
   c. The query language used exclusively for dBASE.
   d. The language used to compile dBASE programs.
3. Fourth generation languages are
   a. Only procedural languages.
   b. Only nonprocedural languages.
   c. Both procedural languages and nonprocedural languages.
   d. Neither procedural languages nor nonprocedural languages.

REFERENCE

MARTIN, J. Fourth Generation Languages, Prentice-Hall, Englewood Cliffs, NJ, 1984.

Section II

SYSTEMS ANALYSIS

Systems analysis is the process of clarifying the nature of existing information systems, the requirements for changes and additions, and how the new can be synthesized with the old to produce a system that meets user needs. This section of the text presents both the tools for systems analysis and the procedures to be followed. The treatment is brief, in large part because it concentrates on the essentials of those tools for systems analysis that are most appropriate in a fourth generation environment rather than attempting to survey the entire field.

Chapter 5 introduces entities and the relationships between them. At the same time, it illustrates the basics of how to produce a physical model of the existing system.

Chapter 6, on event modeling and data flow diagrams, introduces data flow diagrams as an adjunct to data modeling for complete system description. The chapter shows how data flow diagrams can aid the analyst both in understanding the existing system and in communicating with the users who request changes.

Chapter 7 introduces the concepts of data type and structure and the use of data dictionaries. It covers their use in refining physical models, along with their linkage with programming, databases, and programming languages—specifically dBASE III and IV.

Chapter 8, on normalization, introduces an important tool for producing a logical model and refining the earlier designs. The techniques of normalization presented here flow naturally from the earlier discussion of data modeling rather than being based on derivation rules.

Chapter 9, on the user interface, refines the objects representing the system model and introduces the objects from the program model that are obtained directly from the user.

The results of the cases and problems from this section are used throughout the rest of the book as we deal with physical system design and program construction.

One shortcoming of any textbook treatment of systems analysis is that the essence of systems analysis is communicating with the users of a system. Systems analysis is the stage in the system development life cycle where we talk to the users, find out what they want, and integrate their desires into a model of what the final system will be like. Textbooks cannot provide contact with users, hence, we must focus on the tools and techniques that you will use to build the system model rather than on the interactions with users and existing systems that in real-world situations will provide the data you need. This section will teach you what information you need to get to build a system model. It will not teach you how to get that information from the end users; that knowledge comes from real-world experience.

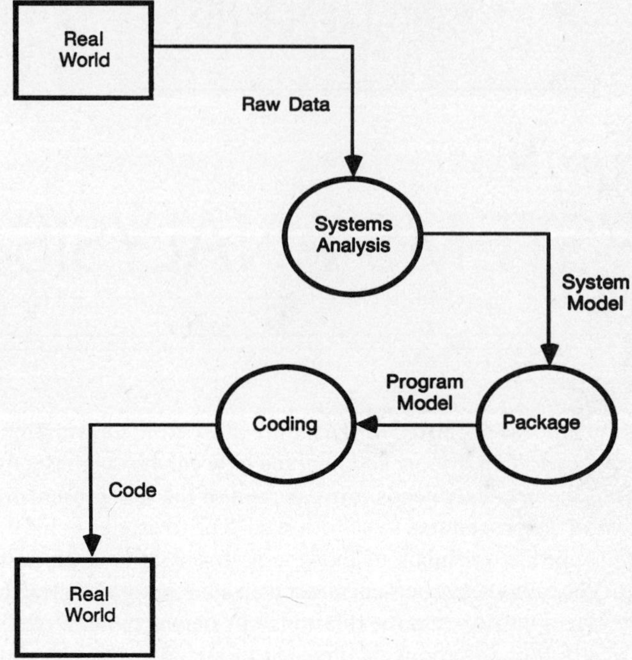

FIGURE S-2-1 Generalized system development life-cycle.

Figure S-2-1 is an abstract view of the systems development process. The systems analysis phase produces an abstract model of the real-world system, with the abstractions chosen for their relevancy both to the real-world problem and to the downstream implementation. The program design phase (Section III, this book) translates this system model into an abstract model of the program, which includes the relevant architecture and other specifications without the unnecessary details and restrictions of actual code. This program design phase is an essential element of "modern" or "structured" approaches to program design. The program model is then translated into code.

Figure S-2-2 shows the same thing in a more graphic form and is intended to emphasize that the particular abstractions chosen for the system model and the program model are relevant only insofar as they provide a smooth transition from the real world to the actual code. In a fourth generation, database environment, there are three problems involved with using traditional systems analysis techniques:

- The system model must provide for database design.
- A smooth transition between the database view at the system model stage and the program model stage is needed.
- Fourth generation languages work with different internal objects than do third generation languages, which causes mismatches when translating from the program model stage.

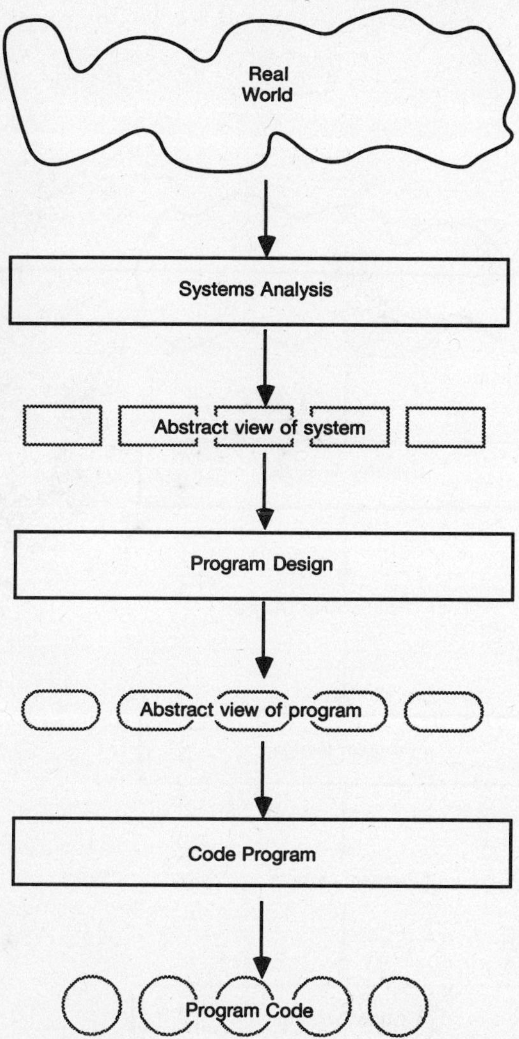

FIGURE S-2-2 Translation in analysis and design.

For a fourth generation environment, this text combines data modeling (Chapter 5) and event modeling (Chapter 6) at the analysis phase (Figures S-2-3). These two approaches to analysis are combined with object modeling at the program design phase (Section III).

Figure S-2-4 illustrates the steps used in deriving a system model. Note that the order in which one actually builds a system model does not correspond exactly to the order of chapters in the book. The reason for this is that the chapters in Section II each present a single tool and its associated notation. These tools are presented in the approximate order

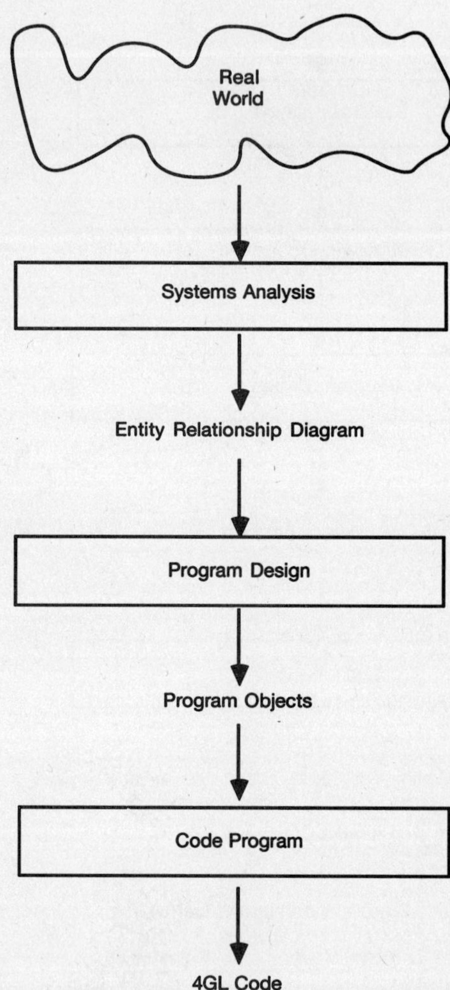

FIGURE S-2-3 Outline of fourth generation design methodology.

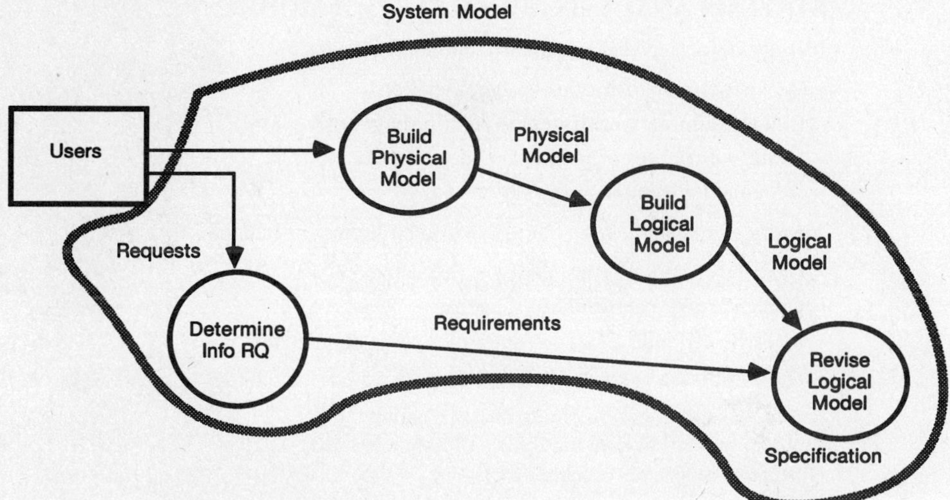

Physical Model = Preliminary Entity Relationship Diagram (Ch. 5) +
Physical Data flow diagram (Ch. 6) +
Data Dictionary (Ch. 7).

Logical Model = Entity Relationship Diagram (Ch. 5 and 6)+
Data flow diagram (Ch. 6)+
Data Dictionary of Entity Attributes (Ch. 7 and 8).

Specification = Database specification (Ch. 7)+
Process object specification (Ch. 9)+
Physical Data Dictionary (CH. 7)+
Screen and Report layouts (Ch. 9)+
Menu structure (Ch. 9)

FIGURE S-2-4 Steps in systems analysis.

in which they are needed, but each step in building the system model actually uses several tools. Thus, in real life we will use the tools of Chapters 5, 6, and 7 at the *Build Physical Model* stage, the *Build Logical Model* stage, and at the *Revise Logical Model* stage.

Repeated from Figure 1-8, the activities that we will carry out and the tools that we will be using in this section are as follows:

SYSTEMS ANALYSIS (BUILD SYSTEM MODEL)

Identify objects in real-world environment (Chapter 5)

- Define permanent entities based on objects
- Build preliminary **entity-relationship diagram**
- Identify attributes of permanent (data elements)
- Document attributes in **data dictionary**

Identify events and actions in real-world environment (Chapter 6)

- Define transient entities spawned by each event
- Update **entity-relationship diagram**
- Identify attributes of transient entities (data elements)
- Document attributes in **data dictionary**

Refine the specification of attributes (Chapter 7)
Produce a physical data dictionary of data elements
Normalize attributes (Chapter 8)
Define views appropriate to end users (Chapter 9)

Chapter 5

HIGH-LEVEL DATA REPRESENTATIONS: ENTITIES AND RELATIONSHIPS

CHAPTER GOALS

- **Learn basics of data modeling.**
- **Learn to use entity-relationship diagrams.**
- **Learn to select appropriate permanent entities.**
- **Learn to analyze forms, reports, and files in existing system.**
- **Learn to assign data attributes to permanent entities.**

Systems analysis (Figure 5-1) is the process of understanding the existing system, understanding the user's needs, and synthesizing from them the logical design of the new system.

There are three alternative approaches to systems analysis in widespread use:

- Traditional input-process-output specification approaches.
- Process approaches ("structured analysis").
- Data-oriented approaches ("data modeling").

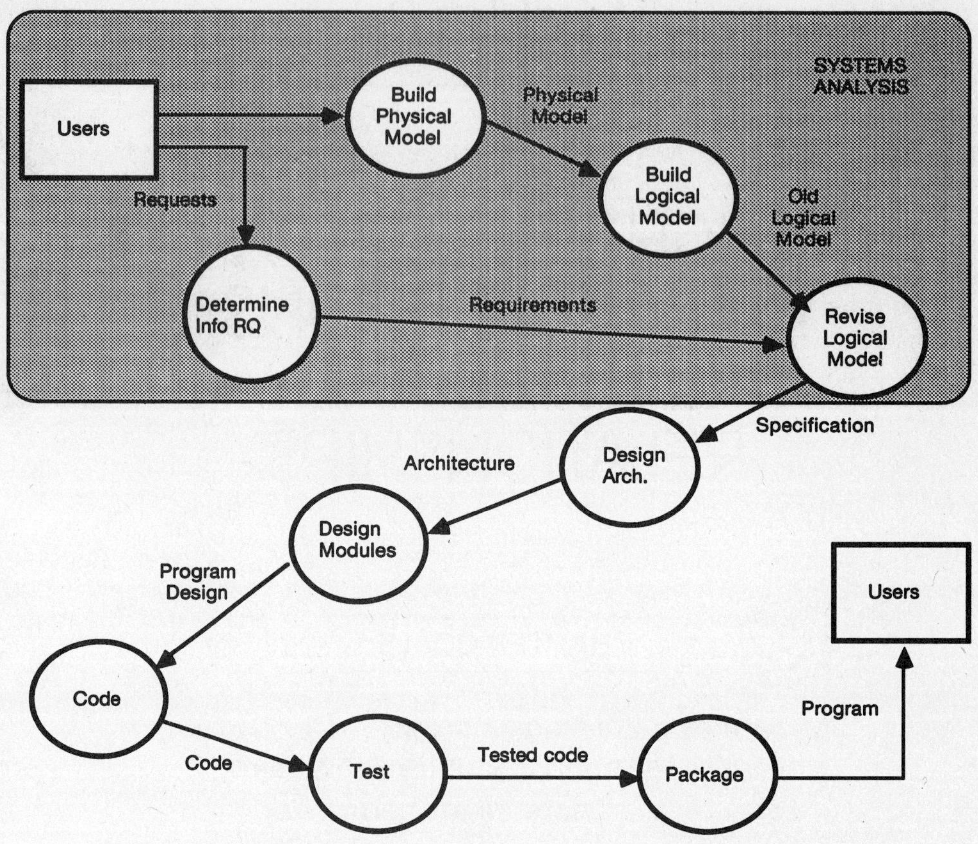

FIGURE 5-1 Systems analysis in the life-cycle.

Traditional approaches
  Flow charts
  I/O charts

Process approaches
  Data flow diagrams
  Data dictionaries
  Action diagrams

Data-oriented approaches
  Entity-relationship diagrams
  Data structure diagrams

FIGURE 5-2 Systems analysis notations.

Traditional input-process-output specification approaches were originally developed for second generation languages; they are still widely taught and used. Process approaches ("structured analysis") were the original "modern" programming practices developed for third generation languages and conventional file processing applications. They are also still widely used. Data-oriented approaches ("data modeling") were developed for database applications and are particularly suited for fourth generation languages. This book will focus on data modeling approaches and includes those process approaches that work well in a fourth generation environment. Figure 5-2 reviews some of the notations used in industry for each approach.

The notations described in *italic* typeface in Fig. 5-2 are high-level (abstract) views of a system. They describe how the parts of a system fit together at a significantly higher level than do the other tools. This chapter introduces the use of entity-relationship diagrams; the next chapter introduces the use of data flow diagrams.

In this section of the book we construct paper models of programs. There are several reasons for this activity, all of which revolve around the strengths and weaknesses of the human information processing system discussed in Chapter 2. The basic goal is to partition a complicated activity into several less complicated tasks. It might be stressed that there are a very large number of competing notations; our selection is premised on four factors:

- What underlying aspect of the program design problem the notation represents.
- Consistency with database environment.
- Consistency with industry practice.
- Maximizing use of pattern matching skills.

WHY BUILD PAPER MODELS?

All of these notations assume that it is important to build a paper model of a system before actually committing it to code. The introduction of this paper modeling stage is, in fact, the major innovation of modern programming practice. The more traditional approach would be to build the system in code directly. There are four reasons for interposing the extra (and time-consuming!) steps of first building a paper model. They are as follows:

- To partition the tasks *between* stages of the life-cycle to minimize cognitive overload.
- To partition the tasks *within* a single stage of the life-cycle to minimize cognitive overload.
- To maximize use of pattern-matching abilities.
- To shield the designer from irrelevant details.

This is not done with code, since computer languages are at best ill-suited to any of these tasks. Any programming language contains a host of extraneous details that are irrelevant to any of the above tasks—indeed, irrelevant to anything except the translation of step-by-step program instructions into machine code. In addition, programming languages require that details of the data, the architecture, and the process be intermixed rather than separated the design task into relatively independent subtasks. Finally, program languages are textually oriented and do not take advantage of pattern-matching skills.

All of this is a roundabout way of saying that we introduce the paper modeling stage because once a program gets above a certain size, the designers and programmers find that they cannot cope with its complexity. These difficulties in coping with complexity are caused by the fundamental limitations in the way people process information, as discussed in Chapter 2. The paper modeling stage allows us to take a large, overly complex problem and split it into a group of smaller, less complex problems. As a result, each stage is more likely to get done right.

There is an analogy in civil engineering. At one time, craftsmen built houses without plans, working from traditional knowledge. Indeed, in many parts of the world, houses and other buildings continue to be so constructed and have changed little over hundreds, and often thousands of years. Such houses tend to be small. Once the size of a building increases beyond a particular threshold of complexity, a builder cannot rely on traditional knowledge but must construct a paper model (plans) before building in masonry and wood.

An additional feature of this example is communication. In a traditional society, all houses are quite similar, with differences being a function of variations in site, materials, and craftsmanship. With more complex buildings, and especially with the additional layer of management in the form of an architect, it is necessary for the architect to communicate with the client and with the builder. The architect and the client must reach an agreement on the design of the building before construction even begins. The role of paper (and physical) models is as a means of communication to make sure that the design is correct from the user standpoint before concrete is poured. As anyone knows who has had a house built, design changes suddenly become very expensive once the foundation is poured and the walls are going up!

The presentation of systems analysis in this book is first tool oriented, and then process-oriented. This means that in this chapter and the next two chapters, we study tools and notations that are useful at several stages of the system development life-cycle illustrated in Figure 5-1. Beginning in Chapter 7 and continuing through Chapter 9, we will discussing the use of these tools in moving from stage to stage in the system development life-cycle.

DATA-ORIENTED APPROACHES

The data-oriented approaches to systems analysis with which we are concerned were developed during the late 1970s. They are thus the most recent of the systems analysis techniques. The process and data flow–oriented techniques that we refer to as the "structured" techniques were developed for a traditional file-processing environment by using third generation languages, such as COBOL. Several data-oriented approaches were also developed for this environment, most notably the Michael Jackson (Chapter 15) and the Warnier-Orr methodologies. The techniques discussed in the rest of this chapter were developed for a database environment and are associated with fourth generation languages. The approach that we are describing here is a version of object-oriented design known as object-based design.

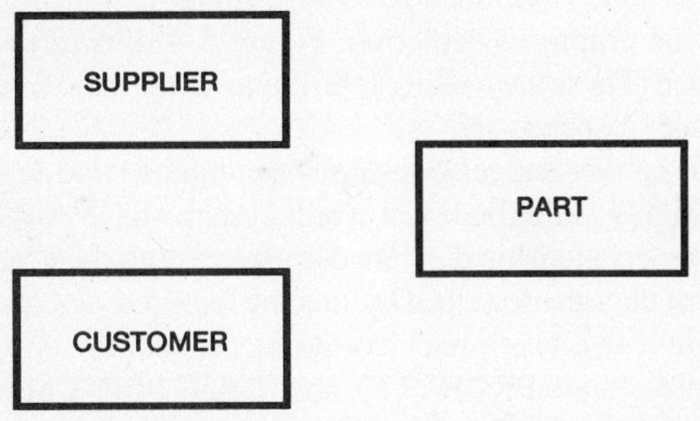

FIGURE 5-3 Entities.

The basic high-level notation used in these database approaches is the *entity-relationship diagram.* There are several closely related notations in use; we will be using one called Bachman diagrams [Martin & McClure 1985].

An *entity* is something in the real world about which we store data. It is represented by a box inside, which is the name of the entity (Figure 5-3). Note that these boxes do *not* refer to files, databases, or other computer-oriented abstractions; they are abstractions of things or objects in the real-world environment about which end users are concerned. Figure 5-3 shows three entities: SUPPLIER, CUSTOMER, and PART.

Entities may be abstractions of many different things in the real world. They may be classes of physical objects, such as parts, automobiles, airplanes, or books. They may be abstractions of roles that individuals play: for instance, suppliers, customers, students, or library patrons. Each entity may have many instances; there may be tens of thousands of instances of the entity STUDENT, for example. To be considered members of the same entity, all of the instances must behave the same way and be described by the same data from the system's point of view. For example, RAW MATERIAL INVENTORY and FINISHED GOODS INVENTORY are probably two separate entities, since their members behave differently. Similarly, CURRENT STUDENTS and ALUMNI are two different entities.

All of the entities in Figure 5-3 have in common that they represent stable, long-term aspects of an organization's environment. It is likely that the organization will keep a permanent record of each customer, of each supplier, and of each part. For that reason, entities where long-term data is kept on each instance (e.g., on each individual customer) are called *permanent entities*

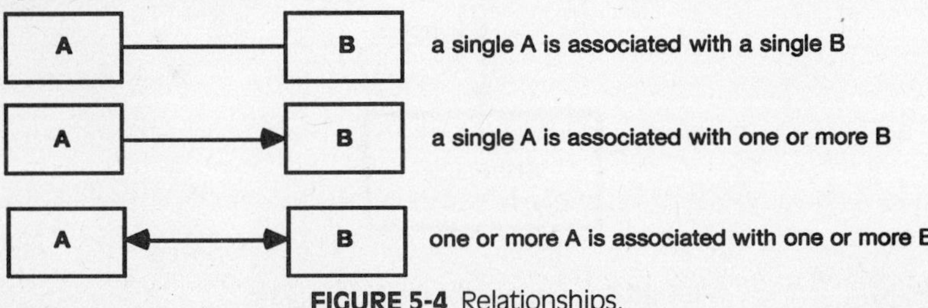

FIGURE 5-4 Relationships.

Entities may have various *relationships*. These relationships are often named by putting the name next to the graphical depiction. Figure 5-4 illustrates the relationships with which we are concerned. These are usually referred to as *one-to-one*, *one-to-many*, and *many-to-many* relationships, respectively.

Figure 5-5 shows how entities and relationships are combined into an entity-relationship diagram. This example is highly simplified; real world systems have dozens or hundreds of entities. The completed entity-relationship diagram describes a high-level, abstract view of the system. Lower level views of data are described by sing the tools discussed in the next chapter.

How does one decide if two given real-world objects should be represented by one or two entities? For example, should PROPERTY and EQUIPMENT be one entity or two? The key to answering this question is that all instances of a given entity have the same data stored about them (the technical term for which is *attributes*). Thus, if we keep different information about PROPERTY and EQUIPMENT, they are two separate entities. If we keep exactly the same information, they are probably one entity. The next section of this chapter explains how we decide which data attributes are associated with which entities.

In designing for a modern system, we want to avoid many-to-many relationships such as those illustrated in Figure 5-5. Usually this can be done by adding additional entities that correspond to transactions; this is covered in the next chapter. However, sometimes the relationship is not described by a transaction. For example, in Figure 5-5, the relationship ORDERS between CUSTOMER and PART corresponds to a transaction and can therefore be ignored until the next chapter. On the other hand, the relationship SUPPLIES between PART and SUPPLIER does not correspond to a transaction; this is knowledge about which

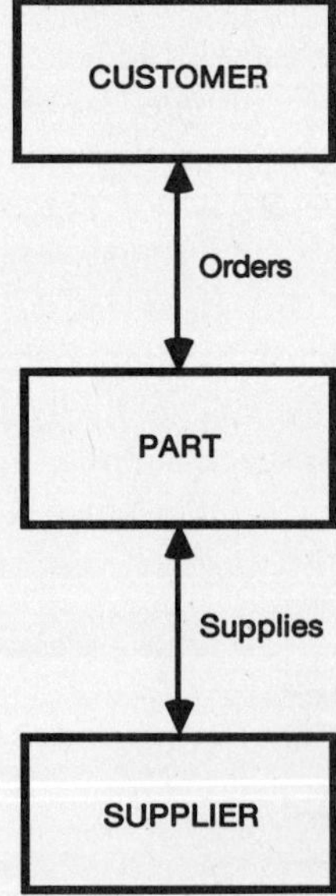

FIGURE 5-5 Entity-relationship diagram.

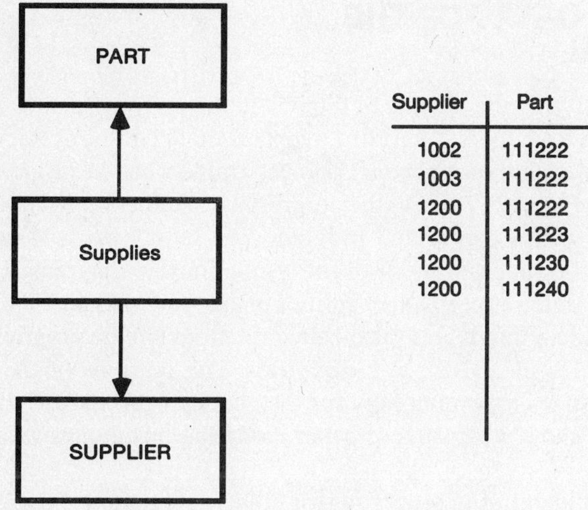

Supplier	Part
1002	111222
1003	111222
1200	111222
1200	111223
1200	111230
1200	111240

FIGURE 5-6 Entity-relationship diagram.

suppliers can supply which parts. This relationship must be revised by introducing a *linking entity* as illustrated in Figure 5-6. This linking entity contains data about SUPPLIER and PART with a record for each possible combination.

	Real World	**System Model**	**Program Model**	**Program**
Item	Objects	Permanent entities	Tables (relations)	`.dbf` files
Notations		Entity-relationship diagram		
Item	Properties	Attributes	Data elements	Data fields
Notations	Old physical data dictionary	Logical data dictionary	New physical data dictionary	dBASE field definitions

FIGURE 5-7 From real world to entity-relationship diagram to program.

DETERMINING DATA FOR THE SYSTEM MODEL

The process of identifying the objects of interest in the real world and creating an entity-relationship diagram from them is building a *logical* model of the system's *data*. The next step in building and revising such a model is to determine what the properties of the objects are in the real world. Figure 5-7 shows the progressive abstraction from real world through system model to program model and program (the latter two will be treated in later chapters). Note that this diagram is *not* an entity-relationship diagram! Roles or objects in the real world are modeled as permanent entities in the system model. Eventually (Chapter 7) we will translate them into tables (also called relations) in the program model and then implement these tables in dBASE as `.dbf` files. The portions of the diagram labeled "Item" show the changes in terminology for the concepts of interest; the boxed portions labeled "Notations" show what sorts of paper modeling techniques we use to show each item.

The process of identifying properties for objects is twofold. First, *assuming that the analyst has a good understanding of the underlying real-world system*, he or she may identify appropriate properties for each object from general knowledge. A more systematic approach is to examine data (forms, reports, files) used for the existing system, document that data in a physical data dictionary as an old physical model, convert it to a new logical model (documented with a logical data dictionary), and then assign data (called attributes in this context) to the appropriate entities. The techniques and the notations are all covered in the rest of this chapter.

It must be emphasized that the analyst must identify objects before analyzing existing data! It is not generally possible to derive a good data model from the raw data in the existing system.

Notation for Systems Analysis

In describing data structure at the systems analysis and program design level, we need a notation that is independent of our programming language, primarily to shield us from unnecessary details (such as length and number of decimal places) at early stages of the process when we are still trying to figure out what the logical structure of the data should be. At this level, there are two major competing notations: data dictionaries and data structure diagrams.

Data dictionaries, as illustrated in Figure 5-8, are alphabetical listings of the data elements that make up records. The notation used is

C = A + B C is composed of A and B.

C = [A | B] C is composed of A or B.

C = {A} C is composed of an unknown number of iterations of A

C = $^{m}_{n}$ {A} C is composed of from n to m iterations of A

C = (A) A is optional

C = *aaa* aaa is a comment

ADDRESS	=	NUMBER + STREET + CITY + [STATE I PROVINCE] + ZIP-CODE + COUNTRY + HOME-PHONE + WORK PHONE
AREA-CODE	=	*3 digit*
CITY	=	*Post Office designation—e.g., "Fairbanks", not "College"*
COUNTY	=	Spell out if not U.S.*
CUSTOMER-FILE	=	{CUSTOMER-RECORD}
CUTOMER-RECORD	=	ID + NAME + ADDRESS
EXCHANGE-CODE	=	1 digit internal; 3 digit external*
EXTENSION	=	*Up to 6 digits*
FIRST-NAME	=	*Name by which familiarly addressed*
HOME-PHONE	=	(AREA-CODE) + EXCHANGE-CODE + SUBSCRIBER-CODE + (EXTENSION)
ID	=	*Auto registration*
LAST-NAME	=	*Family name*
MAIDEN-NAME	=	*Self-defined*
MIDDLE-NAME	=	*Anything else*
NAME	=	LAST-NAME + FIRST-NAME + ([MIDDLE-NAME I MAIDEN-NAME])
NUMBER	=	*Leave blank if PO box*
PROVINCE	=	*Spelled out*
STATE	=	*Two-letter abbreviation*
STREET	=	*Include entire PO box number here*
SUBSCRIBER-CODE	=	*4 digit*
WORK-PHONE	=	(AREA-CODE) + EXCHANGE-CODE + SUBSCRIBER-CODE + (EXTENSION)
ZIP-CODE	=	*5 digit U.S.; 6 character Canada*

FIGURE 5-8 Data dictionary

Note that each piece of data is defined, either as part of a structure or as an elementary item defined with a comment.

Data dictionaries are organized alphabetically because they serve as a reference for all of the data defined by the analyst or designer. Data dictionaries are used for all of the data definition at the different stages of system design as illustrated in Figure 5-7. For example, they are used in building the physical model for documenting the contents of forms, reports, and files and for building the logical model by documenting the contents of the entities in an entity-relationship diagram.

First, one decides what entities should be in the system; and then one decides what attributes (data) each entity will contain. These attributes are documented in a data dictionary. For example, if we have a permanent entity called **STUDENT**, it may be defined as:

STUDENT = ID# + Name + Address + Local_phone + Home_phone + School

Each of the attributes (data elements, such as **ID#**, **Name**, **Address**, **Local_phone**, **Home_phone**, **School**) is then defined. Note that there is one data dictionary to document the entire entity-relationship diagram. Also note that if new versions of the entity-relationship diagram are prepared, new data dictionaries must be prepared to match them. In other words, a data dictionary is not a document that stands alone, but rather is used to support other design documents.

The alternative form of notation for attributes is the *data structure diagram*, which is simply a data dictionary in graphical form. Figure 5-9 shows an example (note that ADDRESS is not defined, because of space). Data structure diagrams make it far easier to see and to understand the structure of data in a system; at the same time they lose the information in the comments, and have traditionally been harder to maintain. With modern computing tools, information on data generally can be kept in data dictionary format and the software can draw data structure diagrams from this as needed.

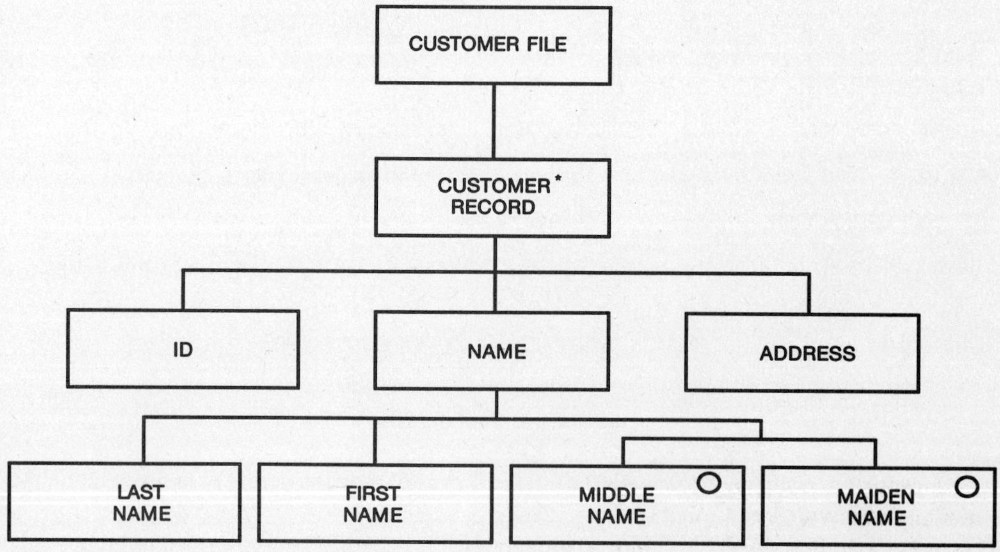

FIGURE 5-9 Data structure diagram.

The star in the CUSTOMER RECORD box in Figure 5-9 means iteration; the circles in the MIDDLE NAME and MAIDEN NAME boxes mean "or" (i.e., MIDDLE NAME or MAIDEN NAME).

Note that the term "data structure diagram" is used for a wide variety of different techniques; the definition used in this book is taken from the Jackson program design methodology (Martin and McClure, in their book *Diagramming Techniques for Analysts and Programmers*, refer to these as "Michael Jackson Diagrams" to avoid confusion). The definition of the term "data structure diagram" seems to be different in each of the dozens of books on systems analysis or program design. Be aware that industry-wide it is a content-free expression, and that in this book it means "Michael Jackson Diagrams." Data structure diagrams (and the associated Michael Jackson program design methodology) will be used in Chapter 15 to design modules. For the rest of this section, we will use data dictionary notation, since it is easier to maintain on an MSDOS computer without special software.

The contents of all containers of data are defined by the data dictionary. There are several advantages to this approach, for example:

- Avoiding redundancy
- Task isolation
- Data abstraction

Avoiding redundancy means that each data element and each data structure should be defined in only one place. This is particularly important for systems where there is more than one person working on the project. It is one of the main features of the "database" approach to designing information systems, which is a major theme of this book. Avoiding redundancy results in greater consistency between the parts of a system.

Task isolation means that at each stage of the design task, one concentrates only on that aspect of the problem that is relevant at that time. The key here is to worry only about one thing at a time. This helps get around the limits of the human information processing system by turning a large problem into many smaller ones.

A major theme throughout this chapter has been data abstraction: using a hierarchy of data definitions at different levels of detail. As one develops a system top-down, at each level of design and for each level of procedural abstraction, there is an appropriate level of data abstraction. A corollary principle is that each level of the program hierarchy should hide at least one detail of data from the levels above. At higher levels, one worries about which data objects a system will deal with but not about which fields and how wide they will be. At more detailed levels, one worries about the particular fields ("should we allow for both maiden name and middle name?"), whereas at the lowest levels one worries about type, size, base, and other low-level tasks (Chapter 7).

Documenting the Current Physical Model

The most tedious, but the most important part of the procedure for building the physical model is identifying the data elements in the existing system (whether manual or automated).

Identify objects in real-world environment.

- Define permanent entities based on objects.

Identify data in the existing system creating physical data dictionary.
Revise to produce logical data dictionary.
For each entity

- Assign attributes (data elements).

FIGURE 5-10 Procedure for implementing entities.

This means taking a census of all of the forms, files, reports, screens, and programs in use and building a database of variable names and definitions. In a real-world system, there may be thousands or even hundreds of thousands of such data items; therefore, building this physical data dictionary by using a database management system (such as dBASE) to keep track of them is highly recommended. The data in question should be analyzed to remove obvious redundancies. The results of this process will be used in the next step of this chapter ("Converting the Current Physical Model to a Logical Model") as well as in Chapter 9.

Often the names of the forms, files, reports, screens, and programs in the current system reflect the physical implementation rather than what tasks are being carried out. Data names may also reflect the physical implementation and are likely to be inconsistent from program to program, file to file, and form to form. Because this view of the system reflects the particular implementation, we call it the "old physical model." Our next task as analysts is to convert this data to a form that is consistent, meaningful, and general.

Converting the Current Physical Model to a Logical Model

The first step in revising the physical model of the system is to eliminate conflicts between inconsistent data names and to make sure that the same data is referred to by the same name throughout the data dictionary. For example, one form may use the term "Last name," another may refer to the same data as "surname," another as "family name," whereas programs may use the abbreviation "LNAME." The analyst should choose one term and apply it consistently.

Other things to look for are undefined items, references to current physical implementation (such as attaching the program name, a paragraph number, or a data structure name to a piece of data), data that appears to be unused, and data that can be calculated from other data. For example, if a report includes totals, the totals should only be included in the logical data dictionary as parts of reports, since they will not be stored in the database.

Assigning Attributes to Entities

One confusing aspect of the conversion of the current physical model to a logical model is that the physical model documents input and output forms and reports as well as data that is used internally by the system. Our interest at the moment is in assigning attributes to entities; hence, we will not use some of the data. Chapter 6 introduces another type of entity that will make use of more of the data items identified in the physical model, and Chapter 9 introduces screens and reports that will make use of additional data used for input and output. The main thing to keep in mind at the moment is that the analysis of forms, reports, files, and so on will document more data than we will use at this point in the analysis.

Figure 5-10 reviews the approach which we use for data modelling.

CASE EXAMPLE

In this example, let us look at a university registration system. Figure 5-11 shows *some* of the high-level entities that may be important in such a system. Our first problem is to draw the boundaries around the target system. A good rule of thumb is: "When in doubt, leave it out." Let us suppose that further investigation of the existing system convinces us that only those entities that are shaded are relevant for our system investigation. This leaves us with four permanent entities.

Figures 5-12 through 5-15 illustrate some of the forms and reports used in the system whose entities are shown in Figure 5-11. Figure 5-2 shows the form of the student record, Figure 5-13 shows the registration form that the student uses to request a class, Figure 5-14 shows the form of the class list that goes to the instructor, and Figure 5-15 shows the format of the course record. As part of the documentation of the original manual system, we need to keep track of the data elements or attributes contained in each entity. In practice, one starts the analysis by gathering together the forms and reports from the existing system and taking a census of the data. Figure 5-16 shows a sample data dictionary constructed from the documents in Figures 5-12 to 5-15.

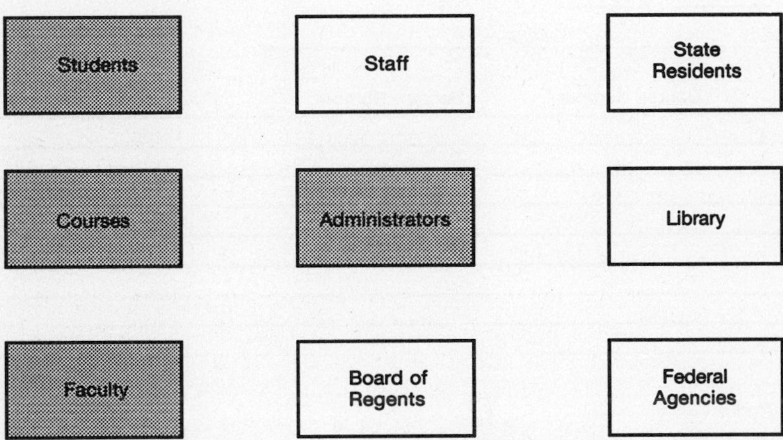

FIGURE 5-11 Regisration entities: stage 1.

Student Record

Last name: ______________ First name: ____________ Middle name: ______________

ID number ______ ____ ______

Permanent Address: ______________________________ ________________________
___ ______________

Street City State Zip

Local Address: ___________________________________ ______________ _____
____

Street City State Zip

Home Phone: (______) _____________ Local Phone: __________________

School: ____________

Degree Program: BA ___ BS ___ BBA ___ BSE ___ MA ___ MS ___ MBA ___ PhD ___

Date of first entry: _____ _____ 19 _____
Month Day Year

Total Credits Towards Graduation: ______

FIGURE 5-12 Student record.

Registration Form

Name: ____________________ ID: ______________________
Date: ____________________

School: __________________ Level: ____________________

Dept.	Course Number	Section Number	Course Title	Credits

Total Credits ____________

FIGURE 5-13 Registration form.

Class List

Year: ______ Term: ______ Dept: ______ Course: ______ Date: ______

Instructor: ____________________ Course

Title: ____________________

Student name	ID	Phone	School	Degree

Total Students: ______

FIGURE 5-14 Class list.

Course Record

Dept: __________ Number: ______ Credits: ______ Section

Type: ____________________

Title: ____________________

College: ____________________

Section: ______ Instuctor: ______________

Meeting Time: ________ Meeting Place: ________

Prerequisite: ____________ ____________

Department Course number

FIGURE 5-15 Course record.

BA	= *Bachelor of Arts*
BBA	= *Bachelor of Business Administration*
BS	= *Bachelor of Science*
BSE	= *Bachelor of Science in Engineering*
Building name	= *self-defined*
City	= *Post Office designation, e.g., "Fairbanks", not "College"*
Class list	= Year + Term + Dept. + Course + Section number + Date + Instructor + Course title + {Student name + ID + Phone + School + Degree} + Total students
College	= ["Liberal Arts" | "Engineering" | "Management" | "Natural Resources"]
Course	= *3-digit course number*
Course number	= *3-digit course number*
Course record	= Dept. + Number + Credits + Section type + title + College + Section + Instructor + Meeting time + Meeting place + Prerequisite
Course title	= *name of course from catalog*
Credits	= *number of credits*
Date	= Month + Day + Year*date of computer run*
Date of first entry	= Month + Day + Year*date first admitted*
Day	= *self-defining*
Degree	= [BA | BS | BBA | BSE | MA | MS | MBA | PhD]
Degree program	= [BA | BS | BBS | BSE | MA | MS | MBA | PhD]
Department	= *name of department from catalog*
Dept.	= *name of department from catalog*
First name	= *personal name*
Home phone	= *include area code*
ID	= *social security number + check digit*
Instructor	= Last name + First name
Last name	= *family name*
Local address	= Street + City + State + Zip
Local phone	= *no area code*
MA	= *Master of Arts*

FIGURE 5-16 Data dictionary for old physical model of registration system. (continued)

MBA	= *Master of Business Administration*
Meeting place	= Room number + Building name
Meeting time	= *24-hour basis*
Middle name	= *any other name*
Month	= *01–12*
MS	= *Master of Science*
Name	= Last name + First name + Middle name
Number	= *3-digit course number*
Permanent address	= Street + City + State + Zip
PhD	= *Doctor of Philosophy*
Phone	= *local phone number*
Prerequisite	= *3-digit course number*
Prerequiste	= Department + Course number
Registration form	= Name + ID + Date + School + Level + {Dept. + Course number + Section number + Course title + Credits} + Total credits
Room number	= *4 digits*
School	= ["Liberal Arts" | "Engineering" | "Management" | "Natural Resources"]
Section	= *2-digit number*
Section type	= ["Lecture" | "Lab" | "Recitation" | "Individual Study"]
State	= *Post Office address*
Student name	= Last name + First name + Middle name
Student record	= Last name + First name + Middle name + ID + Permanent address + Local address + Home phone + Local phone + School + Degree program + Date of first entry + Total credits toward graduation
Term	= ["Fall" | "Spring" | "Summer"]
Title	= *name of course from catalog*
Total credits	= *sum of credit hours on this page*
Total credits toward graduation	= *as of previous term*
Total students	= *nuimber of students in class*
Year	= *last two digits only*
Zip	= *5-digit*

FIGURE 5-16 Data dictionary for old physical model of registration system.

Entities

STUDENT RECORD	=	Last name + First name + Middle name + ID number + Local address + Home address + Home phone + Local phone + College + Degree program + Date of first entry + Total credit toward graduation
COURSE	=	Year + Term + Dept. + Course number + Course title + Section number + Section type + Date + Last name + First name*Instructor* + Course title + Credits + Prerequisite + Meeting time + Building name + Room number
INSTRUCTOR	=	ID number + Last name + First name + Middle name + Building name + Room number + Home phone + Local Phone + College + Dept.

Attributes

Compound

Instructor	=	Last name + First name
Local address	=	Street + City + State + Zip
Home address	=	Street + City + State + Zip
Prerequisite	=	Dept. + Course number

Elements

Building name	=	*abbreviation from campus map*
City	=	*Post Office designation, e.g. "Fairbanks", not "College"*
College	=	["Liberal Arts" | "Engineering" | "Management" | "Natural Resources"]
Course title	=	*Name of course from catalog*
Credits	=	*number of credits*
Course number	=	*3 digits*
Date	=	*self-defined*
Date of first entry	=	*date first admitted*
Degree program	=	[BA | BS | BBA | BSE | MA | MS | MBA | PhD]
Dept.	=	*name of department from catalog*
First name	=	*personal name*
Home phone	=	*include area code*
ID number	=	*socal security number + check digit*

FIGURE 5-17 Revised data dictionary for registration system. (continued)

Last name	=	*family name*
Local phone	=	*no area code*
Meeting time	=	*24-hour basis*
Middle name	=	*any other name*
Room number	=	*3 digit*
Section number	=	*3 digit*
Section type	=	["Lecture" I "Lab" I "Recitation" I "Individual Study"]
State	=	*2-character post office abbreviation*
Street	=	*Post Office address*
Term	=	["Fall" I "Spring" I "Summer"]
Total credits toward graduation		=*as of previous term*
Year	=	*Last two digits only*
Zip	=	*allow for Canadian postal codes*
		Miscellaneous Data
Class list	=	Year + Term + Dept. + Course + Section number + Date + Instructor + Course title + [Student name + ID + Phone + School + Degree] + Total Students
Course Record	=	Dept. + Number + Credits + section type + title + College + Section + Instructor + Meeting time + Meeting place + Prerequisite
Registration form	=	Name + ID + Date + School + Level + Graduating this term flag + {Dept. + Course number + Section number + Course title + Credits} + Total Credits
Meeting place	=	Room number + Building name
Total credits	=	*sum of credit hours on this page*
Total students	=	*number of students in class*

FIGURE 5-17 Revised data dictionary for registration system

The data dictionary in Figure 5-16 reflects the existing registration forms, but has several problems. The most obvious is inconsistent data names; for example, **Course** and **Course number** represent the same data, as do **Course title** and **Title.** The first step in revising the physical model of the system is to eliminate these conflicts and make certain that all of the data documented in the data dictionary is internally consistent. Are there undefined items? Are there multiple names for the same things?

Figure 5-17 shows the data dictionary revised to remove these inconsistencies and to document the contents of three of the four entities identified in Figure 15-1. Where possible, multiple levels (e.g., **Record = Name**; **Name = Last name + First name + Middle name**) have been flattened, so that each permanent entity consists of only elementary data items. In some instances (such as with **Local address** and **Home address** in STUDENT RECORD), this is not possible because the same data element name would occur several times in a single record. The entity ADMINISTRATOR is not defined with attributes, since the forms shown did not contain any data that applies to administrators. This means either that ADMINISTRATOR is not a relevant entity for this system or that we have not analyzed all of the possible data sources. For the rest of the case study, we shall assume that administrators are not relevant.

Note that the permanent entities COURSE and INSTRUCTOR are not based on a particular record or report in the manual system, but were identified as important objects in Figure 5-11. The attributes for COURSE and INSTRUCTOR were selected by going through the data and selecting those attributes that appear relevant.

SUMMARY

This chapter presents the concept of entities as abstractions of real-world objects. Modeling entities, their attributes, and the relationships between them is the first step in designing a new system.

This modeling is done in three stages. They are:

- Identify the entities in the existing system.
- Identify the data attributes of all entities in the existing system
- Modify the resulting model to reflect desired changes in the system.

QUESTIONS AND EXERCISES

1. What is a permanent entity?
   a. An abstraction of a real-world object that an organization is concerned with for the long term.
   b. An abstraction of a real-world object that impacts a transient entity.
   c. An object that a firm owns.
   d. A permanent piece of data.
2. What is the first step in designing a new system?
   a. Talking to the management involved.
   b. Determining the problems in the system.
   c. Modeling the entities and the relationships between them.
   d. Modeling the transient entities.
3. A work order is a example of a
   a. Permanent entity.
   b. Transient entity.
   c. Data entity.
   d. Transient relationship.

4. Data-oriented approaches to systems analysis include
   a. Entity-relationship diagrams.
   b. Data flow diagrams.
   c. Flow charts.
   d. Hierarchy.
5. An example of a permanent entity is
   a. Work order.
   b. Customer.
   c. Purchase order.
   d. Class schedule.
6. What approaches were developed for database applications and are particularly suited for fourth generation languages?
   a. Process approaches
   b. Data-oriented approaches.
   c. Traditional approaches.
   d. Radical approaches.
7. Something in the real world about which we store data is
   a. An entity.
   b. A relationship.
   c. A section.
   d. A file.
8. What are the four reasons for interposing the extra steps involved in first building a paper model?
   a. To partition the task between stages of the life-cycle to minimize cognitive overload.
   b. To partition the task within a single stage of the life-cycle to minimize cognitive overload.
   c. To maximize use of pattern matching abilities.
   d. To shield the designer from irrelevant details.
9. A permanent entity
   a. Is a supernatural being.
   b. An unfixable bug in a program.
   c. The hardware to run a system.
   d. Contains similar long-term data.
10. Systems analysis:
   a. Details what hardware is being used.
   b. Figures out what the user wants, what the system can do, and finds the middle ground where both can work.
   c. Determines where the program coding can be improved
   d. Attempts to determine why the current system went insane
11. Data-oriented approaches to system analysis
   a. Were developed for fourth generation languages.
   b Are usable only with COBOL.
   c. Require some knowledge of engineering.
   d. Are referred to as “structured“ techniques.

DISCUSSION QUESTIONS

1. Why build paper models before starting the coding?
2. What is systems analysis?

NORTHSTAR AVIATION

Part 2

1. Identify the entities for Northstar as described in Part 1 of the case. Create an entity-relationship diagram for them.
2. Create a logical data dictionary for the forms discussed in Part 1 of the case and revise your entity-relationship diagram as necessary. The major decisions that you have to make in this process are as follows:
   a. What information should be kept on customers, and what key should be used for the customer file?
   b. What information should be kept on suppliers, and what key should be used?
   c. Should separate information be kept on airplanes, or should that information be included with the customer data? If it is kept separately, how should it be linked to customers?

By way of supporting information, each airplane has a unique federal registration number (called an "N-number" because U.S. registrations begin with "N"). Approximately 10% of customers own more than one airplane, and about the same number sell airplanes annually. Of those who sell their airplanes, most buy a replacement (usually used) within a year. About 75% of used airplanes are bought and sold locally (which for airplanes means in-state); the rest are acquired or disposed of outside of the state.

REFERENCES

MARTIN, J. and C. MCCLURE. *Diagramming Techniques for Analysts and Programmers*. Prentice-Hall, Englewood Cliffs, NJ, 1985.

SHLAER, S., and S. MELLOR. *Object Oriented Systems Analysis*. Prentice Hall- Yourdon Press, Englewood Cliffs, NJ, 1988.

Chapter 6

HIGH LEVEL DATA REPRESENTATIONS: DATA FLOW DIAGRAMS AND EVENT MODELING

CHAPTER GOALS

- Learn to develop high-level data flow diagrams.
- Learn to identify logical events from data flow diagrams.
- Learn to identify transient entities from data flow diagrams.
- Learn to select attributes for transient entities.

This chapter discusses an alternative approach to systems analysis: the process-based approach. This is important for two reasons. First, it is the standard modern approach for analysis and design in a third generation environment, widely used in real life. Second, it aids the analyst in completing the data model begun in the previous chapter and provides an important link used in deriving the program model of a system after the analysis is completed.

Process approaches to systems analysis are typified by the Yourdon data flow diagramming approaches (Demarco 1979, Gane & Sarson 1979, Powers, et al. 1984). They were assembled into the first modern system development methodologies in the mid-1970s. This approach is often referred to as "structured analysis." The methodology

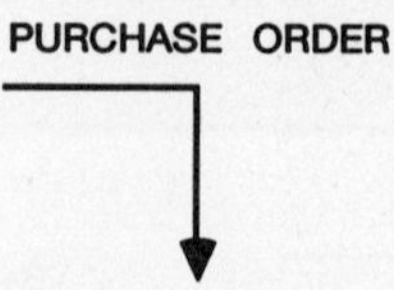

FIGURE 6-1 Data flow.

concentrates on determining the flow of data between parts of the system. A specification from the systems analysis phase consists of the following:

- Data flow diagrams.
- Data dictionary.
- Structured English.

Data dictionaries were discussed in the previous chapter; "structured" English will be discussed in Chapter 14. The next few paragraphs introduce the data flow diagram, which is the basic feature of "structured analysis." The rest of the chapter describes how to integrate data flow diagrams with data modeling in a fourth generation environment.

A data flow diagram is a network model of a system; it describes the processes that occur and the data flows between them. The notation is designed to be easily drawn using only paper and pencil and to be close enough to user views that a non–computer-oriented user can understand the diagram.

The basic element of the data flow diagram is the data flow, represented as an arrow (Figure 6-1). The arrow should be thought of as a pipe through which streams of data flow. Arrows do not indicate control (as they would on a flowchart) but only flow of data. The contents of the data flows are documented in a data dictionary.

The other major component in a data flow diagram is the process (Figure 6-2), which is represented by a circle or an oval (referred to as a "bubble"; hence, data flow diagrams are often referred to as "bubble charts"). The process represents something that transforms a data flow. In our plumbing model of a system, the data flows are pipes and a process may

FIGURE 6-2 Process.

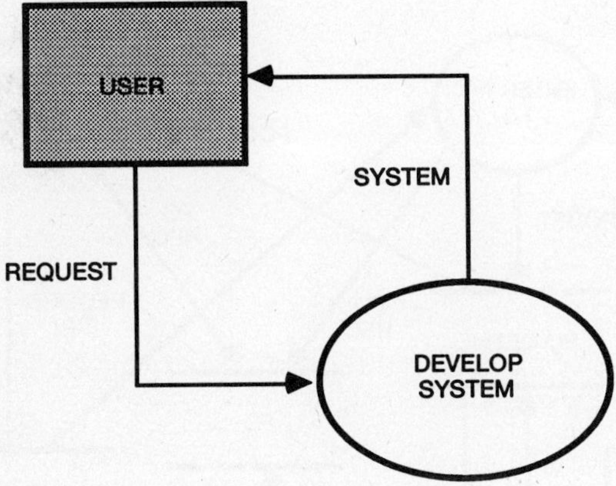

FIGURE 6-3 Sources and sinks.

be thought of as a filter. Chapter 14 discusses notations for describing what goes on in the bubbles. The name of the process should be a verb–object expression that describes the action that is performed on the data, for example:

Compute square root.

Get supplier data.

Check supplier validity.

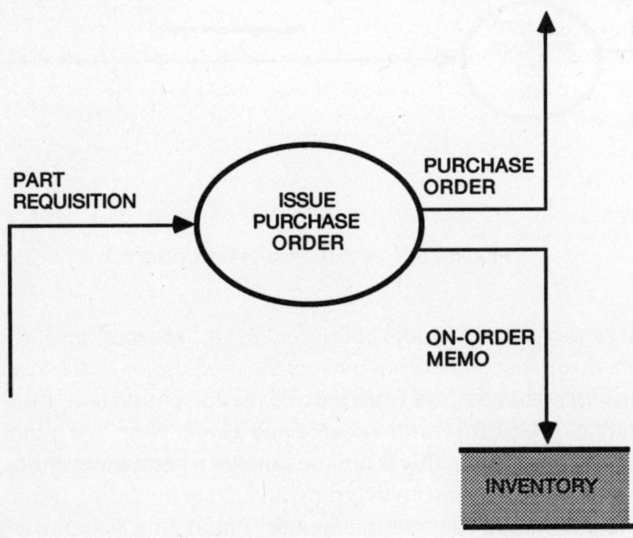

FIGURE 6-4 Data store.

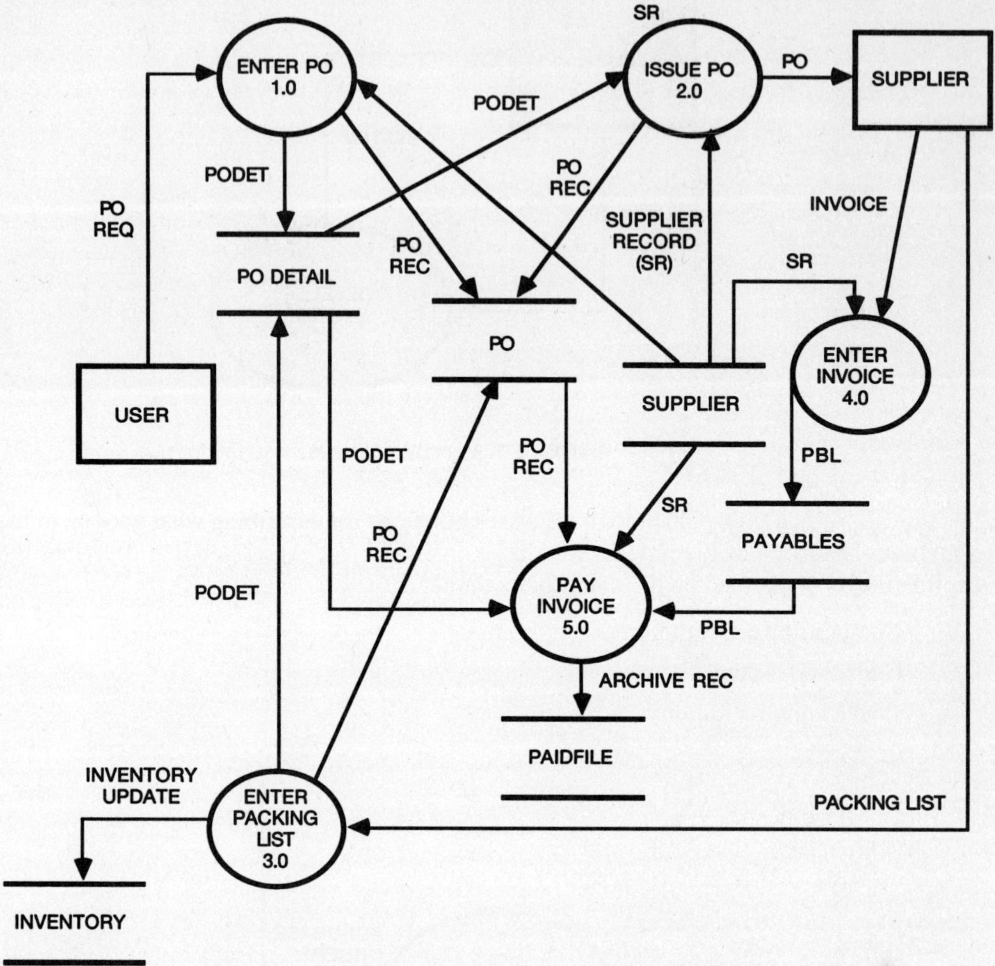

FIGURE 6-5 First-level data flow diagram.

Additional elements in the model of the system are "sources" and "sinks." A "source" is a source of data flows that come from outside the boundaries of the system under study. A "sink" is a consumer of data flows from outside the current system. Both are represented by boxes. In Figure 6-3, USER is both a source and a sink. Note that although the notation for source and sink is a rectangle, this is not the same as a permanent entity. Data modeling (represented by an entity-relationship diagram) and event modeling (represented by a data flow diagram) are alternative (but complementary) modeling systems with incompatible notations. The notations presented here are those used in the real world; they are incompatible, since the two approaches were developed separately.

The boundaries of the system under study are determined by the task assignment or the problem; they are not absolute. For example, at a university the system under study might be the registration system, or the Office of the Registrar. The former is a subset of the latter. Similarly, for a small company, the system under study could be order entry, or it might be the entire transaction processing system. Beginners at systems analysis often cast their nets too widely; they are not willing to restrict themselves to the relevant subset of the overall system.

Sometimes data flows are not used directly by other bubbles but are stored for later use in another part of the system. The place where they are stored is known as a "data store" (most of us call it a file). The symbol for a data store (Figure 6-4) is a pair of lines with the name of the data store between them. The contents of data stores are described in the data dictionary.

Figure 6-5 illustrates how all of the parts fit together *with* a first-level flow diagram for a sample purchase order system. One thing to note at this point is that a realistic detailed system description requires dozens or hundreds of bubbles—far more than can easily fit on a sheet of paper. To get around this problem, data flow diagrams are "leveled" or constructed hierarchically. Each numbered bubble in Figure 6-5 has associated with it a more detailed second-level data flow diagram on a separate page.

To make the overall structure of the system more obvious, most process modeling starts with an overview (or "level zero") data flow diagram, as illustrated in Figure 6-6. *This diagram should be the starting point of event modeling, since the most important part of the model is to determine what are the flows of data into and out of the system.*

In expanding an overview data flow diagram to a first-level data flow diagram, we will generally add a process bubble to take care of each data flow that enters or leaves the overall system and will then add bubbles as needed to make this second set of bubbles work together.

Process-oriented approaches as described above are probably the most common approach to systems analysis today; certainly they are the most widely taught. They were originally developed for third generation languages by using conventional file designs rather than database management systems. They are, however, still useful; the change in language level means primarily that processes need not be split into subfunctions in as much detail, since each bubble can do more. Many analysts find that in a fourth generation language environment, a first-level data flow diagram as illustrated in Figure 6-6 is helpful at both the Build Physical Model and the Determine User Requirements stages. At that point, once the user agrees that the data flow diagrams are an accurate description of reality, the analyst can use data modeling to check and improve the entity-relationship diagram.

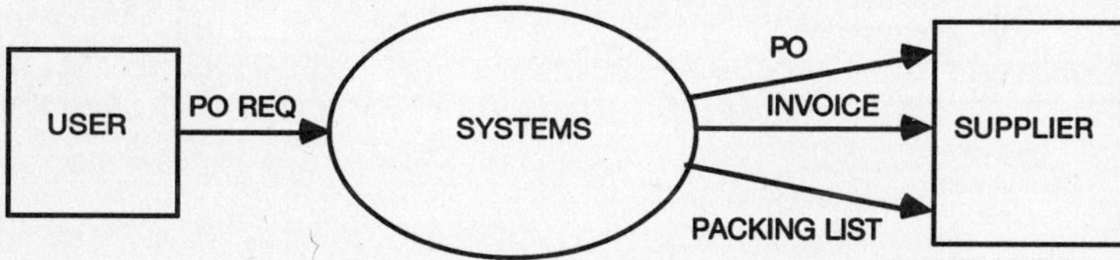

FIGURE 6-6 Overview data flow diagram.

The key phrase here is "once the user agrees." A major benefit of data flow diagrams is that they are close to the user's point of view; most users view their systems as flows of documents between people. Data flow diagrams are thus useful to document existing systems and to combine different user views of the systems in such a way that the analyst can understand the whole.

When data flow diagrams are used to document existing systems, often they will highlight problems that had gone unnoticed. The most common situation is a dead-end data flow.

Dead-end data flows are very common in systems that have been used and changed over a long period of time. They often represent data that was needed at some time in the past but that is no longer used. Often the system goes on gathering this data long after it is no longer useful.

Figure 6-7 illustrates an example of this in a student registration system. Until the 1960s, colleges and universities were legally *in loco parentis*; a legal doctrine that held that

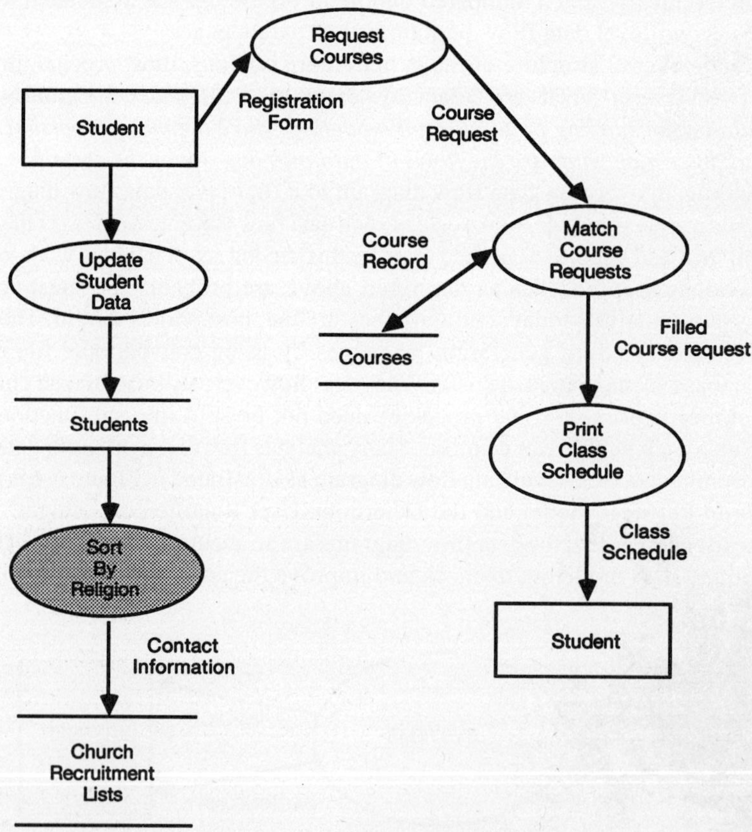

FIGURE 6-7 Dead-end data flow.

Identify events in real-world environment. • Define transient entities spawned by each event. Identify actions (responses to events) in real-world environment. • Define transient entities spawned by each action. Assign attributes to transient entities. Determine constraints in the order of the events and actions.

FIGURE 6-8 Event modelling methodology.

they had parental responsibilities towards their students, especially with respect to moral guidance. Thus, for example, it was common to encourage church attendance. Figure 6-7 shows data on religious preferences being gathered as part of registration so that student data could be sorted by sect and distributed to local ministers. As both the law and social concepts of privacy changed, this data could no longer be sent out, but the system continued to gather it. The dead-end data flow highlighted in Figure 6-7 is a hint to the analyst to examine the contents of the data flow and to determine whether there is a problem. Sometimes dead-end data flows are not errors, but are included for audit purposes or because a government entity requires that the data be gathered even though it is not used.

USE OF DATA FLOW DIAGRAMS WITH DATA MODELS

The second advantage of data flow diagrams is that they are useful in identifying *events*, *actions*, and *reports*. All of these are important in translating between the system model and the program model (Chapter 11). Reports are the way in which system data looks to outside users. Events are those occurrences in the real world that give rise to changes in permanent entities. Actions are activities carried on inside the system that cause changes to permanent entities.

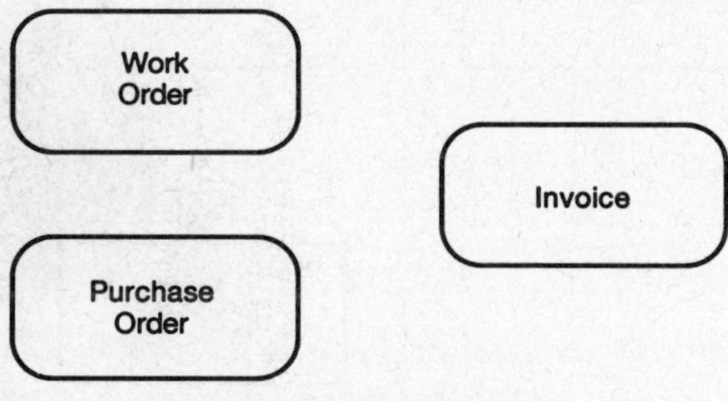

FIGURE 6-9 Transient entities.

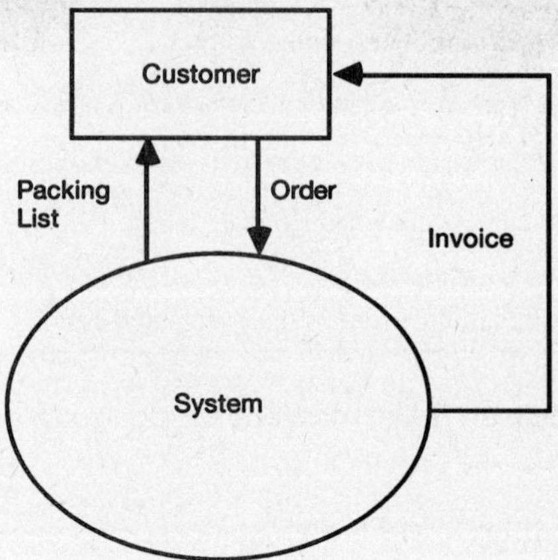

FIGURE 6-10 Overview data flows.

The procedure for using events to complete the system model is shown in Figure 6-8. A reminder—although we use data flow diagrams to build entity-relationship diagrams, a data flow diagram cannot be transformed into an entity-relationship diagram. They represent very different views of a system. An entity-relationship diagram is a view of static, unchanging data structures and relationships. A data flow diagram is a view of action: what happens to a piece of data as it flows through the system. We emphasize entity-relationships diagrams in this book because they are more easily transformed into fourth generation languages systems.

Define Transient Entities Spawned by Each Event

Accounting theory tells us that in addition to the permanent entities, described in the previous chapter, there are also transient entities such as work order, where each instance

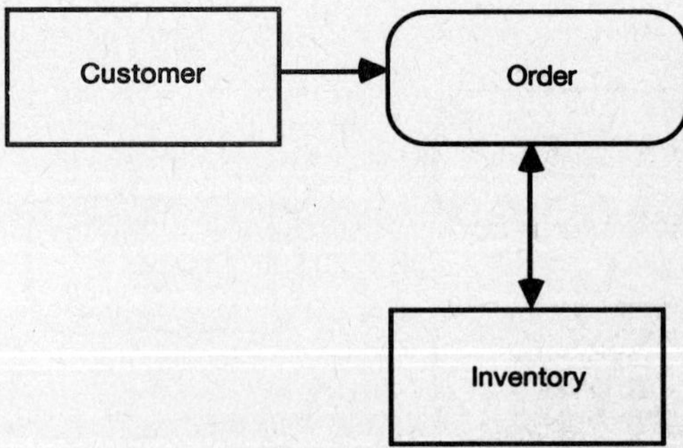

FIGURE 6-11 Event as single transient entity.

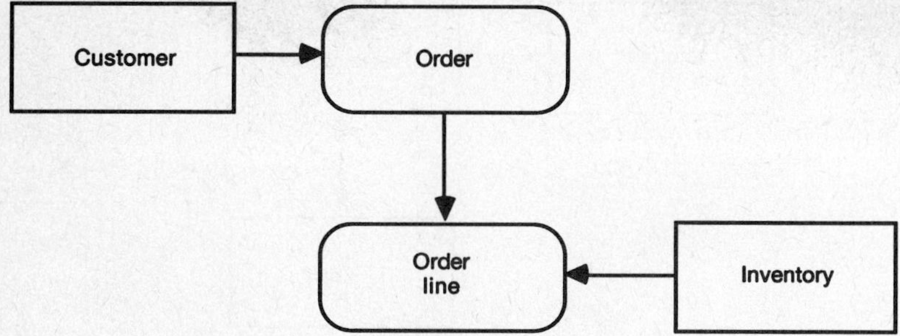

FIGURE 6-12 Modified representation of transient entities .

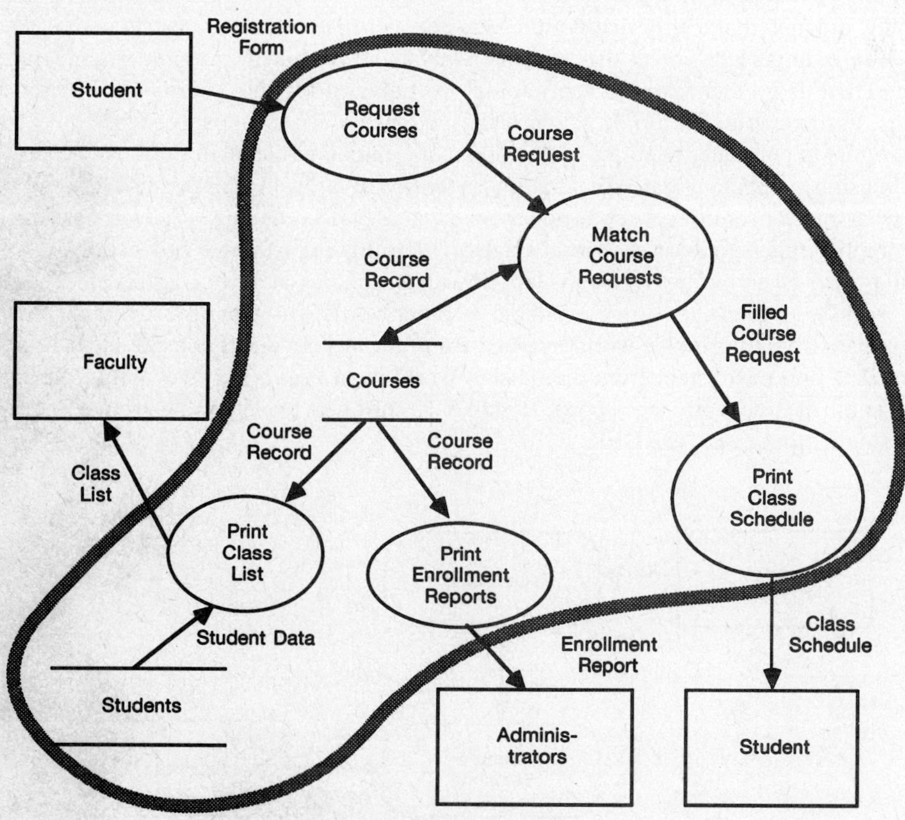

FIGURE 6-13 Registration system data flow diagram.

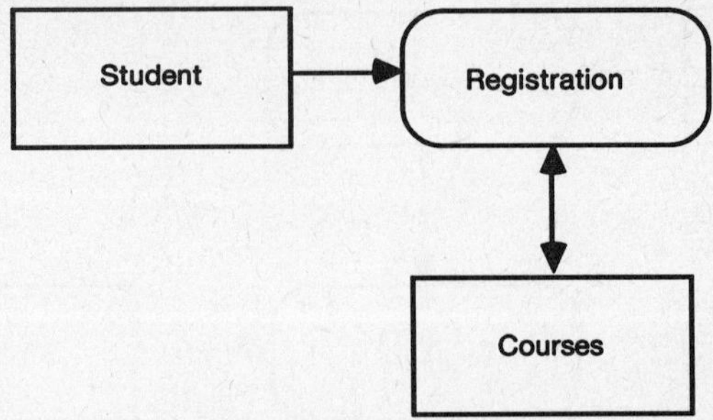

FIGURE 6-14 Registration as single transient entity.

is relevant for a short period of time and is of interest primarily for its effects on permanent entities. Such entities are illustrated in Figure 6-9. As you can see, transient entities often correspond to transaction types discussed in Chapter 3. The original version of data modeling did not make this distinction between permanent and transient entity; the distinction is important not in the systems analysis stage, but in program architecture design. There is no standardized terminology or notation for this approach to systems analysis. For example, UNISYS, which makes extensive use of the approach [UNISYS 1986], refers to permanent entities as "components" and to transient entities as "events."

In using events to update the data model (entity-relationships diagram), we need to know what transient entities are spawned by the event REGISTRATION. A fairly easy way to accomplish this is to do it in several stages. The following example shows how.

Figure 6-10 shows an overview data flow diagram, one at such a high level that all of the processes are subsumed in one bubble. In other words, this data flow diagram shows flows of data from the outside world into and out of the system under consideration. Each flow of data into the system from the outside world is an event. Flows of data from the system to the outside world are reports. Figure 6-10 shows an overview data flow diagram with a single input event: ORDER.

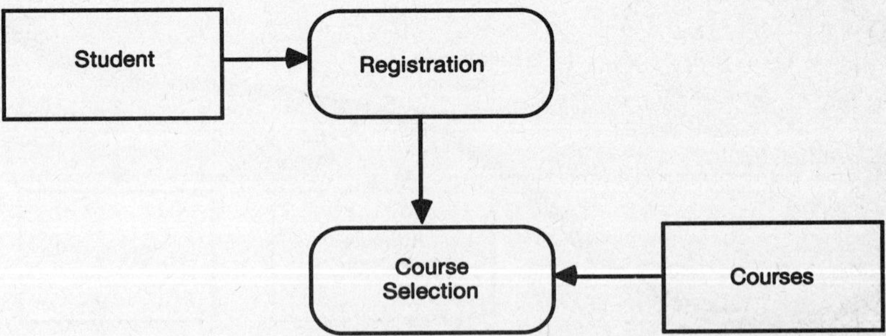

FIGURE 6-15 Modified representation of transient entities.

First we assume that each event spawns a single transient entity that impacts one or more permanent entities. In this case, we assume that the event ORDER spawns a transient entity by the same name. We add that transient entity to the data model, as illustrated in Figure 6-11.

The next step is to remove many-to-many relationships by splitting the compound transactions that have them into transactions that deal with only one permanent entity. In our example, a single order (associated with a customer) has multiple order lines, each of which is associated with a single item in inventory (Figure 6-12).

There are two reasons for the extra step depicted in Figure 6-12. The major one is that it helps us distinguish between events and actions. For example, in our example above, a customer ordering something is an event that spawns a transient entity called ORDER. Each time an item is picked to fill the order, we have an action. When we implement the program, the original event and the actions that represent the system's response to it are likely to be separate parts of the program, to be carried out at separate times.

The other reason is closely related; a transient entity spawned by an event may exist separately and independently from one spawned by an action that responds to that event. For example, an instance of a particular order from a customer may exist for some time before the first action is taken to respond to it; the order exists independently of work that is done in response to it.

At this stage we must decide which data elements should be used to describe each of the new entities in our system. The basic rules are the following:

- All data about a permanent entity is assigned to that entity.
- Transient entities refer to permanent entities only by keys (Chapter 7).

CASE EXAMPLE

Figure 6-13 shows a preliminary data flow diagram for the Build Physical Model stage of the student registration system discussed in Chapter 5. The heavy gray line represents the boundary between the system and its environment (this is not part of the usual data flow diagram notation).

What this says in English is as follows. A source called **Student** submits a document called **Registration form** to a process called **Request courses**. That process passes each **Course request** to a process called **Match course requests**. This process uses data called **Course record** from the **Courses file,** and puts the changed record back in the **Courses file.**

Transient entities		
REGISTRATION	=	ID + Date
COURSE SELECTION	=	Dept. + Course number +Section number

FIGURE 6-16 Revised data dictionary for registration system.

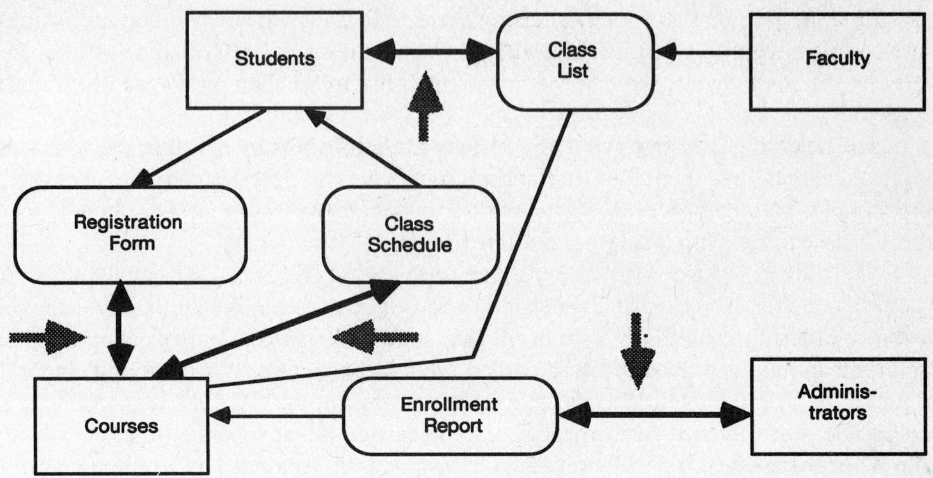

FIGURE 6-17 Registration system entity relationship diagram ready for normalization .

If the record were not changed, there would be no arrowhead showing data going back to the file. **Filled course requests** are passed on to a process called **Print class schedule.** At some other time, **Course records** are taken from the **Courses** file by the process **Print enrollment Reports**, which sends the resulting reports to the sink known as **Administrators.** Similarly, a process called **Print class list** takes data from the **Courses** file and from a **Students** file and generates **Class lists**, which are sent outside the system to **Faculty**.

Figure 6-13 shows four data flows penetrating the boundaries of the system. **Registration Form** is input to the system representing an event (which for grammatical correctness we might call Student Registration). **Class list**, **Enrollment Rrport**, and **Class schedule** are reports which go out of the system.

Figure 6-14 shows the preliminary entity-relationship diagram that results from the assumption that each event spawns a single transient entity. Note that it is identical in form, to the customer order example of Figure 6-11.

Figure 6-15 shows the next step: removing many-to-many relationships by splitting the compound transactions that have them into transactions that deal with only one permanent entity.

We have one incoming event in this system represented by REGISTRATION FORM. Let us design the transient entity spawned by the REGISTRATION EVENT.

In manual systems especially, the forms that document events are likely to contain much information about permanent entities to which the transient entity refers. This information is not needed, because it is already stored in the permanent entities. In our example, as long as we have the student ID number in the transient entity, any other data on the student may be found by looking it up in the permanent entity. Also, **Department** and **Course number** uniquely determine **Course title**, so that is also not necessary. In the example at hand, the elements in *italics* below are redundant.

Registration form = *Name* + ID + Date + *School* + *Level* + {Dept. + Course number + Section number + *Course title* + *Credits*} + Total credits

The revised definition of the transient entity is thus

Registration Form = ID + date + {Dept. + Course Number + Section Number} + Total Credits

This data, as we discussed with Figure 6-15, is divided between two transient entities: REGISTRATION and COURSE SELECTION. The data field **Total credits** is not needed in the database, since it can be calculated from data that is already stored. Figure 6-16 shows the revisions to the data dictionary from the previous chapter after we assign attributes to each entity.

Figure 6-17 shows an example of a more complete entity-relationship diagram where only the first step has been carried out. The shaded arrows point to places where revision is necessary. This revision is left as an exercise for the reader.

SUMMARY

Data flow diagrams are used because they help us understand the existing system and identify events in the real world and from these events, the transient entities that complete our data model. Data flow diagrams are also useful in the translation between the system-level model and the program-level model, as will be discussed in Chapter 11.

QUESTIONS AND EXERCISES

1. A transient entity is spawned by each
   a. Report.
   b. Action.
   c. Event.
   d. Customer.
2. A report is
   a. An input to the system.
   b. The internal system data.
   c. The way system data looks to outside users.
   d. The way systems data look to managers.
3. An example of an event in a transaction processing system is a
   a. Work order.
   b. Customer.
   c Supplier.
   d. Statement.

4. A transient entity spawned by an event may exist ________ and ________ from one spawned by an action which responds to that event.
   a. Together, dependently.
   b. Together, independently.
   c. Separately, dependently.
   d. Separately, independently.

5. When data flow diagrams are used to document existing systems, they often will highlight
   a. Problems that have been unnoticed.
   b. Lazy employees.
   c. Complexity of a simple problem.
   d. Output.

6. Data that was needed at some time in the past but not now is known as a:
   a. Hierarchy.
   b. Pattern recognition.
   c. Dead-end data flow.
   d. Prototype.

7. In a data flow diagram a sink
   a. Is a kitchen appliance.
   b. Consists of temporary entities.
   c. Handles only data in the boundaries of the system.
   d. Can also be a source.

8. An entity-relationship diagram is
   a. A view of the action of the system.
   b. An obsolete method for looking at a system.
   c. An unchanging view of the system.
   d. Easily transformed into a third generation language.

9. A data flow diagram
   a. Is a view of the action of the system.
   b Only shows the flow of data in a system.
   c. Is an unchanging view of what is outside the system.
   d. Is a mirror image of an entity relationship diagram.

10. What is the basic element of the data flow diagram?
   a. Elements.
   b. Dictionaries.
   c. Data flow.
   d. Entity.

11. How is a process represented in a data flow diagram?
   a. A box.
   b. A line.
   c. A triangle.
   d. An oval.

12. A consumer of data flows from outside the current system is a
    a. "Sink".
    b. "Source".
    c. "User".
    d. "Consumer".

DISCUSSION QUESTIONS

1. What are some of the benefits of data flow diagrams?
2. Describe a dead-end data flow and why they exist.

NORTHSTAR AVIATION

Part 3

1. Create a data flow diagram to describe Northstar's system.
2. Determine what are the events, actions, and reports for the Northstar system.
3. What transient entities do they spawn?
4. Update your entity-relationship diagram based on this information.
5. Update your data dictionary from Part 2 of the case to document the attributes of the new transient entities that you have identified.
6. What aspects of the system do you find you miss using a data flow diagram as opposed to an entity-relationship diagram? What aspects of the system do you find it easier to describe?

REFERENCES

DEMARCO, T. *Structured Analysis and System Specification*. Prentice-Hall, Englewood Cliffs, NJ, 1979.

DICKENSON, B. *Developing Structured Systems*. Prentice-Hall (Yourdon Press), Englewood Cliffs, NJ, 1980.

GANE, C., and T. SARSON. *Structured Systems Analysis: Tools and Techniques*. Prentice-Hall, Engleood Cliffs, NJ, 1979.

POWERS, M., D. ADAMS, and H. MILLS. *Computer Information Systems Development: Analysis and Design*. Southwestern, Cincinnati, OH, 1984.

UNISYS. *Logic and Information Network Compiler II (LINC II) Capabilities Overview*. Manual 1198272. August 1986.

Chapter 7

DATA TYPE AND STRUCTURE

CHAPTER GOALS:

- **Learn about types and implementation of data.**
- **Learn translation of data from system to program model.**
- **Learn to create dBASE tables.**

The previous chapters discussed high-level abstractions of data: entities and their relationships. This chapter discusses a more physical view of data: how attributes of data are defined. In other words, in this chapter we translate data models from the system model stage to the program model stage, and then into a dBASE implementation.

ALL ABOUT DATA

There are two properties of data that are of interest to us in this chapter: *type*, and *structure*. These are logical properties that apply to data irrespective of the programming language in use. They are, of course, translated into some real-world programming language—in our case dBASE.

To understand some of the aspects of data type and structure, it is useful to review alternative views of data in the program development process. Figure 7-1 illustrates the hierarchy of data views from the real world level to the dBASE program level and the notations that we will use to describe data at each level. In developing the system, we move from the more abstract views of data at the left to the more concrete (or silicon) views on the right, using the notations at the bottom of Figure 7-1.

REAL WORLD	SYSTEM MODEL	PROGRAM MODEL	dBASE SYSTEM
Properties	Attributes	Data elements	Data fields
Descriptions	Logical data dictionary	Physical data dictionary	dBASE field definitions

FIGURE 7-1 Hierarchy of data.

This figure is important because it illustrates a concept that is often ignored (and that is the source of much confusion in communication with users). That concept is that the proper view of data depends on the problem context. If one is worried about machine operations, the proper context is that of machine encoding: bits, bytes, words, and whatever else the machine provides. From a programming language view, we worry about the data types (integer, real, logical, etc.) provided by the programming language. At the problem

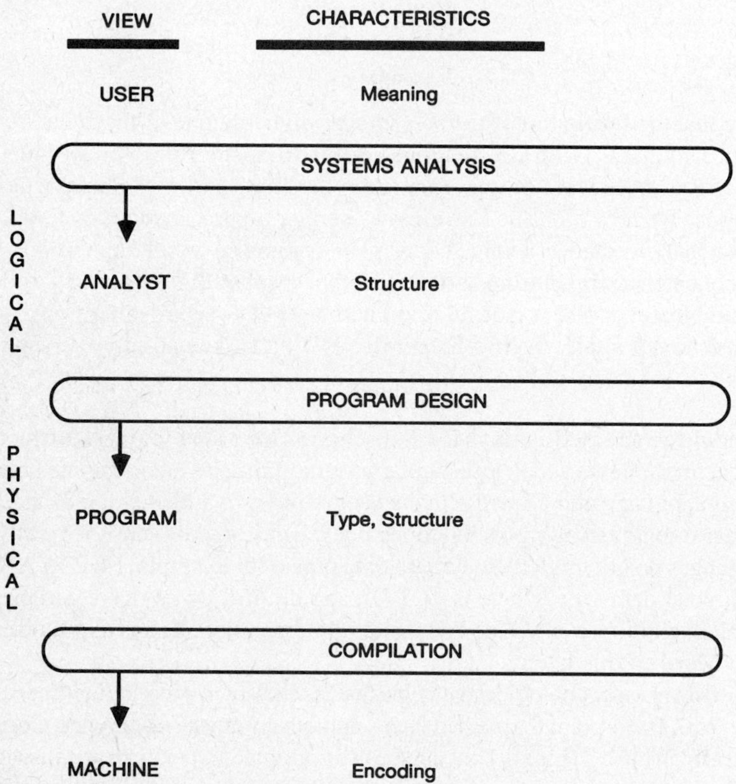

FIGURE 7-2 Data translations.

level and the application level (the focuses of this book), such low-level encoding is not relevant and often gets in the way of solving the problem. The moral here, as elsewhere in the book, is to concentrate on what we need to know at each stage of the process and to ignore extraneous factors. Figure 7-2 illustrates the translation of data from stage to stage in the program development process. The translation processes between data views (framed in oval boxes) are the sources for most of the errors in the program development process.

Data Type

Type is a logical property of data that exists at all levels. It is defined by the set of operations that are valid for a particular piece of data. Suppose we define the variable **Example** to be of type Integer. Most programmers would conclude that this means that **Example** has been defined to be stored as a single word on the target computer (via a DEFINT statement in BASIC, for example). This is not true. When we say that **Example** is of type Integer, what we are actually saying is that the rules of integer arithmetic apply to any values stored in **Example**. If **Example** contains the value 7, then

Example + 3 = 10
Example - 4 = 3
Example * 2 = 14
Example / 2 = 3

Note that the fourth line illustrates integer division, one of the areas where the rules for integer arithmetic (with no fractions) differ from the rules for arithmetic with real numbers. If **Example** were of type Real, then the result of line 4 above would be 3.5.

Suppose we now redefine **Example** as being of type Character (a letter, numeral, or punctuation mark treated as a value for display or printing). Valid operations on **Example** are now concatenation (putting letters together), substringing (setting them asunder), sorting, and whatever else it is legal to do with text in your jurisdiction. Arithmetic rules (operations) do not apply; even if **Example** = "7", it makes no sense to say

Example - 4 = ???

It should be stressed again that our discussion here is of logical data types and not of the physical implementation in a particular programming language. Some languages (such as assembly language and C) will allow a programmer to add characters and integers, but the fact that it is physically possible does not mean it makes sense logically! Similarly, some languages do not implement certain data types (for example, FORTRAN IV does not have a character data type, whereas COBOL and dBASE do not have complex numbers); if the problem requires a data type that is not implemented, one has to program around this difficulty. More on this later.

A low-level aspect of logical data type that is relevant to programmers concerns the base for integer, real, fixed-point (explained later), and other numeric data types. Computers work most naturally in base 2 (binary) but can be programmed to perform arithmetic in any base desired. For business data processing, where we are dealing with financial data, it is often important that operations be performed in base 10 (decimal) to avoid the slight rounding errors in conversion of fractional values between base 2 and base 10. This concern is relevant towards the end of the program design stage, when we get to low-level implementation details.

Implementation

In the discussion of dBASE, the following typographic conventions will be used to signify that actual dBASE code is intended rather than generic descriptions:

DBASE COMMANDS

Dbase variables

DBASE MENU COMMANDS

Dbase file names

<replace with any valid file or variable name>

Non-dbase variables (e.g., in data dictionary)

NON-DBASE ENTITY, RELATION, OR FILE NAMES

dBASE has two sorts of data: memory variables and relational data. Memory variables (called "variables" in most programming languages) are named locations in the computer's main memory (RAM). Their contents exist only while a program is running. Relational data in dBASE are stored on disk in files. Their contents are kept as long as the disk is not changed.

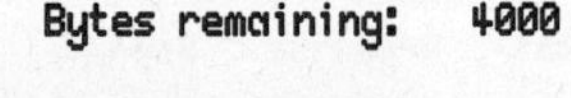

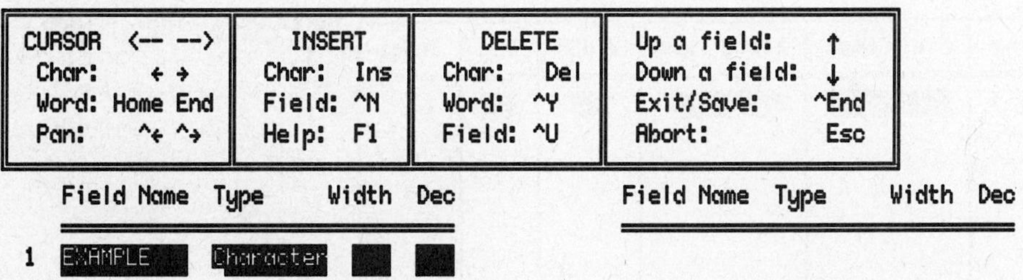

CREATE <D:> TEST Field: 1/1

Press SPACE to change the field type.

Character fields contain character information of a specified length.

FIGURE 7-3 dBASE III Create screen.

In dBASE III, data (whether memory or relational) can be of type *Fixed-length-character*, *Fixed-point*, *Logical*, *Date*, and *Variable-length-character*. The first three were available in dBASE II as well; date and variable-length-character (known as memo) data types were added for dBASE III. dBASE IV adds a *floating-point* data type.

In dBASE, memory variables are defined by using them. For example, to define `yn` as of type *Fixed-length-character*, you would assign a fixed-length-character value to it either in the program (`STORE "YES" TO yn`) or from the keyboard (e.g., `ACCEPT "Do you want to continue? " TO yn`). Relational data is defined in DBASE III by filling in the name, type, and length from the **CREATE DATABASE** or **MODIFY DATABASE** selections in the Assistant (Figure 7-3). You can also use the `CREATE <filename>` command from the dot-prompt. In dBASE IV, use the corresponding selections from the Control Center menu (Figure 7-4).

Fixed-length-character means that a predefined amount of space is reserved for any combination of one-byte values. These values are treated as human-readable elements for display or printing; they are not regarded as having any numeric or logical value. In dBASE III, to declare `Example` of type character with width 32 from the dot-prompt, you would fill in the screen of Figure 7-3 (note that in this figure, the user has not yet entered the width).

Fixed-point data (called numeric in dBASE) are base 10 numbers (technically "binary-coded decimal") with a predefined number of digits after (to the right of) the decimal point. They are the standard representation for business and accounting data. All

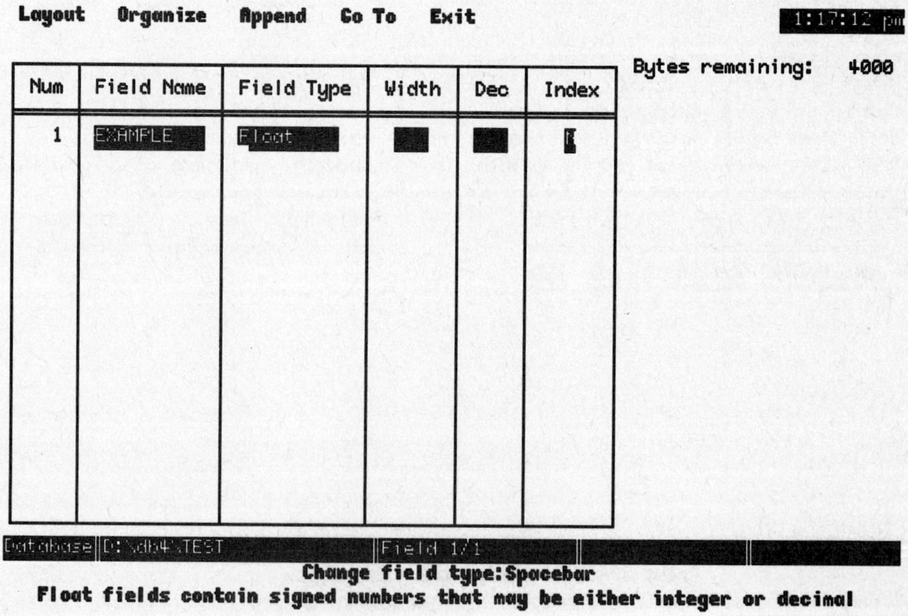

```
Layout   Organize   Append   Go To   Exit                          1:17:12 pm

                                                      Bytes remaining:   4000
| Num | Field Name | Field Type | Width | Dec | Index |
|  1  | EXAMPLE    | Float      |       |     |       |

Database | D:\db4\TEST | Field 1/1
                     Change field type:Spacebar
   Float fields contain signed numbers that may be either integer or decimal
```

FIGURE 7-4 dBASE IV Create screen.

of dBASE's arithmetic operations except for floating point are performed in base 10 so that financial calculations will come out correctly. With fixed-point (numeric) data, you need to specify two parts to the width: the total width and how many of those digits are to the right of the decimal point (the decimal point itself does not count in the total width).

Logical variables have only two values: true and false. In dBASE, these have the values `.T.` and `.F.`, respectively.

Variables of type Date are used to hold valid calendar dates. Width is not necessary for type Date.

Variables of type Memo are character variables the length of which is unknown. They are available as either memory variables or as record fields. Width is not necessary for type Memo.

Variables of type Floating-point ("float") in dBASE IV are numeric variables the length of which is unknown. They are used to describe real numbers and, unlike other dBASE numeric variables, are stored and manipulated in binary form. Width is not necessary; it defaults to 64 bits. In dBASE IV, data definition from the dot-prompt results in a data definition screen where one selects data type by pressing the space bar until the correct type appears (Figure 7-4).

In SQL mode within dBASE IV, data can be of type Fixed-length-character, Short integer, Integer, Fixed-point, Floating point, Logical, or Date. These are standard data types for SQL on any computer system.

Data Structure

Data *structures* are groups of elements that each has a type and that are processed as a unit. The particular structures desirable depend on the application; the structures available depend on the language. As with implementation limitations on data type, if the language that you use does not have a particular structure, you have to program around it.

In most business programming, there are three basic forms of data structures: elements, arrays, and records.

Elements are single pieces of data, such as characters or numbers. They have

1	Lisa
2	Renee
3	Bob
4	Dave
5	Laura
6	Marv
7	Howard
8	Cynthia
9	Becky

FIGURE 7-5 Array of elements.

	PO-Number	Quantity	Cost	Part-#	Received
1	1001	1	45.00	11345	T
2	1001	4	10.00	11678	T
3	1001	23	0.95	11856	F
4	1004	18	1.49	24596	T
5	1004	25	2.29	24555	T
6	1004	1	95.25	72354	T
7	1004	3	12.00	74354	T
8	1008	9	18.29	83454	F
9	1008	10	4.95	23425	T

FIGURE 7-6 Table of records.

individual names and are worked with one at a time. Memory variables in dBASE III are all data elements; the type of a memory variable is implicitly defined the first time an operation is performed on the variable (for example, `STORE "Y" TO answer` defines `answer` as type character).

Arrays are groups of identical elements (or identical substructures). The array can be referenced as a group, or the individual items in an array can be referenced independently. Arrays are commonly used to implement mathematical vectors and matrices, as well as tables. The array data structure in dBASE III is the table (also called a relation) that is stored in a datafile. A table (relation) consists of a series of identical records. Arrays are not available for memory variables. dBASE IV allows arrays of memory variables. Figure 7-5 illustrates an array of elements (of type character in this case).

Tables or *relations* are arrays of *records*, which are groups of elements where the elements may be of dissimilar types. For example, a purchase order system may use a record called **Purchase-order-detail**, the contents of which are as follows:

Element	Type	Length	Decimals
PO-NUMBER	CHARACTER	8	
QUANTITY	NUMERIC	5	0
COST	NUMERIC	8	2
PART-NUMBER	CHARACTER	12	
RECEIVED	LOGICAL	1	

When the program executes the statement that corresponds to the logical function Get-current-record, the **PO-number**, **Quantity**, etc. for the current record are all retrieved at one time. Figure 7-6 illustrates a table.

A logically related group of records make up a *database* (Figure7-7). If all of the records are in the form of tables, the database is *relational*. The program that allows use of a database is called a database management system. In dBASE, there is no separate thing

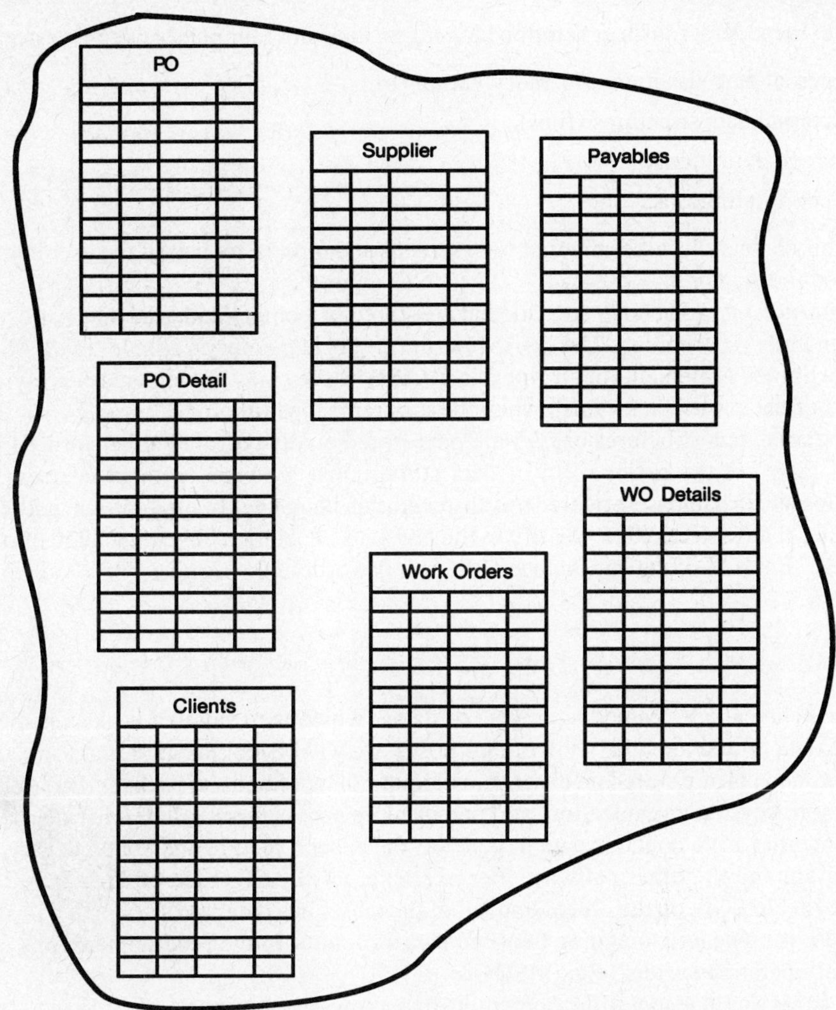

FIGURE 7-7 Database of tables.

called a database; the tables are implemented independently and their relationships are maintained by the programs. In SQL mode within dBASE IV, databases are separate objects, opened with the `START DATABASE` command and closed with the `STOP DATABASE` command. In SQL, tables exist only as components of a database—not independently.

DATA IN PROGRAMS

Data type and structure are relevant to us partly because of their role in the problem definition, but mostly because they eventually become parts of the computer programs that we write. In modern, fourth generation languages, there are four places where we use data:

- Internal data structures (memory variables).
- External data structures (files).
- Screen definitions.
- Report definitions.

This chapter discusses the first two; screens and reports are part of the user interface discussed in Chapter 9.

Internal data structures are data that are stored in memory and used internally by the program while it is running. The dBASE term for this is memory variable. In dBASE III these are limited to elements of all types; in dBASE IV they may be elements or arrays. The contents of these variables vanish when the program stops running.

External data structures or *files* are data stored on disk or some other form of mass storage. Files are the major form of data storage that we work with in business data processing and in database-oriented fourth generation languages like dBASE. In particular, the entities that we learned to identify in the previous chapters will be translated into files in dBASE. Because of the importance of files, it is worthwhile taking a closer look at how they work.

Files

A *file* is technically a "named aggregate of data," which is to say that it has a name and contains data (plural intended). For our purposes, we will be looking at files that are arrays of records and that are stored on disk (or in memory that pretends it is a disk). Each file has one or more keys, an organization, and one or more access types (all defined below).

Note that a file contains data in general; the exact structure and contents vary with the program and the other software. For example, in dBASE, each table is stored as a separate file. In SQL, on the other hand, all of the tables in a database are stored in a single file. There is no generic mapping between data structures in the program and files in the computer operating system (e.g., MSDOS).

A *key* is a unique identifier: something that allows us to uniquely identify or to locate each individual record in a file. For simple files, this may simply be the order of the record in the file—the tenth record for example. But in many files, the order changes from time to time; therefore some other identifier is needed. Ideally this is an element the content of which is different for each record—social security number for example. Unfortunately, such elements are not very common unless they are assigned by some bureaucracy. A common approach is to combine or "concatenate" several elements, the combination of which is unique (one hopes). The reason for having a key is simply so that one can retrieve the correct record when needed. What happens when you do not have a good key is illustrated by the following story.

Some years ago I taught programming at the University of Minnesota in Minneapolis, where it sometimes happened that students delayed doing their assignments until the last moment. One such student had delayed doing a COBOL assignment until the night before it was due, and about 2:00 A.M. found herself thoroughly confused. Confused enough to call me for help (bad move!).

This was not my first time teaching programming, so I had neglected to include my home telephone number on the course syllabus. The student in question decided to use the telephone directory. Unfortunately for her, the predominant ethnic group in Minneapolis is German, "Lehman" is the third most common last name in Germany, and "John" is the most common male first name in the United States. As a result, the Minneapolis telephone directory contains almost a full page of "John Lehman(n)s." You guessed it—at 2:00 A.M. she called every one of them! Except me—I lived in St. Paul at the time. "John" + "Lehman" is not a unique key.

For this reason, most computer systems use some sort of arbitrary identification number. Social Security numbers (arbitrary but unique) used to be popular, but there are legal problems with using them now if you are not a government entity.

Note that a major difference between a permanent entity and a transient entity is that each instance of (record in) a permanent entity requires its own unique key, whereas this is not required for a transient entity. For example, each customer in the permanent entity CUSTOMER requires a unique customer key, while many records in the transient entity WORK-ORDER-DETAIL may have the same value of **Work Order Number**.

File organization describes the order in which records are stored in a file. There are three common strategies: sequential, indexed sequential, and random.

Sequential organization means that the records are stored one after another in physical order by key. This type of organization was popular (indeed necessary) in the days of card and tape mass storage; today it is used because it is faster than alternative methods when the majority of the records in the file have to be accessed each time the file is used. Such systems are usually batch oriented, although fourth generation languages such as dBASE support sequential organization.

In an indexed sequential organization, the records are stored one after another in order by key, and there is an index to the records that can be searched to find the exact location of any selected record. Searching an index is much faster than searching through the entire file.

A related file organization is indexed, but nonsequential. In such files, the records are stored physically out of order (perhaps ordered by a different key), but there is an index organized by the desired key. For example, if PURCHASE-ORDER-FILE is organized sequentially by **Purchase-order-number**, there may be one index ordered by **Purchase-order-number**,(indexed sequential), another ordered by **Purchase-order-date**, and a third ordered by **Supplier-name**. This is similar to a library where the books are stored separately in order by call number but are indexed in the card catalog by author, title, and subject. dBASE supports both forms of indexed organization.

In a randomly organized file, the records are stored in any way, but one hopes, according to some scheme. This organization is similar to that of my desk. To get a record, you have to know where it is.

File access describes how you get a record from a file. Figure 7-8 shows the alternatives. A shaded square means that the access method in that column is available with the organization in that row. Sequential access means one record after another, in order. If

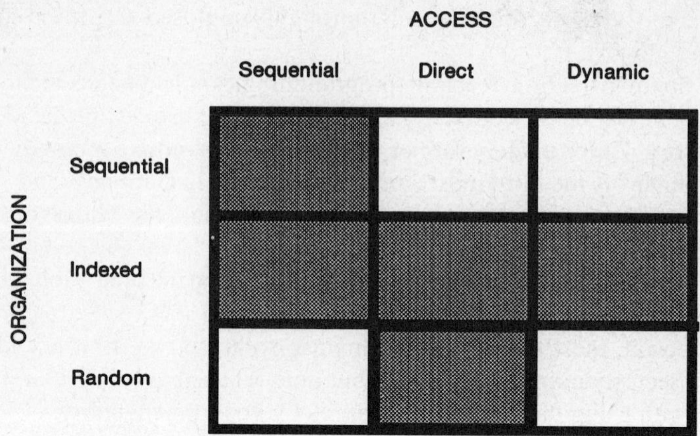

FIGURE 7-8 File organization versus access.

you want to get the 100th record, you first have to get the first 99. Direct means that you can go directly to the record you want. Dynamic means that you can go direct and then go sequentially from there.

Our library example can help clarify this (remembering that a library uses indexed organization sequential by call number). Let us suppose that the library in question uses the Library of Congress cataloging system and that you are looking for *Management Information Systems* by Davis and Olson. To access the stacks sequentially, you would start at A00 and walk along, checking the call numbers until you came to T58. This would be educational, but time consuming. With direct access, you would look in the card catalog, find the call number (T58.6.D38), check the map of locations, go directly to the floor where the book was located, check the stack labels, and go directly to the book. With dynamic access you would do the same, but after retrieving the book would start looking in the same area of the shelves to see if there were anything else of interest on the same topic.

dBASE files usually use indexed organization, sequential where possible. One creates a sorted sequential file with the command `SORT ON <sortfield> TO <filename>`, where `<filename>` is the name of the new file and `<sortfield>` is the name of the data element by which the file will be sorted. One specifies use of a sequential file with the instruction `USE <filename>`, where `<filename>` is any previously defined datafile. Indexed files in dBASE III are specified with `USE <filename> INDEX <indexfile>` where the index file `<indexfile>` has previously been created

Identify objects in real-world environment.

- Define permanent entities based on objects

Identify events in real-world environemnt.

- Define transient entities spawned by each event.

Identify actions (responses to events) in real-world environment.

- Define transient entities spawned by each action.

Identify data in the existing system.
For each entity:

- Assign attributes (data elements).
- Document attributes in logical data dictionary.
- For each attribute:
  Decide on data type.
  Decide on length.
  Decide on number of decimal place, if appropriate.
- Document attributes in physical data dictionary.
- Put in dBASE table.

Determine constraints in the order of the events and actions.

FIGURE 7-9 Procedure for implementing entities.

with the `INDEX` command (`INDEX ON <sortfield> TO <indexfile>`). In dBASE IV, files have a single multiple index, and the information on indexing is automatically associated with the file. Files may be searched or processed sequentially (using the `LOCATE` command or the `SKIP` command). Direct access is possible using the `SEEK` command, followed by either further direct access or by dynamic access.

Building the Physical Model of a System

The revised procedure for analysis, design, and implementation of external objects in dBASE is illustrated in Figure 7-9.

Note that the first part of each of these activities involves paper modeling; we do not actually start translating into dBASE until we have decided on the appropriate structure and type for all data.

Case Implementation in dBASE

In translating the data dictionary of Chapters 5 and 6 into dBASE, we need to do the following for permanent entities:

For unflattened compound structures such as **Local address**

- Define unique names for each element.

For each permanent entity

- Create a table.
- Enter data items, types, and lengths.
- Design the screen.
- Create the screen either with the control center or an editor.

Then, for transient entities, we do the following:

Remove data elements already defined in permanent entities.
Remove data elements which can be calculated from other data.
For each transient entity:

- Create a table.
- Enter data items, types and lengths.

For each event:

- Design the screen (Chapter 9).

Data type and length is determined by analyzing existing or potential data. For example, the maximum required length of **Last name** can be defined by checking either existing files or the telephone directory for long names. For some items, such as **Telephone number** and **Zip code**, one will have to decide whether to allow for non-U.S. data. For example, a typical Canadian postal code is G1V 4P1, which would not fit in a variable designed to hold a five-digit numeric U.S. zip.code.

A rule of thumb is that if a particular data item will be used in more than one entity, it should have the same physical definition application-wide. In our example, the following items are common to more than one permanent entity:

Element	Type	Length	Decimals
BLDGNAME	CHARACTER	6	
COLLEGE	CHARACTER	20	
DEPT	CHARACTER	16	
FNAME	CHARACTER	12	
HPHONE	CHARACTER	14	
LNAME	CHARACTER	16	
LPHONE	CHARACTER	12	
MNAME	CHARACTER	12	
ROOMNUMB	NUMERIC	4	

For unflattened compound structures, define unique names for each element.

In our example, the compound structures are **home address**, **local address**, and **prerequisites**. The data element names for **home address** are identical to those for **local address**, whereas the data element names for **prerequisites** are identical to those used to identify a particular course section. The following example shows the elements for **local address** and **prerequisites** defined with unique names and converted to dBASE format for substitution into the data dictionary:

Local address = LStreet + LCity + LState +LZip

Home address = Street + City + State + Zip

Prerequisite = PDept + PCnumb

Element	Type	Length	Decimals
CITY	CHARACTER	16	
CNUMB	NUMERIC	3	
DEPT	CHARACTER	16	
LSTATE	CHARACTER	2	
LSTREET	CHARACTER	16	
LZIP	CHARACTER	6	
PCNUMB	NUMERIC	3	
PDEPT	CHARACTER	16	
STATE	CHARACTER	2	
STREET	CHARACTER	16	
ZIP	CHARACTER	6	

The three permanent entities in our example with all names converted to follow dBASE rules are listed as follows:

Student = Lname + Fname + Mname +Idnumb + Lstreet + Lcity + Lstate + Lzip + Street + City + State + Zip + Hphone + Lphone + College + Degrprog + Datefent + Totcred

Course = Year + Term + Dept + Cnumb + Ctitle + Sectnumb+ Secttype + Date + lname + Fname + Ctitle + Credits + Pdept + Pcnumb+ Mtime + Bldgname + Roomnumb

Instruct = Instnumb + lname + Fname + Mname + Bldgname + Roomnumb + Hphone + Lphone + College + Dept

Those data elements not already defined in dBASE format are listed as follows:

Element	Type	Length	Decimals
CTITLE	CHARACTER	32	
CREDITS	NUMERIC	1	
CNUMB	NUMERIC	3	
DATE	DATE		

DATEFENT	DATE	
DEGRPROG	CHARACTER	3
IDNUMB	NUMERIC	10
INSTNUMB	NUMERIC	10
MTIME	CHARACTER	5
SECTNUMB	NUMERIC	2
SECTTYPE	CHARACTER	4
TERM	CHARACTER	6
TOTCRED	NUMERIC	3
YEAR	NUMERIC	2

In the previous chapter, on event modeling, we derived the following entity-relationship diagram to describe the target system:

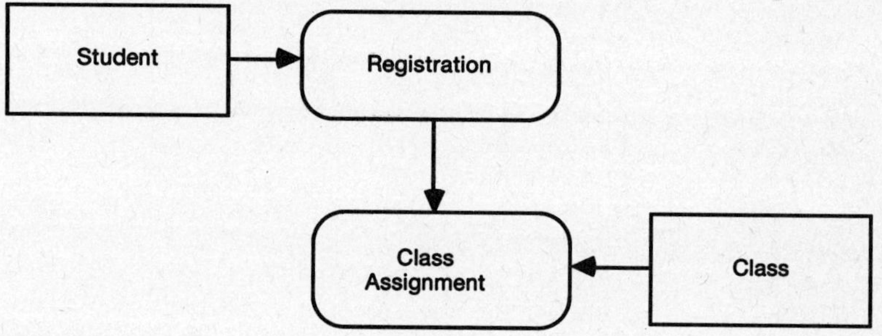

This result is in the following data structures:

Registration = ID + Date

Class assignment = ID + Dept. + Course number + Section number

In this form, each **Class assignment** links a single student with a single section of a course. In dBASE data form, the definition is

Element	Type	Length	Decimals
ID	NUMERIC	10	
DEPT	CHARACTER	16	
CNUMB	NUMERIC	3	
SECTNUMB	NUMERIC	2	

SUMMARY

This chapter has discussed the nature of data elements, how they are put together, and how they can be used in a program. We have seen how to move from analysis of data in the real world to the assignment of attributes to the entities in a database and to the implementation of those entities in dBASE data definitions.

QUESTIONS AND EXERCISES

1. In data modeling, low-level definition of data describes
   a. The data attributes.
   b. The data relationships.
   c. The data models.
   d. The data hierarchy.
2. Two properties of data that are important for data definition are
   a. Type and structure.
   b General and numeric.
   c. Character and floating point.
   d. String and array.
3. Which statement is true about memory variables and relational variables?
   a. Memory variables are named locations in RAM and exist only while the program is running, whereas relational data in dBASE are stored on disk in files and are kept as long as the disk is not changed.
   b. Relational data are named locations in RAM and exist only while the program is running, whereas memory variables in dBASE is stored on disk in files and are kept as long as the disk is not changed.
   c. Relational data can only be of type character, whereas memory variables can only be of type real.
   d. Relational data can only be of type real, whereas memory variables can only be of type character.
4. What is the only type of organization that allows dynamic access to a file.
   a. Sequential.
   b. Indexed.
   c. Random.
   d. Direct.
5. If you have sequential organization, what kind of access do you have?
   a. Sequential.
   b. Indexed.
   c. Random.
   d. Direct.
6. Random organization has only ________ access.
   a. Sequential.
   b. Indexed.

   c. Random.
   d. Direct.

7. Fixed-length-character, fixed-point, logical, date and variable-length-character assigned to data is called its
   a. Value.
   b. Representative.
   c. Type.
   d. Length.
8. A single piece of data, such as characters or numbers is
   a. Structures
   b. Tables.
   c. Details.
   d. Elements.
9. Variables.
   a. Are random glitches in a program design.
   b. Exist in memory only while the program is running.
   c. Are different sets of prototypes.
   d. Cannot be used with fourth generation languages.
10. Data structures are
   a. Pieces of information used to design screens.
   b. Dictionaries stacked in geometric shapes.
   c. Entity relationship diagrams.
   d. Groups of elements of different types processed as a unit.
11. A relational database
   a. Stores all records in tables.
   b. Stores all records sequentially as they are entered.
   c. Analyzes personal problems.
   d. Can only be accessed in batch.
12. A logically related group of records make up a
   a. List.
   b. Database.
   c. Relation.
   d. Program.

DISCUSSION QUESTIONS

1. Describe a data dictionary and what it does.
2. What is a key? Give three examples.

NORTHSTAR AVIATION

Part 4
Data

1. For the elementary items in the data dictionary that you derived in Part 3 of this case, decide what data type and length is appropriate. Restrict yourself to data types available in dBASE and decide based on the use to which the data will be put. Remember that if necessary it is possible to convert from one data type to another.
2 Northstar has decided to integrate the new system with their accounting system, which is also being automated. What should be the data structure for an accounting journal entry?
3. Set up the results of Questions 1 and 2 in dBASE.

Chapter 8

NORMALIZATION

CHAPTER GOALS

- **Learn to normalize entities in the system model.**

Normalization is the design of data and file structures for correct use in a relational database management system. Correct use here means, among other things, making sure that data is correct and consistent between applications by eliminating redundant storage.

An example of what happens with traditional file design, which uses redundant storage, is familiar to anyone who has changed her or his name while associated with a larger organization such as a university. Figure 8-1 shows an idealized (??) view of this situation. In theory, changing one's name at the student records office should be sufficient. In practice, it would take at least a year for the other offices to catch up with the change, and since it was not flagged as a change, they would probably interpret the changed record as a new student and so not update their records. Generally, things would be a mess. In fact, in such a system, previous records may never get updated.

Figure 8-2 shows the first step in eliminating this problem—having everyone use the same database file. This can be done with time-sharing on minicomputers or mainframes, or with a central network server for personal computers. However, this hardware approach is only part of the solution. The design of the database has to be such that data about entities is stored in one place only.

This design (normalization) is part of the process Build Logical Model illustrated in Figure 8-3. It consists of organizing the data in relations to minimize redundancy.

The key to normalizing files is to realize that systems are divided into permanent entities and transient entities (transactions). A permanent entity is something about which the system will always retain information: customers, suppliers, inventory, or students, for example. A transaction (transient entity) is a message or an exchange of data between two

FIGURE 8-1 Redundant records.

or more permanent entities. For example, a purchase order is a message from a buyer to a supplier regarding inventory items.

The key to proper data design is that all data about a permanent entity be stored in one, single relation (file). Data or records concerning transactions do not contain data about permanent entities: rather they contain keys to the records in the files that describe the permanent entities. Let's look at an example.

Figure 8-4 shows our old friend the purchase order. This is a transaction that contains data about two permanent entities: suppliers and inventory. Like most transactions in a manual system, this single paper form actually contains data about three different things: the supplier, the purchase order, and the parts ordered. The purchase order form serves as a link between the supplier entity and the inventory or parts entity (linked via PO detail). In an automated system, only the linkage need be explicit; the system can fill in the details on suppliers and parts. The traditional file design for a purchase order (assuming a language like BASIC or COBOL) would be as illustrated in Figure 8-5. There are a series of problems with this design. One of the most obvious is that the entire supplier record is repeated for each purchase order (of which there will be thousands). This is a problem not only because it takes up large amounts of extra file space (perhaps 200 bytes per record), but because of what happens if any aspect of the supplier record changes.

Since the supplier record is stored as a part of each purchase order, a change in the content of a supplier field (for example, a change in telephone number) means that all

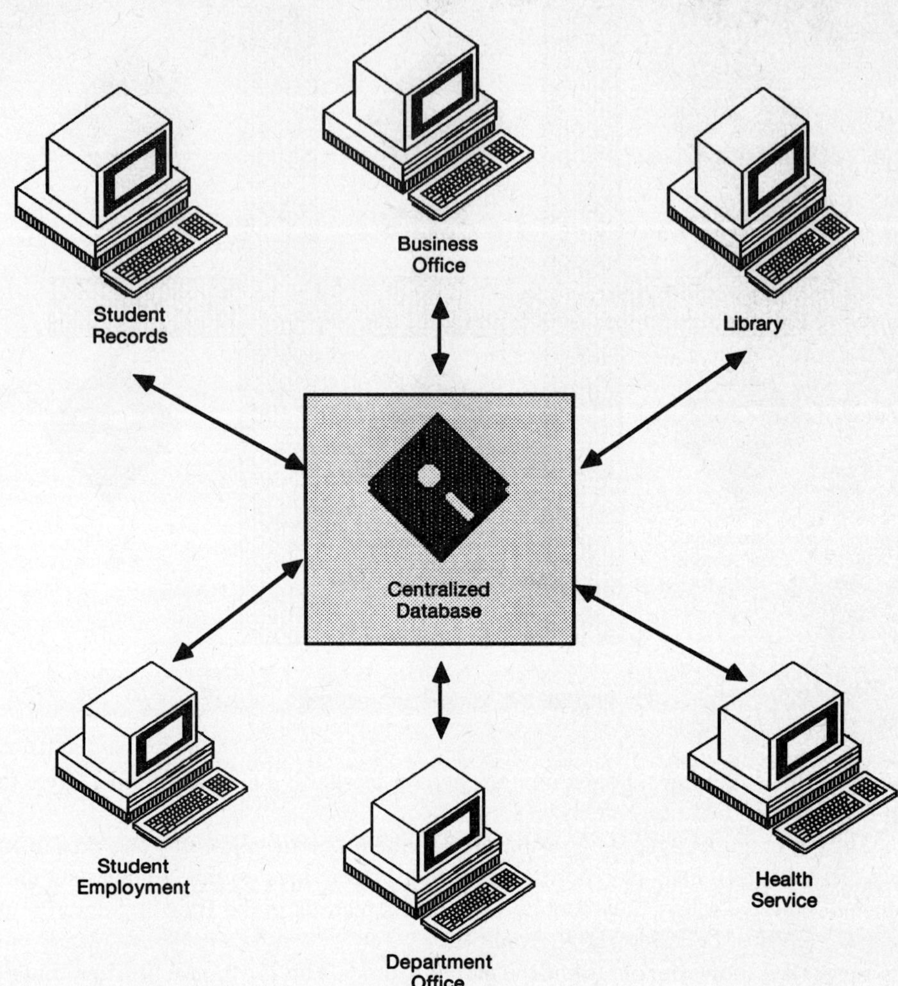

FIGURE 8-2 Reducing redundancy.

previous purchase orders containing this supplier have to be changed. In a large organization, that means that hundreds of thousands of purchase order records will have to be examined and changed if necessary. If a change in the supplier record *structure* is made (such as adding a new field for salesman name), all programs using that record must be changed, and all previous files must be rewritten if they are to be accessed by the new programs. Usually, of course, this does not get done, and thus analysis of previous data becomes much more difficult.

The entity-relationship diagram corresponding to Figure 8-4 is illustrated in Figure 8-6; this is a standard translation for any three-part transaction. In a modern data design,

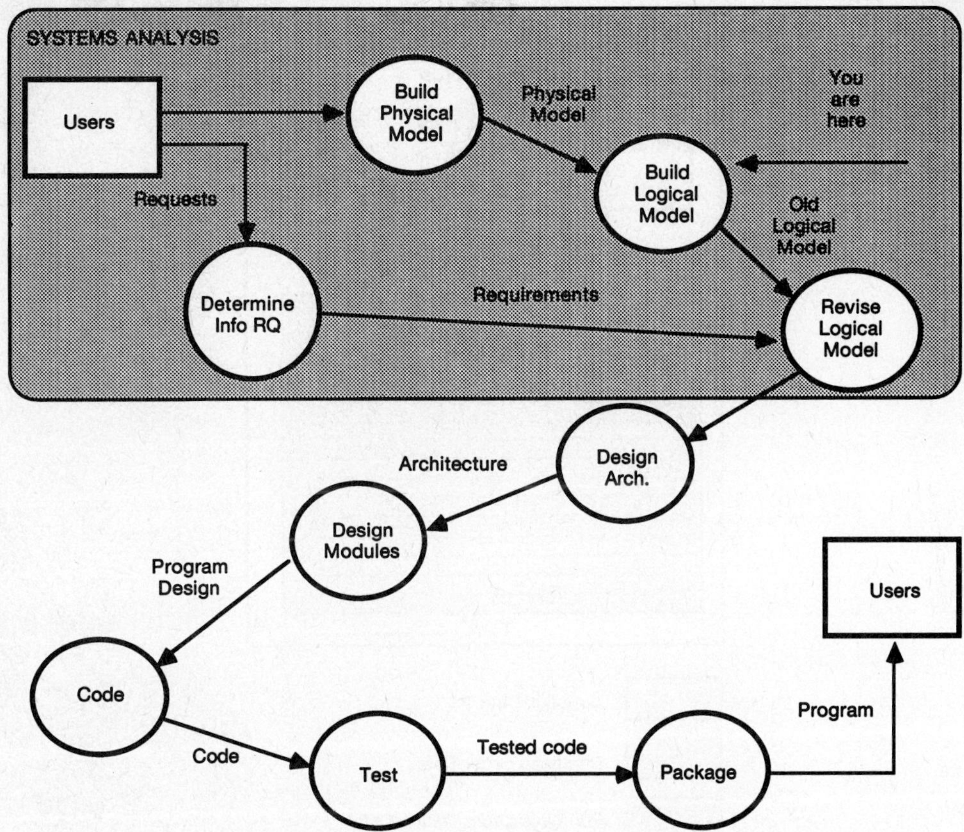

FIGURE 8-3 System development life-cycle.

one would identify suppliers and inventory as permanent entities. The file format would be as illustrated in Figure 8-7. SUPPLIER and INVENTORY are permanent entities. PODET (purchase order detail) indicates how many of each item have been ordered, and how many have been received (to allow for backorders). The only information it contains on the actual item ordered is the key PNUMBER (part number), which allows it to reference the associated record in the INVENTORY file. The only information contained about the purchase order is the PO number, which links the detail records to the appropriate purchase order header (PO).

Similarly, the purchase order file (PO) contains no details about the supplier—only the supplier number which allows information on the supplier to be retrieved from the SUPPLIER file. Any changes to the supplier data may be made in one place and will automatically propagate to any programs, reports, or transactions using supplier data. Only the supplier number need remain constant.

Why not simply link SUPPLIER and INVENTORY with a single transient entity having the structure **Purchase-order = POnumb + POdate + POsupplier +{POquant +**

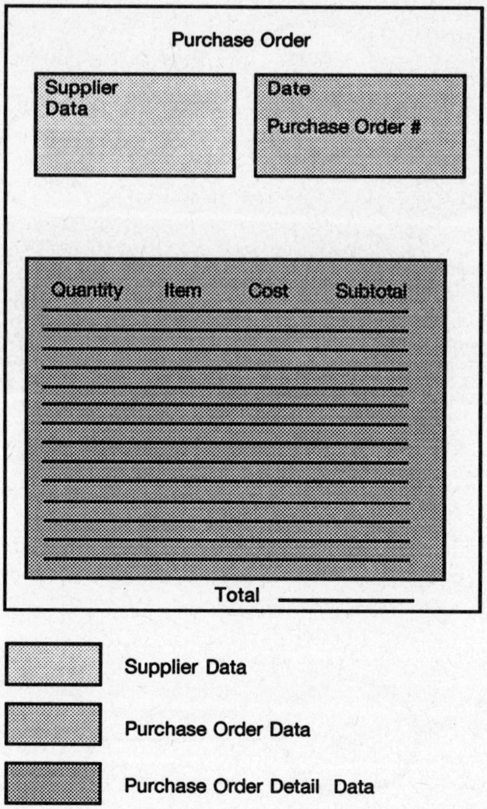

FIGURE 8-4 Purchase order.

Qreceived + Pnumber}? The basic reason has to do with making the database as flexible as possible to reduce maintenance and to allow the database to accommodate alternative user views and queries, even if these have not yet been thought of. In our example, it is likely that any changes to the structure of a purchase order will be made to either PO or PODET but not to both, since they show different things. More important, other parts of the overall information system may make use of one or the other. For example, the inventory subsystem needs to know how many parts are on order irrespective of the purchase order data, an analyst may need to know parts turnover patterns, and an auditor may need to know how many total parts are back ordered. This is all a round-about way of saying that PO and PODET keep data on different "objects" (purchase orders and parts, respectively), that the data on one object may be used independently of the other, and therefore it is better to separate the data on each object.

Purchase Order = PO Header + Supplier Record + {PO Detail} + end of PO flag

PO FILE

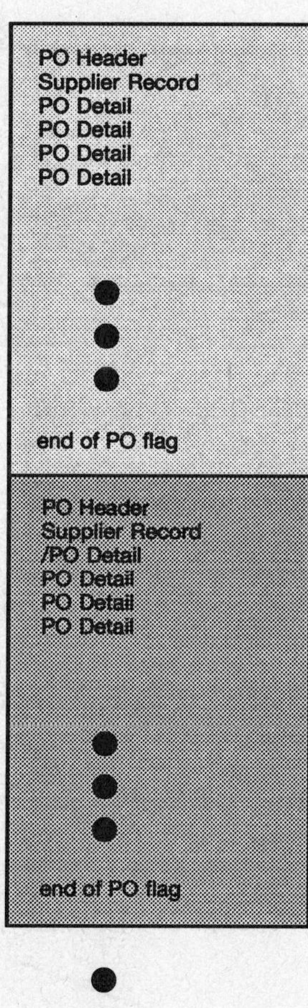

FIGURE 8-5 Old approach to file design.

The basic rules for normalization are as follows:

- **No repeating groups** (any item that is in brackets in the data dictionary or that has arrows on both ends in the entity-relationship diagram must be a separate relation or file).
- **Transaction records should contain no information about permanent entities other than the key to** the appropriate entities.

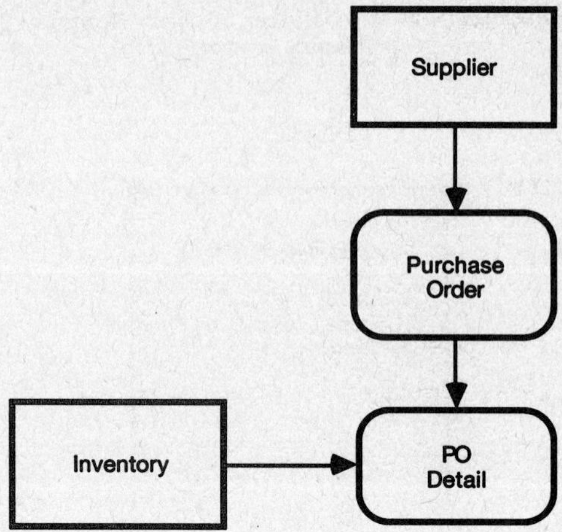

FIGURE 8-6 Entity-relationship diagram for a purchase order.

Normalized file design will not match the structure of the system inputs and outputs, most of which are similar to Figure 8-4. However, as we will see in Section IV, it is not difficult to translate a normalized data structure into the classic three-part structure of most transaction processing system outputs.

The basic rule for modern program design is that all data structures *internal to the system* are normalized. In other words, the databases used by the organization are normalized. The data

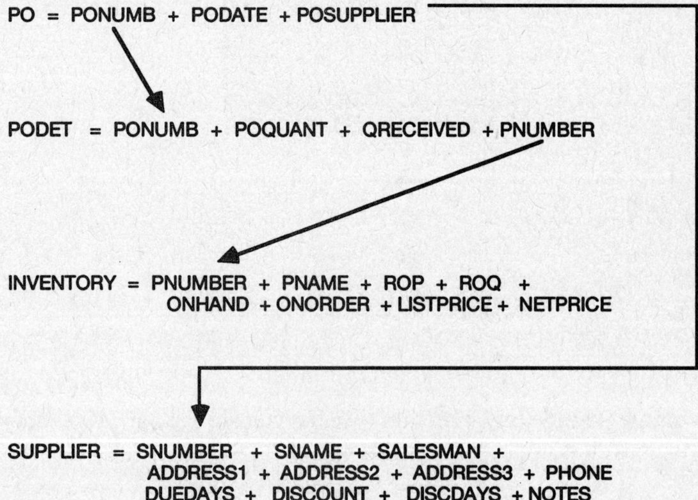

FIGURE 8-7 Normalized purchase order.

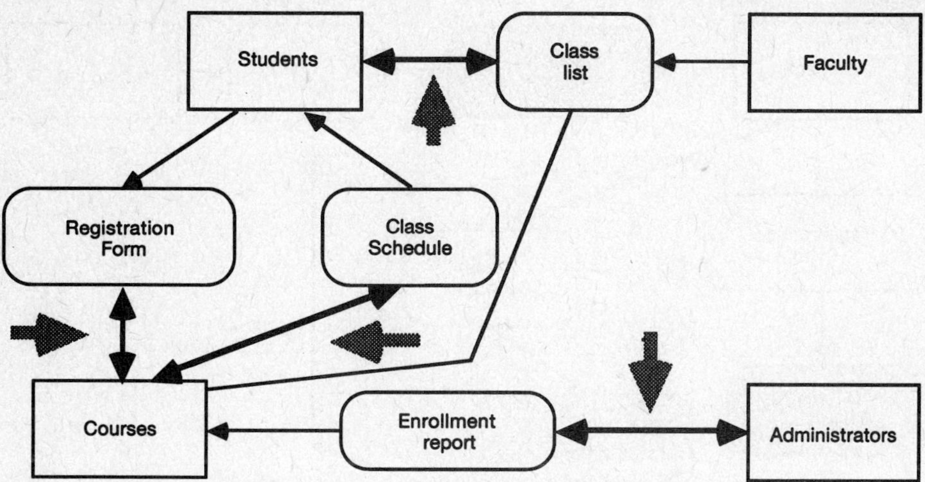

FIGURE 8-8 Registration system entity-relationship diagrm—ready for normalization.

structures of inputs and outputs generally are not normalized; usually they are in the form of three part transactions such as PURCHASE ORDER or four part transactions such as WORK ORDER. Translation between external, nonnormalized data and internal normalized data is done by the programs we write. As we discuss later, this form of translation represents a major class of programming in modern systems. We go to all of this trouble because modules which are designed to deal with normalized data structures make future program maintenance *much* easier.

TRADITIONAL APPROACH TO NORMALIZATION

The techniques presented thus far in this book will generally result in normalized database structures. The traditional approach to normalization is to skip the logical data design and to apply a series of transformations to external data structures. These transformations are useful even with the techniques of data modeling discussed above, since they help ensure that all data is normalized. What we have been referring to as normalized data is technically known as "third normal form."

The first stage in normalization is the conversion of data into *first normal form*. This means removing all repeating groups and putting the data into the form of tables. for example,

PURCHASE-ORDER = **PO-number + PO-date + Supplier-data + {Quantity + Item-number}**

is converted into two tables:

PURCHASE-ORDER = **PO-number + PO-date + Supplier-data**

PURCHASE-ORDER-DETAIL = **PO-number + Quantity + Item-number**

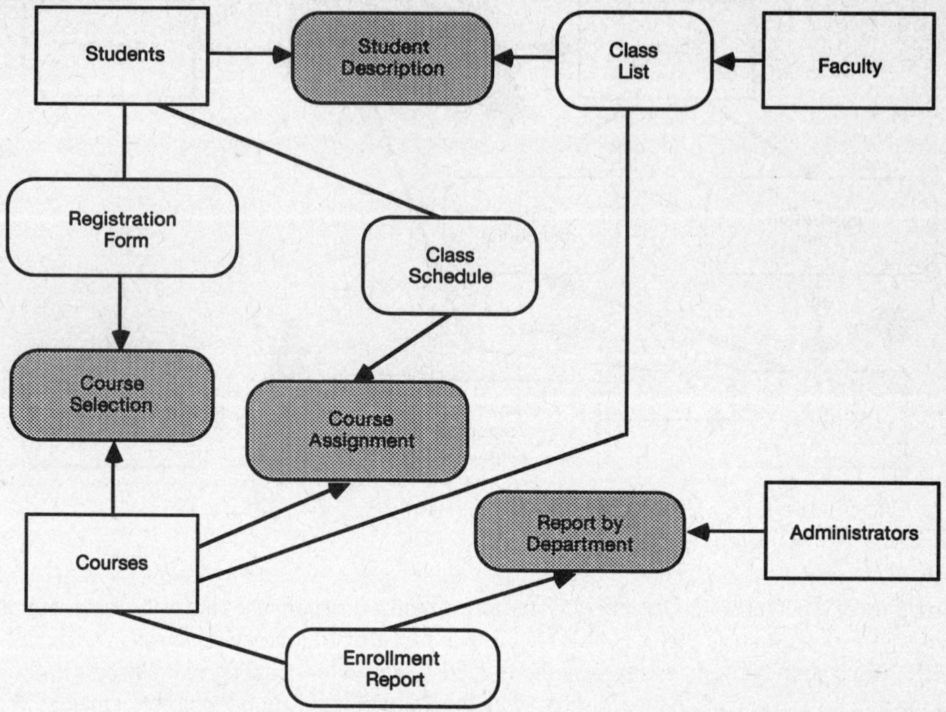

FIGURE 8-9 Registration system enity-relationship diagram—ready for normalization.

Second normal form enforces functional dependence within tables. "B is functionally dependent on A" is another way of saying "A identifies B." For example, in the relation

SUPPLIER-DATA = **Supplier-number** + **Supplier-name** + **Address** + **Phone#**

Supplier-name, **Address** and **Phone#** are functionally dependent on **Supplier-number**, since once one knows the supplier number, all of the other data is determined. In second normal form, every data attribute in a relation (table) is uniquely determined by the key. For example, in the relation

PART-RECORD = **Part-number** + **Supplier-number** + **Supplier-name** + **Address** + **Phone#** + **Quantity-on-hand** + **Item-number** + **Item-name** + **Price**

a separate record is required if there are multiple suppliers; in other words, Part-number does not uniquely determine every attribute in the table (the combination of Part-number and **Supplier-number** does). This would best be translated into three tables:

PART-RECORD = **Part-number** + **Quantity-on-hand** + **Item-number** + **Item-name**

SUPPLIER = **Supplier-number** + **Supplier-name** + **Address** + **Phone#**

PART-SUPPLIED = **Part-number** + **Supplier-number** + **Price**

Class list =	Year + Term + Department + course number + Section number + Date + Instructor + Course title + {Student description} + Total students
Course record =	Department + Course number + Credits + Section type + Course title + College + Section number + Instructor + Meeting time + Meeting place + Prerequisite
Course selection =	Department + Course number + Section number + Course title + Credits
Registration form =	Student name + Student ID + Date + College + Level + Graduating this term flag + {Course selection} + Total credits
Student description =	Student name + Student ID + Local phone + College + Degree
Student record =	Last name + First name + Middle name + ID + Permanent address + Local address + Home phone + Local phone + College + Degree program + Date of first entry + Total credits toward graduation

FIGURE 8-10 Registration system partial normalized data dictionary.

Third normal form removes transitive dependence within tables. Transitive dependence is the case where one item is functionally dependent on another, and a third item is functionally dependent on the second item. For example, in the relation

PURCHASE-ORDER = **PO-number + PO-date + Supplier-number + Supplier-name + Address + Phone#**

Supplier-number is functionally dependent on PO-number, and **Supplier-name** is functionally dependent on **Supplier-number**. This should be restructured to

PURCHASE-ORDER = **PO-number + PO-date + Supplier-number**

SUPPLIER = **Supplier-number + Supplier-name + Address + Phone#**

In summary, the traditional approach to normalization has us

- Remove repeating groups to convert to first normal form. In other words, store the data as tables.
- Enforce functional dependence to convert to second normal form. In other words, make sure there is a single key for each table.
- Remove transitive dependence to convert to third normal form. In other words, make sure each table contains data on only one thing.

CASE EXAMPLE

In Chapter 6 we discussed a simple physical model of a student registration system using an entity-relationship diagram (Figure 8-8). In this model of the existing system, the relationships indicated by the shaded arrows are repeating groups or "many-to-many" (polygamous) relationships. In order to represent this properly in a relational database system, these relationships need to be translated to "one-to-many" (monogamous) relationships.

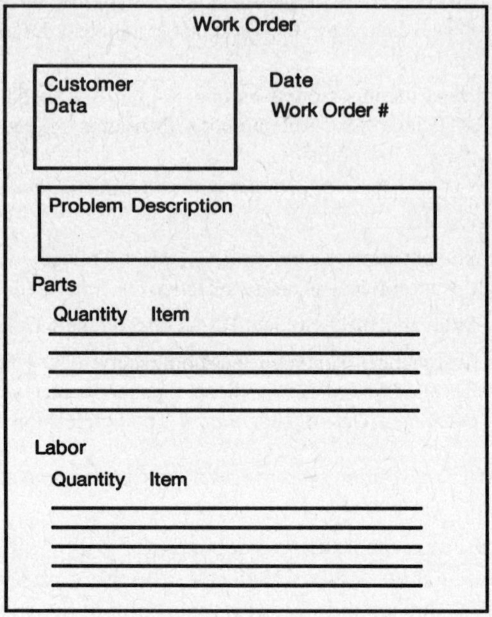

Work Order

Customer Data | Date | Work Order #

Problem Description

Parts

Quantity Item

Labor

Quantity Item

FIGURE 8-11 Work order.

The technique for doing this is to insert new relations corresponding to the individual lines in the manual forms. We have already seen this where PURCHASE ORDER was linked to PURCHASE ORDER DETAIL, which contained the information for each line of the purchase order. Figure 8-9 shows how this can be done for our registration system. The shaded transient entities are additional relations inserted to normalize the system.

Figure 8-10 shows the data dictionary entries for the entities STUDENT RECORD, COURSE RECORD, REGISTRATION FORM, and COURSE SELECTION, as well as the reports CLASS LIST and REGISTRATION FORM, which are not normalized, since they represent manual outputs from the system. Note also that COURSE RECORD has a compound (concatenated) key: one needs **Year + Term + Department + Course number + Section number** to identify a unique record.

Work order =	Work order number + Date + Problem description + Customer ID + Customer name + Address + Phone + {Part quantity + Part number} + {Labor amount + Labor type{

FIGURE 8-12 Work order data dictionary.

SUMMARY

Normalization is making sure that data is correct and consistent between applications by eliminating redundant storage of the data. Each entity contains data about one thing only, meaning that there are no repeating groups within records. Data about permanent entities is stored only as a part of those entities; transactions contain only the values of the key to the appropriate permanent entity. Transactions themselves contain no data that can be derived from other data already stored.

EXERCISE

Design normalized file structures for the customer work order system illustrated in Figures 8-11 and 8-12. Use data dictionary notation.

QUESTIONS AND EXERCISES

1. The basic rules for normalization are
   a Transient and permanent entity data is stored in the same database file.
   b. There should be no repeating groups, and transaction records should contain only the key to the appropriate entities.
   c. There should be many repeating groups, and transaction records should contain the key and several other pieces of data from the appropriate entities.
   d. Transient and permanent entity data is stored together in many database files.
2. Normalization is the design of data and file structures in relational database management systems that
   a. Creates redundant storage.
   b. Creates redundant storage only of transient entity data.
   c. Creates redundant storage only of permanent entity data.
   d. Makes sure data is correct and consistent between applications by eliminating redundant storage.
3. Normalized file design
   a. Always matches the structure of the system inputs and outputs.
   b. Does not match the structure of the system inputs and outputs.
   c. Contains only invoices and statements.
   d. Contains only transient entity records.
4. An example of normalization in a college context is
   a. Having all classes taught by one professor.
   b. Having one class taught by many professors.
   c. Having all departments pull data from one database.
   d. Having all departments pull data from many databases.
5. A purchase order file contains
   a. Supplier.
   b. Inventory.

c. Supplier number.
d. Customer data.

6. All data structures should be normalized if
   a. They are internal to the system.
   b. They aren't required for immediate use.
   c. It will match the system input screens.
   d. There is time after the coding is complete.
7. A transient entity is
   a. Information on infrequent customers.
   b. Always stored in a single file.
   c. A message or exchange of data.
   d. A system design moved from one machine to another.
8. If a change is made in a record structure
   a. Nothing need be done elsewhere in the system.
   b. Only programs accessing that record need be changed.
   c. The entire system will need to be redesigned.
   d. New hardware will be needed.
9. What is the design of data and file structure for correct use in a relational data base management system?
   a. Normalization.
   b. Rationalization.
   c. Structure.
   d. Storage.
10. The key to proper data design is that all data about a permanent entity is stored in
    a. Several relational files.
    b. Two relational files.
    c. One single relational file.
    d. An element.
11. The basic rule for modern program design is that all data structures internal to the system are
    a. Numbered
    b. Structured
    c. Listed
    d. Normalized

DISCUSSION QUESTIONS

1. Give an example of a traditional data design that uses redundant storage of data.
2. What is normalization?

NORTHSTAR AVIATION

Part 5

In previous exercises you created and revised an entity-relationship diagram for Northstar and defined the attributes (definitions) of the data using a data dictionary. Revise your entity-relationship diagram and your data dictionary as needed to make sure that all of Northstar's internal database is normalized. Set up the results in dBASE.

Chapter 9

DESIGN OF THE USER INTERFACE

CHAPTER GOALS

- **Learn to design effective screens, menus, and reports.**
- **Learn to implement screens.**
- **Learn to implement menus.**
- **Learn to implement reports.**

The user interface describes the way the program will look to users. It involves defining screens, printed outputs, and menu structures. The information to do this comes from the forms analysis discussed in Chapters 5 and 6 as well as from interviews with the user.

This chapter covers the design of screens, printed outputs, and menu structures. It also introduces the dBASE code required to define and to manipulate these objects. More details on dBASE coding will be covered in Section V.

Most modern programming languages provide support for user-interface–oriented objects. dBASE III provides direct support for

- Screens
- Reports
- Views

dBASE IV adds support for

- Windows
- Pop-up menus
- Bar menus (as in Lotus 123)

Before defining these objects, we must first design them.

GUIDELINES FOR USER INTERFACE DESIGN

As computers have become more common and used by more non–data processing professionals, ease of use has become increasingly important. The following guidelines, adapted from the Apple *Human Interface Design Guidelines*, are widely accepted.

- Real world metaphors
- Selection rather than remembering
- Consistency
- User control
- Feedback
- Forgiveness
- Perceived stability

Real world metaphors means basing the user view of the system on things in the real world rather than on things internal to the computer system. For example, input screens should be designed to reflect the paper forms that people use in real life rather than to reflect the structure of the database or files inside the computer.

Selection rather than remembering means that users should not have to remember the names of commands, files, and the like. This is usually dealt with by using menus. The user should never be prompted for information that he or she must remember about the system. For example, a module to maintain entities that gives the users a choice of add, change, and delete should not ask for the name of the file to be used; it should instead provide a list of valid files.

Consistency means that all screens and menus should look and work as similarly as possible. If you use function keys, the same key should mean the same thing for each menu. On any menu, the same command should be in the same place (for example, selection 9 might always be "Return to MSDOS.")

User Control means that users should be able to choose what they want to do in the order in which they want to do it. For example, a system should not require that all new records be added before any existing records (or errors in new entries!) can be changed. Similarly, if operations will take a long time (such as sorting and indexing a large file), users should have the choice of starting the operation when convenient rather than having it forced on them as part of another task.

Feedback means that users should be kept informed of what the system is doing. For example, screens should have titles (and sometimes different-colored backgrounds) so that users know that the correct screen has been selected. Similarly, if a long operation such as a sort is in progress, the screen should display a message so that the user knows that the machine is not hung up. Similarly, when a user selects a record for deletion, the record should be displayed on the screen for confirmation that it is the correct one.

Forgiveness means that the system should not take actions without allowing the user to recover. For example, after a user selects a record for deletion, the system should ask for confirmation. Then, when the user exits the menu, the system should again ask for confirmation before it actually issues the dBASE `PACK` command to delete records.

Perceived stability means that users should not notice changes to the system unless those changes impact the users' tasks. For example, adding new transactions or new entities should not impact the structures of existing menus and *absolutely* should not change the meaning of user inputs to carry out other tasks. For example, adding a transaction **PRINT CHECK** to a menu should not change the meaning of "P" from "Purchase Order" to "Print Check."

SCREENS

Screens are predefined "forms" that display information and allow users to input predefined types of information. They are widely used in business system design, since they allow the predefinition of data to be entered. The Assistant in dBASE III+ and the Control Center in dBASE IV are examples of predefined screens, whereas the dot prompt allows free-form input. The use of screens constrains the user's flexibility but makes using (and learning) the system much easier.

Principles of Screen Design

Careful design of screens can be important; research has shown that a well-designed screen improves productivity about 25%. Most of the principles of screen design arise from considerations of the strengths and weaknesses of human information processing. There are four basic types of screens:

- *Data entry screens* are used to enter data into a component or for a transaction. They may be used either with or to enter data without source documents.
- *Inquiry screens* are used to display selected contents of the database.
- *Multipurpose screens* are a combination of inquiry and data-entry screens. Multipurpose screens are used to update a database.
- *Menu screens* are used to choose between alternative actions.

General Principles

Although the principles of screen design in this chapter are a good start, it is important to involve the actual user both in the design of screens and in testing them. Fortunately dBASE screens are easy to paint using the Assistant or Control Center; hence, it is fairly easy to design a prototype screen, have the user try it out, and make modifications as needed. Appendix A in Chapter 10 shows how to create such a prototype system.

The first general principle of screen design is consistency—screens throughout a system should look and act consistent. For example, on menus, the same number should always be used to exit the system. Also, data that is displayed on several screens should always be in the same place so that the user will know where to look for it automatically. Screen titles should be centered at the top of the screen.

The second general principle is cohesion — each screen should do one complete task. All relevant information needed for a given task should be on the screen, but *only* relevant information. For example, on a screen for entering students' course selections, the student name is relevant (to make sure the ID number is correct), but the student address and phone number are not relevant and should not be displayed.

Fields should be built left to right and top to bottom, starting with the upper left corner. Instructions on how to use the screen should precede the data entry portion. The caption for a field should immediately precede the field rather than being above or below it (except for multi part transactions, as described later).

Screens should appear balanced and symmetrical. The design should be horizontal rather than vertical; this usually means multiple columns. No more than 25% of the screen should be used; the rest should be "white space." Items on the screen should not be densely packed; there should be at least some "white space" between every item.

Data fields should be left-justified and should be visually highlighted in some way. Captions for the data fields can be either right- or left- justified. Thus, both of the following are OK:

```
Department:_______________
Course number:____
Section:____
```

or

```
   Department:_______________
Course number:____
      Section:____
```

The following display features are often used in screen design:

- High brightness
- Reverse video
- Color

High brightness is good for getting the user's attention and is not distracting. It is good to use for data-entry fields, with the captions in regular brightness.

Reverse video is also good for getting the user's attention but can reduce legibility and increase eye fatigue. It should be used for data-entry fields or for error displays.

Color is very good for getting attention but can also be distracting and reduce legibility. An understanding of color theory is very helpful for professional-looking screen design. Two basic rules are to avoid mixing dark colors and never to combine a dark blue background with red foreground or vice-versa.

Specific Screen types

Data-entry screens are used either with an input source document or by themselves. The basic rule in any data-entry screen is that the screen sequence should follow the transaction sequence; data should be entered in the order in which it is encountered. If there is a source document associated with the screen, the items on the screen should be in the same positions as on the source document. In fact, the screen should be as exact an image of the source document as is possible. Ideally the document and the screen should be designed together. Data fields on the screen should be highlighted. Captions for multiple-transaction screens (for example, multiple classes selected by a registering student) should be above the columns.

Inquiry screens should display only the information needed for the activity in question; there should be a group of special purpose inquiry screens rather than one general purpose screen. The data should be organized in the order in which it will be used. Codes should be spelled out. Data fields should be displayed in high intensity, and captions should be displayed in low intensity.

Multipurpose screens should be used only to update permanent entities. Otherwise, it is generally better to combine an inquiry screen with a separate data-entry screen.

Menu screens should be organized to reflect the natural organization of the users' tasks. All menus should be carefully labeled to help prevent the user from getting lost.

Editing screen inputs

"Editing" is the process of checking inputs for errors. There are five common forms of editing used in screen design:

- Mixed mode checks
- Range checks
- Reasonableness checks
- Check digits
- Visual verification

Mixed mode checks are used to make sure that a data element is of the correct type. For example, if the type has been specified as numeric, such a check will refuse to accept any entry that contains an input other than a number. These checks are especially helpful in catching problems that occur when the person doing data entry is looking at the source document rather than the screen and accidentally skips a field.

Range checks are used where data must be within a specific range. Input data is compared with a stored set of valid values and rejected if it does not meet the criterion. For example, if job levels can range between 1 and 24, such a check would reject an input of 42. Similarly, if the highest pay level is $150,000 per year, such a check would refuse to accept an value of 1,500,000. A related test is to ensure that a record with a particular key value exists before accepting the screen.

Reasonableness checks are used to identify data entries that do not make sense. They are often implemented by checking one variable against another. In doing this, the values of the comparative variables are stored in a table in memory. For example, job grade could be checked against pay level. If an entry contains a job level of 5, for which the pay range is $10,000 to $15,000, then the program would refuse to accept an entry of $25,000.

A *check digit* is a number added on to the end of a code that can be calculated from the rest of the code. Check digits usually involve a series of multiplications, additions, and

Order Form

Date ____________ Customer ____________

Name ____________

Address ____________

Phone ____________

Quantity | Item number | Item name | Size | Price

FIGURE 9-1 Sample multipart transaction form.

divisions performed on the data. They are often used to construct keys, since the use of a properly designed check digit will catch any single-digit entry error.

Visual verification is the display of a record when the key is entered. For example, if an operator enters a student ID number, the system might then display the student's name and address at the top of the screen. If the wrong ID was entered, the fact that the name on the screen does not match the input form will be obvious to the operator.

None of these techniques ensure that there will be no input errors, but in combination they can significantly reduce the number of such errors.

Multipart Transaction Screens

Most input events in the real world involve multipart transactions. For example, a customer usually orders several items at a time, and a single purchase order often is issued for multiple items. An input screen for such an event should allow the entry of multiple items on a single screen.

Figure 9-1 shows a typical multipart form with information on the customer and the different items ordered. Figure 9-2 shows the poor way in which most database systems encourage programmers to automate the form. The first screen is for the customer and is attached to the appropriate permanent entity. Then there is a second screen, corresponding to the transient entity ORDER ITEM, and this is repeated once for each order item on the form. This type of program is easy to write using screen definition facilities but is difficult to use.

From the point of view of user interface, Figure 9-3 is a far better design; it reflects manual forms, which reduces the need for operator training and makes data entry easier. Even more important, a distracted operator is less likely to forget what he or she was doing, reducing the chance of duplicates or skipped entries.

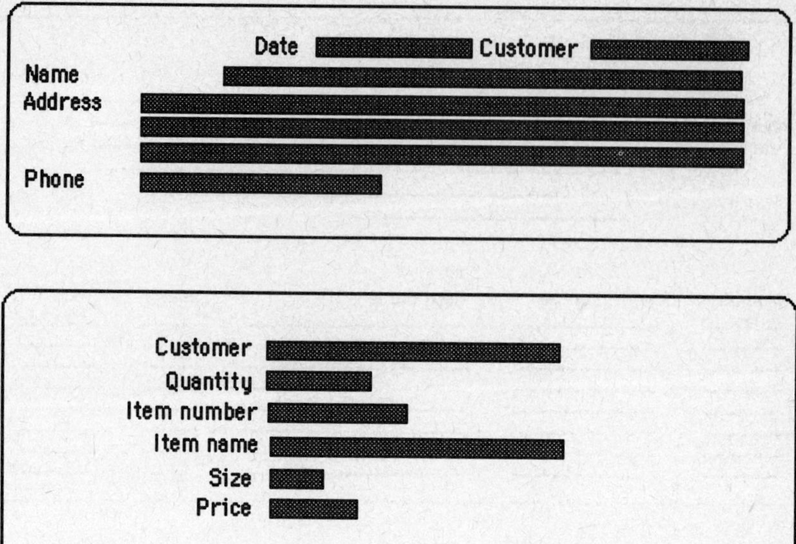

FIGURE 9-2 Typical multipart transaction screens.

Order Form

Date ______________ Customer ______________

Name ____

Address ____

____

____

Phone ______________________

Quantity	Item number	Item name	Size	Price
______	____________	__________________	____	______
______	____________	__________________	____	______
______	____________	__________________	____	______
______	____________	__________________	____	______
______	____________	__________________	____	______
______	____________	__________________	____	______
______	____________	__________________	____	______
______	____________	__________________	____	______

FIGURE 9-3 Better multipart transaction screen.

Additional information on screen design can be found in *Handbook of Screen Format Design* by Wilbert Galitz.

Implementing Screens in dBASE

Screens are predefined formats for data input or output. They are associated with entities, and in fourth generation languages they are usually defined and stored separately from the procedural code. A screen defines how data will be presented. Traditional programming languages, such as COBOL, had no facilities for predefined screens; instead, they implemented the user interface as part of the program. Modern versions of fourth generation languages allow separate screen definitions. For example, one might define a screen for CUSTOMER-RECORD and then use that one screen for modules such as **ADD-CUSTOMER-RECORD, CHANGE-CUSTOMER-RECORD, DELETE-CUSTOMER-RECORD**, and **DISPLAY-CUSTOMER-RECORD**. In that way, any change in the screen format (such as changing the order of the fields) will automatically propagate to every module that uses that screen. This is important in maintaining a consistent user interface to the program. In dBASE III, screens are defined in **`.fmt`** files (created with the **`CREATE FORMAT`** menu selection in the Assistant) and connected to a module with the `SET FORMAT TO` command. In dBASE III there is a Format for Screen design utility as part of the Assistant; in dBASE IV one uses the **`CREATE FORMS`** selection in the Control Center. Figure 9-4 shows a sample screen definition, and Figure 9-5 shows how it is used in a program (the `SET FORMAT` command is highlighted). Figure 9-6 shows the results on the screen.

```
@ 5,5 SAY "Supplier name?"
@ 5,55 SAY "Supplier number"
@ 6,5 SAY "Salesman name"
@ 7,5 SAY "Address line 1?"
@ 8,5 SAY "Address line 2?"
@ 9,5 SAY "Address line 3?"
@ 10,5 SAY "Phone number?"
@ 11,5 SAY "Days until due?"
@ 11,25 SAY "Discount?"
@ 11,40 SAY "Discount days?"
@ 12,5 SAY "Notes?"
@ 5,22 GET SNAME
@ 6,22 GET SNUMBER
@ 7,22 GET SADDR1
@ 8,22 GET SADDR2
@ 9,22 GET SADDR3
@ 10,22 GET SPHONE
@ 11,21 GET DUEDAYS
@ 11,35 GET DISCOUNT
@ 11,55 GET DISCDAYS
@ 12,12 GET SNOTES
```

FIGURE 9-4 Screen definition (`supp.fmt`).

```
*******************************
* Enter Supplier data SUPPENT *
*******************************
USE SUPPLIER
DO WHILE .T.
  CLEAR
  APPEND BLAND
  GO BOTTOM
  SET FORMAT TO SUPP.FMT
  READ
  @ 16,5 SAY " "
  ACCEPT "Another supplier? (Y or N)  " TO YN IF YN="N"
         DO SUPPSORT
         SET DEVICE TO SCREEN
         RETURN
     ENDIF
  ENDDO T
RETURN
```

FIGURE 9-5 Module that uses the screen definition in `supp.fmt`.

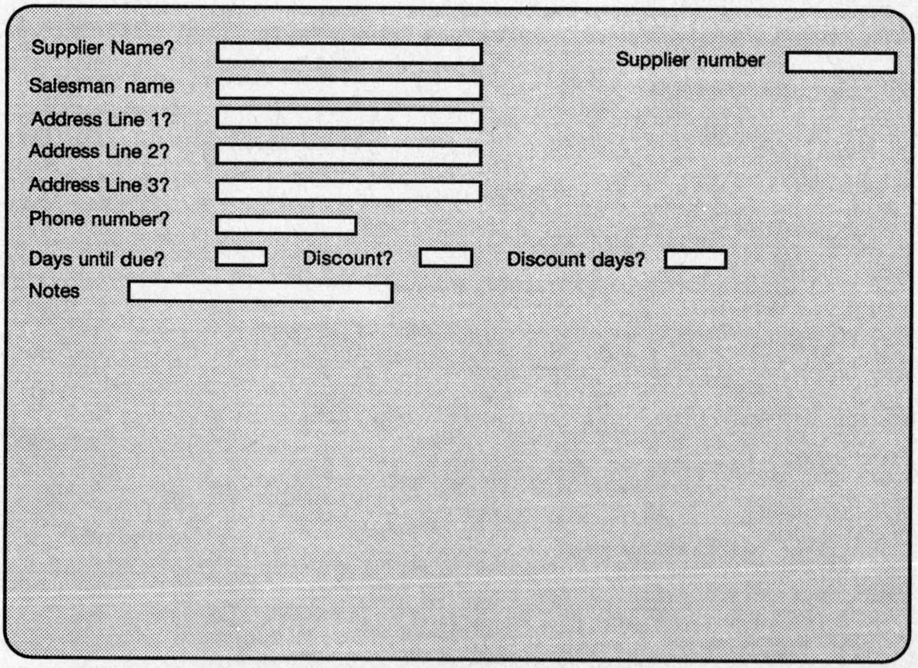

Supplier Name?
Supplier number
Salesman name
Address Line 1?
Address Line 2?
Address Line 3?
Phone number?
Days until due?
Discount?
Discount days?
Notes

FIGURE 9-6 Screen created by `supp.fmt`.

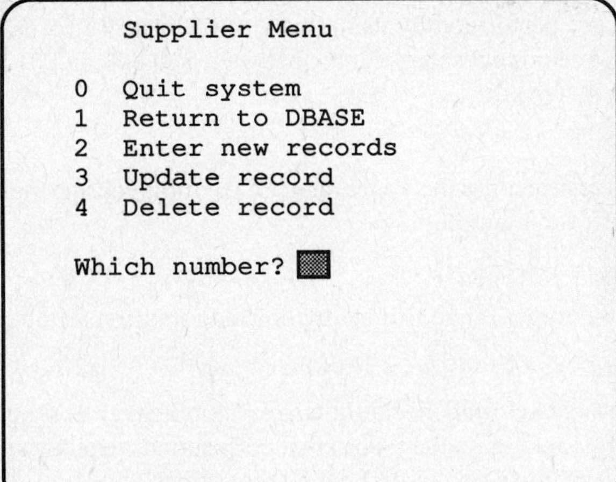

FIGURE 9-7 Typical dBASE III menu.

Editing Screen Inputs in dBASE

Mixed mode checks are performed automatically when one defines data. dBASE will refuse to accept character data in a numeric field or inappropriate data in date or logical fields. Character fields can be made to accept only letters rather than numbers by using the `PICTURE` clause in a `GET` command, that is

```
@ 8,5 GET lastname PICTURE "AAAAAAAAAAAA"
```

Other versions of the `PICTURE` command are available for formatting output.

==== MAIN MENU ====
Databases:
EMPLOYEES
CUSTOMRS
VENDORS
INVENTORY
ORDERS
ACCOUNTS RECEIVABLE
AREA CODES
Utilities:
PRINT INVOICES
BACK UP/RESTORE DATA
RETURN TO dBASE
QUIT TO DOS

FIGURE 9-8 Pop-up menu.

Range checks are performed by using the RANGE clause in a GET command. For example, if an employee annual salary can be between $10,000 and $150,000, one could check input with the statement:

```
@ 8,5 GET salary RANGE 10000,150000
```

If one wants to restrict only the lower range (e.g. employee age must be over 18), the last number,is left off, for example,

```
@ 8,5 GET age RANGE 18,
```

whereas restricting the upper range is done by omitting the first number, for example,

```
@ 8,5 GET salary RANGE ,150000
```

Reasonableness chekcs and check digits are implemented as program code. Visual verification is done by looking up the record that corresponds to a key and displaying that record in a window (or full screen in dBASE III) for verification.

dBASE Screen Highlighting

dBASE works with either a color or a monochrome monitor. The appropriate command is SET COLOR ON or SET COLOR OFF.

dBASE internally recognizes two types of screen output that are relevant for programming:

Normal is the output from the SAY command

Fields are input from the GET command

In a program, the command SET COLOR OF FIELDS TO <attribute> or SET COLOR OF NORMAL TO <attribute> can be used to control the output of GET and SAY commands. To set both normal and background color, the command is SET COLOR TO <standard attribute> ,,,<background attribute>. The attribute alternatives are the following:

N	black
B	blue
G	green
BG	cyan
X	blank (nothing, this is useful for passwords)
N+	gray
R r	ed
RB	magenta
GR	brown
GR+	yellow
W	white
I	causes the item to be displayed in reverse video
*	blinking (after another letter
+	high intensity (after another letter)

FIGURE 9-9 Bar menu.

MENUS

Menus in the Program Design Process

A menu is a predefined list of choices that is displayed on the screen. Menus implement the design principle of "selection rather than remembering," since at any point, the user sees a list of what he or she can do with the system.

In a modern interactive system, the menu structure represents a large part of the way in which the user views the system. Thus, in the MSDOS world, companies such as Lotus go to great legal lengths to defend their proprietary menu structures from competitors. Similarly, in the Macintosh world, Apple's *Human Interface Design Guidelines* enforce a common menu structure on all applications, and Macintosh users generally reject any product that does not follow the common menu structure.

Menus determine how the system is organized and what a user's choices are at any point in using the system. In a custom system automating day to day work, the menu structure should be based on the user's task structure. For example, if in a small business the same clerk sends out purchase orders, enters incoming shipments, and enters data on incoming invoices, then all of these choices should be grouped together. On the other hand, a more common structure would be for ordering, receiving, and accounts payable to be separate; therefore, a system might have separate ordering, receiving, and accounts payable menus (perhaps, with some sort of password protection to enforce accounting controls).

Since menu structure is such an important part of the user interface, it should be tested as part of a prototype before the rest of the program is constructed. Fortunately, menus in dBASE are easy to build.

Implementing Menus in dBASE

dBASE III has no predefined menu object class; instead, we write short programs (Chapter 19). The results usually look like Figure 9-7.

dBASE IV has two types of predefined menu objects: pop-up windows and bar menus (Figures 9-8 and 9-9).

Pop-ups are special windows that contain menus. Like other menus, they are defined, activated, and cleared. When a pop-up menu is defined, each of the lines (bars) in the menu must also be defined. The syntax is as follows:

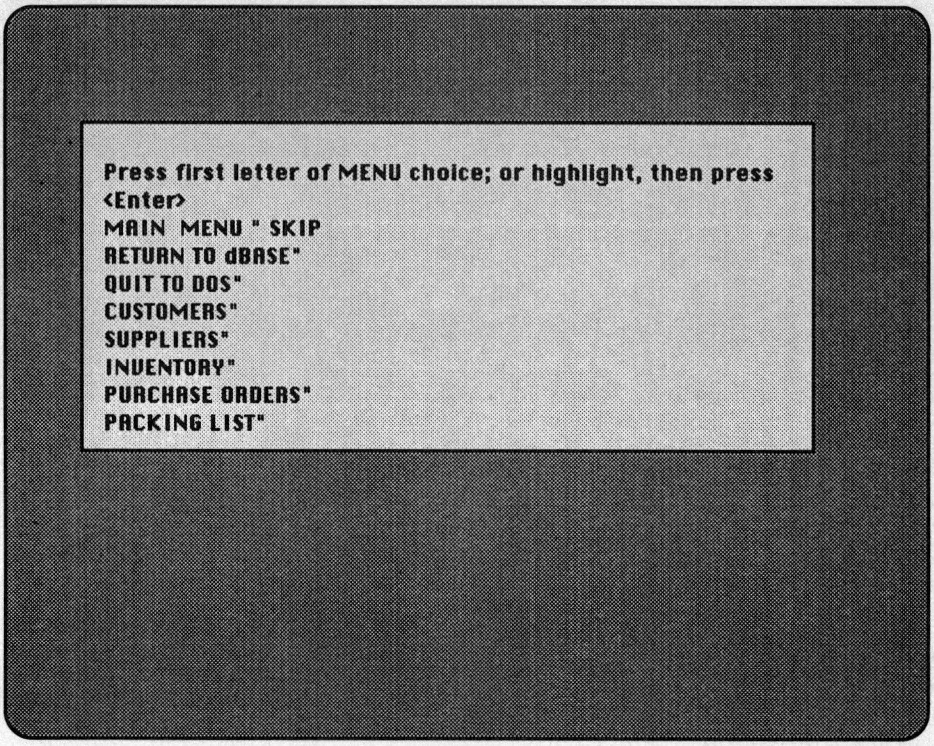

Press first letter of MENU choice; or highlight, then press
<Enter>
MAIN MENU " SKIP
RETURN TO dBASE"
QUIT TO DOS"
CUSTOMERS"
SUPPLIERS"
INVENTORY"
PURCHASE ORDERS"
PACKING LIST"

FIGURE 9-10 Pop-up menu.

```
DEFINE POPUP <popup name> FROM <row> <column>
DEFINE BAR <line number> OF <popup name> PROMPT <message>
```

For example:

```
DEFINE POPUP main FROM 10,2 TO 20,70;
MESSAGE "Press first letter of MENU choice; or high light, then press <Enter>"
DEFINE BAR 1 OF main PROMPT "MAIN  MENU " SKIP
DEFINE BAR 2 OF main PROMPT " RETURN TO dBASE"
DEFINE BAR 3 OF main PROMPT " QUIT TO DOS"
DEFINE BAR 4 OF main PROMPT " CUSTOMERS"
DEFINE BAR 5 OF main PROMPT " SUPPLIERS"
DEFINE BAR 6 OF main PROMPT " INVENTORY"
DEFINE BAR 7 OF main PROMPT "PURCHASE ORDERS"
DEFINE BAR 8 OF main PROMPT "PACKING LIST"
ON SELECTION POPUP main DO Main
```

This results in the pop-up menu represented in Figure 9-10.

Pop-up menus, like windows, are not active when first defined. To activate a pop-up menu, one uses the command: `ACTIVATE POPUP <popup name>`, for example:

```
ACTIVATE POPUP main
```

Pop-up menus are deactivated with the command `DEACTIVATE POPUP`. They are erased from memory with the command `CLEAR POPUPS`.

The other sort of predefined menu in dBASE IV is a bar menu (similar to those in Microsoft Windows, in the OS/2 Presentation Manager, and on the Apple Macintosh. As expected, the appropriate commands are `DEFINE MENU, ACTIVATE MENU, DEACTIVATE MENU, and CLEAR MENU`. In addition, one has to define the "pads" on each bar—the selections. This is done with the `DEFINE PAD` command. Actions to be taken if a pad is selected are defined with the `ON PAD` command. Syntax is

```
DEFINE MENU <menu name>
DEFINE PAD <pad name> OF <menu name> PROMPT <message>
ACTIVATE MENU <menu name> [PAD <pad name>]
DEACTIVATE MENU
CLEAR MENUS
RELEASE MENUS <menu name list>
ON PAD <pad name> OF <menu name> <action>
```

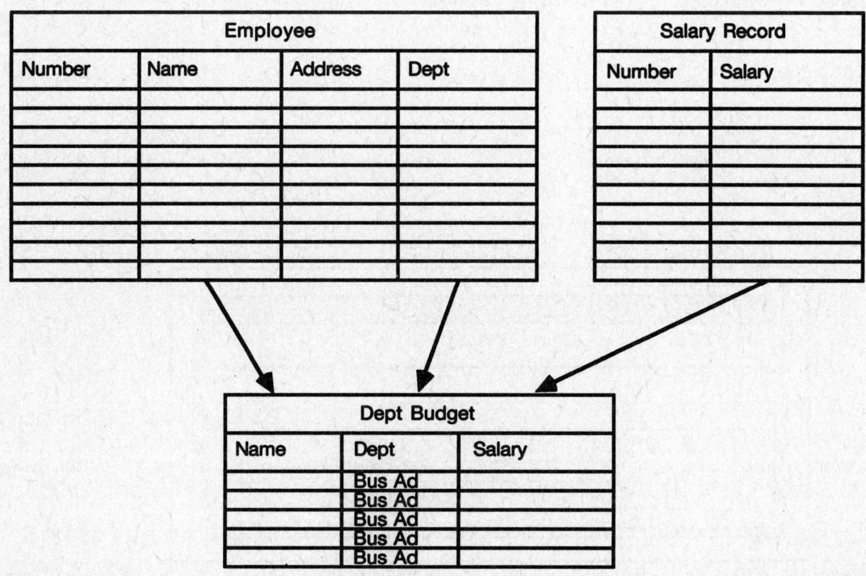

FIGURE 9-11 Views.

Often bar menus are combined with pop-up menus.

```
ON PAD exit OF pomenu ACTIVATE POPUP exit
```

REPORTS

Reports in the Program Design Process

A report is a predefined output that can be generated at any time. Most of the paper coming out of a system is in the form of reports.

Reports in dBASE

Report definitions are similar to screen definitions, except that they are for written output rather than video output. Most fourth generation languages (and even COBOL) allow the definition of predetermined report types. In dBASE III, reports are defined with the **CREATE REPORT** menu selection in the Assistant. In dBASE IV, use the **CREATE REPORT** selection in the Control Center. In both languages, reports are invoked with the `REPORT FORM` command. For example, the command

```
REPORT FORM supprpt
```

generates a predefined report that has been stored in the file `SUPPRPT.FRM`.

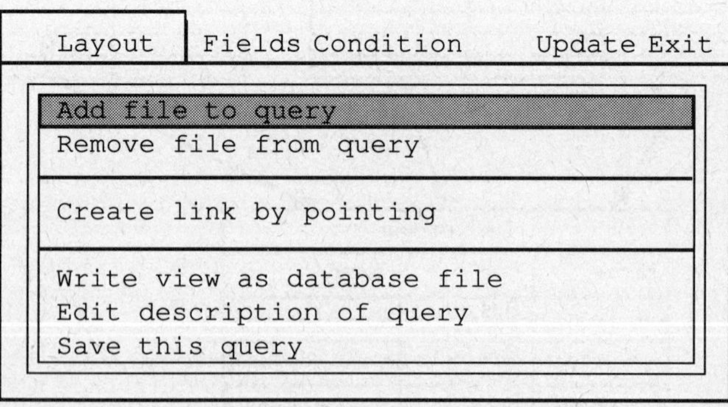

FIGURE 9-12 Query definition in dBASE IV.

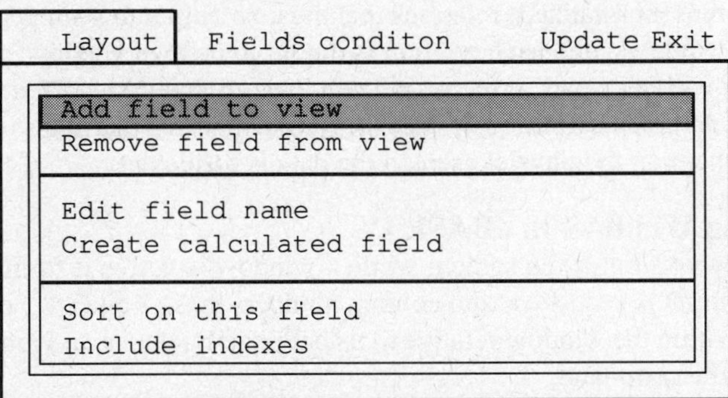

FIGURE 9-13 View definition in dBASE IV.

VIEWS

Views in the Program Design Process

Views are familiar to database designers, since one of the fundamental dogmas of database design is that user views need not be the same as system views. A view is simply a definition of how the data is organized from the point of view of a particular user. Figure 9-11 shows some possible examples. A view may be a subset of fields (e.g., omitting salary), a subset of records (e.g., only those in a given department), or a combination of data from different tables or relations.

Views in dBASE

Views in dBASE are created by using two related facilities: views and queries. A query in dBASE is a predefined retrieval from a single file. An example might be extracting all employees whose department is "BusAd." A view in dBASE is a virtual (i.e., "imaginary") database that may be the combination of several existing relations (`xxx.dBF` files). Both queries and views in dBASE are created from the `Create Queries` section of the Control Center (Figure 9-12).

A view is created from a query with the Layout submenu's **`ADD FILE TO QUERY OPTION`** (Figure 9-13). The two files must be linked together by a common key. Figure 9-14 shows the final dBASE view that implements the diagram of Figure 9-11.

WINDOWS

Windows in the Program Design Process

Windows are virtual screens. Translated into English, this means that they are sections of a real, physical screen that are treated as separate logical screen. In Figure 9-15, there are three windows defined: A, B, and C. When a window is active, all output that is supposed to go to the screen goes to that section of the screen inside the window. Windows are often used for prompts, error messages, and supplementary information. Figure 9-16 shows one of the most common uses for windows in a database environment. In this example, we have data from three different (normalized) relations that must be output to a single form. The form is divided into windows, and each relation is output to its own window.

Figure 9-17 shows how views, screens, and windows are integrated. A view defines what data a user sees. A screen definition defines the format in which that data is displayed. A window defines where on the physical screen the data is displayed.

Implementing Windows in dBASE IV

Windows may be any portion of the screen; while a window is active it forms a virtual screen to which all output is sent. Row and column numbers in SAY and GET commands refer to coordinates within the window relative to its boundaries, that is, in Figure 9-18, if window B is active, the command

```
@ 1,1 SAY "Error, please reenter item"
```

will appear at the upper left hand corner of window B toward the right of the screen rather than in the upper left hand corner of the screen, as would be true if no window were active.

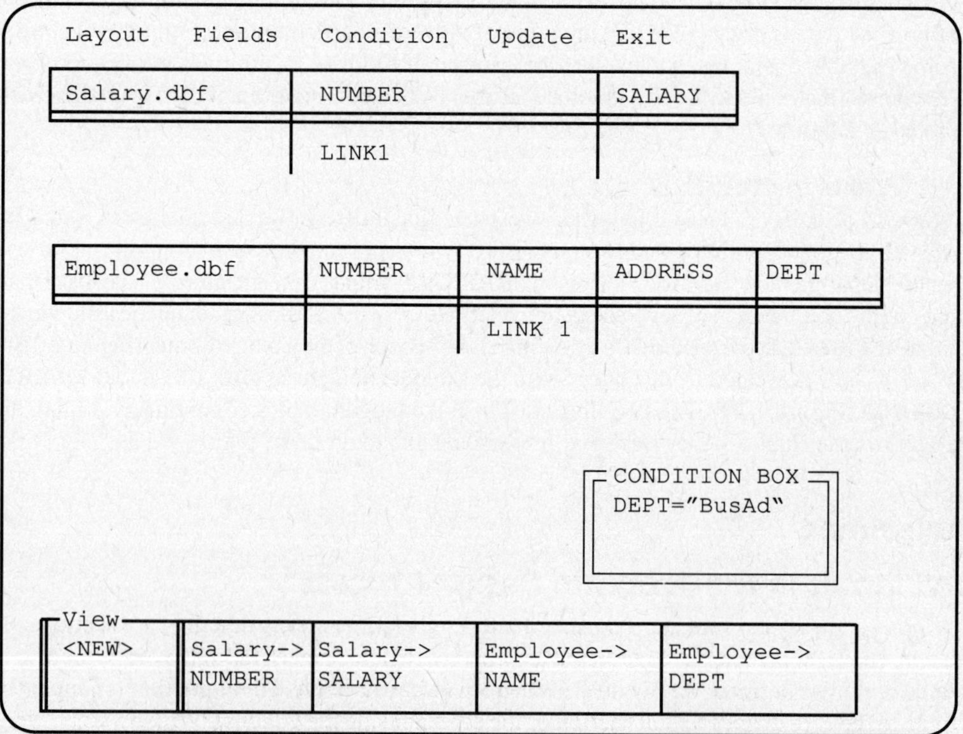

FIGURE 9-14 Completed view definition in dBASE IV.

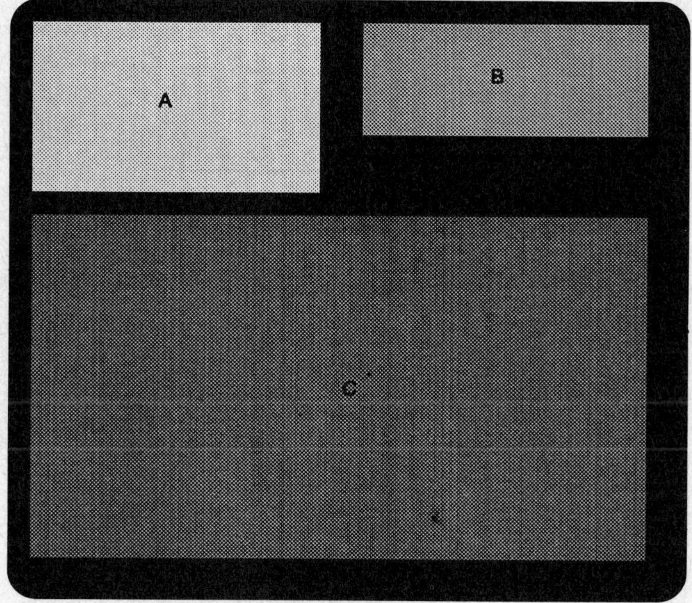

FIGURE 9-15 Windows.

In using windows, a window must first be defined, giving its position on the screen in terms of upper left corner and lower right corner. For example, the command

```
DEFINE WINDOW poheader FROM 2, 33 TO 10,70
```

defines a window named `poheader` located with its upper left corner in row 2 column 33 and its lower right corner in row 10 column 70 (about the location of window B in Figure 9-15). Once a window is defined, it exists as a potential object until deleted with a `RELEASE WINDOW windowname` command (to erase a specific window) or a `CLEAR WINDOWS` command (to erase all windows). It does not, however, take effect until it is activated.

A window is activated with the `ACTIVATE WINDOW` command. Once this command is issued, all subsequent screen operations refer to the window until such time as it is deactivated. In the following example, the three `SAY` commands output to the window called `poheader` (upper right-hand corner of the screen). Windows are deactivated with the `DEACTIVATE WINDOW` command. Alternatively, the command `ACTIVATE SCREEN` may be used to redirect output from the last defined window to the screen as a whole. This

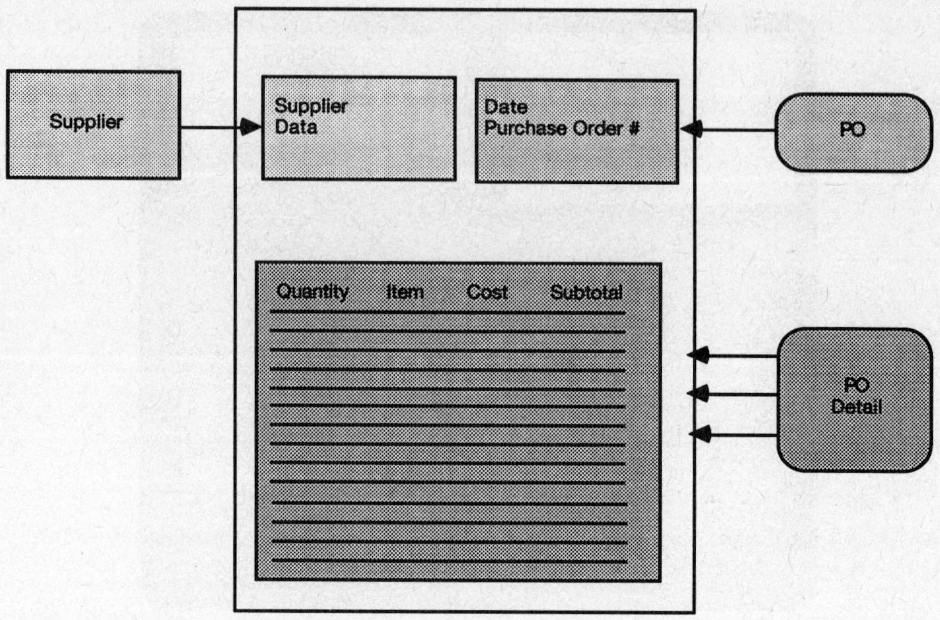

FIGURE 9-16 Three-part form implemented by windows.

is especially useful when one wants to keep a window (or a pop-up menu) on the screen for reference, but not use it.

```
ACTIVATE WINDOW poheader
   @ 0,0 SAY ponumb
   @ 2,1 SAY podate
   @ 3,1 SAY posupp
DEACTIVATE WINDOW poheader
```

Window definitions may be saved to a file with the `SAVE WINDOW` command and restored with the `RESTORE WINDOW` command. This is useful when defining standard windows for use throughout a large system.

SUMMARY

In this chapter we have seen how to define the elements of the program's user interface: menus and screens or paper reports. These can be used to assemble a prototype for the user and thus to get feedback on whether we have really understood what needs to be done.

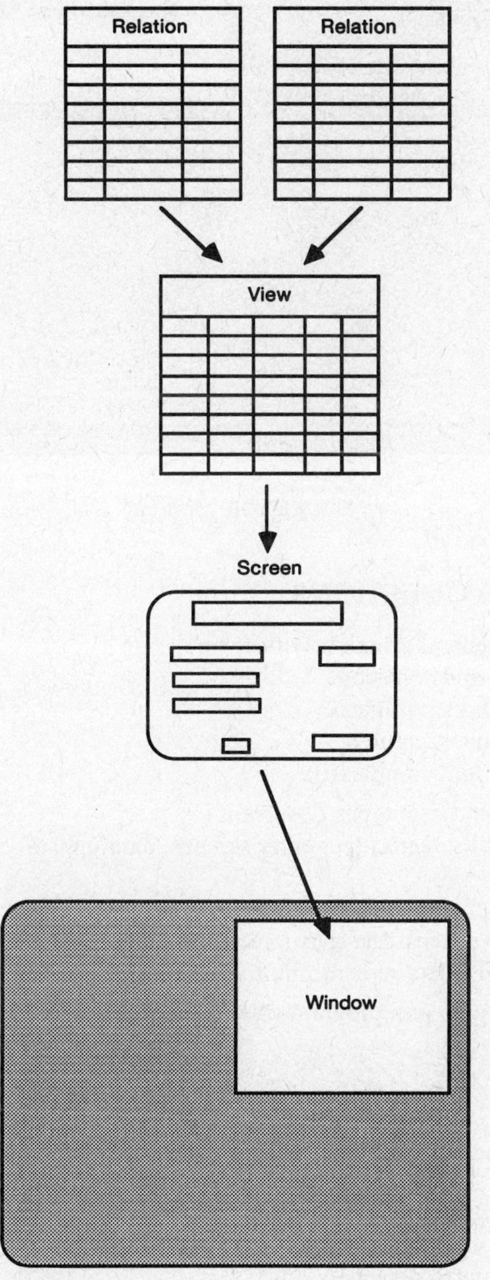

FIGURE 9-17 Views, screens, and windows integrated.

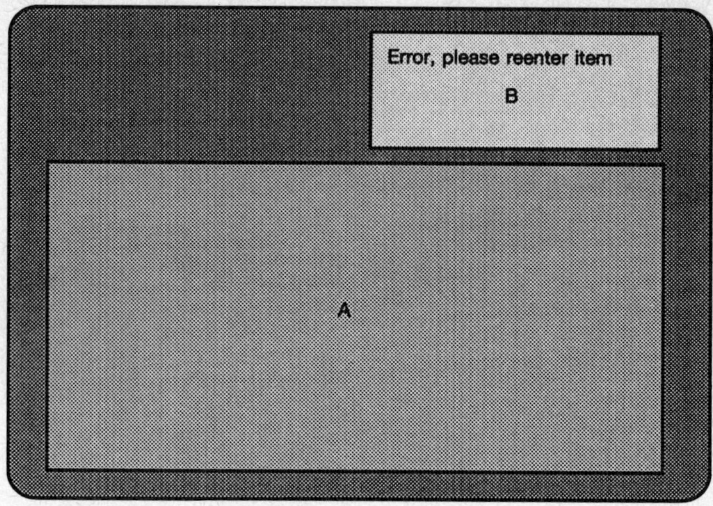

FIGURE 9-18 Windows.

EXERCISES AND QUESTIONS

1. What are two general principles of screen design?
   a. Consistency and cohesion.
   b. Simplicity and lengthiness.
   c. Organized and structured.
   d. Hierarchical and complexity.
2. What are the four basic types of screens?
   a. Data-retrieval screens, data-entry screens, data-update screens, and data-delete screens.
   b. Data entry-screens, inquiry screens, multipurpose screens, and menu screens.
   c. Data-retrieval screens, data-entry screens, multi-use screens, and data-delete screens.
   d. Entity screens, data screens, multiuse screens, and event screens.
3. What is an example of a program-oriented object?
   a. Screen.
   b. Event.
   c. Action.
   d. Entity.
4. The two major classes of object of concern in the program model is program-orientated objects and
   a. Application-oriented objects.
   b. Screen-orientated objects.
   c. Hardware-orientated objects.
   d. Disk-orientated objects.

5. What type of screen is used to choose between alternative actions?
   a. Data-entry screens
   b. Menu screens
   c. Multipurpose screens
   d. Inquiry screens
6. Carefully designed screens
   a. Look nice, but need to be altered often.
   b. Should be balanced and consistent throughout the system.
   c. Take too much time to design.
   d. Aren't important since they don't improve productivity.
7. In a fourth generation environment a window is
   a. A section of a screen that is treated as a separate logical screen.
   b. The part of the screen that is in use.
   c. A part of a program module.
   d. A module.
8. A predefined formatsfor data input or output is a
   a. Screen.
   b. Monitor.
   c. Menu.
   d. Records.

DISCUSSION QUESTIONS

1. What does a user interface consist of?

FOR NORTHSTAR AVIATION

2. Identify events, updates, actions, reports, and inquiries.
3. Design screens, menus, and reports.

REFERENCES

GALITZ, W. *Handbook of Screen Format Design*, 3rd Edition. QED, Wellesley, MA, 1989.

APPLE. *Human Interface Design Guidelines*. Addison-Wesley, Reading, MA, 1987.

Section III

DERIVATION OF PROGRAM ARCHITECTURE

This section discusses how to derive a program architecture from a system specification (Figure S-3-1). In more graphic terms, it describes how to transform a data flow diagram or an entity-relationship diagram into a program structure chart (introduced in Chapter 10). This derivation is the essence of "top-down" design; to repeat a quotation from Chapter 1, it is "deciding which components, interconnected in which way will best solve some well-specified problem" [Constantine & Yourdon 1977]. The approach is also known as problem decomposition. In terms of traditional systems analysis, it is the design of a new physical model—the last step in systems analysis and the first step in program design. In terms of problem solving, we are translating an abstract model of a system to an abstract model of a program.

Approaches to the derivation of program architecture range from ad hoc to formal methodologies (a methodology is an integrated selection of methods used to solve a particular type of problem). All of these approaches are related to the concept of cohesion discussed in Chapter 12. The modules in the architecture have to be related by some concept. Formal approaches to problem decomposition may be based on functional abstraction, on data abstraction, or on procedural abstraction. *Abstraction* here means that we are dealing with models of reality that have a hierarchy; higher level modules deal with *what*, and lower level modules deal with *how*.

Each of these techniques is traditionally presented in isolation as the "correct" way to do program design. In fact, there is no best method to derive a program architecture, and most practical projects can benefit from the use of multiple design approaches. Many of the approaches used in industry are parts of commercial system-development methodologies whose vendors have a vested interest both in maintaining the universal usefulness of their methods and in differentiating their methods from those of other vendors (or perhaps more importantly, from public-domain approaches). Moreover, there is much confusion about the level of design for which a particular method is appropriate, since many versions of the

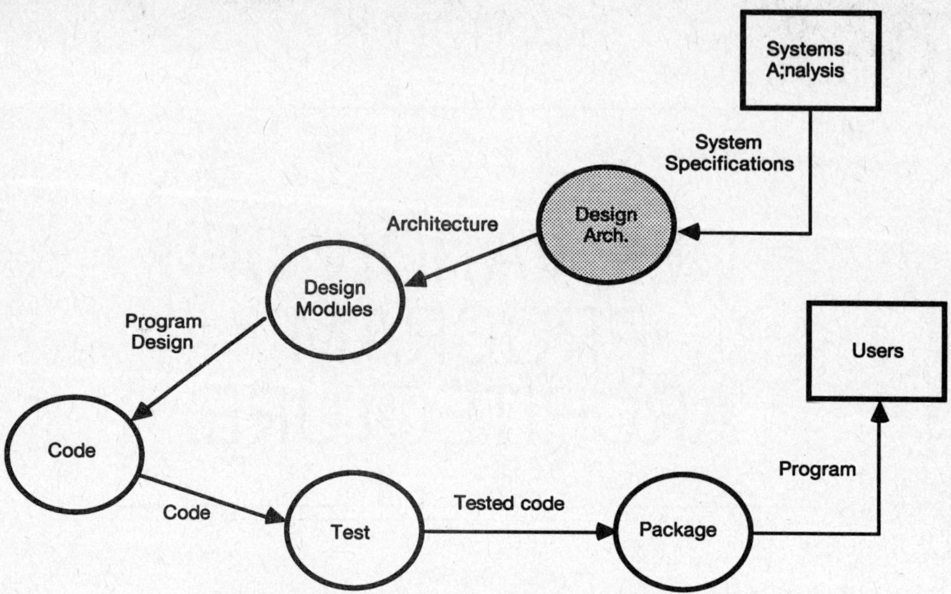

FIGURE S-3-1 Derivation of program architecture.

systems-development life-cycle do not differentiate between derivation of program architecture and design of individual modules.

As an example of both of these problems, in industry the Michael Jackson data structure–based program design methodology [King 1988] and the Yourdon, Inc., data flow–based methodology [Page-Jones 1988] are considered direct competitors. In a fourth generation environment, the latter is an approach to designing program architectures that provides very little help at the module design stage, while the former is an approach to designing modules which does not really address program architecture issues. Figure S-3-2 illustrates these two common third generation approaches. In the Yourdon approach (left) the relevant abstraction of the real-world system is data flow (Chapter 6), documented by the systems analysis process, and the abstraction for the program is process structure (Chapter 14), produced by the program design process. In the Jackson approach (right) the relevant abstraction of the real-world system is data structure (Chapter 7), documented by the systems analysis process, and the abstraction for the program is program flow of control (Chapter 14), produced by the program design process.

Figure S-3-3 illustrates a fourth generation approach. The relevant abstraction of the real-world system is a model of the data (Chapter 5), documented by the systems analysis process, which is then translated into the relevant abstractions of the program, produced by the program design process. This section shows what the relevant abstractions are, and how to do the translation.

This text integrates the common approaches to program architecture derivation. The next seven chapters discuss these approaches as they are used for fourth generation languages in general and for dBASE III and IV in particular.

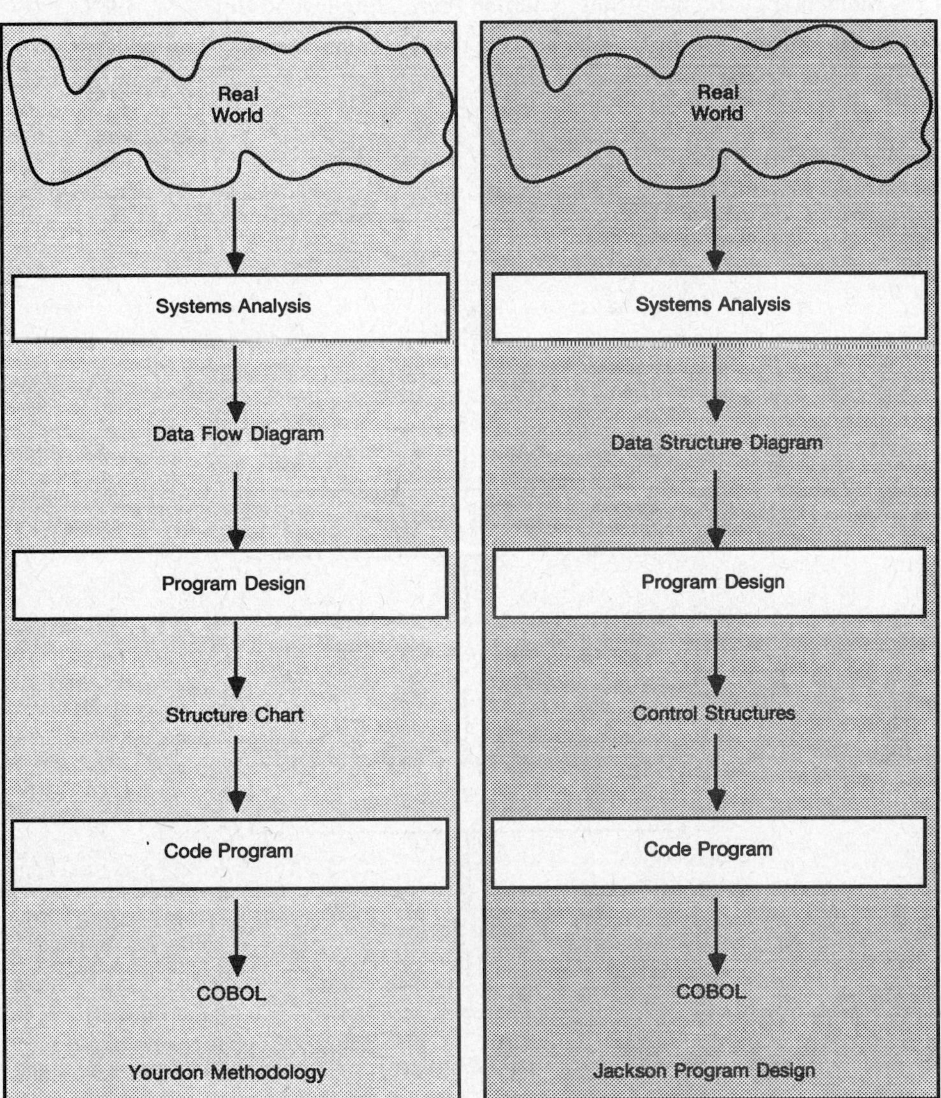

FIGURE S-3-2 Third generation approaches.

REFERENCES

KING, D. Creating Effective Software: Computer Program Design Using the Jackson Methodology. Prentice-Hall (Yourdon Press), Englewood Cliffs, NJ, 1988.

PAGE-JONES, M. The Practical Guide to Structured Systems Design, Prentice-Hall (Yourdon Press), New York, 1988.

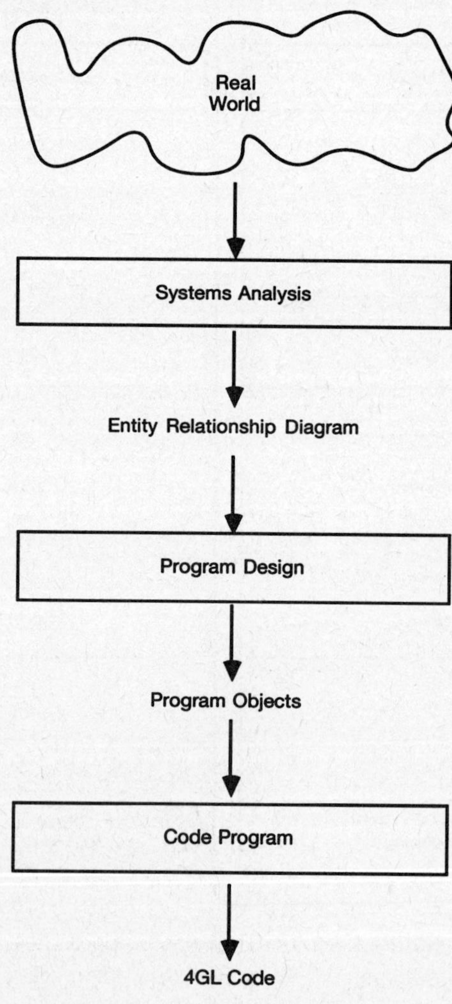

FIGURE S-3-3 Fourth generation approa ch.

Chapter 10

PROGRAM ARCHITECTURE AND MODULARITY

CHAPTER GOALS

- Learn what functional modules are
- Learn to choose functional modules
- Learn notation for structure charts
- Learn to assemble functional modules into a system
- Learn dBASE implementation of modules
- Learn to build prototype systems to get user feedback

This chapter discusses the concept of modularity, the notation that we will use for modularity at the program design stage, and how modularity is implemented in dBASE.

The first step in program design is determining the architecture of the program: What are the subtasks to be accomplished? How shall they be put together? This is the same task faced by a writer who has to determine what the organization of a paper will be before starting to write the paragraphs and sentences. Generally, the architecture of the program will be hierarchical,—partly because that is the way in which most programming languages are organized, but mostly for the reasons discussed in Chapter 2 on the human information processing system. Figure 10-1 shows as an example the outline for part of this book hierarchically arranged. Each of the low-level statements in the outline becomes a paragraph in the final work. For program design, the equivalent of a paragraph is a module, and the equivalent of an outline is a structure chart.

1. **Structured programmikng**
   1.1 Limited number of building blocks
   1.2 Standard representations
2. **Structured design**
   2.1 The "right" modules
   2.2 Minimal connections
   2.3 Program architecture
3. **Control structure role**
   3.1 Data
   3.2 Operations
   3.3 Control structures
   3.4 Algorithm = Operations + Control structures
4. **Presentation of control structures**
   4.1 Flowchart
   4.2 Structured English
   4.3 Pseudocode (PDL)
   4.4 Canonical Pseudocode (Formal PDL)
   4.5 Action diagrams

.

.

.

FIGURE 10-1 Outline.

Figure 10-2 shows the basic attributes of a module. Each module in a system has a *function*: it carries out some task or part of a task. Corresponding to that function is a *name* that describes the module function. The module may use *input* data from the rest of the system, and it may produce *output* data which is used elsewhere in the system. In performing its function, the module probably will use *internal data* that is not used elsewhere in the system.

The concept of modularization has been around for quite awhile, but computer languages differ considerably in their support for the technique. Some, such as COBOL and BASIC, provide only what is known as "lexical separation," which means that all of the statements in a module are located together, but are part of a larger program. In such languages, nothing prevents a programmer from jumping into the middle of a module, and there is no isolation of data within modules from the program as a whole. Other, more modern languages, including dBASE, separate the code for each module. dBASE stores the code for each module in a separate `.prg` file, or as part of a `.pro` (procedure) file identified by a `PROCEDURE` statement. In dBASE, data within a module is private to that module and its subordinates unless it has been declared available to the entire program via a `PUBLIC` statement. Input and output data may be shared via the `PARAMETERS` statement. In short, dBASE provides excellent support for program modularity. Figure 10-3 gives an example of how a module is implemented in dBASE III, with the program statements annotated for

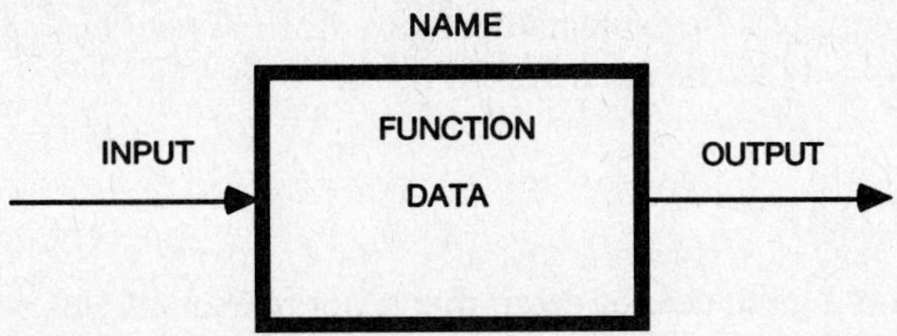

FIGURE 10-2 Parts of a module.

	`**********************************`
	`* Correct Inventory Items INVUP *`
	`**********************************`
	`USE INVENTRY`
	`DO WHILE .T.`
Get value for INB from keyboard	`    ACCEPT "Item number to up-`
`date?" TO INB`	
Find this record in the file	`    LOCATE FOR INUMB = INB`
	`    IF EOF ()`
Print message on screen	`      ? "Can't find that number"`
	`    ELSE`
Use predefined screen format	`SET FORMAT TO INV.FMT`
Clear screen	`      CLEAR`
Read the record onto the screen	`      READ`
for editing	`    ENDIF`
Position cursor on screen	`    @ 18,5 SAY " "`
Get value for YN from keyboard	`    ACCEPT "Update another item`
`(Y or N)"`	
	`TO YN`
	`    IF YN="N"`
Go back to default screen	`      CLOSE FORMAT`
Return to higher-level module	`      RETURN`
	`    ENDIF`
	`ENDDO`
	`CLOSE DATABASES`
	`RETURN`

FIGURE 10-3 dBASE III module.

clarity. The statements will be explained in more detail in later chapters; at this point the module code shows why we do not start our design with code!

STRUCTURE CHARTS

Figure 10-3 contains a great deal of detail that is not relevant at this point in the program development life-cycle. At the program architecture design stage, we do not want to be bothered with the details of any programming language or, for that matter, with the details of how module functions are carried out. All we need to know about the module in Figure 10-3 is what it does (corrects inventory items) and how it is related to other modules. What is of interest is what hierarchical structure of modules will best describe the solution to our problem. The notation used for this is a structure chart. It shows the organization of modules and the data exchanged between them.

Figure 10-2 showed the parts of a module; a structure chart is simply a hierarchical (tree) diagram composed of modules represented like those in Figure 10-2. Figure 10-4 shows the way in which the notation of Figure 10-2 is modified; Figure 10-5 shows a simple example with three modules. Note that the direction of the arrows rather than their position to the right or the left determines input versus output. Note also that the ellipses (. . .) in Figure 10-5 are not part of the structure chart notation, but are added to the figure to indicate that the structure chart is incomplete.

In words, Figure 10-5 means that we have a module called **REVIEW CUSTOMER RECORD**, which receives the data element **ID** from higher in the structure chart. Besides the program statements inside **REVIEW CUSTOMER RECORD**, this module makes use of two subfunctions: **GET CUSTOMER RECORD** and **DISPLAY CUSTOMER RECORD**. **GET CUSTOMER RECORD** is sent the data element **ID** and returns **Customer record**, which is then sent to **DISPLAY CUSTOMER RECORD**.

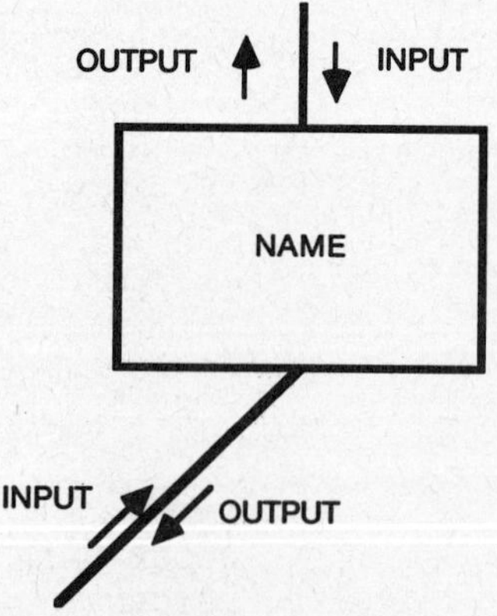

FIGURE 10-4 Structure chart module representation.

Additional Examples

Figure 10-6 shows the structure chart for an application that many of us would rather not learn about—preparing income tax forms. As shown, to perform the task **PREPARE FORM**, one must first perform the five lower-level tasks **PREPARE SCHEDULES A–E** which furnish necessary data to **PREPARE FORM 1040**. Similarly, one cannot **PREPARE SCHEDULE C** without carrying out the necessary subtasks (**PREPARE FORM 4562** and **PREPARE FORM 4797**) that furnish data necessary for schedule C. Note that each of the modules illustrated in Figure 10-6 performs its own processing, but also uses data prepared by lower-level modules. Note also that vertical position in the structure chart is not rigid—the subordinate tasks for **PREPARE SCHEDULE A** are at the same logical level as those for **PREPARE SCHEDULE C** although they are physically placed lower in order to fit on the page. The format of the connecting lines is also not important; either diagonal lines or squared lines are acceptable.

Figure 10-7 illustrates an additional use for structure charts with modern programming, especially for programs likely to be developed in a fourth generation environment. As illustrated, the older approach to programming (a holdover from batch days when end users did not run programs) was to package each task as a separate program. Today, systems are usually designed with the individual tasks selected from a menu; at the highest level the structure chart illustrates what the major tasks are, and at lower levels it illustrates how those tasks are carried out.

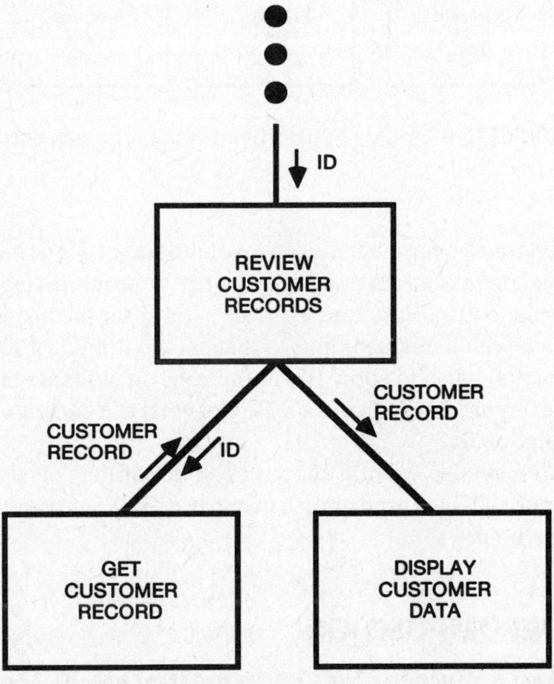

FIGURE 10-5 Simple structure chart.

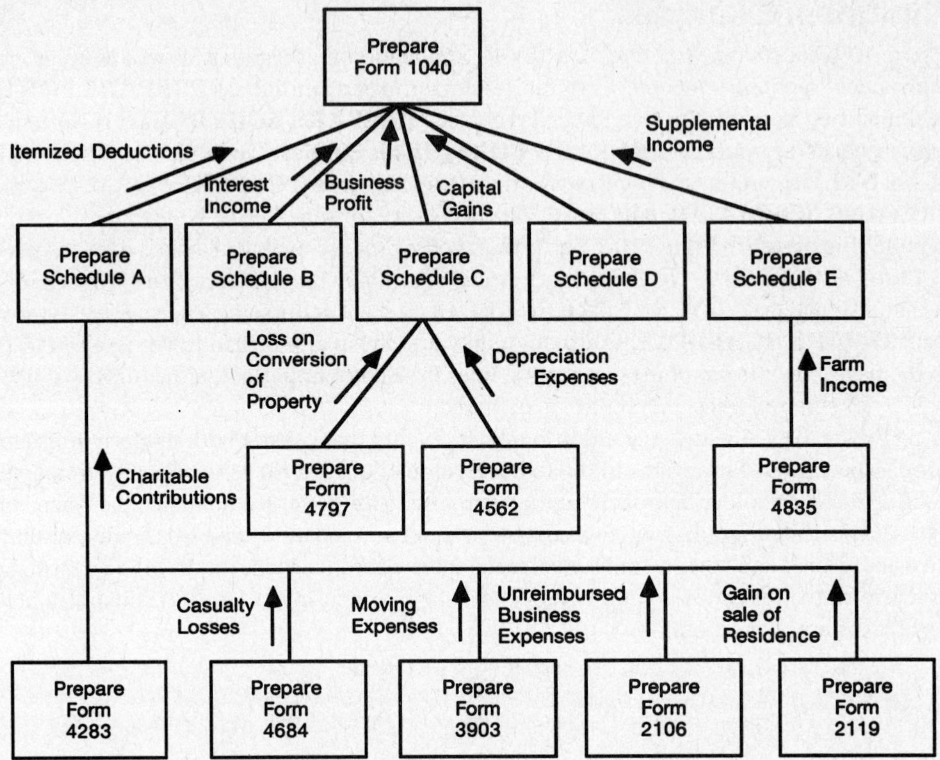

FIGURE 10-6 Structure chart for income tax preparation.

Figure 10-8 illustrates a possible higher-level program for our income tax example. Note, incidentally, that there is no data associated with the program fragment in Figure 10-8. This is typical of the sort of structure chart derived from menus. Figure 10-8 would typically be associated with a menu similar to that shown in Figure 10-9.

Sometimes you may wish to show file definitions on structure charts. The notation shown in Figure 10-10 is used in such instances. Note that the contents of the file are then defined in the data dictionary.

Sometimes you may also wish to show screen definitions on structure charts. The notation shown in Figure 10-11 is used in such instances. The contents of the screen are then defined in the data dictionary.

FUNCTIONAL DECOMPOSITION

How does one produce a structure chart from a program specification? The traditional approach is called "functional decomposition."

Functional decomposition is the production of a program architecture based on functional abstraction. In other words, the highest level module in a system describes what the system does, the second level modules each describe one of the major subtasks, and each level down describes the higher level in more detail. Figure 10-12 details the steps in the approach.

The above process is carried out until the decomposition is sufficient (as discussed in Chapter 12).

Functional decomposition was the first method of modern program design, and in many respects it is still the best. Program architectures derived via *well-done* functional decomposition are functionally cohesive (Chapter 12) and have a problem-based structure that makes them relatively easy to maintain. Moreover, most expert designers use functional decomposition. Why bother with other approaches?

Functional decomposition does have some major shortcomings. It is more a guideline than a method, and results from its use are inconsistent. In other words, if the same problem is given to five different designers, all of whom use functional decomposition, it is very likely that they will come up with five different designs. These designs will probably vary in quality from excellent to awful. Hence the italics in the previous paragraph. One learns to do functional decomposition well by practice and by understanding the problem context. A designer using functional decomposition must be somewhat of an expert in the program domain.

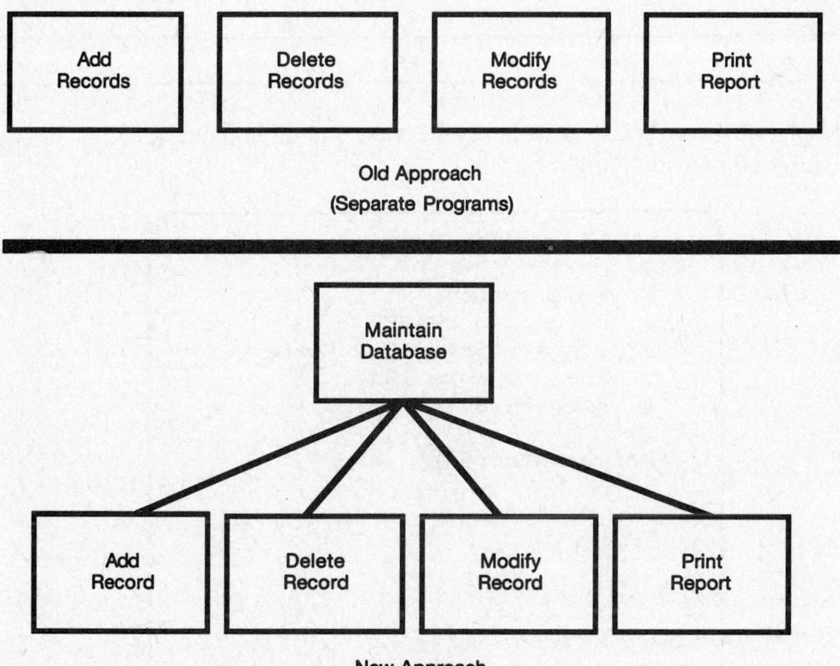

FIGURE 10-7 Old and modern approaches to task management.

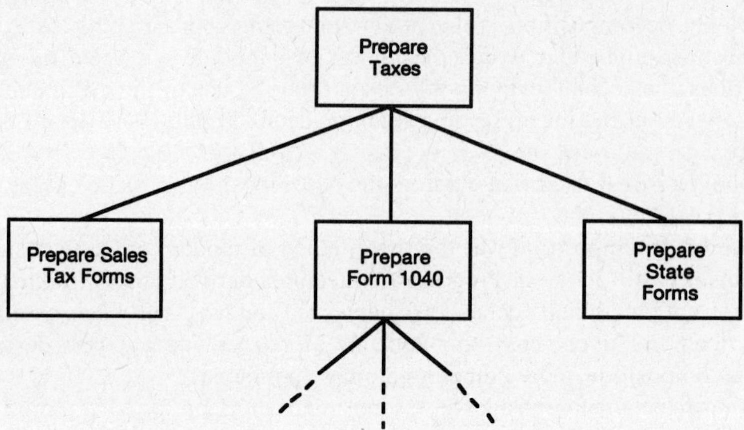

FIGURE 10-8 application of Figure 10-10 to income tax example.

For example, let us suppose that you are going to design a program to perform multiple regression. Figure 10-13 illustrates the general idea here—fitting a straight line to a series of points such that the average distance of the line from the points is as low as possible. The algebra for the simple example in Figure 10-13 is

$$y = a + bx$$

For example, if *X* were height in inches and *Y* were weight in pounds, the relationship to predict weight for an adult might be

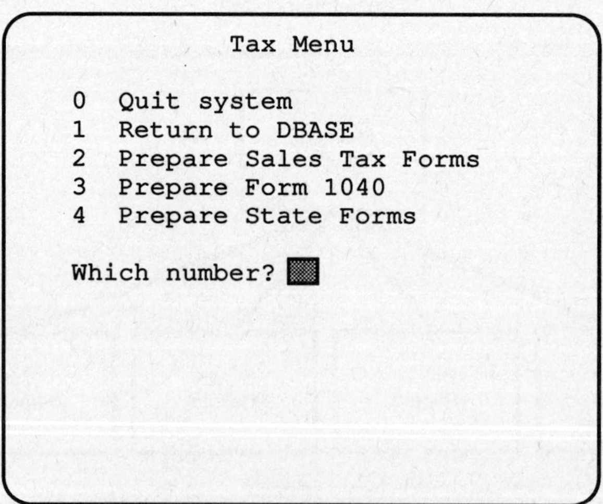

FIGURE 10-9 Menu corresponding to Figure 10-10.

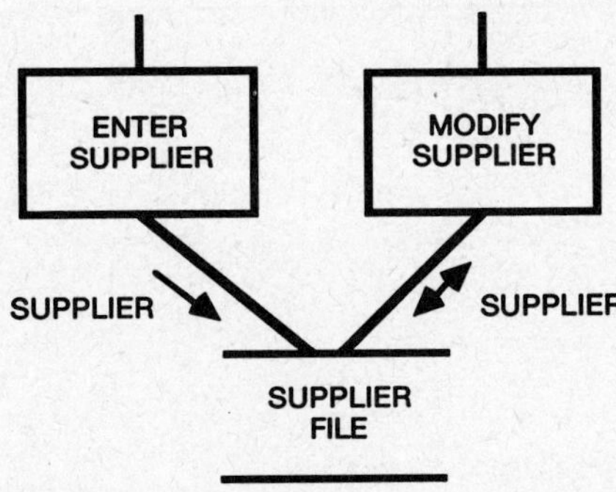

FIGURE 10-10 File depicture on structure charts.

$$\text{Weight} = -60 + 3*\text{Height}$$

Incidentally, this is a made-up relationship, so don't go on a diet if you don't match the forecast!

Our sample task is to produce a program design that will fit data to a model of the form:

$$y = a + b_1 x_1 + b_2 x_2 + \ldots + b_n x_n$$

using the goal of minimizing the sum of the squared distances between the hyperplane and the points. If you have never studied statistics, your reaction is probably to skip to the next chapter. That is part of the point here: you cannot use functional decomposition in a subject area that you do not understand.

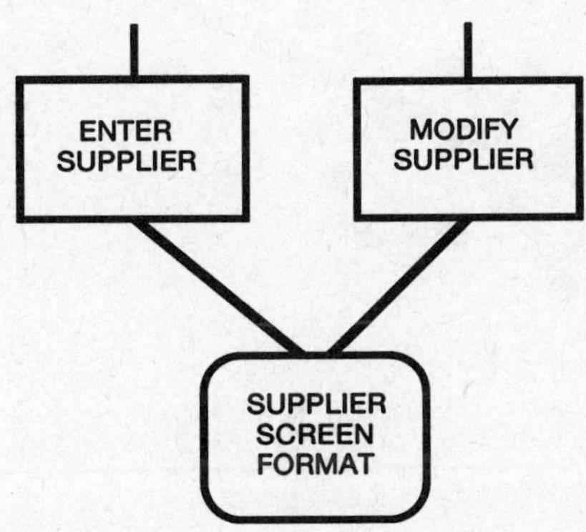

FIGURE 10-11 Screen definitions on a structure chart.

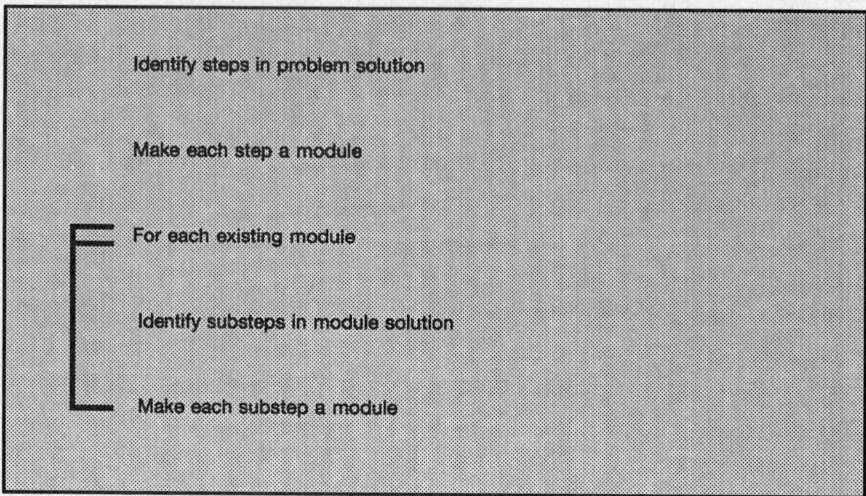

FIGURE 10-12 Steps in functional decomposition.

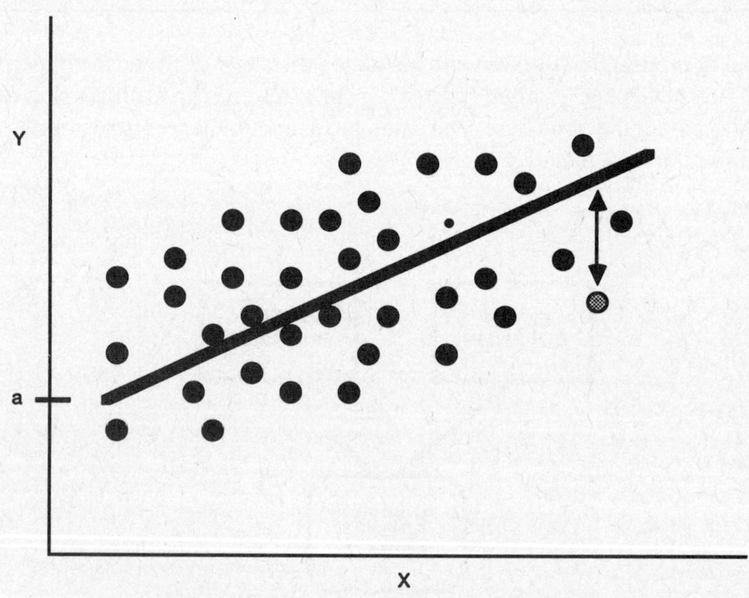

FIGURE 10-13 Simple linear regression.

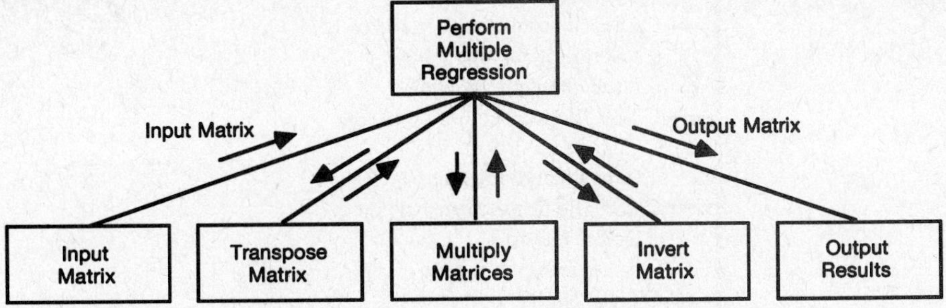

FIGURE 10-14 Architecture for multiple regression.

Suppose you have studied statistics. Going back to your textbook, you probably found an involved computational formula for simple regression (one X variable) and possibly a worse formula for multiple regression with two X variables. Textbooks for introductory statistics seldom include a general formula, since it requires matrix algebra. The formula in question is

$$(X^T X)^{-1} (X^T Y)$$

where ^{T} stands for matrix transformation and $^{-1}$ stands for matrix inversion. Given this knowledge, you can determine that the subtasks in determining the equation are

- Input the data.
- Transform a matrix.
- Multiply two matrices.
- Invert a matrix.
- Output the results.

The program architecture will be as illustrated in Figure 10-14.

The foregoing discussion is not meant to imply that a designer who uses functional decomposition need be a quantoid but rather that such a designer needs a good understanding of the problem domain in which he or she is working. One cannot design the architecture for accounting systems without understanding accounting and cannot design the structure for a word processor without understanding writing and document construction. Anyone doubting the latter is advised to try writing a book using EDLIN on the IBM PC!

An illustration of this problem is what happened to a small company in Detroit in the mid-1970s. This company had acquired midwestern distribution rights for a new model of minicomputer and had decided to sell the system as part of a package with a general ledger system. They hired a certified management accountant (me) to design the system, and then hired a pair of computer science majors to program it. The programmers had never dealt with accounting before and were horrified at the mathematical inelegance of it. They proceeded to implement an improved version in which all debits were subtractions and all credits were additions (for nonaccounting types, whether a debit or a credit means addition or subtraction depends on the type of account). Needless to say, the resulting general ledger

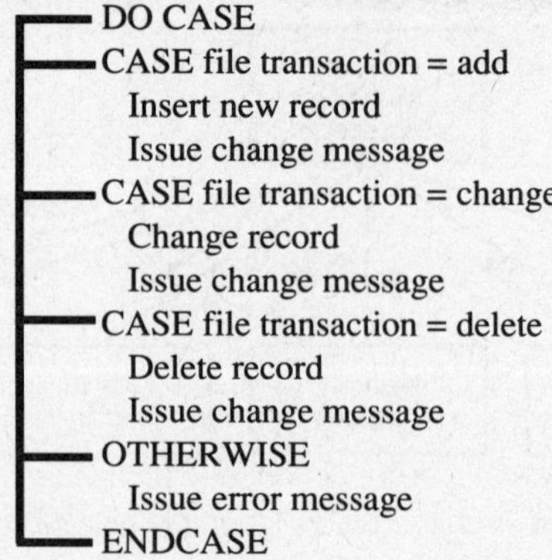

FIGURE 10-15 CASE control structure.

system had more debits than credits! The company went bankrupt (and I never got paid). One has to understand the problem context!

The best way to learn functional decomposition is to do it for several years. For many of us, this is impractical. The next best alternative is to study (not just read) either *Software Tools* [Kernighan & Plauger 1976] or *Software Tools in Pascal* [Kernighan & Plauger 1981]. These books walk a reader through the construction of text processing programs, explaining what the decisions were and why they were made.

Transaction-based Design

The above discussion on knowledge required for functional decomposition does not apply to one subset of the method, which often is referred to as transaction-based design (the name comes from Constantine and Yourdon). This is the implementation of a *CASE* control structure (Chapter 14). A *CASE* control structure is used to describe situations where one has a data element that can take on multiple values and where there is a separate action required for each value. For example, a variable

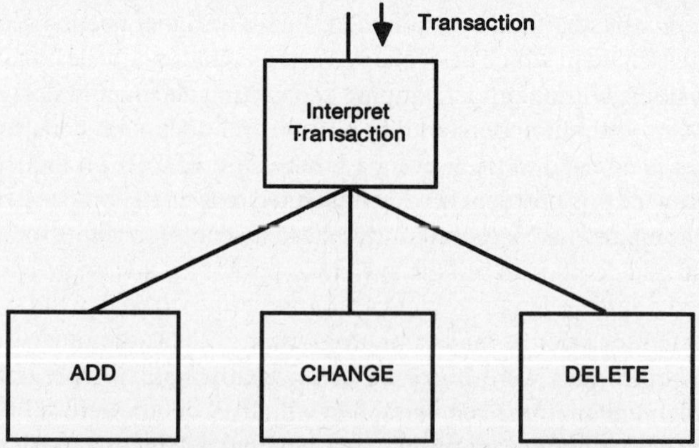

FIGURE 10-16 Implementation of CASE control structure.

called **Command** or **File-transaction** might take on the values **add**, **change**, or **delete**, and the program would add a record, modify a record, or delete a record depending on the value of the variable. The procedure is to make each alternative a module. This is, of course, the approach we have been taking in creating menus. Figures 10-15 and 10-16 illustrate the approach.

Sources of Algorithms for Module Design

In the preceding multiple regression example, the functional structure of the problem was defined by the underlying mathematics; often the functional structure of the problem is not evident even if one understands the problem context. In the following discussion, we describe some common strategies for finding inherent process structure. Such structure can come from different sources, the most common being mathematical structure (as in the regression example) and business problem structure.

Mathematical structure is a common source of functional specification for program architecture design. If there is a mathematically derived way to calculate a required value, the sequence of steps in the module is determined. Note that there are often two different ways to calculate mathematical and statistical functions. The derivational forms are those that make sense in terms of mathematical theory. For example, the equation given for variance in statistics is

$$s^2=\Sigma(\mu_i-\mu)^2 / (n-1)$$

Such equations are often in a form difficult to calculate. For example, the above formula requires one to calculate first μ, which means carrying out the operation $\mu=\Sigma(\mu_i)/(n-1)$. An easier approach is to use the calculational formula:

$$s^2=[(\Sigma\mu_i^2)-(\Sigma\mu_i) / n]^2(n-1)$$

This allows both sums to be calculated as part of the same WHILE loop. Such calculational formulas are available for many functions, and simplify the module design.

Business problem structure is another source for module design. For example, when dealing with any form of accounting system, the rules and procedures inherent in generally accepted accounting principles specify how to carry out the desired operations. Whether the task is a simple one such as checkbook balancing or cash flow reconciliation, or a more complicated one such as merging subordinate statements, the procedural logic is defined with the problem. Standard examples include systems for receivables, customer invoicing, customer cash receipts, accounts receivable, materials control, order entry, finished goods inventory, purchasing and receiving, materials requirements planning, general ledger, budget reconciliation, payables, accounts payable, fixed assets, and employee payroll. Anyone going into business system design obviously ought to know how these systems work [Eliason 1987].

Management science models are a combination of mathematical algorithms and business processes. In these problems (such as optimization, assembly line balancing, and

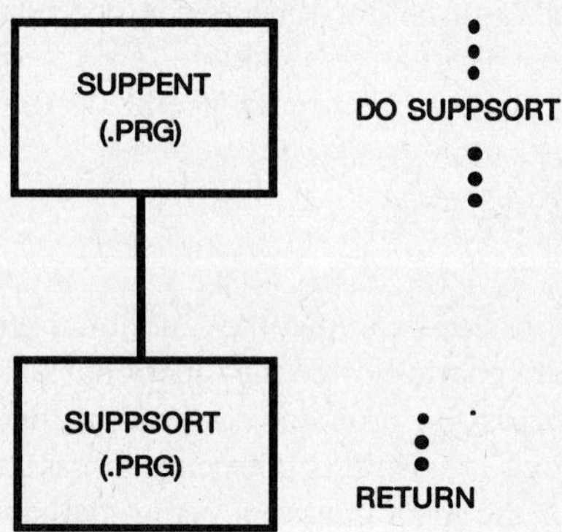

FIGURE 10-17 Basic dBASE modularity.

inventory management), the textbook formulations of the problems and their mathematical solutions guide the module designer. For example, in solving an optimization problem for allocating resources, the simplex method of linear programming provides a step-by-step logical design. Analysts who are not familiar with such models can find them described in standard operations research textbooks [Baumol 1972; Markland & Sweigart 1987].

Many common file operations (e.g., transaction/master file update, merge, sorting, and indexed file processing) are built into fourth generation languages like dBASE III; hence, modules requiring them can be implemented as single statements (UPDATE, APPEND, SORT, INDEX, etc.).

Even if a program designer has extensive training in a particular topic area, occasions will arise in which she or he does not know the best way to solve a particular problem. The first place to look is in textbooks and handbooks that cover the topic areas. Handbooks are especially useful; there are large reference books designed for practitioners in an area who may need to look up procedures that they have forgotten. An example is the *Accountant's Handbook*, 6th edition, published by Wiley. Collections of algorithms are also published for this purpose. The best known are the ACM *Collected Algorithms* series, which covers most mathematical, statistical, and system programming problems. Other good sources are programming textbooks and magazines. Magazines aimed at programmers such as *Byte*, *Dr. Dobb's Journal of System Software*, and more specialized journals such as *ACM Transactions on Computer Graphics* are good possibilities.

DBASE AND PROGRAM MODULARITY

The reason for putting so much effort into deriving structure charts is that structure charts reflect the organization of computer programs. Specifically, modern programs are divided into modules, each of which implements one box on a structure chart. Thus, by building a structure chart of a problem, we are building an outline of the program. Modules in dBASE

```
                                    ********************************
                                    * Enter Supplier data SUPPENT *
                                    ********************************
                                    USE SUPPLIER
                                    DO WHILE .T.
Clear screen                            CLEAR
Add a blank record to file              APPEND BLANK
Use prefdefined screen format           SET FORMAT TO SUPP.FMT
Get new record from screen        READ
                                        @ 16,5 SAY " "
Get value for YN from keyboard          ACCEPT "Another supplier? (Y
or N)" TO YN
                                        IF YN="N"
Perform the module SUPPSORT              DO SUPPSROT
Return to calling module                 CLOSE FORMAT
                                         RETURN
Return to calling module                END IF
                                    ENDDO T

                                    ********************************
                                    * Sort Supplier file SUPPSORT *
                                    ********************************
Use file named SUPPLIER             USE SUPPLIER
Set content of YN to "Y"                STORE "Y" to YN
Get new value for YN                    ACCEPT "Sort supplier file?
(Y or N)" TO YN

                                        IF YN="Y"
Sort to file named SXXX                  SORT ON SNAME TO SXXX
Use no file                               USE
Rename old supplier file                  RENAME SUPPLIER.DBF TO
SYYY.DBF
Rename sorted file                 RENAME SXXX.DBF TO SUPPLIER.DBF
Delete old file                           DELETE FILE SYYY.DBF
Use new file                              USE SUPPLIER
Build index to new file                   INDEEX ON SNAME TO SUPPLID
                                        END IF
Return to calling program           RETURN
```

FIGURE 10-18 dBASE III code for Figure 10-17.

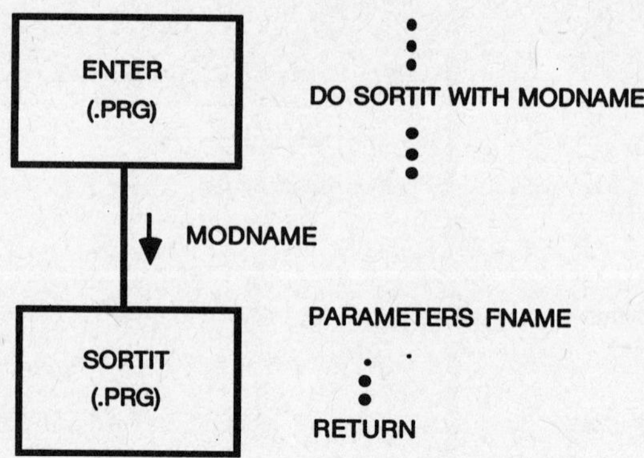

FIGURE 10-19 dBASE modularity with parameters.

are sequences of program statements contained in a file; they are created with the built-in text editor.

Specifically, `MODIFY COMMAND` **`xxx`** is used to create a module named **`xxx.prg`**. As described in Chapter 4, this instruction to the dBASE system brings up an editor with which you can enter program statements into a file. Using the editors packaged with dBASE III and IV, pressing the **Ctrl** key and the **W** key simultaneously will save your file and return to dBASE.

A module that has been created in dBASE may be executed (run or invoked) either from the dot prompt or from another module. The statement `DO START`, for example, executes the program in the module **Start.prg**.

Figure 10-17 illustrates the basic approach to implementing modules in dBASE III.

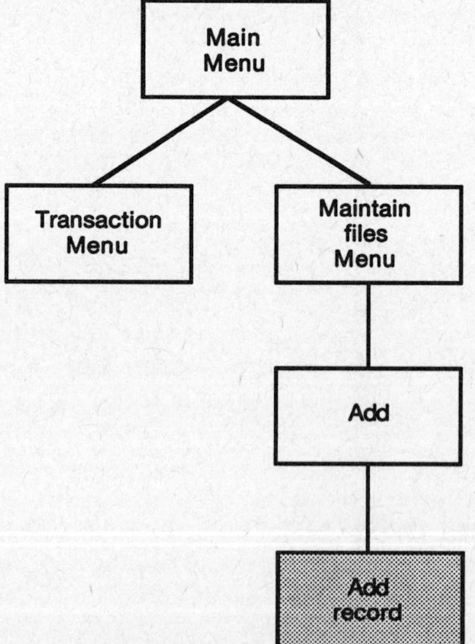

FIGURE 10-20 Abbreviated structure chart for sample prototype.

```
* PROCEDURE MAIN
STORE .T. TO RUN
DO WHILE RUN
CLEAR
@ 2,15 SAY "Main Menu"
@ 5,10 SAY "0 Quit system"
@ 6,10 SAY "1 Maintain Files"
@ 7,10 SAY "2 Transactions"
?
ACCEPT ' Which number? ' TO CHOICE
DO CASE
CASE CHOICE='0'
QUIT
CASE CHOICE='1'
DO MAINTAIN
CASE CHOICE='2
DO TRANSACT
ELSE
? "Invalid choice — please enter one of the above"
ENCASE
LOOP
ENNDO
RETURN
```

FIGURE 10-21 Prototype dBASE code for **MAIN** menu.

Each module is implemented as a separate file with a `.prg` filetype (this happens automatically if you create modules with the `MODIFY COMMAND` instruction). If no data is being passed between modules, the higher-level module calls the lower-level one with the `DO` command, followed by the name of the lower-level module. In Figure 10-17, **SUPPENT** calls **SUPPSORT** with the command `DO SUPPSORT`. The lower-level module terminates with a `RETURN` command. Figure 10-18 illustrates the annotated code for these two modules.

dBASE IV is similar except that all of the modules are normally stored in a single file and each is identified with a line containing the word `PROCEDURE` and the name of the procedure, for example:

```
PROCEDURE suppent
```

Figure 10-19 illustrates the situation in which data is passed between modules. The higher-level module calls the lower-level one with the `DO WITH <parameters>` command where "parameters" are the memory variables from the higher-level module that correspond to the arrows on the structure chart. The lower-level module begins with a `PARAMETERS` statement that lists the memory variables (names for data in memory) that it expects to either receive or return. These also correspond to the arrows on the structure chart. Note that the names of the memory variables used by the two modules need not

```
* PROCEDURE MAIN
STORE .T. TO RUN
DO WHILE RUN
CLEAR
@ 2,15 SAY "Main Menu"
@ 5,10 SAY "0 Quit system"
@ 6,10 SAY "1 Add record"
@ 7,10 SAY "2 Change record"
@ 8,10 SAY "3 Delete record"
?
ACCEPT ' Which number? ' TO CHOICE
DO CASE
CASE CHOICE='0'
QUIT
CASE CHOICE='1'
DO ADD
CASE CHOICE='2'
? "Not yet implemented"
WAIT
CASE CHOICE='3
? "Not yet implemented"
WAIT
ELSE
? "Invalid choice — please enter one of the above"
ENCASE
LOOP
ENNDO
RETURN
```

FIGURE 10-22 Prototype dBASE code for **MAINTAIN FILES** menu.

match; only the number of variables and their type. In this book, our convention will be that the names of the data flows on the structure chart match the names of the memory variables in the higher-level module.

PROTOTYPING THE SYSTEM

In the previous chapter we discussed how to create objects in the user interface: screens, menus, and windows. We now are ready to assemble these objects into a prototype system: a system that will demonstrate the user interface but not yet do much work. This stage is especially valuable, since it allows us to get feedback from users on whether or not they are satisfied with the way the system works.

```
* PROCEDURE MAIN
STORE .T. TO RUN
DO WHILE RUN
CLEAR
@ 2,15 SAY "Inventory System Main Menu"
@ 5,10 SAY "0 Quit system"
@ 6,10 SAY "1 Supplier file"
@ 7,1- SAY "2 Customer file"
?
ACCEPT ' Which number? ' TO CHOICE
DO CASE
CASE CHOICE='0'
QUIT
CASE CHOICE='1'
DO ADDSUPP
CASE CHOICE='2
DO ADDCUST
ELSE
? "Invalid choice – please enter one of the above"
ENCASE
LOOP
ENNDO
RETURN
```

FIGURE 10-23 Prototype dBASE code for **ADD** menu.

```
***********************
* Add SUPPLIER record *
***********************
USE SUPPLIER
DO WHILE .T.
CLEAR
APPEND BLANK
SET FORMAT TO SUPPLIER
READ CLOSE FORMAT
@ 23,5 SAY "Another? (Y or N)"
@ 23,40 GET YN
READ
IF YN="N"
RETURN
ENDIF
ENDDO T
RETURN
```

FIGURE 10-24 Prototype dBASE code for **ADD SUPPLIER** menu.

A prototype system consists of the menus and any screens required for maintaining permanent entities. Figure 10-20 shows a simplified structure chart for part of Northstar's system. The unshaded modules are menus; the shaded module illustrates one of the screens. Each module will be implemented as a program file in dBASE by issuing MODIFY COMMAND from the dot prompt. Figures 10-21 to 10-25 show the resulting dBASE code (this will work in either dBASE III+ or IV).

The example is simplified in that there is only one file to be maintained (**supplier.dbf** in this case, along with its associated screen **supplier.frm**), and there are no transactions implemented. Also, only the procedure to add a record is implemented, and we do not worry about sorting, indexing, and other aspects of file maintenance. Again, this prototype is only used to test the user interface. Appendix A at the end of this chapter shows how to expand the prototype to maintain any file. Transactions are not part of the prototype; Chapter 11 shows how to add them to the real system.

```
* PROCEDURE TRANSACT
STORE .T. TO RUN
DO WHILE RUN
CLEAR
@ 2,15 SAY "TRANSACTION MENU"
@ 5,10 SAY "0 QUITE SYSTEM"
@ 6,10 SAY "1 GET WORK ORDER
@ 7,10 SAY "2 ISSUE PURCHASE ORDER"
@ 8,10 SAY "3 ISSUE INVOICE"
@ 9,10 SAY "4, ISSUE STATEMENTS"
?
ACCEPT ' WHICH NUMBER? ' TO CHOICE
DO CASE
CASE CHOICE='0'
QUIT
CASE CHOICE='1'
? "Not yet implemented"
WAIT
CASE CHOICE='2
? "Not yet implemented"
WAIT
CASE SENDINVC='3
? "Not yet implemented"
WAIT
ELSE
? "Invalid choice — please enter one of the above"
LOOP
ENDDO
RETURN
```

FIGURE 10-25 Prototype dBASE code for **TRANSACTION** menu.

SUMMARY

A structure chart functions as the outline for a program, the basic notation for program architecture. It shows the organization of the modules and the data flows between them. The data flows between modules are important; Chapter 12 entitled "Measures of Program Quality," discusses why.

When we translate from the program model to the actual program, each box on the structure chart becomes a procedure in dBASE.

EXERCISES AND QUESTIONS

1. What is the function of a structure chart?
   a. The function of a structure chart is to outline the program.
   b. The function of a structure chart is to create the program.
   c. The function of a structure chart is to code the program.
   d. The function of a structure chart is to design the program.
2. To successfully use functional decomposition, a systems designer must
   a. Have a good understanding of the problem domain in which he or she is working.
   b Know how to code in any fourth level language.
   c. Know how to transform matrices.
   d. Know output results in advance.
3. Generally, the program architecture will be
   a. Difficult to follow.
   b. Organized hierarchically.
   c. Organized by the end user.
   d. Programmed using multipurpose screens.
4. Older approaches to system design used ________ programs.
   a. Linked.
   b. Separate.
   c. Modified.
   d. Printed.
5. A ________ chart functions as the outline for a program.
   a. Flow.
   b. Structure.
   c. Computer.
   d. Functional.
6. A module
   a. Has a specific function.
   b. Does many functions.
   c. Is useful only in a paper model.
   d. Uses only internal data.

7. Modularization
   a. Has been supported extensively in all computer languages.
   b Support among computer languages varies greatly.
   c. Is not used in fourth generation languages.
   d. Works only with COBOL.
8. Generally, the architecture of the program will be
   a. Descending.
   b. Spontaneous.
   c. Spiatic.
   d. Hierarchical.
9. What is used to describe a situation where one has a data element that can take on multiple values and in which there is a separate action required for each value?
   a. A Data control structure.
   b. A Variable control structure.
   c. A CASE control structure.
   d. A dBASE control structure.

DISCUSSION QUESTIONS

1. In dBASE, what is `MODIFY COMMAND` used for?
2. What are the steps in functional decomposition?
3. Why is modularity important?

NORTHSTAR AVIATION

Part 6
Modularity

Not surprisingly, the owner of Northstar Aviation has decided to install a custom computer system to support his transaction processing needs. Rather than buying a version of an existing system, he has hired you to develop one (after all, you are better qualified than 75% of the computer consultants who sell their services). In preparing for the design tasks, authorities in the field (i.e., the author of the text and your professor) recommend the following task:

1. Based on the information in Part 1 of the case, and based on the material in Chapter 3 of the text (especially Figure 3-2), create a two- or three-level structure chart for the transaction processing system. Be sure to show data flows.
2. Use functional decomposition to design a structure chart for the task **Issue Paycheck**. Use a sample pay stub to determine the necessary information, and assume that all necessary files exist. Be sure to show both process decomposition and the data flows between the modules.

REFERENCES

Collected Algorithms, Association for Computing Machinery, New York, 1976.

BAUMOL, W. *Economic Theory and Operations Analysis*. Prentice-Hall, Englewood Cliffs, NJ, 1972

ELIASON, A. Online Business Computer Applications, 2nd ed. Macmillan, New York, 1987.

KERNIGHAN, B., and P. Plauger. S*oftware Tools*. Addison–Wesley, Reading, MA, 1976.

KERNIGHAN, B. and P. PLAUGER. *Software Tools in Pascal*. Addison–Wesley, Reading, MA, 1981.

MARKLAND, R., and J. SWEIGART. *Quantitative Methods: Applications to Managerial Decision Making*. Wiley, 1987.

SEIDLER, L.L. and D.R. CARMICHAEL. *The Accountants' Handbook*, 6th ed. Wiley, New York, 1981.

Chapter 11

OBJECT ORIENTED DESIGN

CHAPTER GOALS

- Learn definitions of object-oriented and object-based programming.
- Learn the basic program objects.
- Learn to translate program objects into modules.

OBJECT-ORIENTED DESIGN IN GENERAL

Object-oriented design is the latest hot topic in program design, recent enough that neither the vocabulary nor the methods have been standardized. In other guises, it is called data-abstraction-based design and entity-relationship-based design. In all instances, it is an attempt to produce a program architecture (expressed in this book by a structure chart) that is decomposed based on abstraction from the data rather than the processes.

Object-oriented design is the selection and implementation of conceptual objects rather than of functions. It is similar to electronic hardware design, where each chip implements a complete object in the design. The key difference between object-oriented design and functional design for software is that software objects hide most of the details of their data structures from other modules. Communication between objects is via messages rather than via data passing as in functionally oriented design. This means that there is little data flow between modules.

Object-oriented languages allow the definition of arbitrary object types; these include languages such as Smalltalk. *Object-based* languages provide a set of predefined object types that are suitable for a particular type of problem (such as business data processing). A language

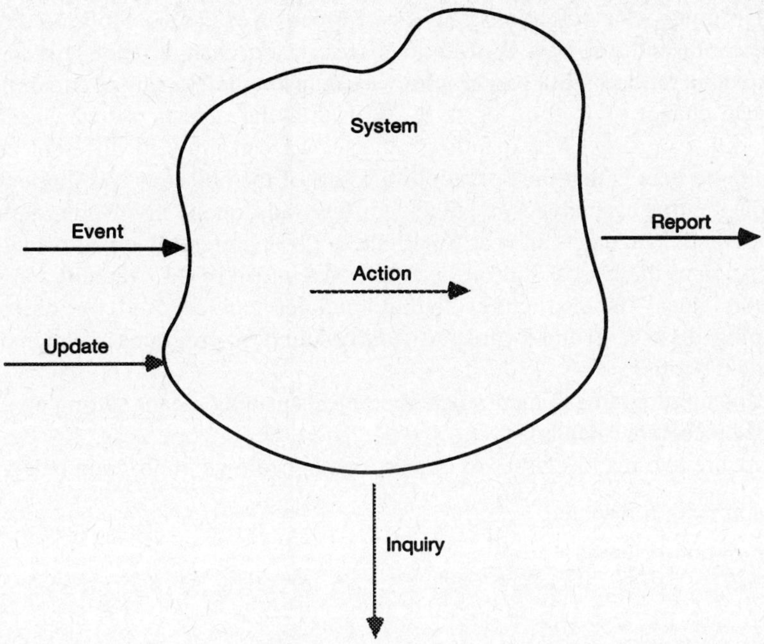

FIGURE 11-1 Parts of a physical system model.

may *facilitate* object-oriented programming (make it easy), or it may *enable* object-oriented programming (make it possible). dBASE enables object-based programming.

- Determining what operations can be performed on each object.
- Implementing each object as a black box.
- Setting up programs to manipulate the objects.

Determining what conceptual objects a user works with means viewing the problem in user rather than computer terms. We have already seen this approach with entities, where the analyst identifies objects such as supplier, customer, and work order. An additional example comes from the field of writing; a writer deals with objects having to do with documents: documents, including sections, sentences, paragraphs, and words. An alternative view is that a writer deals with parts of a typewriter, including letters, tabs, and carriage returns. If we are developing a word processor, the "feel" will be very different depending on which set of objects we adapt.

Yet another example of objects is the selection of what objects make up a drawing. "Object-oriented" drawing packages such as MacDraw on the Apple Macintosh and GEM Draw on MSDOS machines assume that drawings are made up of lines, boxes, letters, circles, arcs, text, and similar "objects." Paint packages (MacPaint, Microsoft Paint) assume that drawings are made up of colored points formed with objects such as pens, brushes, and air brushes.

Determining what operations can be performed on each object follows directly from the identification of the objects. With entities, we can add, change, delete, list contents, and other related operations. With paragraphs, we can insert, delete, move, cut, or paste. With text, we can change size, font, or style. With drawing objects we can insert, stretch, duplicate, fill, or group. With painting objects, we can draw in different colors. The important point here is that the operations are part of the object as it is implemented.

Implementing each object as a black box has traditionally involved programming in "object-oriented" languages such as Smalltalk or C++, preferably on an "object-oriented machine" such as the Xerox Star or the Apple Macintosh series. Actually, any language that supports local data structures within modules can be used for object-oriented programming. dBASE III and IV are particularly suited for programs in which objects are data-oriented entities.

Setting up programs to manipulate the objects usually means setting up a hierarchy of transaction centers (menus).

There are two major classes of objects that concern us in program design:

- application-oriented
- program-oriented

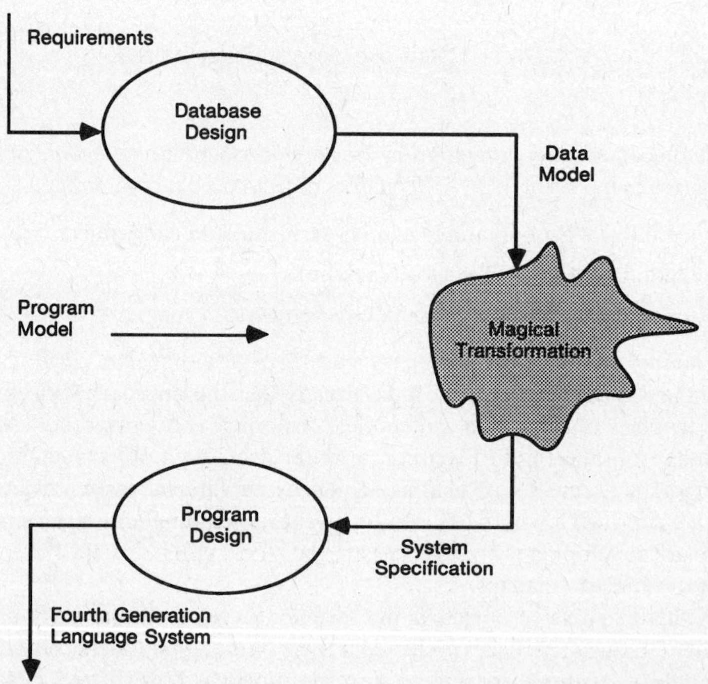

FIGURE 11-2 Program model in the system development life-cyle.

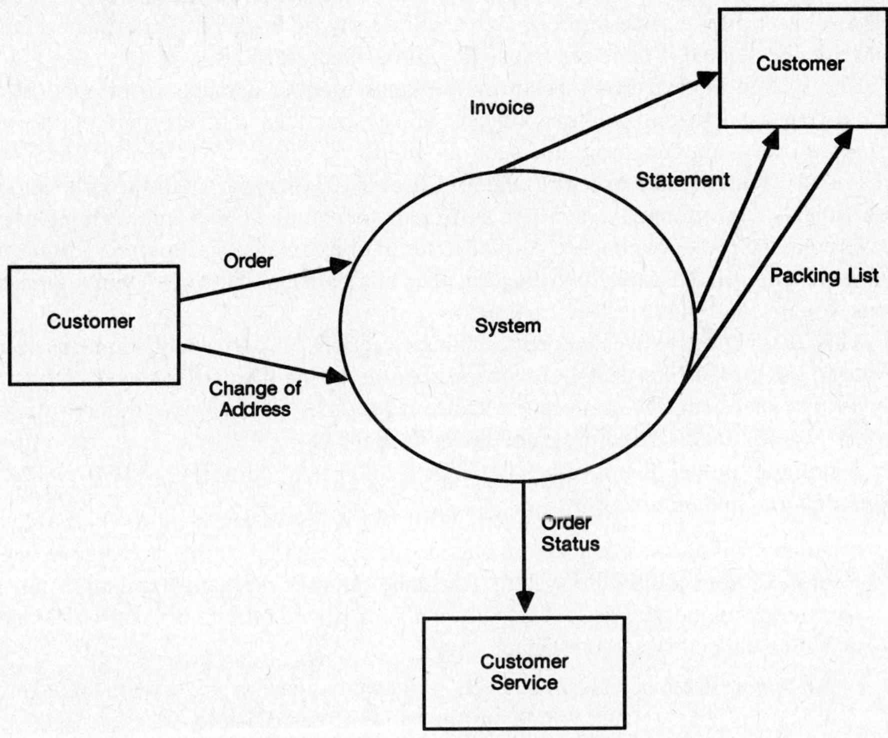

FIGURE 11-3 Data flow diagram for order system.

Application-oriented objects are those (such as entities) that are abstractions of parts of the problem that is being solved. Program-oriented objects are abstractions that are part of the computer-based solution to the problem, such as windows, screens, and reports. Often these objects are part of the user interface to the computer program. The program designer's task is to select and design the appropriate program-oriented objects to work with the application-oriented objects.

There are two sets of constraints that must be met in implementing and linking the program objects. One is the order constraints based on real-world event logic; one should not, for example, sell something until it has been acquired. The other is based on referential integrity constraints if a relational model is being used; one should not be able to delete permanent entities that are referenced by currently outstanding transient entities.

Referential integrity means in general that no transient entities should refer to an instance of a permanent entity that does not exist. For example, if a part number is included in a purchase order, then a record for a part with that part number must be present in the inventory relation. Implementing referential integrity constraints means that when an instance (record) in a transient entity is created, the system should check to make sure that all permanent entities that are referenced exist. Similarly, no instance of a permanent entity should ever be deleted if there are transient entities that refer to it.

The system model, discussed in the previous section, is made up of application-oriented objects. Program-oriented objects are abstractions that are part of the user interface to the computer program, such as windows, screens, and reports, and were discussed in Chapter 9. The structure chart of Chapter 10 is also part of the program model. These objects, unfortunately, are not sufficient to complete the architecture, as we discovered in the previous chapter. A final series of object classes is required (Figure 11-1): an extension of the data flow diagram that distinguishes between events, updates, actions, reports, and inquiries (defined below).

This distinction between events, updates, actions, reports, and inquiries is not relevant to the user, so we were not worried about it during the earlier stages of systems analysis. The distinction is important because it provides the "magical transformation" between systems analysis and program design (Figure 11-2).

A program model distinguishes between five types of data flows: *events*, *update*s, *actions*, *reports*, and *inquiries*.

- An *event* is a flow of data from outside the system that causes a change to one or more entities within the system. It usually requires reorganizing data from external nonnormalized form to internal normalized form. It is usually associated with a data entry screen (Chapter 9).
- An *update* is a special form of Event—one that impacts a single permanent entity. It is usually associated with a multipurpose screen (Chapter 9).
- An *action* is a flow of data internal to the system that causes a change to one or more entities. It is usually associated with a menu screen (Chapter 9).
- A *report* is a flow of data from inside the system to the outside world. It usually requires reorganizing data from internal normalized form to external nonnormalized form. Reports usually involve a batch of transactions and are normally scheduled. It is usually chosen from a menu screen (Chapter 9) and may be associated with a predefined dBASE report.
- An *inquiry* is a special form of report—one that returns data on a single entity or transaction on an unscheduled basis. It is usually associated with an inquiry screen or with a predefined dBASE query (Chapter 9).

Figure 11-3 shows part of a data flow diagram for an order entry and billing system; Figure 11-4 shows the associated program model.

Figure 11-5 reviews where we have been and where we are going. Section II discussed how to design and implement the database and the program objects. Chapter 10 discussed structure charts and their use for representing program architecture. The first part of this chapter discussed how to interpret a data flow diagram in terms of events, updates, actions, reports, and inquiries. The rest of this chapter shows how this interpretation of a data flow diagram, along with an entity-relationship diagram, can be turned into a structure chart.

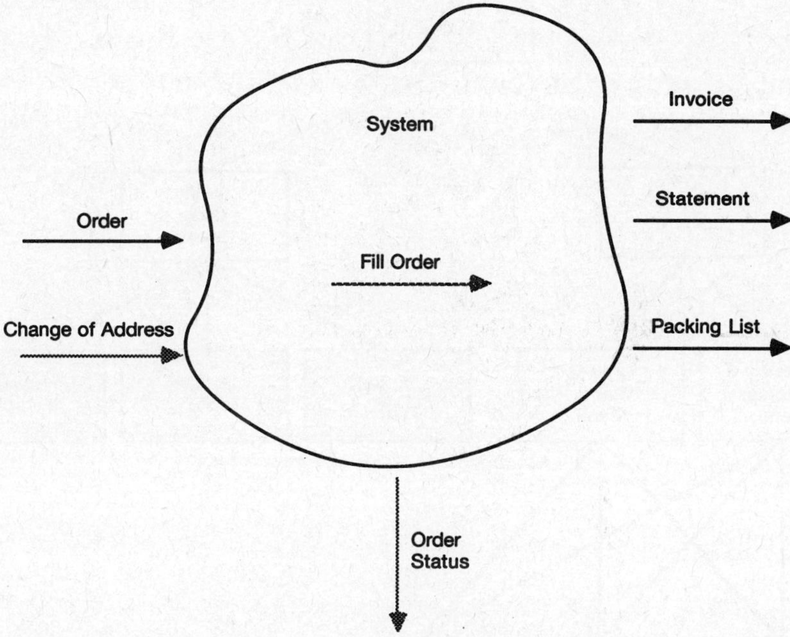

FIGURE 11-4 Program model for order sytem.

- Create permanent entities based on data model.
- Create transient entties based on data model.
- Determine constraints in the order of the events and reports.

For each event:

  - Define views appropriate to events.
  - Define screens or reports appropriate to events.
  - Define windows appropriate to events.
  - Link views to screens or reports.
  - Link screens to windows.
  - Define menus.

- Build structure chart based on event and report types.
- Build action diagrams (Section IV).

FIGURE 11-5 Algorithm for fourth generation language program design.

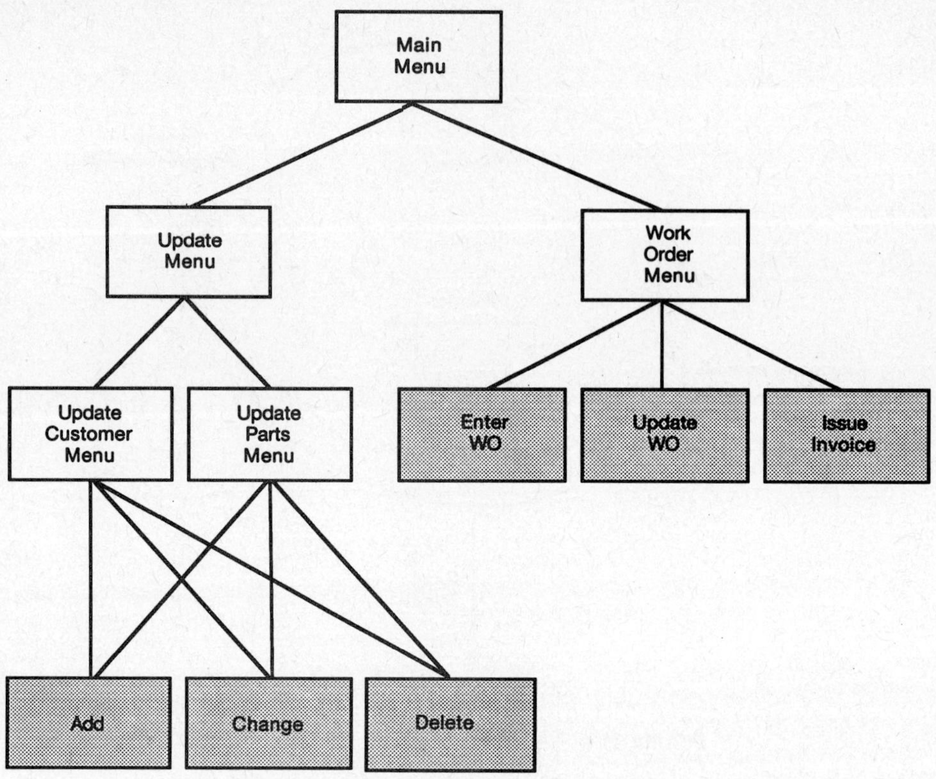

FIGURE 11-6 High-level menu structure.

Our goal in program design is to translate the system model into a program model. In Chapter 9, we saw that a program model includes the definition of a user interface (made up of menus and screens). The menu structure that we designed in Chapter 9 in conjunction with the end users forms the first few levels in our structure chart, as discussed in Chapter 10. At this stage, the user is choosing what to do. Figure 11-6 shows a typical menu hierarchy. In Chapter 10, we saw that we were able to set up a prototype system with menus and some screens but that we were not able to define structure charts for transactions (corresponding to the events and reports of Figure 11-1). The shaded modules at the bottom of Figure 11-6 correspond to those transactions and do the actual work; these are the subject of the rest of the section.

The "work" modules at the bottom of the structure chart derived from the menus have to be further decomposed. In object-based design, we do this based on the entity-relationship diagrams or on the events, updates, actions, reports, and inquiries derived from the data flow diagram.

Figure 11-7 shows an entity-relationship diagram for a work-order subsystem. A customer is associated with one or more work orders, each work order is associated with

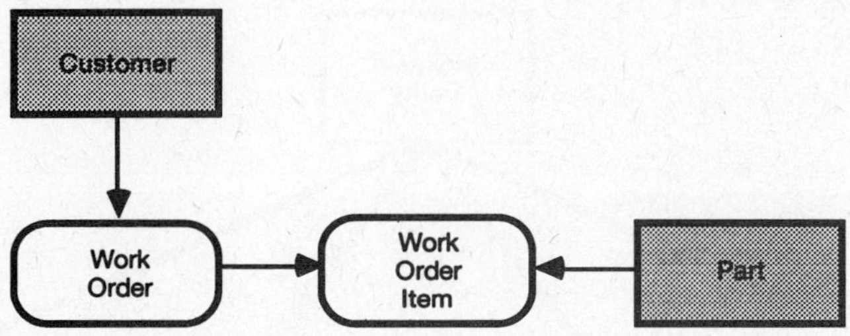

FIGURE 11-7 Entity-relationship diagram for work order sybsystem.

one or more line items, and a part from inventory is associated with one or more line items. In converting this entity-relationship diagram to a structure chart, one first needs to distinguish between the two different types of entities.

This distinction is important because permanent entities give rise to a single standard program structure that does not apply to transient entities. The reason for this is that permanent entities correspond to objects in the real world, whereas transient entities do not correspond to real-world objects; rather they are data about relationships between real-world objects that are spawned by events, actions, and reports.

In Figure 11-7, the two permanent entities (CUSTOMER and PART) are shaded. These entities represent aspects of the system environment which are important in and of themselves. Put another way, managers in the organizations are likely to want information on stand-alone entities without connecting them with other information. One may well wish to analyze inventory by itself, irrespective of work orders. Each permanent entity translates into the standard structure chart of Figure 11-8.

This standard structure to maintain entities is so common that almost all program generators support it. However, the use of a program generator for such applications is not necessary. Since current versions of dBASE III and IV support parameter passing, it is possible to write a general-purpose dBASE program that will maintain any file. Appendix A in Chapter 10 showed how to do so.

In other words, structure chart fragments for maintaining permanent entities are constructed as in Figure 11-8 and implemented as in Appendix A in Chapter 10. These parts of the program can also be generated automatically. Our difficulty is not in dealing with permanent entities, but with the entities that arise as a result of transaction processing. It is in dealing with the results of these transactions that automatic program generators fail, and we have to resort to the forms of design discussed in this section.

Figure 11-9 illustrates this situation—in which several entities and the relationships between them represent a compound transaction. To produce a structure chart corresponding to this transaction, we make use of the program-level objects (events, actions, inquiries, and reports) identified above. Each of these objects, except actions, translates into the structure chart segments of Figures 11-10 to 11-14. Actions other than simple menu choices must be translated by using the functional decomposition techniques of the previous chapter or the techniques to be presented in Chapter 15.

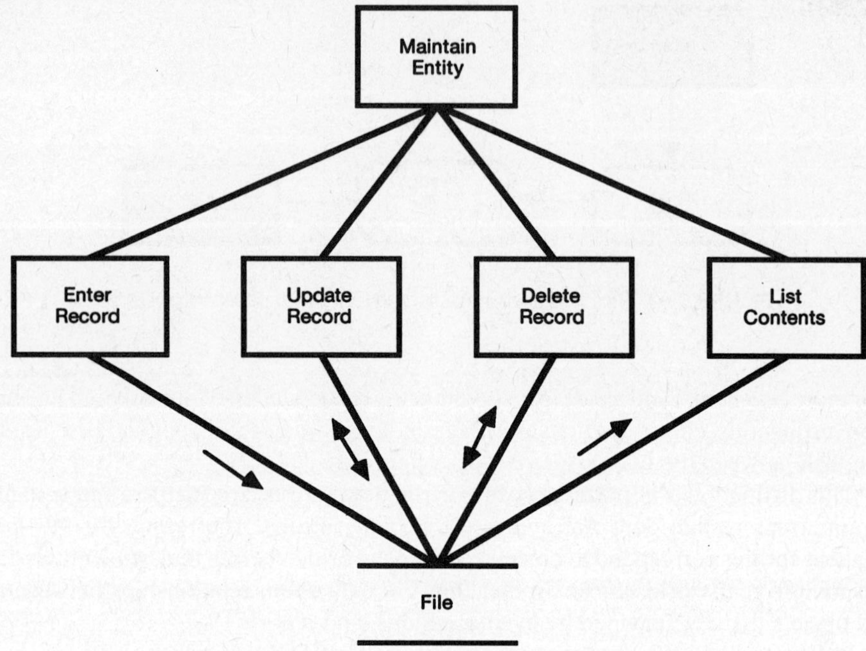

FIGURE 11-8 Structure chart for permanent entity.

Previously we discussed program models which distinguished between the following objects:

- An *event* is a flow of data from outside the system that causes a change to one or more entities within the system. It usually requires reorganizing data from external non-normalized form to internal normalized form. The structure chart for an event is illustrated in Figure 11-10.
- An *update* is a special form of event—one that impacts a single permanent entity. The structure chart for an update is illustrated in Figure 11-8.
- An *action* is a flow of data internal to the system that causes a change to one or more entities. There is no standard structure chart for an action, although many actions are simply a single box in a menu.
- A *report* is a flow of data from inside the system to the outside world. It usually requires reorganizing data from internal normalized form to external nonnormalized form. Reports usually involve a batch of transactions and are normally scheduled. The structure chart for a report is illustrated in Figure 11-12.
- An *inquiry* is a special form of report—one that returns data on a single entity or transaction on an unscheduled basis. The structure chart for an inquiry is illustrated in Figure 11-14. In dBASE, we often use predefined views (Chapter 9) to implement inquiries.

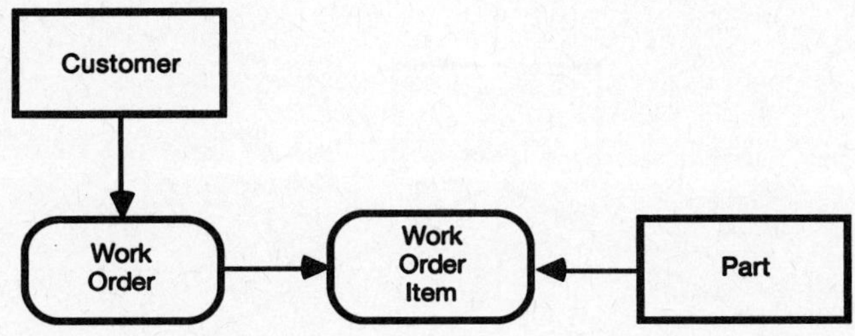

FIGURE 11-9 Entity-relationship diagram for compound transaction.

An event usually links a permanent entity outside the system with a permanent entity inside the system. Nonnormalized data comes from outside the system boundaries and is linked to the normalized relations in the database. The structure of the task is to confirm that data is being stored about the current external object (DISPLAY PERMANENT ENTITY), to then enter data corresponding to the event itself (GET HEADER DATA), and finally to enter data about changes to the internal permanent entity (GET BODY DATA). The internal structure of this last module is discussed at length in Chapter 15.

An example would be a program to enter a customer order (Figure 11-11), where an order is received and the person taking it gets the customer's number (we will ignore the mechanics of how he or she does this for the moment). The program then displays selected information from the CUSTOMER RECORD so that the order-taker can confirm that the correct customer record is being used. The program then enters the appropriate data into

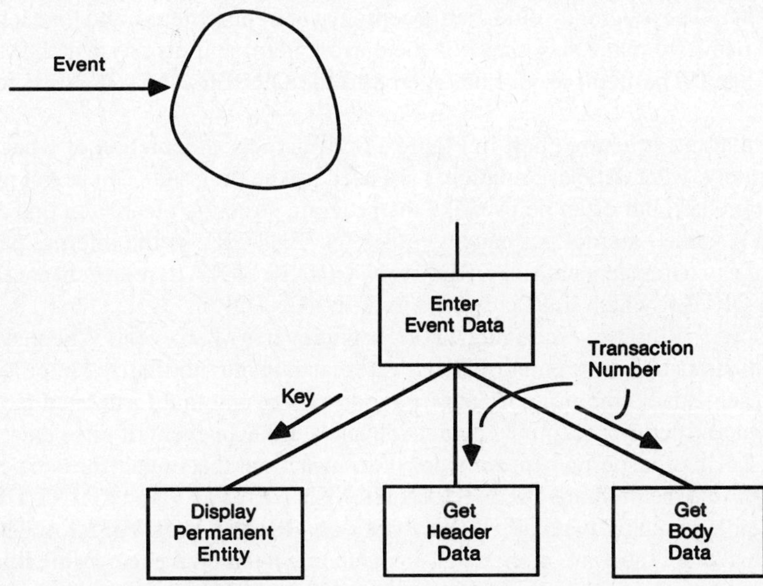

FIGURE 11-10 Structure chart for an event.

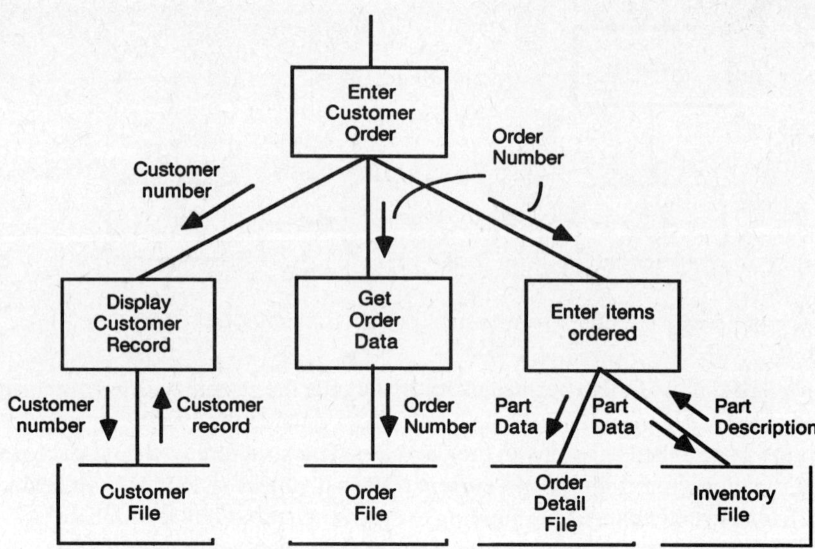

FIGURE 11-11 Structure chart for the event **CUSTOMER CORDER**.

ORDER FILE; this would typically include **Date**, **Customer number**, **Order number**, and **Clerk number**. The program would then accept a list of items ordered, and for each of them display the name (to make sure that it is the correct item) and display whether there are enough on hand. The items would be entered in the ORDER DETAIL FILE for future reference.

Note that the structure chart in Figure 11-11 includes a depiction of what files (or more accurately, what database relations) are used by the program. This is not necessary in a structure chart, but often helps make the program structure clearer. In this example, CUSTOMER is the external permanent entity, INVENTORY is the internal permanent entity, and the two transient entities ORDER and ORDER DETAIL represent data from the transaction ORDER which links customer with INVENTORY.

A report, as illustrated in Figure 11-12, is the reverse of an event. Whereas an event represents the translation of nonnormalized external data into normalized internal form, a report represents the combining of data from normalized internal form from parts of the database into a structure acceptable by outside users. Like an event, it links data about an external and an internal permanent entity via the transactions that impact the two permanent entities. Note that the modules **PRINT PERMANENT ENTITY** and **PRINT HEADER DATA** are called both by **PRODUCE REPORT** and **PRINT BODY DATA**. The reason for this is that when there are more detail items than will fit on a page, **Print Body Data** needs to be able to go to the top of the next page, print header information, and resume printing detail lines.

Figure 11-13 shows an example; the generation of a CUSTOMER INVOICE. This program fragment is called from another module that provides an order number. The **PRINT INVOICES** module then prints the relevant customer data on the invoice (name, address, etc.), the appropriate header data (order date, invoice date, order number, invoice number, etc.), and then prints each item ordered with the name and list price extracted from the INVENTORY FILE. If the total invoice is less than a page, the **Print Invoices** module then prints the totals. If there are more items than will fit on one page, however, the **PRINT ITEMS ORDERED** module skips to the top of the next page, prints required header information, and then continues listing items. This continues until the items ordered with the current **Order number** are exhausted, at which point the **PRINT INVOICES** module prints totals and returns.

A variation here would be to have **Order Data** as passed down from on high include all of the data from ORDER FILE, in which case **PRINT INVOICE HEADER** would not need to access ORDER FILE. Note also that the reason for passing **Order Number** to **PRINT INVOICE HEADER** each time is that **PRINT INVOICE HEADER**, being a black box, does not know (and should not know) if it is being called for the first page of the order or the nth page.

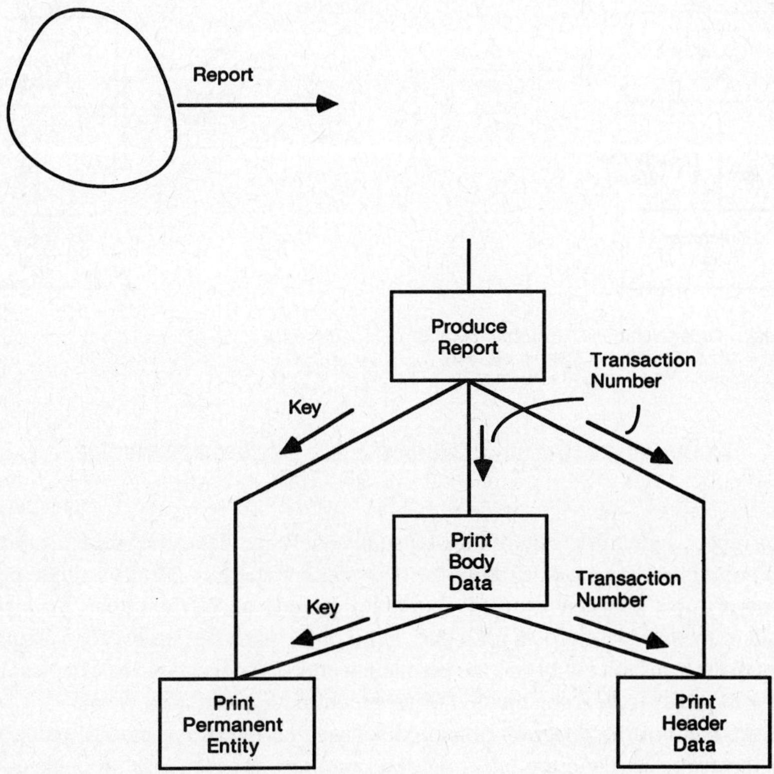

FIGURE 11-12 Structure chart for a report.

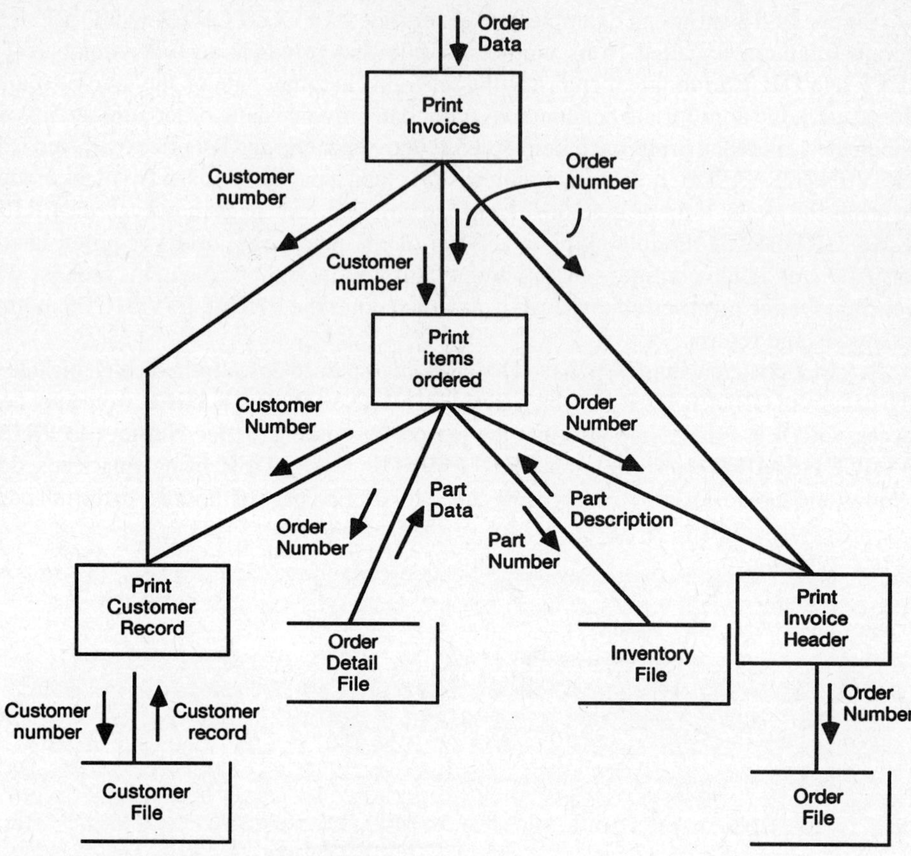

FIGURE 11-13 Structure chart for the report **CUSTOMER INVOICE.**

Like a report, an Inquiry (Figure 11-14) usually combines data about several entities in the database in order to satisfy a user external to the system. Generally it links a single permanent entity to one or more transient entities. Examples include all of the orders for a particular customer, all of the purchase orders for a part, or all of the purchase orders for a supplier, with data from both the transient entity and the permanent entity. As discussed in Chapter 9, dBASE allows many inquiries to be implemented using predefined queries and views.

In short, each of the program objects discussed above is associated with a standard structure chart fragment, and the building of a complete program architecture consists of assembling these fragments into an integrated whole. This is perhaps best illustrated with an extended example.

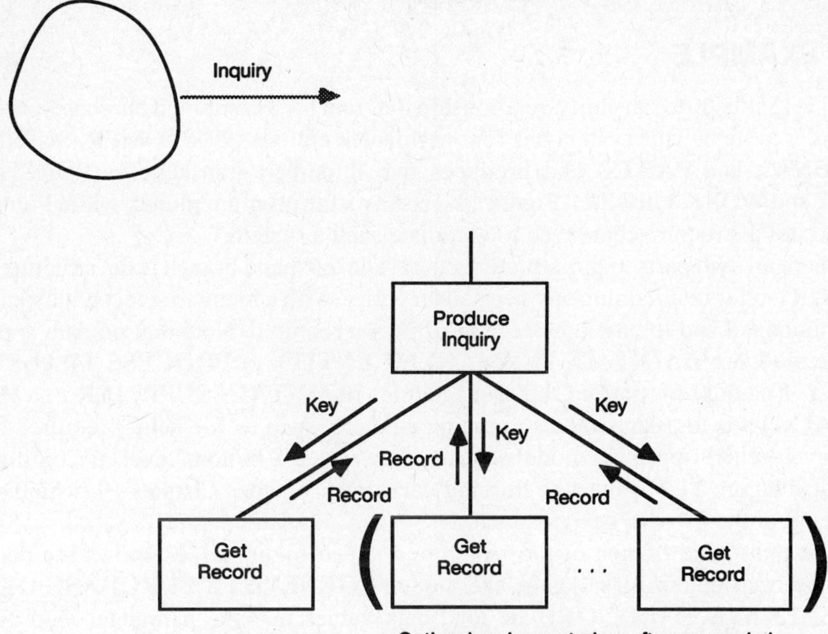

FIGURE 11-14 Structure chart for an inquiry.

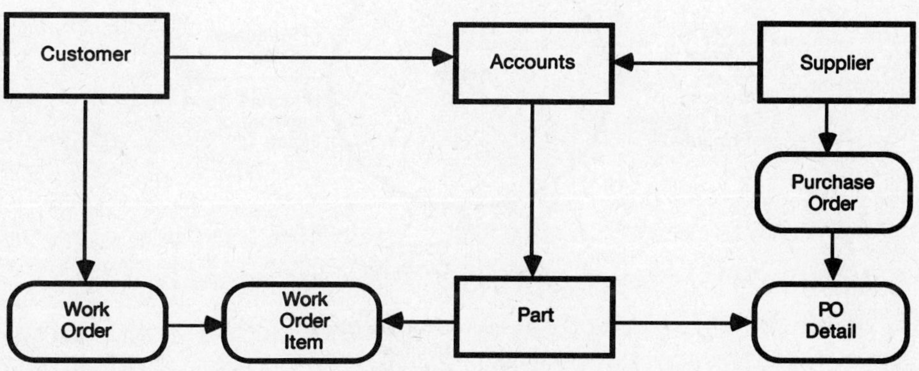

FIGURE 11-15 Entity-relationship diagram for more complex system.

CASE EXAMPLE

Figure 11-15 illustrates an entity-relationship diagram for a combined purchase-order and work-order system. This system has four permanent entities (CUSTOMER, SUPPLIER, ACCOUNTS, and PARTS) and produces two three-part transactions (PURCHASE-ORDER and WORK-ORDER). Figure 11-16 shows the program model, while Figure 11-17 illustrates a structure chart used to automate such a system.

There are two parts to this structure chart. The left-hand branch is the structure chart of Figure 11-6 for maintaining any permanent entity, with a menu to select which entity is to be maintained and to pass down the information required. Note that no data is passed from the modules **MAINTAIN PERMANENT ENTITY** or **PROCESS TRANSIENT ENTITY**. The only purpose of the four modules **MAINTAIN SUPPLIER . . . MAINTAIN ACCTS** is to assign values to the parameters (such as file name) required by the lower-level general-purpose modules. Data flows at the bottom level are omitted for simplicity; Figure 11-8 shows the missing data flows, as does Chapter 19, which shows more detail of the dBASE design and code.

The right-hand branch of the structure chart in Figure 11-17 shows the code for processing transient entities. Again, the modules **GENERATE PURCHASE ORDER** and **GENERATE WORK ORDER** load data values into the parameter slots for the general-purpose module **PRODUCE TRANSACTION**, such as the actual names of the generic NAME FILE, TRANSACTION FILE, and DETAIL FILE.

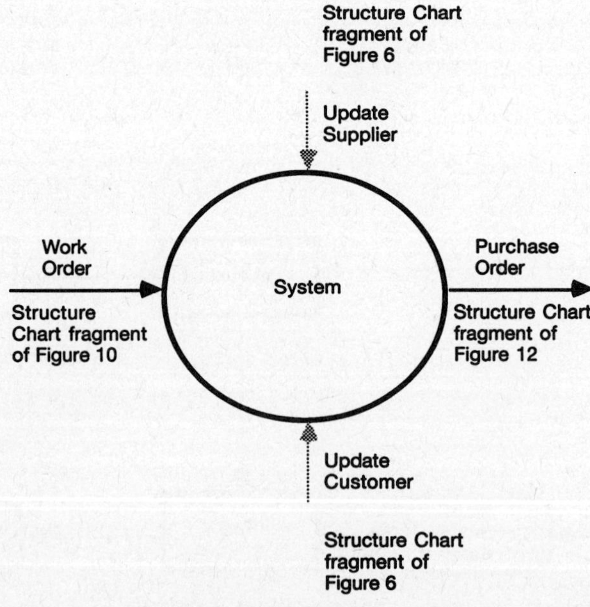

FIGURE 11-16 Program model.

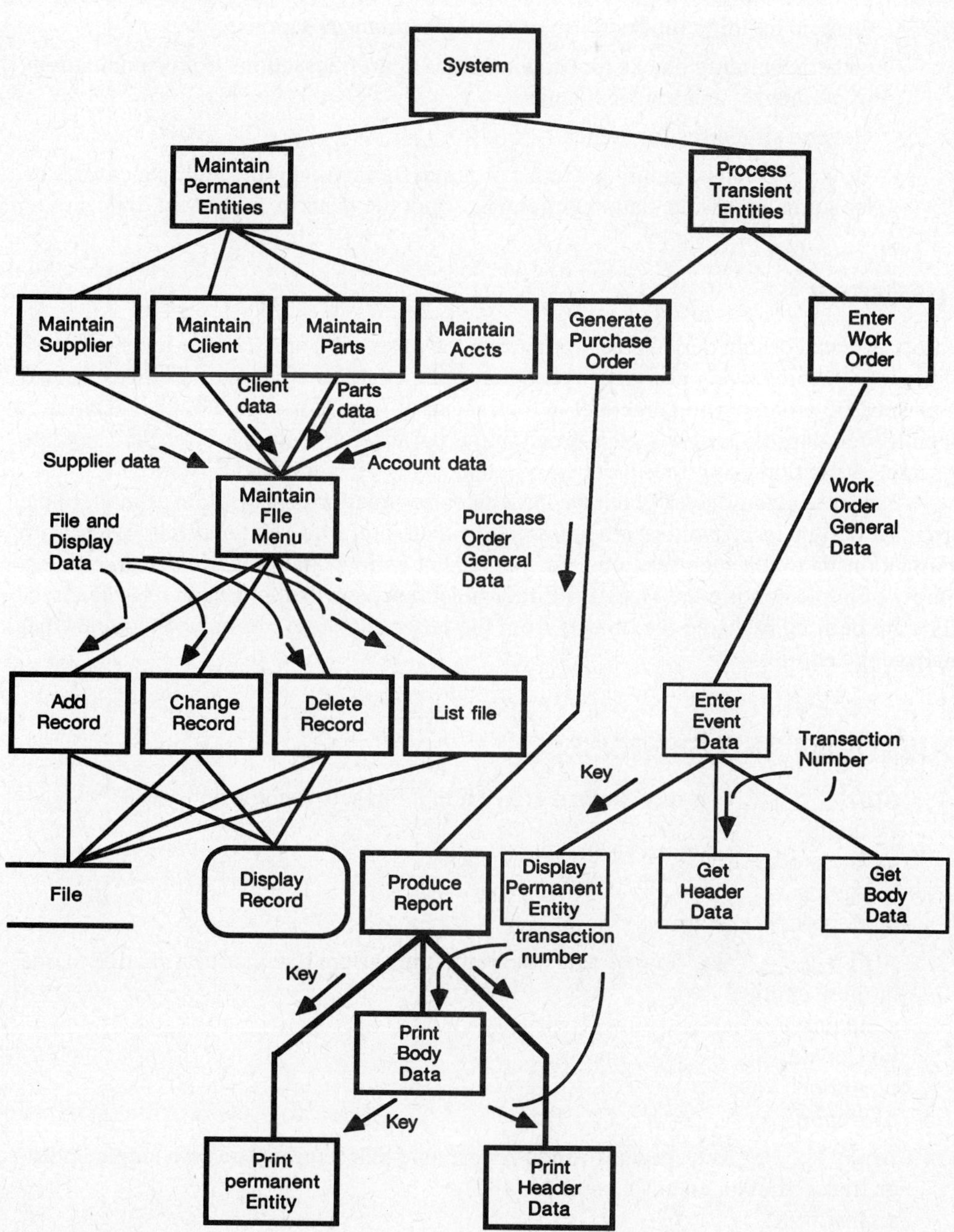

FIGURE 11-17 Structure chart for combined purchase-order and work-order system.

The structure chart in Figure 11-17 thus illustrates the following things:

- Generic building blocks for maintaining permanent entities.
- Generic building blocks for producing multipart transactions from combinations of permanent and transient entities.
- Generic structures for menus.
- How these can be combined into a program for manipulating multiple entities by isolating the unique data requirements from the generic processing logic.

SUMMARY

Object-oriented design derives the structure of the program from the high-level structure of the data. It is relatively new, so general purpose methods are only now being extracted from specific programming practice. In the case of objects as modeled by the techniques of entity-relationship analysis, translation into program architecture is direct and suitable for implementation using fourth generation languages such as dBASE III and IV.

For those situations in which we have an entity-relationship diagram as input to the program design task, entities are translated either into data relations (tables) or into transactions between such relations. For permanent entities, the program design consists simply of implementing the Maintain Entity functions described in Chapter 10. Transactions are built up by using the objects from the program model to produce modules that manage the entities.

QUESTIONS AND EXERCISES

1. A(n) ________ is a special form of event that impacts a single entity.
   a. Inquiry.
   b. Update.
   c. Action.
   d. Report.
2. A(n) ________ is a flow of data internal to the system that causes a change to one or more entities.
   a. Inquiry.
   b. Update.
   c. Action.
   d. Report.
3. A(n) ________ is a special form of report: one that returns data on a single entity or transaction on an unscheduled basis.
   a. Inquiry.
   b. Update.
   c. Action.
   d. Report.

4. A flow of data from outside the system that causes a change to one or more entities within thesystem is a(n)
   a. Inquiry.
   b. Action.
   c. Event.
   d. Report.
5. An event is
   a. Scheduled after every completed system design.
   b. A flow of data from inside the system.
   c. Requires no normalization before being used by the internal system.
   d. A flow of data from outside the system.
6. An action is
   a. A flow of data in the system.
   b. A flow of data outside the system.
   c. Only affects a permanent entity.
   d. An outdated method for moving information.
7. Object-oriented design is the selection and implementation of
   a. Permanent entity relationships.
   b. Conceptual objects rather than of functions.
   c. Transient entity relationships.
   d. Events rather than actions.
8. What is the key difference between object-oriented designed software and functional designed software?
   a. There is little data flow between modules in object-oriented designed software.
   b. There is less data in functional designed software.
   c. There is more data in functional designed software.
   d. There is less data in object-oriented designed software.
9. There are two major classes of objects that concern us in program design: ________ oriented and ________ oriented.
   a. Application, orientation.
   b. Application, program.
   c. User, design.
   d. Direct, indirect.
10. A special form of event—one that impacts a single permanent entity is
    a. Action.
    b. Report.
    c. Update.
    d. Inquiry.
11. What are the steps to deriving a program structure from an object-oriented design?
    a. Determine what conceptual objects a user works with.
    b. Determine what operations can be performed on each object.

c. Implement each object as a black box.
d. Set up programs to manipulate the objects.

12. Compound transactions are made up of several
a. Entities and the relationships that exist between them.
b. Inputs into a system.
c. Screens linked together.
d. Supervisors giving you conflicting orders.

13. Object oriented design tries to
a. View the problem from the programmer's viewpoint.
b. View the problem from the user's viewpoint
c. Solve the problem with more hardware
d Make student's lives more difficult while using it

DISCUSSION QUESTION

1. What is object-oriented design?

NORTHSTAR AVIATION

Part 7

1. Identify all of the events, reports, and inquiries for Northstar's system.
2. Design structure charts for all of the events, reports, and inquiries in Northstar's system. Prepare an integrated structure chart (multiple pages!) for Northstar.

Chapter 12

MEASURES OF DESIGN QUALITY

CHAPTER GOALS

- Learn measure of quality in program design.
- Learn to use those measures in evaluating programs.

Once we get a program architecture, we have to decide how it can be improved. As discussed in the section on the human information processing system in Chapter 2, people do not do very well at generating perfect designs on the first try but do fairly well at revising their early attempts. It helps, however, to have some formal approaches to aid in the process.

Before discussing current approaches to measuring program quality, it is appropriate to discuss how measures are constructed. Coupling and cohesion, the first measures that we will discuss, are examples of scales—an effort to assign numerical values to real-world conditions. There are four levels of scales: nominal, ordinal, interval, and ratio. A nominal scale is the simplest and most limited. It allows us to assign a boolean (true/false) value to a condition. An example is the variable **State-resident**, which can be either "yes" or "no." An ordinal scale is somewhat stronger. It allows us to rank real world entities. An example is the variable **Student-level** ranging from undergraduate to Ph.D. An interval scale is an ordinal scale which also contains information about how far apart real world entities are. An example is **GMAT-score.** A ratio scale is an interval scale which has a definite beginning point. An example is **Number-of-credits**. Measures on nominal and ordinal scales are not additive: the measure of the whole is not necessarily the sum of the parts.

There are three basic measures of program design quality: coupling, cohesion, and correspondence. Additionally, there is a group of heuristics—characteristics of good

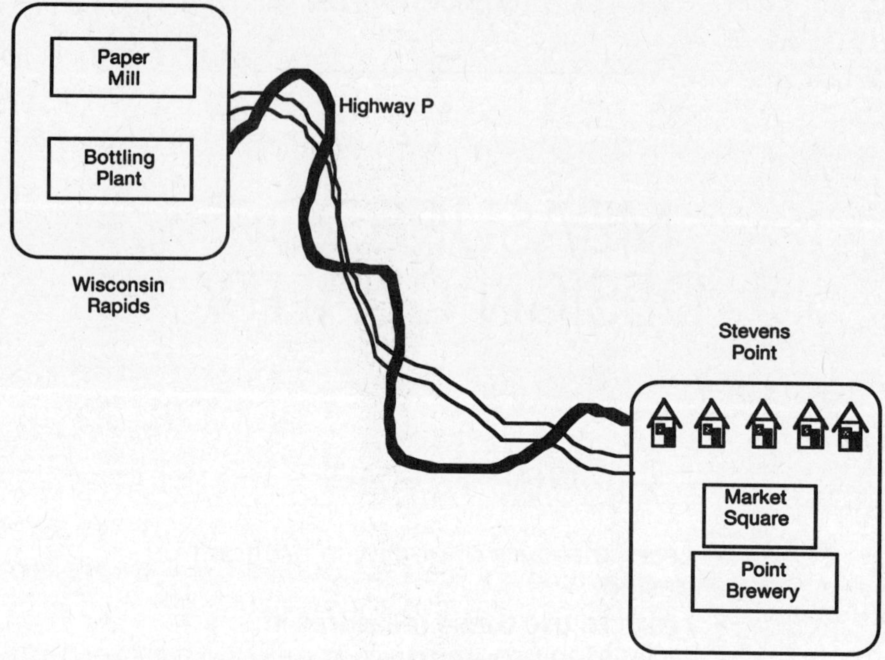

FIGURE 12-1 Fictional urban design.

programs that have not, thus far, been turned into measurement scales. These can be used to evaluate programs but not, strictly speaking, for comparison.

Ideally all of the measures of program quality would produce compatible results. In other words, a program that ranked high in terms of coupling would also rank high in terms of cohesion, correspondence, and all of the evaluation heuristics. Alas, in the real world, such a situation is rare—in part because our "measures" are at best imperfect surrogates for the underlying qualities, in part because there are many different types of programs which differ substantially in their construction, and in part because we do not really understand what program quality is.

Let us examine the measures that we do have. Coupling, cohesion, and correspondence can all be illustrated by a familiar example. Figure 12-1 is the map of a fictional area in north central Wisconsin. In this land of sky blue waters, there are two towns: Stevens Point and Wisconsin Rapids. As illustrated in Figure 12-1, Wisconsin Rapids is home to the Consolidated Paper Plant and the bottling plant for the Point Brewery. Stevens Point is home to the Point Brewery, a market square full of bars, and the workers who work at Consolidated Paper (for reasons that you will have no trouble imagining if you have ever lived near a paper mill!). Connecting them is Highway P, which S-turns across the Wisconsin River Valley, crossing the river about half a dozen times.

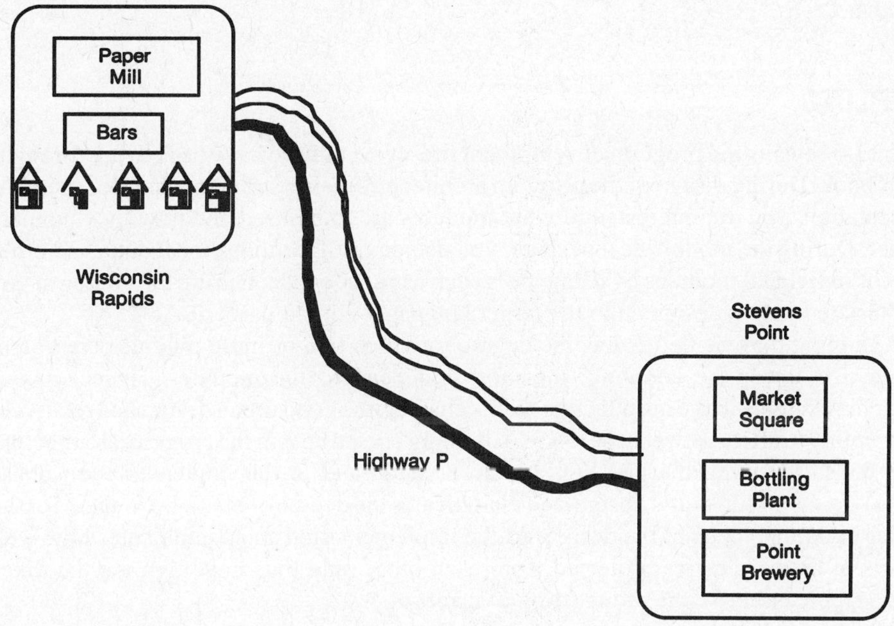

FIGURE 12-2 Actual town layout.

In this fictional urban design, Highway P carries a great deal of traffic. Every morning the paper mill workers commute from Stevens Point to Wisconsin Rapids, and every evening they commute back. All day, tank trucks of beer go from the brewery to the bottling plant along Highway P. Trucks continually carry bottled beer back to Stevens Point for consumption in the market square. All of this traffic is slowed down by the narrow bridges over the river. Neither town contains all it needs for the tasks it performs, hence the high traffic. The towns have poor cohesion internally, and there is high coupling (traffic) between them. Furthermore, the highway routing does not correspond to the local geography; hence, the reason for all of the bridges. This represents a good way not to design something.

Figure 12-2 shows things as they really are. Wisconsin Rapids produces paper and contains both the mill and the workers (as well as the watering holes). Stevens Point produces Point Special Beer; the brewery and the bottling plant are collocated. The Highway follows the river valley. Traffic on the highway is only as necessary — bottled beer to Wisconsin Rapids and cardboard beer cartons to Stevens Point. Each town has high cohesion (does one task) and there is low coupling (traffic) between them. The layout corresponds to the local geography. We shall not speculate whether all the women are strong, the men good looking, and the children above average. I tend to think so, but then a steady diet of Point Beer in my formative years may have clouded my judgment somewhat.

COUPLING

Figure 12-3 revisits the program development life-cycle that we have been using throughout this book. During design of the program architecture, using structure charts or a similar representation, you are interested in what modules are to be used and how they connect together. During the module design stage, you decide on algorithms, local data, and other details of individual modules by using tools such as pseudocode. During the coding stage, you translate module designs into the target language—in our case, dBASE.

Coupling may be defined as the degree to which two or more modules are bound together; the lower the coupling, the more independent the modules. Hence, in our geographic example in the introduction to this chapter, the good urban design had relatively little coupling (traffic) between the towns. Coupling is used both in the program architecture design phase (deriving the program structure chart) and in the implementation phase (coding). At the architectural design stage it indicates the degree of black-boxedness for the modular building blocks of the design. At the implementation stage it indicates how well the parts of the system are protected from each other (and thus how high are the dikes against "ripple effect"—the propagation of errors).

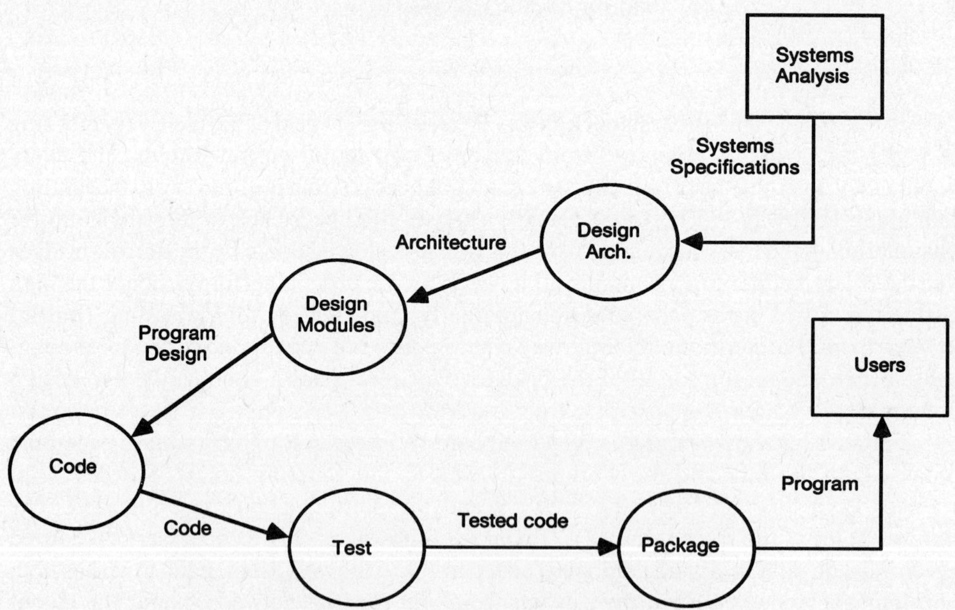

FIGURE 12-3 Program design life-cycle.

The stage of the program development process at which coupling is to be used determines in large part which aspects of coupling are relevant. Two scales are needed, one at the architecture level (corresponding to this and the next sections of the book) and one at the implementation level (Figure 12-4). At the implementation level, the scale measures the way in which actual connections between modules are made, primarily because in a given language there may be several choices. At the design level, the scale measures the variety of data flowing between modules.

At the *design* (program architectural) level, the forms of coupling are data-element coupling, data-stamp coupling (data-structure based), control-element coupling (control-structure based), and control-stamp coupling.

Data-element coupling (usually referred to simply as data coupling) means that modules have access only to the data items that they need. This is the best form of coupling, since it minimizes interconnections between modules. Figure 12-5 illustrates data-element coupling. In this example, the program fragment represented by **PRINT ADDRESS LABELS** needs only the name and address from the customer record (the contents of which are documented in the attached data dictionary entry). No other information from the customer record is sent to **PRINT ADDRESS LABELS**. In the example, a reason for this might be security; customer balance might well be an item which the clerk sending out letters is not authorized to know.

Stamp coupling means that modules have access to the data structures that contain the data elements needed in the module, as well as other data elements that are not needed. For example, in Figure 12-6 the data structure **Customer record** contains other data besides name and address. **PRINT ADDRESS LABELS** in Figure 12-6 only uses name and address, but it has access to the entire record. Stamp coupling is not as good as data-element coupling, since connections between modules are not minimized and sensitivity to ripple effect*s* (changes in one part of a program causing problems elsewhere) from program change is greater. Security can also be a problem.

Control-element coupling refers to the use of flags and other elements of control rather than data. It is usually a symptom of designing modules that cross control structure boundaries. In Figure 12-7, the highlighted flow **End-of-file** is a flag that passes control rather than data.

Design level (Sections III and IV)
Data-element
Data stam
Control element
Control stamp
Implementation level (Section V)
Parameter passing
Information clusters
Common coupling

FIGURE 12-4 Coupling scales.

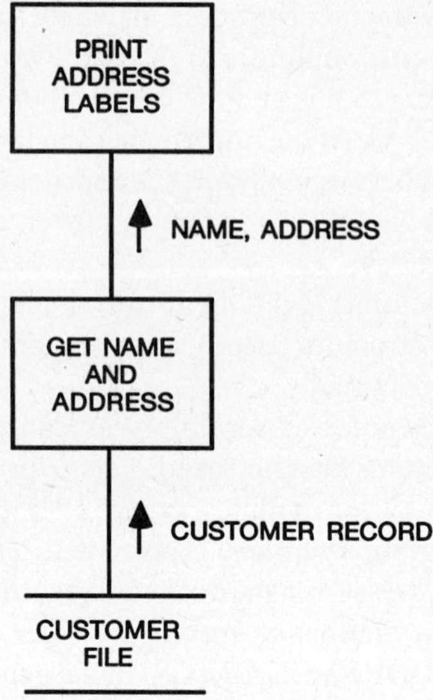

CUSTOMER-RECORD = NAME + ADDRESS + PHONE + MAKE + MODEL + DATE-NEXT-CHECK + BALANCE

FIGURE 12-5 Data-element coupling.

Control-stamp coupling is the passing of records containing flags and switches between modules that use a subset of the control elements in the record. For example, the record PROGRAM-SWITCHES may contain flags for all of the conditions that may occur in a program, even though only one of those conditions might be relevant for a given module.

Note that control coupling of any sort refers to the use of *data* that is passed between modules. Control coupling is where that data is used as a message to tell the module what to do. It has nothing to do with the passing of control between modules. If one module calls another but the two share no data, there is no control coupling between them.

At the *implementation level*, there are three basic possibilities: parameter passing, information clusters, and common coupling.

Parameter passing (Figure 12-8) is the explicit definition of each data item going between modules. At the design stage, data flows between modules are named and defined. At the implementation stage, parameter passing ensures that modules cannot refer to data within other modules unless the data items appear as parameters in module calls. Either data elements or data structures may be transferred. dBASE provides these facilities via the `DO WITH` and the `PARAMETER` statements (see Chapter 10). The parameters in the code correspond directly to the arrows on the structure chart. In discussions of implementation-level coupling, this form of design is best, since it minimizes connections between modules, makes those connections explicit, and thus minimizes the ripple effect of subsequent changes.

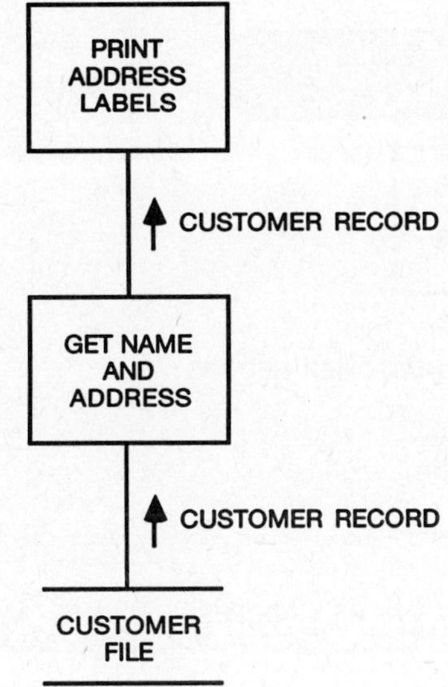

CUSTOMER-RECORD = NAME + ADDRESS + PHONE + MAKE + MODEL + DATE-NEXT-CHECK + BALANCE

FIGURE 12-6 Data–stamp coupling.

Localization (use of information clusters; Figure 12-9) is the grouping of variables into data structures, and the explicit sharing of these data structures between modules. The major difference between parameter passing and localization is the lack of hierarchy by the latter; the structure of the data is not assumed to correspond with the structure of the program as with parameter passing. Thus, lower-level modules may share data without passing it through higher level modules. dBASE provides localization through the `USE` command for data relations. This form of coupling is the standard approach to coupling with fourth generation languages and often produces even lower levels of interconnection between modules than does parameter-based coupling. It is placed below parameter-based coupling, because its presence is an indication that the program structure may not match the data structure of the problem. This occurs frequently in database environments, because the database is organized to be general purpose and not to support a particular program.

Common coupling is use of global data; any module within the system can use any data item. Examples of implementation in third generation languages are any data in BASIC, the `DATA DIVISION` in COBOL, and blank `COMMON` in FORTRAN. dBASE provides common coupling through the `PUBLIC` statement (Figure 12-10), which makes `PUBLIC` memory variables available to all modules in a program. Common coupling is often used at the highest level of a program to set program-wide constants. It is the worst form of implementation coupling for a modular program. There are two reasons for this. The first is that there are no barriers to the "ripple effect;" a change in one part of the program can propagate throughout the program. The other problem is that when you are

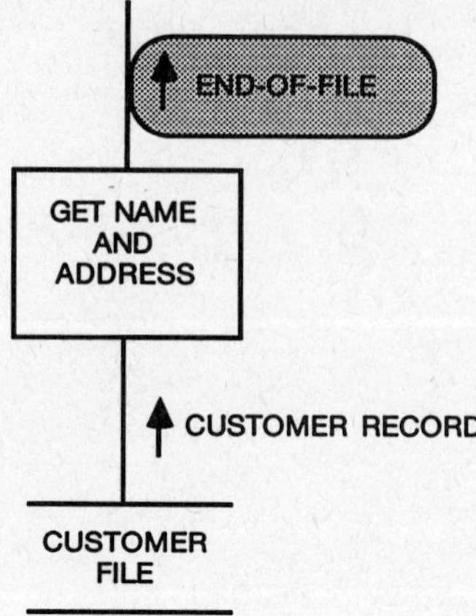

CUSTOMER-RECORD = NAME + ADDRESS + PHONE + MAKE + MODEL + DATE-NEXT-CHECK + BALANCE

FIGURE 12-7 Control–element coupling.

maintaining a program, you have no idea what modules are using what data, since all data is accessible to all modules.

Based on the discussion thus far, it would appear that these three implementation approaches should not affect the design. There is a complication, however, in the case of localization (information clusters). It turns out that this technique has two uses:

- As a way to improve common coupling or to compensate for efficiency considerations with parameter passing.
- As a supplement to program architecture in cases where the program structure does not match the data structure.

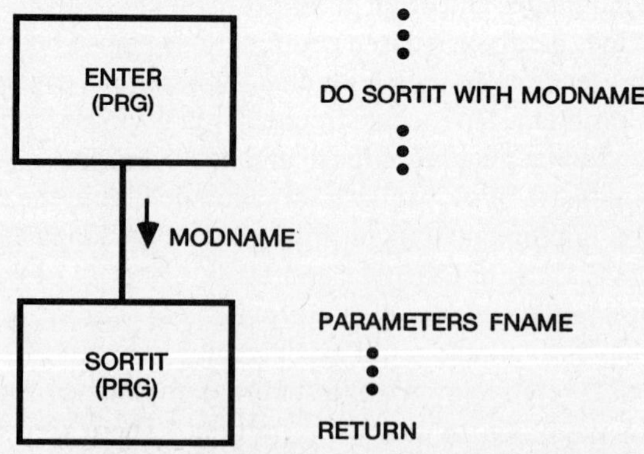

FIGURE 12-8 Parameter passing in dBASE III.

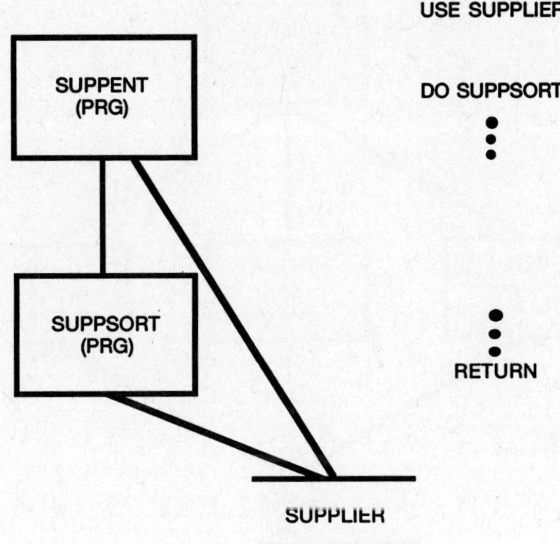

FIGURE 12-9 Data localization in dBASE III.

```
**************************************
* CONFIGUR set up initial configuation *
**************************************
PUBLIC
CONDENSE,PICA,ELITE,NORMAL,EXPAND,PRESET,WIDTH,MDATE
*
* Set up Epson Printer
*
STORE CHR(15) TO CONDESNE
STORE CHR(27)+"P" TO PICA
STORE CHR(27)+"M" TO ELITE
STORE CHR(18) TO NORMAL
STORE CHR(14) TO EXPAND
STORE CHR(27)+"@" TO PRESET
STORE CHR(27)+"Q"+CHR(233) TO WIDTH
*
* Get date
*
STORE DTOC (DATE()) TO MDATE
*
.
.
.
RETURN
```

FIGURE 12-10 dBASE III `PUBLIC` variables.

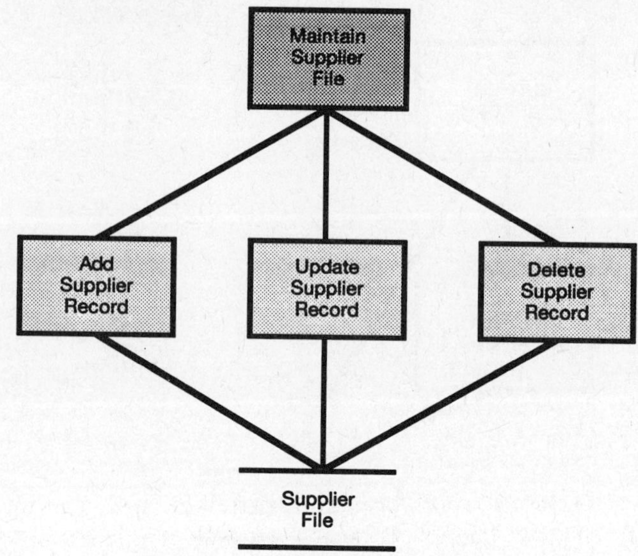

FIGURE 12-11 Sample module calls.

This last is most often found in database environments and is quite common with designs intended for implementation using database-oriented fourth generation languages such as dBASE.

COHESION

As discussed in the introduction to this chapter, cohesion is a measure of the strength of association of the elements within a module. It is thus a measure that is used at the module design stage of the program development life-cycle. Before looking at how this strength of association is measured, let us look first at what exactly we mean by elements.

The concept of module is nothing new, of course—all of Chapter 10 was devoted to it. The elements in a module may be either instructions in our chosen language or calls to another module. Instructions are no problem, since we have been using them all along; it is probably fairly clear what is meant when we talk about how the instructions within a module should work together. Treating calls to another module as elements may be a bit harder to understand.

Basically, a call to another module (e.g., `DO GETCUST`) is treated as a custom instruction in the language; the function of our custom instruction is whatever the module in question does. Figure 12-11 illustrates this concept; in it we see a high level module (**MAINTAIN SUPPLIER FILE**) that does three things: **ADD SUPPLIER RECORD, UPDATE SUPPLIER RECORD**, and **DELETE SUPPLIER RECORD**. Each of these modules is a function performed by **MAINTAIN SUPPLIER FILE** and is thus an element of the module **MAINTAIN SUPPLIER FILE**.

Functional
Sequential
Communicational
Procedural
Temporal
Logical
Coincidental

FIGURE 12-12 Levels of cohesion.

Thus, when we talk about measuring the strength of association of all of the elements within a module, what we are saying is that we want to measure how strongly everything that that module does is tied together, and it does not matter if what the module does is done via statements that are built into the language or via statements that are custom built using lower-level modules.

Now that it is clearer (one hopes!) just what is measured by elements, let us look at this "strength of association." Our concern is similar to that of a writer evaluating a paragraph who wonders: "Do all of the sentences in this paragraph concern one complete idea?" As program designers, we want all of the statements within a module to solve one complete problem.

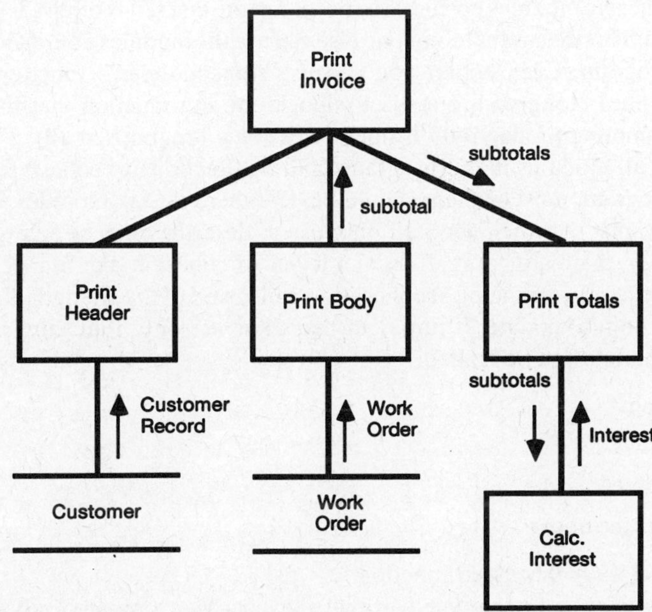

FIGURE 12-13 Example of functional cohesion.

Figure 12-12 illustrates the levels of cohesion that are generally recognized in the industry today. Let us briefly review these levels, and then discuss how to determine the level of cohesion for a particular module.

Functional cohesion is the best sort. Here, the elements are like the sentences in a well-written paragraph: each contributes to the solution of one complete task (or function, hence, the name). The name of the module completely and accurately describes what task the module performs. This name is usually stated in the form of a simple imperative sentence with a single direct object (e.g., **CALCULATE SQUARE ROOT** or **DELETE SUPPLIER RECORD**). In fact, one of the characteristics of a functionally cohesive module is that it always can be described with such a sentence.

The main advantages of a functionally cohesive module is that it makes the program easy to understand and maintain. Just by looking at the structure chart or at the listing of modules you can determine what each module does. Moreover, it is clear where each task is performed, since tasks are not split between modules unless the task is split into subtasks and each subtask is made into a subordinate module. Figure 12-13 is an example of such a situation. The function **PRINT INVOICE** has three subfunctions: **PRINT HEADER**, which uses information from the **CUSTOMER** file; **PRINT BODY** which uses information from the **WORK ORDER** file; and **PRINT TOTALS**. **PRINT TOTALS** has a single subfunction: **CALCULATE INTEREST**. Basically, then, with functional cohesion you always know where to find the part of a program that performs a particular task. Moreover, the structure of the program will probably match the structure of the problem, which makes it even easier to find what modules do what. To add icing to the cake, since functionally cohesive modules perform single, complete tasks, it is often easy to make them general purpose. This means that someone else can use the modules you write at some other point in the program. Even better, you can use someone else's functionally cohesive modules. This goes along with our discussion in the introduction that the best way to improve programming productivity is not to write new programs at all.

Alas, not all modules in our programs will be functionally cohesive, although in a well-written program, most of them should be. But there are six more levels of cohesion to get through (most of which you will only use to describe other people's programs, of course). Actually, there are not really seven levels of cohesion, but four. Confused?

Going back to first principles, cohesion is a measure of the strength of association of the elements within a module. It turns out that there are only four things by which the elements in a module can be related:

- function
- data
- procedure
- none of the above

We have already discussed function.

If the elements are not related in that they perform one and only one complete function, they are likely to be related because they all work with the same data. For example, the module **VERIFY AND INSERT SUPPLIER RECORD** performs two functions, but everything it does is done to the same data. Similarly, **ADD NAME, ADDRESS, AND PHONE NUMBER TO SUPPLIER RECORD** performs all (or maybe part) of three functions, but everything is done to the same data.

Most discussions of cohesion break down data-oriented cohesion into two subtypes: sequential and communicational cohesion. *Sequential* cohesion is data-oriented cohesion in which the order of execution makes a difference. For example, in **VERIFY AND INSERT SUPPLIER RECORD** we want to verify the record before it is inserted. Sequential cohesion often is shown by module names with the word "and" in them, or by other forms of complex sentence structures. Modules with sequential cohesion are usually the result of turning a detailed data flow diagram into a structure chart without sufficient revision.

In *communicational* cohesion the elements all deal with the same data, but it doesn't matter in what order they are performed. For example, in **ADD NAME, ADDRESS, AND PHONE NUMBER TO SUPPLIER RECORD**, the fields can be put into the record in any order. Communicational cohesion is often produced by data-structure–oriented design methodologies such as the Jackson and the Warnier-Orr approaches to program design (Chapter 15).

The careful reader may have noticed at this point that the modules in Figure 12-12 are all related by data, yet the discussion implied (correctly) that they are functionally cohesive. When discussing any level of cohesion, a module has that level of cohesion if it meets the criteria for that level, and ***not*** for any higher levels. Thus, if a module meets the criteria for procedural, communicational, and functional cohesion, it is functionally cohesive. Hence, when we say that sequential and communicational cohesion describe

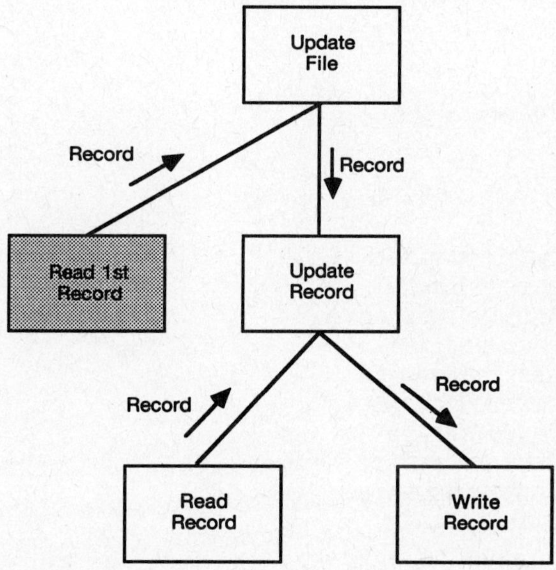

FIGURE 12-14 Example of procedural cohesion.

modules whose elements are related because they all manipulate the same data, it is implied that those elements do not perform one complete function.

Similarly, when we say that the elements in a module are related by *procedure*, and thus have procedural or temporal cohesion, we are also saying that those elements are not related by data or by function. The distinction between procedural and temporal cohesion is similar to that between sequential and communicational cohesion. With procedural

```
****************************************
* CONFIGUR set up initial configuation *
****************************************
PUBLIC
CONDENSE,PICA,ELITE,NORMAL,EXPAND,PRESET,WIDTH,MDATE
PUBLIC
NAVLAB,PULSLAB,INSTLAB,RADLAB,AUTOLAB,TAXRATE,XPRATE,ALTRATE
PUBLIC ENCRATE,INTRATE,WOD
*
* Set up Epson Printer
*
STORE CHR(15) TO CONDENSE
STORE CHR(27)+"P" TO PICA
STORE CHR(27)+"M" TO ELITE
STORE CHR(18) TO NORMAL
STORE CHR(14) TO EXPAND
STORE CHR(27)+"@" TO PRESET
STORE CHR(27+"Q"+CHR(233) TO WIDTH
*
* Get date
*
STORE DTOC(DATE()) TO MADATE
*
* Get current labor and interest rates
*
USE COFNIG
STORE NAVCOM TO NAVLAB
STORE PULSE TO PULSLAB
STORE INSTALL TO INSTLAB
STORE RADAR TO RADLAB
STORE COMPASS TO AUTOLAB
STORE SALESTX TO TAXRATE]
STORE XPONDR TO XPRATE
STORE ALTIMETR TO ALRATE
STORE ENCODER TO ENCRATE
STORE IRATE TO INTRATE
RETURN
```

FIGURE 12-15 Example of temporal cohesion.

cohesion, the order in which things are done makes a difference; with temporal cohesion, the order in which things are done does not make a difference.

Figure 12-14 shows a procedurally cohesive module (**READ FIRST RECORD**) that is not a logical part of the function **UPDATE FILE**; it is included because it is a separate paragraph in the underlying COBOL code. Such modules usually come about when a program is designed using flowcharts. Flowcharts show procedure (operations and control structures) rather than data or tasks. If a flowchart is broken into modules, often based on visual clues, it is likely that many of the resulting modules will have procedural cohesion.

Temporally cohesive modules are those in which all of the elements are carried out at about the same time (hence, the name, since temporal means "time-oriented"). Figure 12-15 shows the dBASE III code for a temporally cohesive module that initializes all of the memory variables at the beginning of a program. Initialization and termination modules are the most common form of temporally cohesive modules.

What is wrong with procedural and temporal cohesion? There are two major problems, both of which make programs with many procedure-oriented modules hard to maintain. The first problem is that such modules do not perform a complete task; hence, it is difficult to determine either what relationship the module at hand has to the overall problem or, conversely, what module is affected by a task within the problem. The other difficulty with such modules is that there is high coupling between them, since the modularization is done without regard for data usage.

An example of the difficulties in maintaining such modules is a problem I once had with a business simulation game. This game had been written during the early 1970s and established wage and price controls for the game environment if the rate of inflation rose above 5%. A few years later, with inflation well into double digits and no wage and price controls, this was no longer a reasonable assumption. Therefore, the game administrator asked me to remove it from the program.

The program in question consisted of about 10,000 lines of FORTRAN spaghetti code. It was "modularized," but the "modules" averaged 1500 lines each! I finally found the equation that applied wage and price controls but did not dare remove it, since everything in the program was common coupled and I didn't know what other modules might make assumptions about the variables. So I changed the trigger inflation rate to 999%, figuring that would eliminate wage and price controls for mere double-digit inflation.

A week later I got a long distance phone call from a panicked game administrator—wage and price controls were still in force. It turned out that the report-generating module also was involved in determining whether to impose the controls. Hence, even though they had been taken out of the econometric simulation proper, the report generator was putting them back in.

This business game program was an example of traditional program design, which does not produce functionally cohesive modules. Such programs, as discussed in the introduction, are not easy to maintain and modify. But it could be worse; at least modules with procedural and temporal cohesion have elements that are connected by procedure! The next set of modules have elements with even less meaningful relations.

Modules in which the elements do not perform a single complete function, are not related because they work with the same data, and are not related because they are part of the same procedure are pretty awful. There are two types of such modules. Those with logical cohesion have the elements related by something; an observer with a vivid imagination can at least figure out why a benighted programmer might have put these things together. For example, all of the input statements may be in one module, and all of the output statements in another. The original programmer may have thought that this would simplify translating the program into languages other than English (there are better ways to do that).

Coincidental cohesion is the situation in which the elements in a module have no meaningful relationship whatsoever—this is functional confusion at its worst level. Very few modules are ever produced with this form of defect. Modules that have only coincidental cohesion are probably the result of "midnight maintenance" by programmers who were not sure what they were doing. These programmers probably did their work in machine code and were on the lookout for any cubbyholes in memory that could serve as

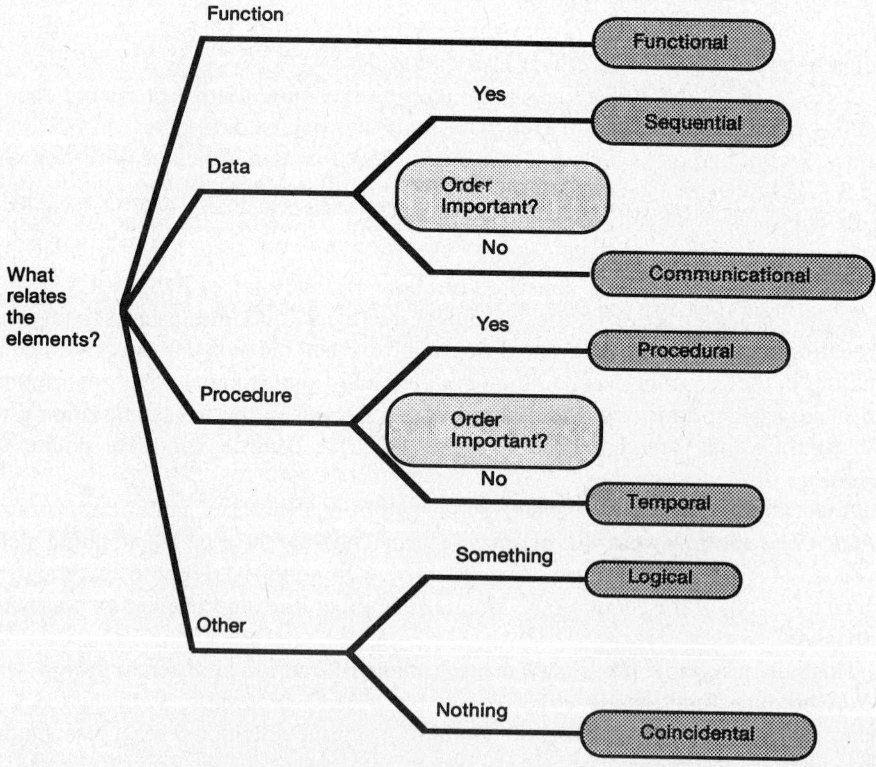

FIGURE 12-16 Decision tree for module cohesion.

repositories for their ill-conceived endeavors. This sort of situation makes respectable program designers shudder. Fortunately, it is rare; programs that evolve this way do not usually live to reproduce.

Figure 12-16 is a decision tree showing how to determine what is the level of cohesion for a module? Start at the left and answer the questions. And remember, when a module has several levels of cohesion, the highest applies.

Most people treat cohesion as an ordinal scale: one where we know that functional is better than sequential, for example, but we do not know by how much. Some authorities, such as Constantine and Yourdon [1979], suggest that cohesion is not only ordinal but interval (numbers can be assigned to each level of cohesion) and that programs can be compared numerically. Figure 12-17 shows their recommended values for the scale.

OTHER MEASURES

The previous two sections have discussed the basic measures of design and program quality that are used in the Yourdon "structured" approaches to analysis and design, and that are widely accepted in industry. This section discusses additional measures of design and program quality. Some of these measures are derived from methodologies that compete with the Yourdon approach in the systems development marketplace; others are derived from collective experience concerning what makes a good program.

The warning from the introduction to this chapter still applies: there is no overall theory of measurement for program quality; the measures that we use in the industry are ad hoc. They are based on intuition and experience rather than on formal empirical testing derived from accepted theory. What this means in English is that our measures are like the blind men's view of the elephant—each describes accurately the part of the problem at hand but not the whole. Moreover, the fact that a program or a design does well on one measure is no guarantee that it will do well on another, since we measure aspects of program quality rather than program quality itself. Cynics in the industry would probably argue that our measures are like the view of the blind man behind the elephant who reached down and declared that "the elephant is soft and mushy."

Coupling measures one aspect of data quality: cohesion measures one aspect of procedural quality. Given the split in the industry between data-oriented and procedure-oriented views of design, it is not too surprising that the other measures of program quality are either data-oriented

Functional	7
Sequential	5
Communicational	4
Procedural	3
Temporal	2
Logial	1
Coincidental	0

FIGURE 12-17 Suggested numeric values for cohesion.

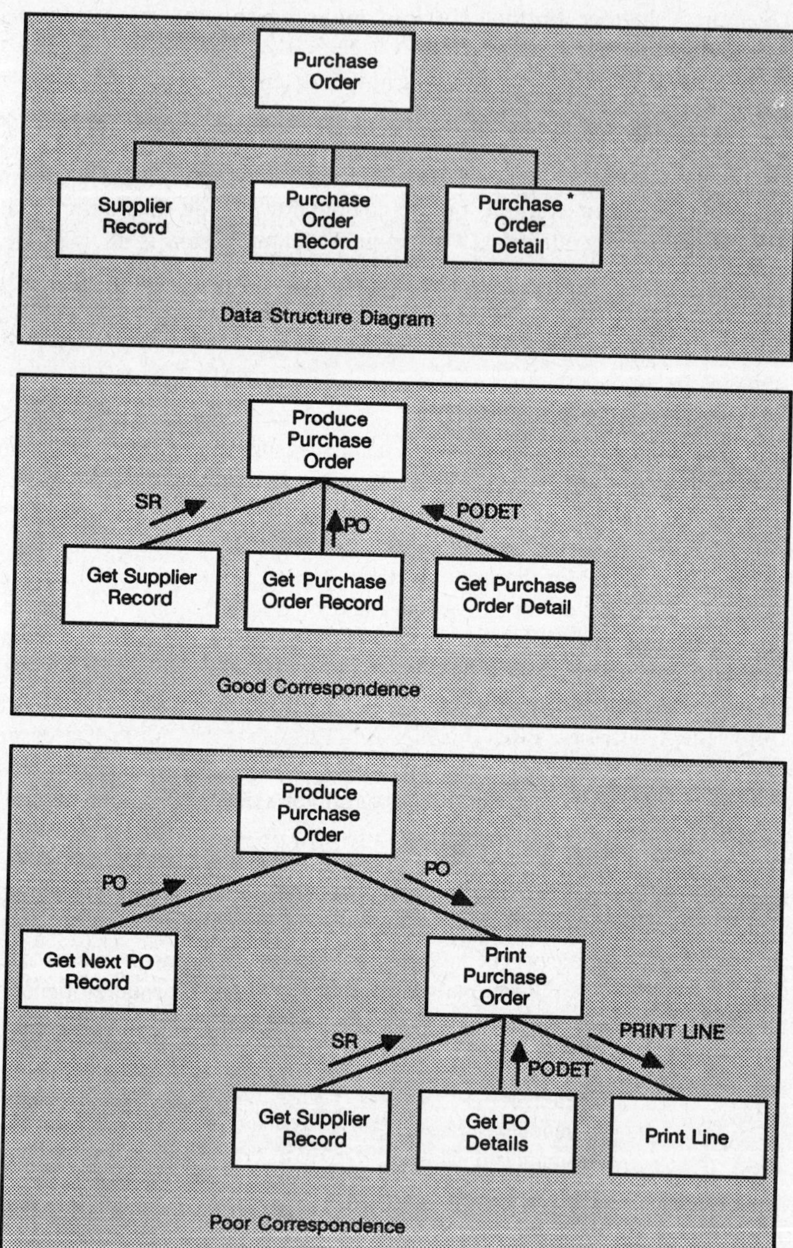

FIGURE 12-18 Correspondence.

or procedure-oriented. The rest of this chapter examines these two groups.

Data-Oriented Measures

There are three commonly used measures other than coupling that involve data. *Correspondence* is a measure of overall design quality. *Static memory* is a measure of module quality. *Data hiding* is a measure of both.

Correspondence means that the structure of the problem matches (corresponds to) the structure of the program. It is a measure used in the various data-structure–oriented approaches and is particularly applicable to database-oriented designs. Signs of poor correspondence include high coupling and the use of localization at the design stage. When a program is designed based on a data-structure diagram or an entity-relationship diagram, correspondence is usually good. Other techniques, especially process-oriented ones, may or may not produce good correspondence. Figure 12-18 illustrates good and bad correspondence for a simple problem. Correspondence is a measure that relies on pattern-matching skills; it is not quantifiable.

Static memory is a measure of the quality of individual modules; a module contains

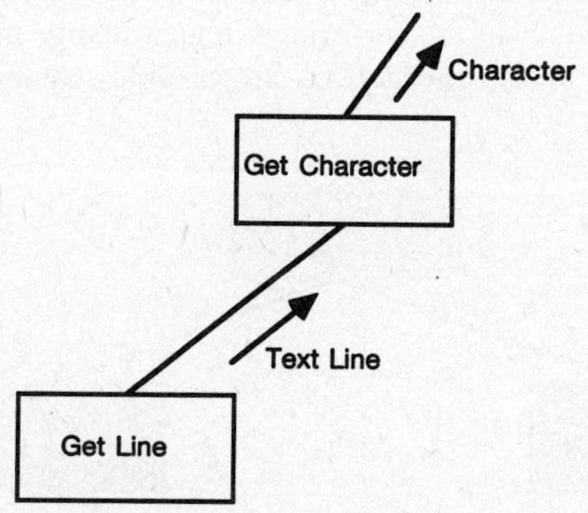


```
Procedure: Get Character
Static i
if i <= end of line
then return ith character in line
    i=i+1
else Get line
      i=i+1
endif
return
```

FIGURE 12-19 Static memory.

static memory if the values of any of the module's internal data are retained between invocations of the module. Note that static memory does not refer to data passed as parameters between modules but only to that data that is internal to a module. Static memory is undesirable, since it hinders the reusability of modules within a program. Figure 12-19 illustrates part of a design that uses static memory. In this case, **GET CHARACTER** must remember the value of **i** so that it knows where in the line to look. The disadvantage is that **GET CHARACTER** cannot be used elsewhere in the program unless the calling module wants characters from the same input stream.

Data hiding is a measure of data abstraction. The idea is that each module will hide some aspect of the implementation of data from the modules above. It is nonquantifiable.

Procedure-Oriented Measures

Measures of procedural quality other than cohesion are degree of factoring, fan-in, fan-out, generality, and size.

Factoring (Figure 12-20) means splitting a task into subtasks such that the higher-level modules concentrate on the logic of the problem solution and the lower-level modules carry out the actual tasks. There are two major advantages to this approach. The first is that changes in the environment that result in changes to the program are likely to affect either the way in which low-level tasks are performed (e.g., a change in tax rate) or the high-level logic (e.g., a change in which transactions are taxable). A factored design is easier to

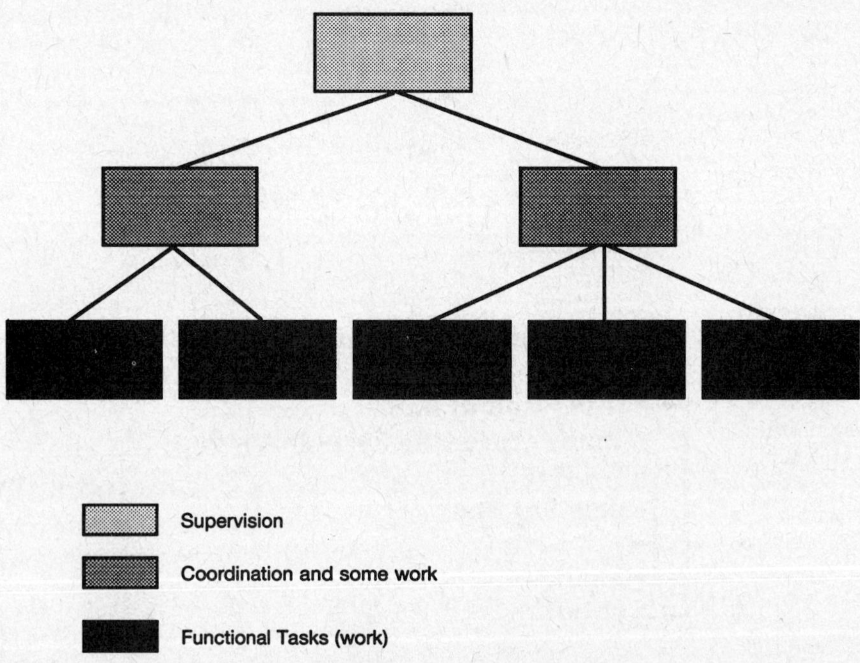

FIGURE 12-20 Factoring.

maintain under such circumstances. The other advantage is that the low-level modules are likely to be general purpose, and can be borrowed from someone else or from a library of standard routines. This makes program development far easier, since the best approach to programming productivity is to use an existing program!

Fan-out is a count of how many immediate subordinates a module has. Fan-out should be limited to seven plus or minus two except when the modules implement the alternatives in a CASE control structure. The reason for the general limitation is that in a functionally cohesive design, subordinate modules indicate subtasks, and if a task has more than about seven subtasks, it is hard to understand and should be factored more. The reason for exempting the CASE control structure is that subordinate modules there represent alternatives, not subtasks. Since only one alternative can be chosen at a time, there is no danger of overloading short term memory. In Figure 12-21, panel A has a fan-out of five, and panel B has a fan-out of seven. Fan-out is a measure of individual module quality; it is not applied to systems as a whole.

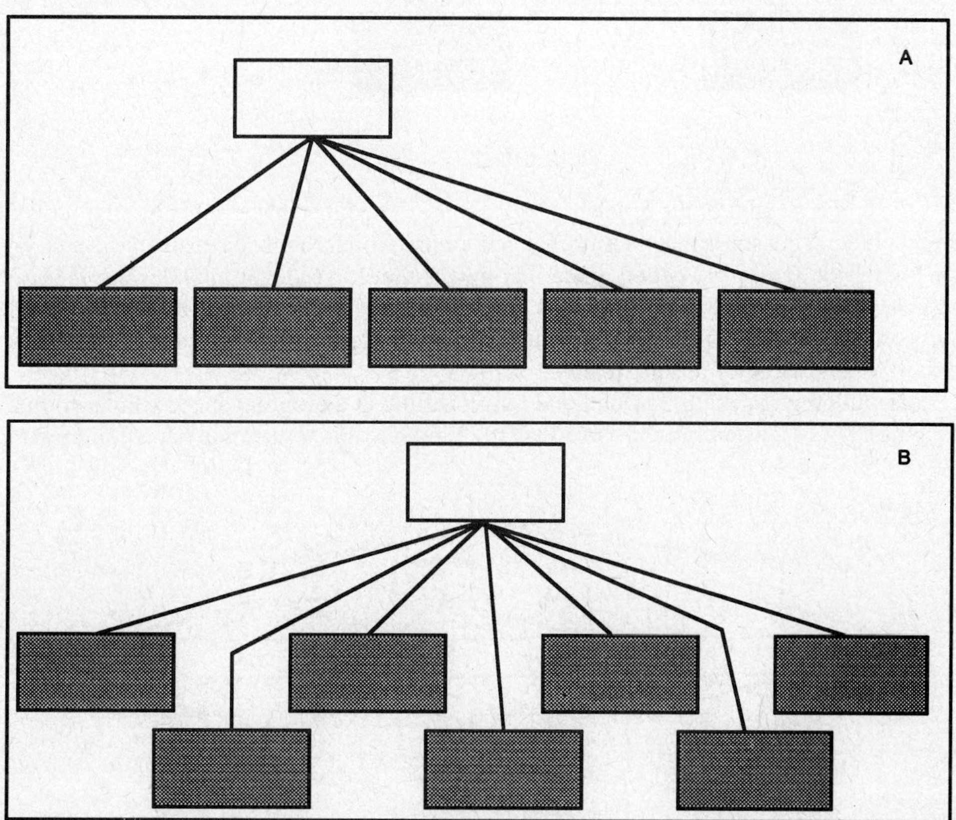

FIGURE 12-21 Fan-out

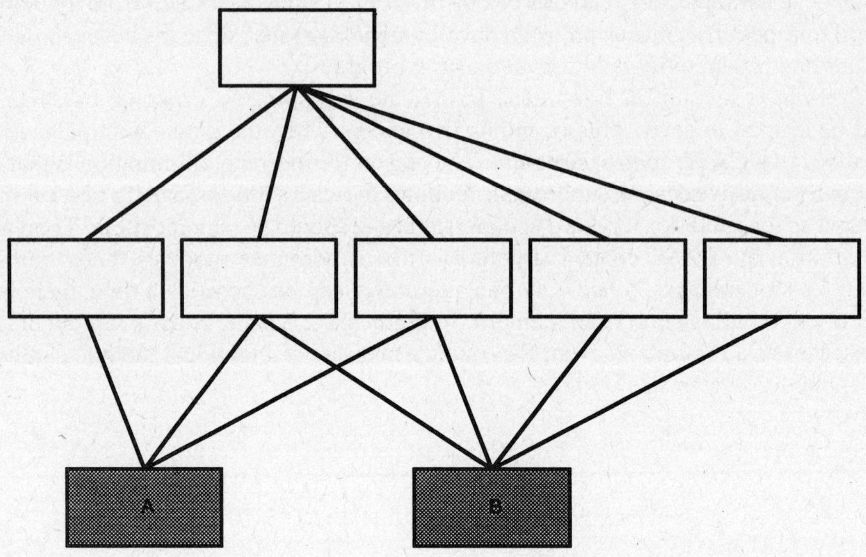

FIGURE 12-22 Fan-in.

Fan-in is a count of the number of *higher-level* modules that use a particular lower-level module. It is a substitute measure for generality (which cannot be measured directly). The higher the fan-in the better, since this means that lower-level modules are general purpose. In Figure 12-22, module A has a fan-in of three while module B has a fan-in of four. Fan-in is basically a measure of the quality of a single module, but average fan-in may be used as a measure of design quality.

Combining factoring, fan-out, and fan-in results in a program shape similar to that in Figure 12-23. Constantine and Yourdon [1979] refer to this as mosque shaped, since with

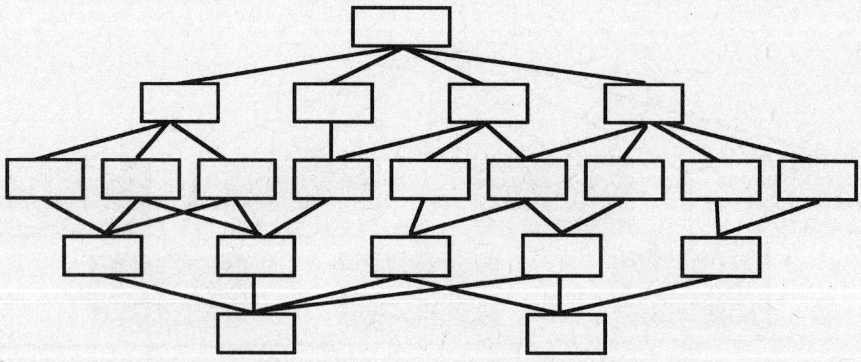

FIGURE 12-23 Mosque-shaped program.

an active imagination one can see a resemblance to the shape of the building in Figure 12-24. There is some empirical evidence that programs of this shape are easier to maintain than are programs that are not mosque shaped.

Generality is the overall quality that static memory and fan-in attempt to measure and that factoring attempts to produce. In the ideal situation the designer has access to a large number of general-purpose, plug-in modules and the design task consists of deciding how those modules should be connected together, and under what circumstances each should be invoked. An analogy here is computer hardware design, where a circuit designer chooses from among a few hundred standard integrated circuits rather than designing new chips from scratch. Ideally, an organization can buy or develop the modules it needs; and programming then is a matter of simply plugging together the pieces.

In reality this does not happen as much as it should; most programmers and most organizations spend a great deal of time reinventing the wheel. To the extent, however, that modules ***can*** be made general purpose (which is a fairly easy technical problem) and to the extent that programmers and designers ***will*** reuse them (which is a fairly difficult organizational problem), productivity can be greatly increased.

A final measure of module quality is module *Size*, defined in number of lines of source code or number of statements in an action diagram. Most of the traditional arguments about module size revolve around issues of packaging efficiency, which we discuss in Chapter 21. Such issues are irrelevant at the design stage. Ideally, size is not an issue—one partitions a system until each of the lowest-level modules does one single complete task. Often, however, one can continue partitioning after a fairly small size is reached, so it is relevant to ask when to stop. This question has upper bounds, lower bounds, and a few guidelines.

As discussed above, I once had the job of maintaining a "modular" FORTRAN program whose average module size was over 1500 lines! One of the modules was over 2500 lines. This is not modularity. (It turned out that the program had been split up that way only because it could not otherwise fit into memory on the minicomputer for which it had been developed.) Clearly, several hundred or several thousand lines is too big for a module.

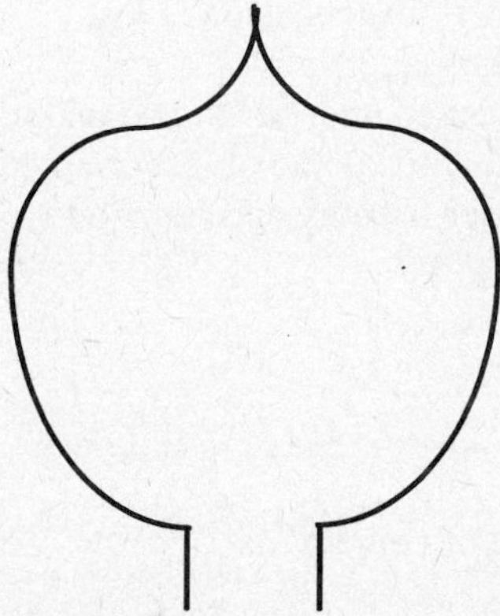

FIGURE 12-24 Mosque-shaped mosque.

At the implementation stage one line is too small. However, at the design stage one may not know that a module will have only one or two lines, since it may depend on the target language. For example, a word-processing program done in C may have several 25-line modules that shrink to a single line each when the system is recoded in PL/1, since PL/1 has many built-in text manipulation functions. Similarly, a 50-line COBOL program may shrink to a single line of dBASE. The rule of thumb here is to factor as much as makes sense from the problem point of view. If at the coding stage you discover that some of the modules are very small, it is easy to unfactor the design by one level where needed. Always err on the side of overfactoring at the design stage; unfactoring later is trivial.

In the best of all possible worlds, a module will be 24 lines or less. This is because most modern programs are developed on a computer terminal, and the average CRT has a 24-line display. So long as the entire module can be seen at one time, short-term memory limitations are not relevant, since the display functions as an extension of short term memory. As modules get longer than 24 lines, they become harder to work with, since more mental processing (and more paging back and forth at the CRT) are required. Note that 10 or 15 years ago, the recommended maximum module size was 55 lines (one sheet of paper).

QUESTIONS AND EXERCISES

1. What are the three basic measures of program design?
   a. Correctness, structure, and simplicity.
   b. Coupling, simplicity, and structure.
   c. Coupling, cohesionn and correspondence.
   d. Cohesion, structure, and correspondence.
2. Coupling is defined as
   a. The measure of strength of association of elements within a module.
   b. The degree to which two or more modules are bound together.
   c. A measure of overall design quality.
   d. A measure of module quality.
3. The main advantage of functional cohesion is that
   a. It makes the program short and simple.
   b. It makes the program easy to understand and maintain.
   c. It makes the program functional and object oriented.
   d. It makes the program user friendly and functional.
4. Program quality is measured by
   a. Menus.
   b. Colors.
   c. Speed.
   d. Cohesion.
5. At the design level, a form of coupling is
   a. Entity
   b. Parameter passing.
   c. Information clustering.
   d. Control element

6. Static memory is a measure of ________ quality
   a. Data.
   b. RAM.
   c. ROM.
   d. Module.
7. Data coupling means
   a. Modules have access only to data needed.
   b. Database records of similar nature are linked together.
   c. Screens are used only with a specific data record.
   d. All database records are linked together.
8. Common coupling means
   a. Any module can use any data item.
   b. Similar modules can only use similar data items.
   c. All modules are linked together.
   d. Any data item can be used from outside the system.
9. Cohesion is
   a. How strongly a module does its job.
   b. How a module works in different languages.
   c. How closely different prototypes resemble each other.
   d. How closely the current prototype resembles what the users want.
10. The degree to which two or more modules are bound is known as
    a. Retracting.
    b. Coupling.
    c. Interaction.
    d. Bonding.
11. The forms of data-element coupling, data-stamp coupling, control-element coupling, and control-stamp coupling are used at what level of program design?
    a. Implementation level.
    b Ground level.
    c. Design level.
    d. Prototype level.
12. A measure of strength of association of the elements within a module is known as
    a. Correspondence.
    b. Reflection.
    c. Division.
    d. Cohesion.

DISCUSSION QUESTIONS

1. What is cohesion
2. What is coupling, and how is it used?

3. Define static memory, and how do you identify a module that has it?

NORTHSTAR AVIATION

Part 8

1. In Chapter 11, you created a structure chart for Northstar Aviation. For each pair of connected modules in this system, analyze the coupling.
2. Continuing with the Northstar Aviation structure chart,
   a. What is the cohesion of each module?
   b. How closely do cohesion of modules and the coupling between them correspond?
3. Analyze the Northstar Aviation structure chart in terms of the measures presented in this chapter. How well do these measures correspond to the results of measuring quality with coupling and cohesion?

REFERENCES

YOURDON , E. and L. CONSTANTINE. *Structured Design*. Prentice-Hall, Englewood Cliffs, NJ, 1979.

Chapter 13

CASE STUDY FOR PROGRAM ARCHITECTURE

CHAPTER GOALS

- Present an integrated example using the techniques presented in the previous three chapters.

In this chapter we apply some of the techniques studied in Section III to a sample problem: designing a simple system to manage inventory. The system that we are designing is as depicted in Figure 13-1. Note that there is no description of how the parts in inventory are used for anything; that data model is outside the boundaries of the system that we are designing, as are the accounting aspects.

Figure 13-2 shows the attributes (data structure and type) for the SUPPLIER entity in dBASE format. Figure 13-3 shows the attributes (data structure and type) for the PARTS entity. Based on this information, we can construct the partial structure chart shown in Figure 13-4 to maintain the permanent entities.

The next step in designing the program architecture is to examine how the permanent entities change. This is traditionally done via process modeling using data flow diagrams. The basic question is: What occurs to change the state of permanent entities? Figure 13-5 shows a data flow diagram for the system under discussion.

The structure chart of Figure 13-4 can be evaluated in terms of the measures discussed in Chapter 12, specifically coupling, cohesion, and generality.

Between the module **MAINTAIN ENTITIES** and the modules **LOAD PART DATA** and **LOAD SUPPLIER DATA**, there is no coupling, since no data is transferred. Between

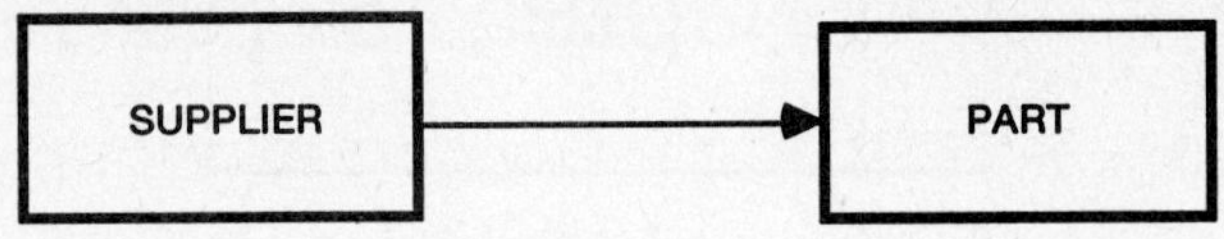

FIGURE 13-1 Entity-relationship diagram: permanent entities.

the modules **LOAD PART DATA**, **LOAD SUPPLIER DATA**, and **MAINTAIN ENTITY** there is data-element coupling, since all of the data items passed are used in lower level modules.

Each module in the chart performs a single complete task, so each is functionally cohesive.

The modules **ENTER RECORD**, **UPDATE RECORD**, **DELETE RECORD**, and **LIST CONTENTS** are examples of general purpose modules; indeed, the whole point of the higher-level modules **LOAD X DATA** is to set up the data required by the lower-level general purpose modules. This way, a new entity can be added without writing new versions of **ENTER RECORD**, **UPDATE RECORD**, **DELETE RECORD**, and **LIST CONTENTS**; only the top-level system menu need be changed.

Figures 13-6 and 13-7 show the attributes (data structure and type) for the **PO** and PO Detail data stores illustrated in Figure 13-5.

ORDER PARTS represents two things in this system: a message to a supplier (not the entity SUPPLIER, but a real-world instance of that entity) and a set of messages to the PARTS entity. The message to the supplier is an output from the system to the outside world and is therefore not normalized. It is, in fact, our old friend the three-part transaction. The messages to the PARTS entity are internal to the system and should be normalized. Figure 13-7 shows the relevant message to the PARTS entity, which is concerned with changes in the status of a particular part (from on-order to on-hand).

Figures 13-8 and 13-9 show partial structure charts derived from the objects PO (report) and PACKING LIST (event) via the object-oriented techniques of Chapter 11. Figure 13-10 shows the two combined into a single structure chart segment to deal with transactions.

Figures 13-4 and 13-10 include most of what we need for our program architecture; now they need to be put together to form a single structure chart.Since the combined structure chart will not fit easily on one page (as is often the cas in real life), the combination of Figures 13-4, 13-10, and 13-11 is left to the reader's imagination.

Field	Field Name	Type	Width	Dec
1	SNAME	Character	32	
2	SNUMBER	Character	4	
3	SALESMN	Character	32	
4	SADDR1	Character	32	
5	SADDR2	Character	32	
6	SADDR3	Character	32	
7	SPHONE	Character	20	
8	DUEDAYS	Numeric	2	
9	DISCOUNT	Numeric	4	
10	DISCDAYS	Numeric	2	
11	SNOTES	Character	3	

FIGURE 13-2 Supplier data definitions.

Field	Field Name	Type	Width	Dec
1	INAME	Character	40	
2	INUMB	Character	40	
3	ISUPPL	Character	2	
4	ROP	Numeric	4	
5	ROQ	Numeric	4	
6	ONHAND	Numeric	4	
7	ONORDER	Numeric	4	
8	IPRICE	Numeric	8	2
9	NPRICE	Numeric	8	2

FIGURE 13-3 Supplier data definitions

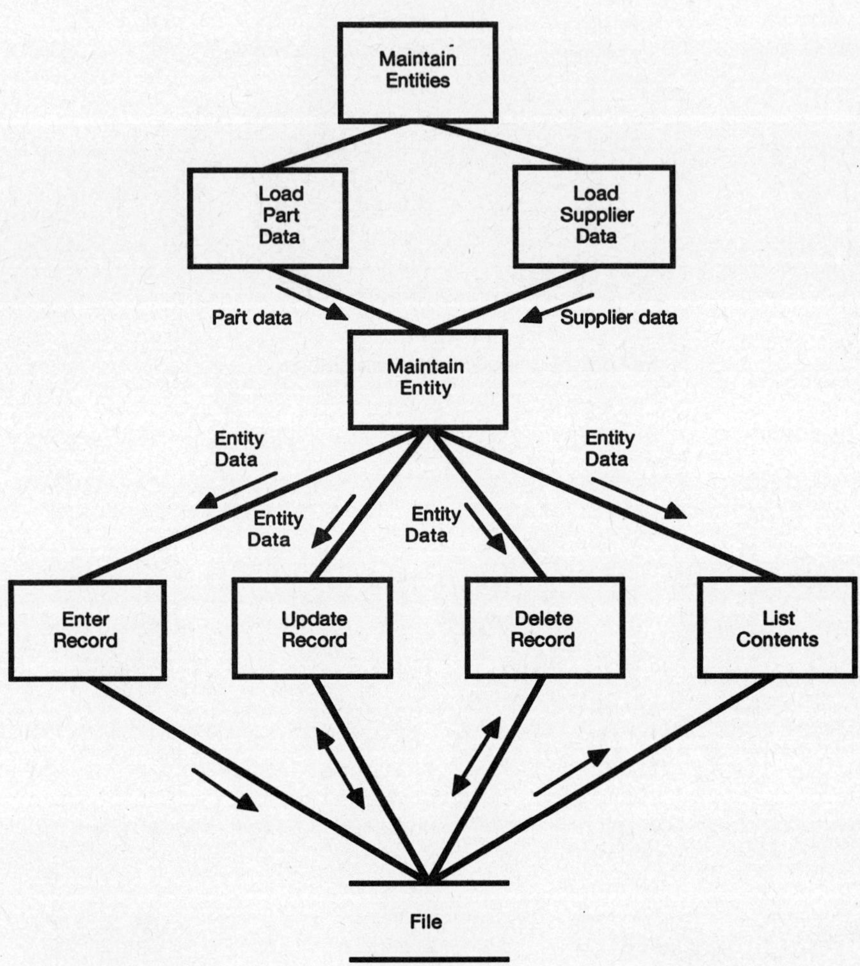

FIGURE 13-4 Structure chart fragment: maintain permanent entities.

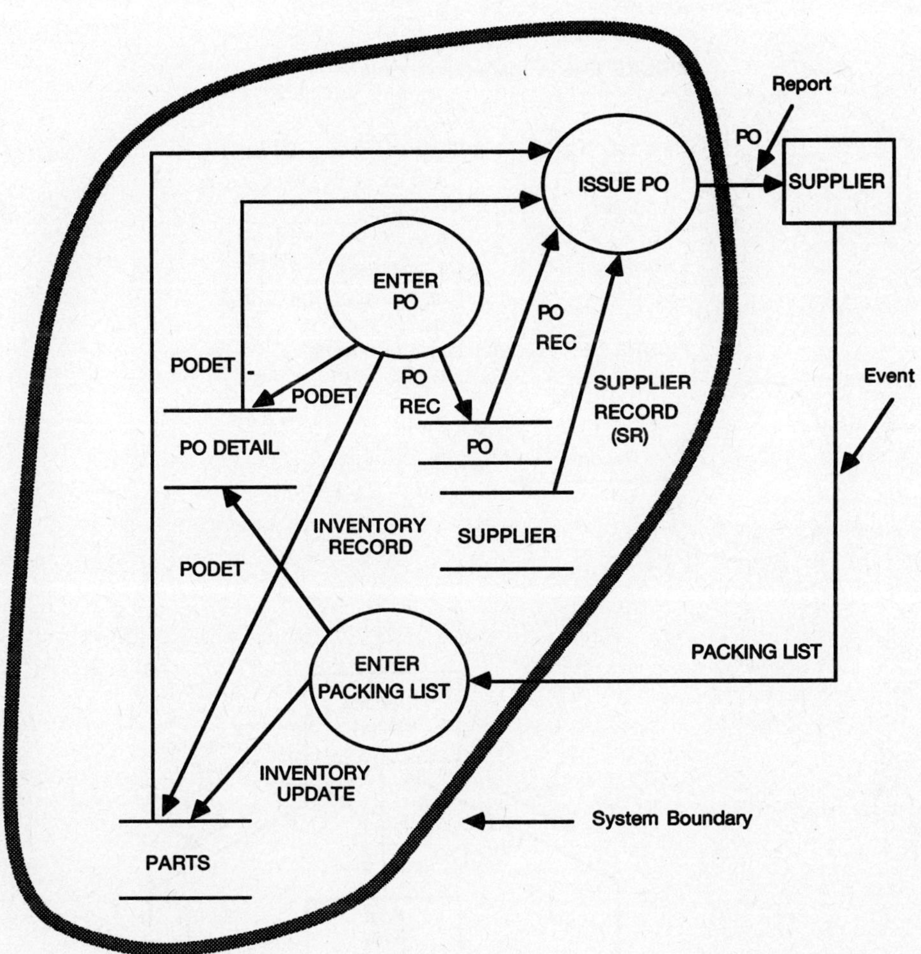

FIGURE 13-5 Data flow diagram.

Field	Field Name	Type	Width	Dec
1	PONUMB	Character	6	
2	PODATE	Character	8	
3	POSUPP	Character	40	
4	POPAID	Character	1	

FIGURE 13-6 PO data definitions.

Field	Field Name	Type	Width	Dec
1	PONUMB	Character	6	
2	POQUANT	Numeric	84	
3	QRECEIVED	Numeric	44	
4	INUMB	Character	40	
6	IPRICE	Numeric	8	2

FIGURE 13-7 PO detail data definitions.

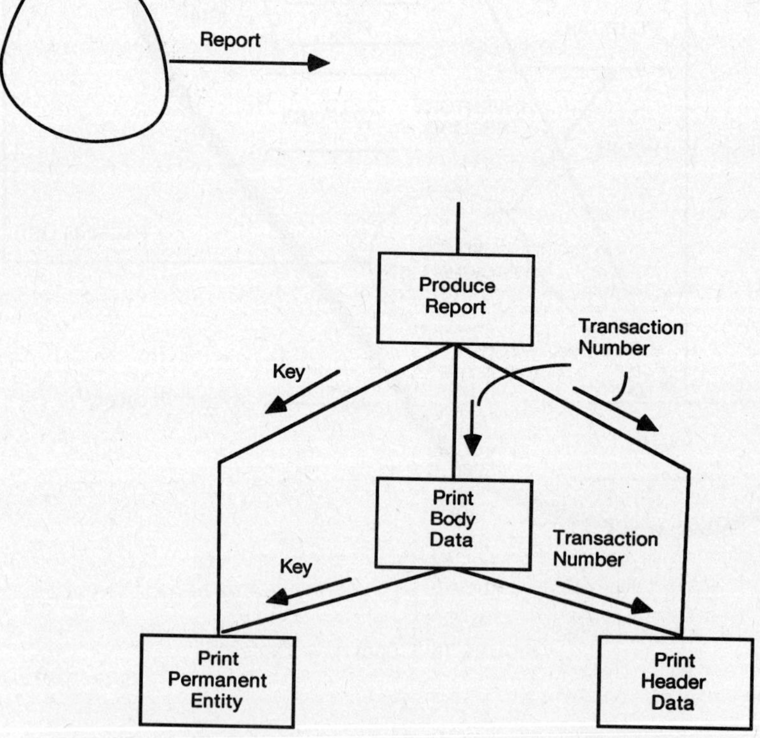

FIGURE 13-8 Structure chart for report from object-based design.

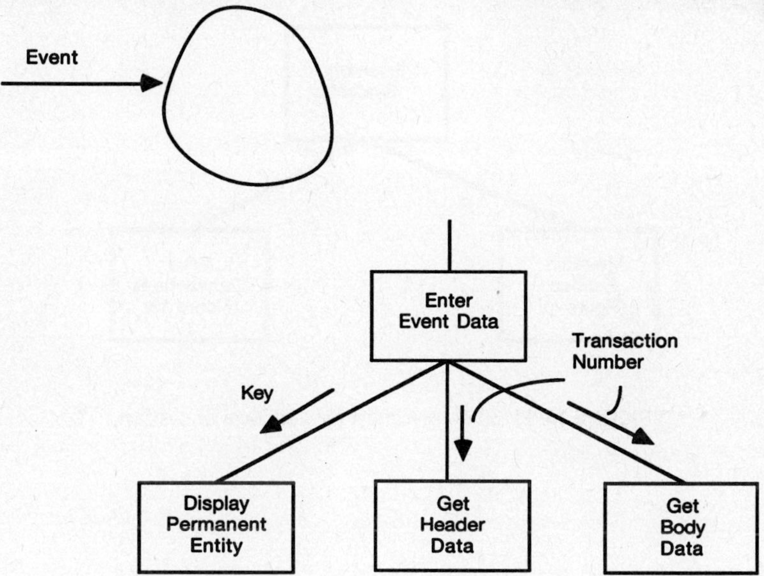

FIGURE 13-9 Structure chart for event from object-based design.

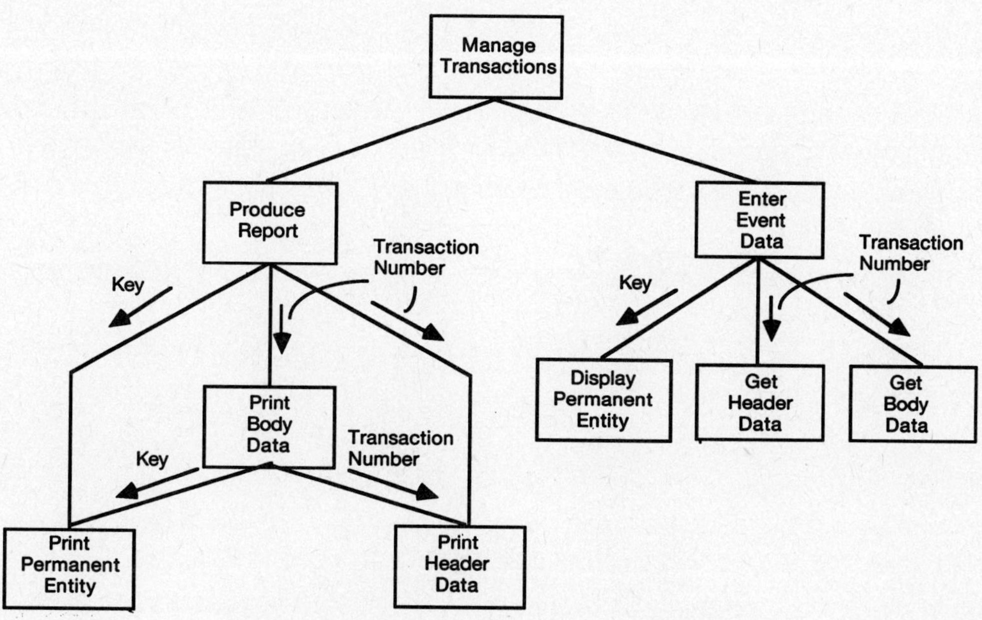

FIGURE 13-10 Structure chart segment for transactions.

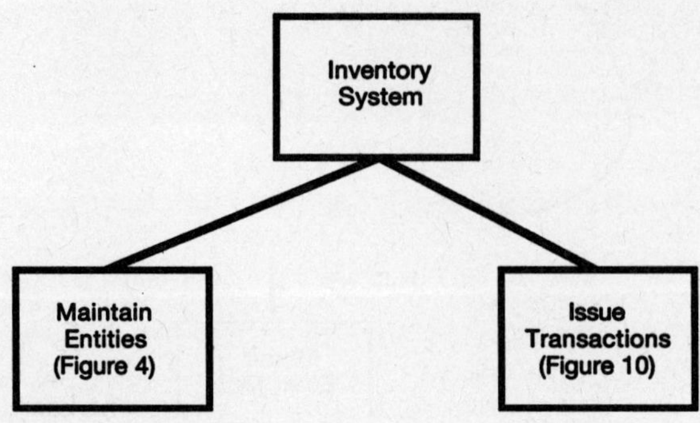

FIGURE 13-11 Structure chart for top level of system.

Section IV

DESIGN OF INDIVIDUAL MODULES

This section discusses how to design the contents of individual modules once the architectural design has been completed. Figure S-4-1 reviews where we are in the program development life-cycle.

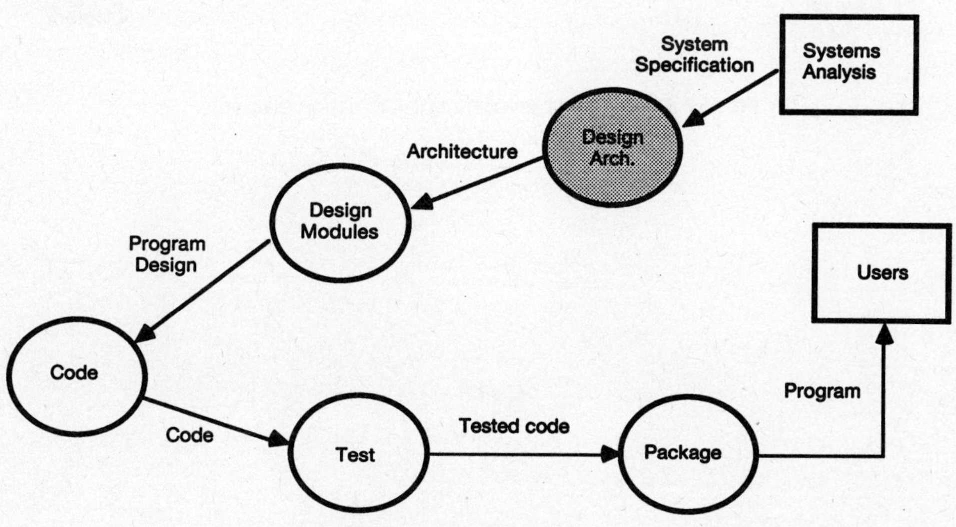

FIGURE S-4-1 Where we are.

Module designs consist of action diagrams (Chapter 14) and data dictionary entries. There is one action diagram for each module (Figure S-4-2); this shows what operations get done in what order to solve the task assigned to a module. In other words, this is the stage at which modules cease to be black boxes. Given that the overall problem solution has been established, the designer now has only to take each smaller subtask and solve it in isolation from larger issues. In other words, at this stage we are designing a series of small programs, the interrelationships of which have been defined in previous stages of the design process.

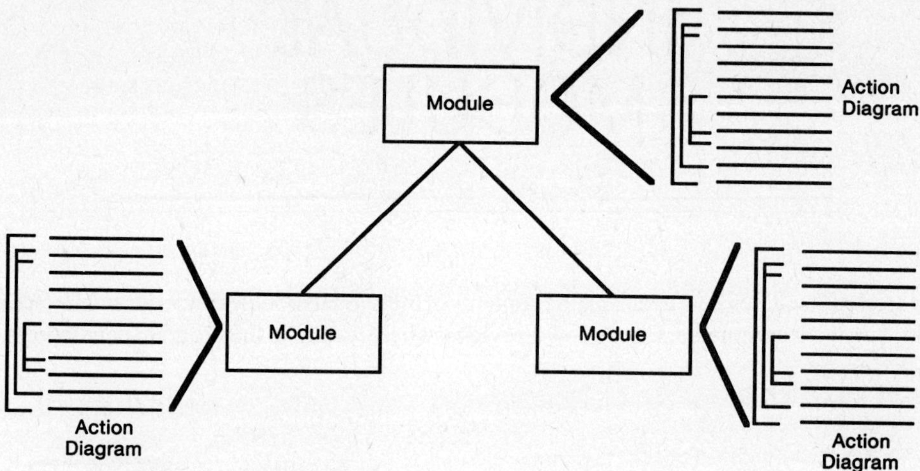

FIGURE S-4-2 Expansion of modules to action diagrams.

Chapter 14

CONTROL STRUCTURES, OPERATIONS AND STRUCTURED PROGRAMMING

CHAPTER GOALS

- Learn detailed design of modules using action diagrams.
- Learn use of standard control structures.
- Learn use of standard operations.
- Learn to translate simple action diagrams into dBASE code.

Up to this point, we have looked at notation to describe system architecture, program architecture, and data structure. We still need a notation to describe the content of modules. Figure 14-1 reviews where we are in the program development life-cycle.

The notation used to describe the details of the Design Modules phase of program design was at the center of the "structured programming" controversy of twenty years ago. The problem was in establishing which control structures to use and how to represent them. Before going into these issues, let us review what is meant by an operation and what is meant by a control structure.

In Section II, we discussed *data*—what a program processes. *Operations* are the manipulations which can be performed on data. *Control structures* determine which operations get performed on which data under what conditions. Operations and control

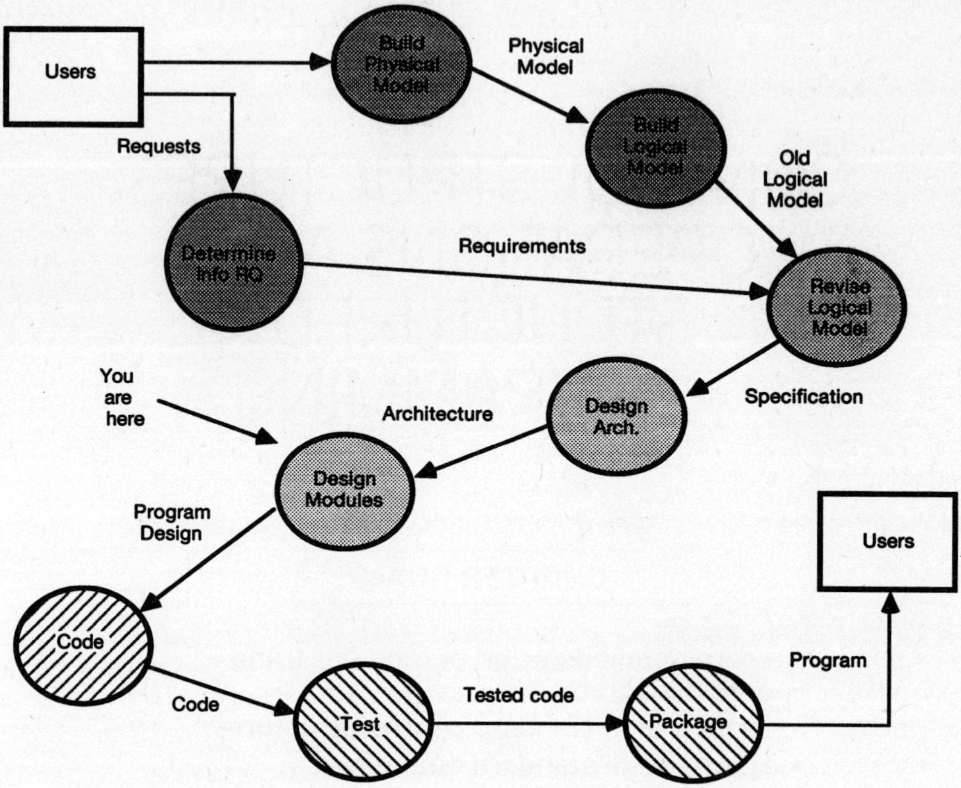

Users
Build Physical Model
Physical Model
Build Logical Model
Requests
Old Logical Model
Determine Info RQ
Requirements
Revise Logical Model
You are here
Architecture
Design Arch.
Specification
Design Modules
Program Design
Users
Code
Program
Tested code
Code
Test
Package

System Architecture Specification = Entity-relationship diagram + data dictionary + overview data flow diagram

Program Architecture = Structure chart + data dictionary + screen definitions + views + report layouts

Program Design = Structure chart + action diagrams + data Dictionary + screen definitions + views + report layouts

Section II
Section III
Section IV
Section V
Section VI

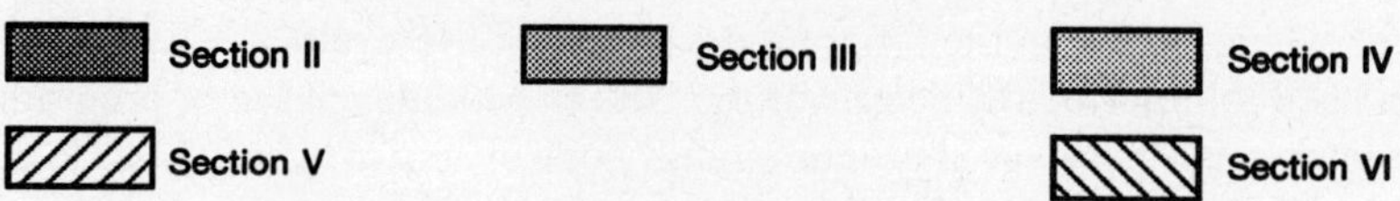

FIGURE 14-1 control structures and operations in the program developmetn life-cycle.

structures are combined to specify *algorithms*, the logical steps taken to perform a task. A *program* is made up of *modules*; each of which contains data and an algorithm.

OPERATIONS

The things that one can do to a piece of data depend primarily on the level of language in use (second, third, or fourth generation). Figure 14-2 shows the operations that are provided by most assembly-level languages. Figure 14-3 shows the operations provided by most third generation languages, such as COBOL, BASIC, or PASCAL. Figure 14-4 shows the operations normally provided by fourth generation languages. The syntax (way in which the statement is written) will vary from language to language, but the operation types are the same.

1. MOVE
   1.1 LOAD REGISTER
   1.2. STORE REGISTER
   1.3. EXCHANGE
   1.4. PUSH
   1.5. POP
2. ARITHMETIC
   2.1. COMPLEMENT
   2.2. ADD
   2.3. SUBTRACT
   2.4. MULTIPLY
   2.5. DIVIDE
   2.6. INCREMENT
   2.7. DECREMENT
3. LOGICAL
   3.1. AND
   3.2. OR
   3.3. NOT
   3.4. XOR
   3.5. SET
   3.6. BIT
   3.7. SHIFT
   3.8. ROTATE
4. CONTROL
   4.1. CALL
   4.2. RETURN
   4.3. BRANCH
   4.4. TEST
   4.5. LOOP

FIGURE 14-2 Operations at the assembly level

Note that each level of language is cumulative—third generation languages contain many of the same types of operations as those found in second generation languages and fourth generation languages contain many of the same types as those found in third generation languages. What differs is partly the addition of new, more powerful operations (e.g., relational operations in fourth generation languages) and partly the application of the same types of operations to higher-level data structures (e.g., databases in a fourth generation language as opposed to a machine register in a second generation language).

1. MOVE
2. ARITHMETIC
   2.1. ADD
   2.2. SUBTRACT
   2.3. MULTIPLY
   2.4. DIVIDE
   2.5. FUNCTIONS
3. STRING
   3.1. EXTRACT SUBSTRING
   3.2. CONCATENATE
   3.3. COMPARE
4. LOGICAL
   4.1. AND
   4.2. OR
   4.3. NOT
   4.4. BIT
5. CONVERT DATA TYPES
6. INPUT/OUTPUT
   6.1. OPEN
   6.2. CLOSE
   6.3. READ
   6.4. WRITE
   6.5. REWRITE
7. CONTROL
   7.1. CALL
   7.2. TEST
   7.3. BRANCH
   7.4. IF-THN-ELSE
   7.5. DO-WHILE
   7.6. REPEEAT-UNTIL
   7.7. FOR
   7.8. CASE

FIGURE 14-3 Operations at the high-level language level.

Movement Operations

Movement of data is the basis of most business data processing. There are three types of containers for data: memory, disk, and input/output devices. Devices in dBASE can include the keyboard, the screen, and the printer. Operations for movement can move data between any combination of these, giving the following possibilities:

1. MOVE
2. ARITHMETIC
    2.1. ADD
    2.2. SUBTRACT
    2.3. MULTIPLY
    2.4. DIVIDE
    2.5. FUNCTIONS
3. STRING
    3.1. EXTRACT SUBSTRING
    3.2. CONCATENATE
    3.3. COMPARE
4. LOGIAL
    4.1. AND
    4.2. OR
    4.3. NOT
5. CONVERT DATA TYPES
6. INPUT/OUTPUT
    6.1. OPEN
    6.2. CLOSE
    6.3. READ
    6.4. WRITE
    6.5. REWRITE
7. RELATIONAL
    7.1 SELECT
    7.2. PROJECT
    7.3. JOIN
    7.4. UPDATE
    7.5. SORT
8. CONTROL
    8.1. CALL
    8.2. TEST
    8.3. BRANCH
    8.4. IF-THEN-ELSE
    8.5. DO-WHILE
    8.6. REPEAT-UNTIL
    8.7. FOR
    8.8. CASE

FIGURE 14-4 Operations at the very-high-level language level.

Memory-to-memory moves in dBASE are accomplished with the `STORE` or = operator.

Memory-to-disk moves in dBASE are accomplished with the `REPLACE` operator.

Memory-to-devices moves in dBASE are accomplished with the `PRINT` or `SAY` operator.

Disk-to-memory moves in dBASE are accomplished with the `STORE` or = operator.

Disk-to-disk moves in dBASE are accomplished with the `REPLACE` operator or `COPY` command.

Disk-to-device moves in dBASE are accomplished with the `PRINT` or `SAY` operator or `COPY` command.

Device-to-memory moves in dBASE are accomplished with the `READ` operator.

Device-to-disk moves in dBASE are accomplished with the `READ` or `GET` operator.

Device-to-device moves in dBASE are accomplished with programs that use memory variables as intermediate storage. Such moves can be accomplished directly in MSDOS.

All of these operators are described in more detail in Chapter 18.

Arithmetic Operations

Arithmetic operations in dBASE allow the performance of common mathematical operations (addition, subtraction, multiplication, division, and exponentiation). More complicated mathematical operations (statistical, financial, and trigonometrical) are performed with built-in functions. Along with the rest of the dBASE operations, these operators are described in more detail in Chapter 17.

Functions Operations

Functions are calls to predefined modules that return a single value. They may be mathematical, string, or logical. They may also involve the conversion of data types (e.g.,

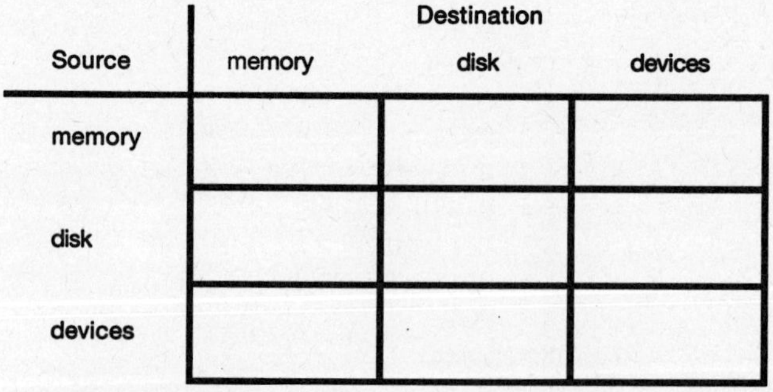

	Destination		
Source	memory	disk	devices
memory			
disk			
devices			

FIGURE 14-5 Types of move operations.

Structured Programming (Coding)

1. Limited number of building blocks
2. Standard representations
3. Procedures for construction

Structured Design

1. The right modules
2. Minimal connections
3. Program architecture

FIGURE 14-6 Structured programming versus structured design.

between date and character). Along with the rest of the dBASE operations, these operators are described in more detail in Chapter 17.

Relational Operations

Relational operations work with entire tables. They involve either the step-by-step specification of how data in tables should be combined or set asunder (dBASE native mode, also known as "relational algebra") or the specification of the results without step-by-step instructions (as in SQL mode in dBASE IV, also known as "relational calculus"). These operators are described in more detail in Chapters 17 and 18.

CONTROL STRUCTURES

Control structures specify in what order and under what conditions the program will perform operations. The appropriate choice of control strucures was at the heart of the "structured programming" movement of the late 1960s. Figure 14-6 summarizes the essentials of the movement and how it differs from what is popularly known as "structured design."

Structured programming was the first of what this book calls "modern programming practices". By itself it did not do much to solve the programming problems outlined in Chapter 1, although it did help improve program maintainability. It was, however, successful enough that the program development methods and methodologies that followed during the 1970s and 1980s were referred to as "structured" even though they have no connection with control structures.

Basically, structured programming meant eliminating the unrestricted use of the "test-and-branch" control structure from assembly language (also known as GOTO—Figure 14-7). The restriction imposed was that each higher-level control structure (which was constructed from test and branch) could have a single procedural entry point and a single exit. Figure 14-8 shows the theory in flowchart form.

```
1000 'UPDATE MEMORY
1005 CURRENTCOLUMN = 2
1010 COLOR 7,0;:LOCATE I,1,0:PRINT MENU$(MENUPOS)
1015 IF WHICHMEMORY <>0
THEN I=WHICHMEMORY-BEGINMEM:LOCATE I,COLUMN(1),1:GOSUB 600
1020 I=2
1030 J=COLUMN(1)
1040 LOCATE I,J
1050 GOSUB 600'PRINT line
1060 J+COLUMN(1)
1065 LOCATE I,J
1070 GOSUB 700' get key
1080 IF SELECTION = 0 THEN 1130'ELSE ENTER key pressed
1090 WHICHMEMORY=I+BEGINMEM
1100 I=MENUSTART+1
1110 J=1
1115 LOCATE I,J
1120 RETURN
1130 LOCATE I,J' begin THEN clause
1135 IF A$>"*" THEN 1200'is letter or number
1136 IF I=K THEN 1178' no change in row
1137 IF K+BEGINMEM > LASTENTRY THEN LASTENTRY = K+BEGINMEM
1140 GOSUB 600
1145 I=K:J=COLUMN (1)
1150 COLOR 15,0
1155 LOCATE I,J
1160 GOSUB 600
1162 COLOR 7,0
1163 J=COLUMN(CURRENT COLUMN)
1166 LOCATE I,J
1168 GOTO 1070'no change in row
1178 J=COLUMN(CURRENT COLUMN)
1179 LOCATE I,J
1180 GOTO 1070
1200 PRINT A$;
1201 GOSUB 900'get rest of keyboard string
1210 FOR N=1 TO 8:IF J>COLUMN(N) THEN CURRENTCOLUMN=N:NEXT N
1200 ON (CURRENT COLUMN) GOSUB 1300,1320,1340,1360,1390,1400
1230 COLOR 15,0
1240 GOSUB 600
1250 COLOR 7,0
1255 CURRENTCOLUMN=CURRENTCOLUMN+2
1256 J=COLUMN(CURRENTCOLUMN)
1257 IF CURRENTCOLUMN>8 THEN CURRENT COLUMN=2
1259 LOCATE I,J
1260 GOTO 1070
```

FIGURE 14-7 Test and branch (BASIC language; GOTOs highlighted).

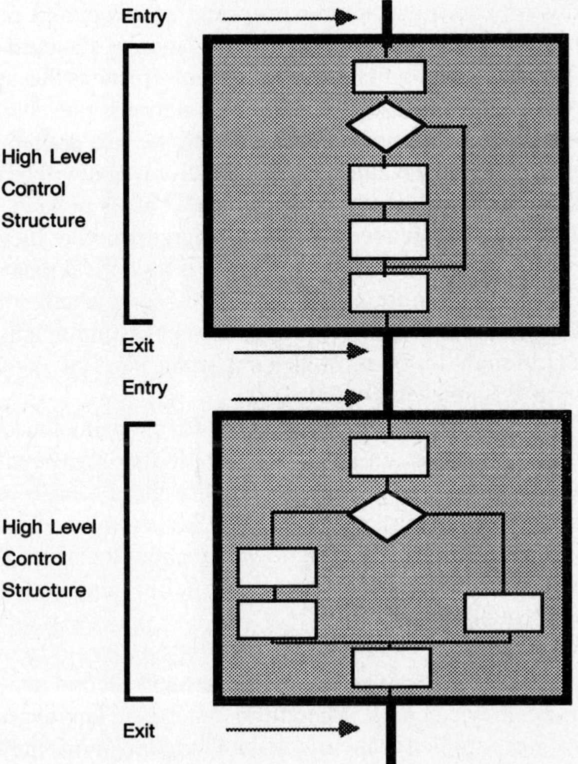

FIGURE 14-8 The basic structured programming restriction.

Flowcharts
Structured English
Informal Pseudocode
Formal Pseudocode
Nassi-Shneiderman Charts
Action Diagrams

FIGURE 14-9 Alternative notations for control structures.

The restrictions on control structures proposed by structured programming have taken two forms: specification of notation and specification of standard control structures for use. We discuss here the notation first, then the control structures that are currently in use.

Figure 14-9 shows the major contenders for notations, presented in approximate order of development. For the remainder of this book we use *action diagrams*. Before presenting these, let us examine the alternatives. The discussion will be organized around the section of dBASE III code illustrated in Figure 10. This is in some ways backwards, since all of these notations are intended to design programs before they are coded rather than to document existing programs. However, there is no logical reason why we cannot work backwards. The code in Figure 14-10 is probably somewhat confusing, especially since I have made no effort to explain it! It illustrates the reason for using noncode design tools; Figures 14-11 through 14-14 show the important parts of Figure 14-10 without getting us caught up in the unnecessary details.

This series of figures illustrates the two reasons for choosing to work with a notation other than code at the module design level. The first is that many real-world computer languages do not have features we might like, so their use unduly constrains the design. The other, more important reason is that using one of these notations allows the designer to concentrate on the algorithm without having to worry about the syntactical details of the coding language. In other words, this is an approach to partitioning the program design task into more manageable chunks.

Flowcharts were first developed during the 1950s as an aid to understanding and documenting the structure of programs written in first and second generation languages (which need all the help they can get). When third generation languages were adopted in the 1960s, flowcharts were applied to them—in many organizations they were required as a form of systems documentation. Figure 14-11 shows the program of Figure 14-10 in flowchart form.

There are several problems with flowcharts. The first, and most serious, is that at the program detail level, they were developed to represent primitive assembly-language level control structures and therefore are not really suited to modern programming languages. They are also tedious to draw and more tedious to maintain. Hence, they are seldom kept up to date (although that problem has been alleviated by automated graphics packages). Moreover, research has shown that they are not useful as a design aid. We now know that this is because their use produces programs with *procedural cohesion* (discussed in Chapter 12), which is a fairly low level of module quality. At the overall systems level, they produce premature physical packaging (but this is a systems analysis problem and therefore not relevant here).

Flowcharts were at one time widely accepted (and often required) in industry. They are still fairly popular among community colleges (which teach them) and garage-shop programmers (who produce programs to automate them). Robert Glass, in his excellent book *The Power of Peonage*, tells an amusing story about how flowcharts fell from grace at a major corporation a long time ago in a universe far, far away [Glass 1979].

It seems that this organization, like many others at the time, required that all programs be flowcharted—a requirement that was unpopular with the programmers. The require-

```
*************************
* Client Entry CUSSTEND *
*************************
USE CLIENT
DO WHILE .T.
   CLEAR
   @ 1,1 SAY "Customer entry"
   APPEND BLANK
   SET FORMAT TO CUST.FMT
   READ
   STORE CNUMBER TO NN
   IF SUBSTR(NN,1,1)="NA"
       STORE HPHONE TO TEMP
       IF SUBSTR(TEMP,1,4)=""
              STORE WPHONE TO TEMP
       ENDIF
       IF SUBSTR(TEMP,9,1)="
              STORE SUBSTR(TEMP,7,3)+SUBSTR(TEMP,5,4) TO TEMP 1
       ELSE
              STORE SUBSTR(TEMP,7,3)+SUBSTR(TEMP,11,4) TO TEMP1
       ENDIF
       REPLACE CNUMBER WITH TEMP1
   ENDIF
   @ 16,5 SAY ""
   ACCEPT "Another customer (Y or N) " TO YN
   IF YN="N"
       CLOSE FORMAT
       ACCEPT "Do you want to index added record(s) now (Y or N)?" TO YN
       IF YN="Y"
              ? "Please stand by for sort and index"
              SORT ON LNAME TO TEMP
              USE WO
              RENAME CLIENT.DBF TO XXXX.DBF
              RENAME TEMP.DBF TO CLIENT.DBF
              DELETE FILE XXXX.DBF
              USE CLIENT
              INDEX ON CNUMBER TO CLIDE
              INDEX ON LNAME TO CLNAME
       ENDIF
       RETURN
   ENDIF
ENDDO T
```

FIGURE 14-10 dBASE III code segment used for control structure examples.

ment became even less popular after the publication of academic studies showing that flowcharts were, at best, useless. These studies did not, of course, change the requirement, which had become written into official corporate Standard Operating Procedures, which were subject to the usual glacial rate of change.

However, times were different then, and the programmers, most of whom were young, had recently graduated from universities where they had been involved in civil disobedience to reform society and bring about Truth, Justice, and World Peace. As a result, it seemed natural to take direct action—in this case, collecting the polystyrene flowcharting templates and piling them in symbolic protest in the middle of the computer room floor. By the standards of the day, this was a very mild protest, so no one paid attention. Making a bonfire out of the symbolic protest worked much better, due in large part to the combination of dense black smoke from burning polystyrene and the use of automatic sprinkling systems in computer rooms! After a certain amount of unpleasantness, the flowcharting requirement was abolished.

Structured English was one of the more popular replacements for flowcharting. It is the module documentation method of choice in the Yourdon system design methodology, so it has become very widely used. The rules are:

- All sentences are imperative
- All nouns are from the Data Dictionary

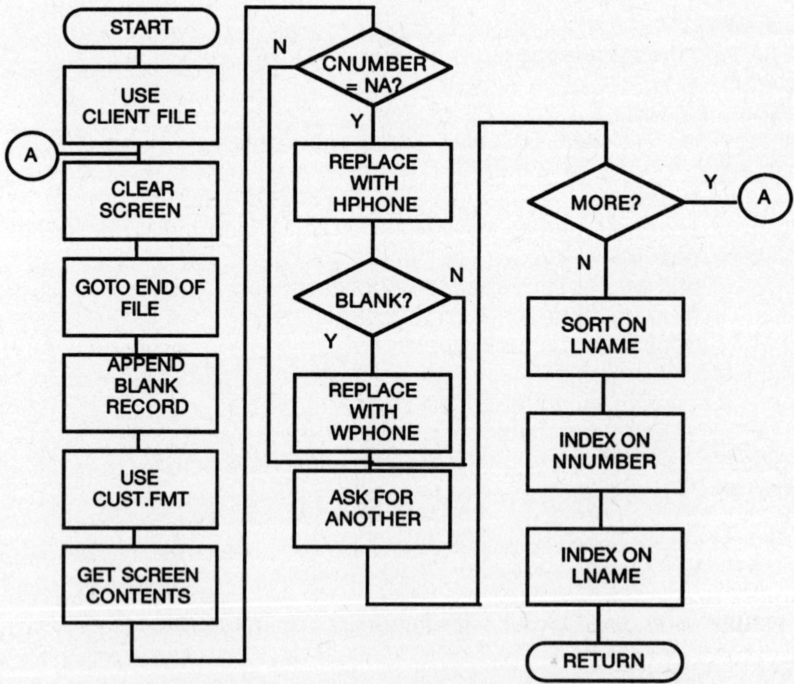

FIGURE 14-11 Flowchart example.

Figure 14-12 is our example in structured English.

The major advantage of structured English is that end users can read it, in many cases without realizing that they are reading design documentation. Thus, the user can be more involved in making sure that the system under construction is indeed the one desired. The major disadvantage of structured English is that it can be almost as unclear as normal English, especially where control structures are concerned.

Informal pseudocode is structured English with the additional requirement that all control structures be specified in a standard fashion. Figure 14-13 shows our example. There is no standard for the control structure representation; most authors suggest using the notation from the language PASCAL. An alternative suggestion is to use the control structure notation from whatever fourth generation language you are using—in our case dBASE. That is the convention used in this book. In the example, control structures and nouns from the data dictionary are in capital letters. Informal pseudocode is probably the most widely used notation in the "real world" today. It is easy to produce, easy to maintain, maps readily into programming languages (often mechanically) and, at higher levels, users can understand it. Its only major disadvantage is that it is nongraphical, so it does not take advantage of the human information processing system's strengths at pattern recognition. *Action diagrams* (discussed later) overcome this problem through a simple extension of informal pseudocode.

Formal pseudocode is a version of pseudocode that follows a rigorous set of rules—about as rigorous as a programming language. Its major use is in mathematical proofs of correctness and in automatic translation from pseudocode to programming language. The major disadvantages are that end users have no hope of understanding it (and are not likely to even look at it!) and that the level of concentration on syntax is such that one might as well program directly in the target language.

Nassi-Shneiderman charts are a modern form of flowchart. They use a more modern set of control structures and preserve the advantages of graphical format. The disadvantages are that end users cannot understand them and that they are tedious to maintain.

```
use CLIENT datafile
clear screen
goto end of file
append blank record
use CUST.FMT screen
get screen contents
if CNUMBER="NA" replace CNUMBER with HPHONE
if HPHONE is BLANK replace CNUMBER with WPHONE, as for another customer
if there are no more customers, sort on LNAME, index on CNUMBER, and index on LNAME
otherwise, repeat the above.
```

FIGURE 14-12 Structured english example.

Action diagrams as illustrated in Figure 14-14 are informal pseudocode with a simple graphical overlay. They preserve the advantages of informal pseudocode and add the advantages of pattern recognition. They will be used throughout the rest of this book.

Choice of Control Structures

There are two sets of modern control structures in common use. The first is a minimum set of three control structures that theoretically are sufficient for all tasks. These are illustrated in Figure 14-15 (details will be discussed later). The second is a somewhat larger set of control strutures that have been found to be useful in practice. These are illustrated in Figures 14-16 through 14-25.

Sequence, as illustrated in Figure 14-16, is the simplest control structure; operations are executed one after another in order. The action diagram notation is a bracket, showing that the statements are a group. Often the bracket is omitted.

IF-THEN-ELSE (true/false condition), illustrated in Figure 14-17 is another basic structure. Statements following the THEN clause are executed if the condition is true; those following the optional ELSE clause are executed if the condition is false. The block ends with ENDIF so that there is no question as to which statements are included. The action diagram notation is a bracket with branches to both the THEN and the ELSE clauses. dBASE follows this syntax, except that the THEN is omitted, as illustrated in Figure 14-26.

```
use CLIENT datafile
DO FOREVER
  clear screen
  goto end of file
  append blank record
  use CUST.FMT screen
  get screen contents
  IF CNUMBER="NA"
  THEN replace CNUMBER with HPHONE
      IF HPHONE is BLANK
      THEN replace CNUMBER with WPHONE
  ENDIF
ENDIF
ask for another customer (YES or NO)
IF NO
  THEN sort file on LNAME
      index on CNUMBER
      index on LNAME
  ENDIF
  BREAK
ENDDO
RETURN
```

FIGURE 14-13 Pseudocode exmple.

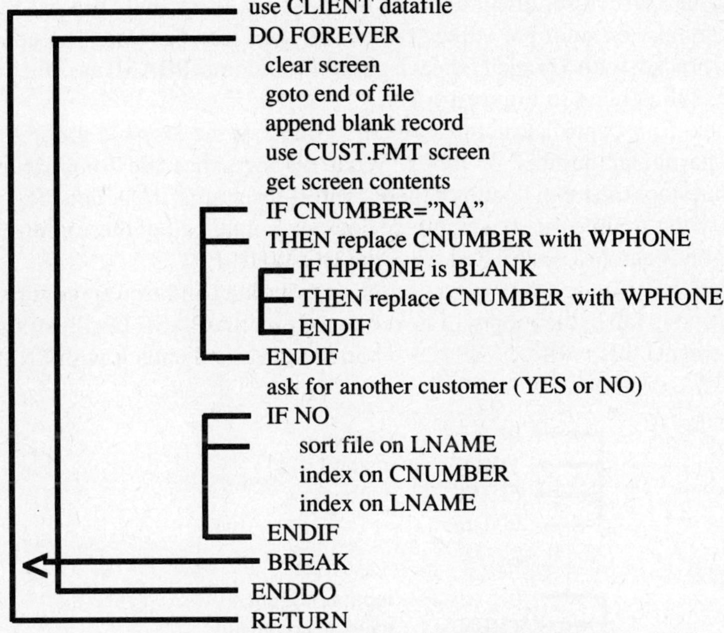

FIGURE 14-14 Action diagram example.

SEQUENCE
IF-THEN-ELSE-ENDIF
DO WHILE

FIGURE 14-15 Minimum set of control structures.

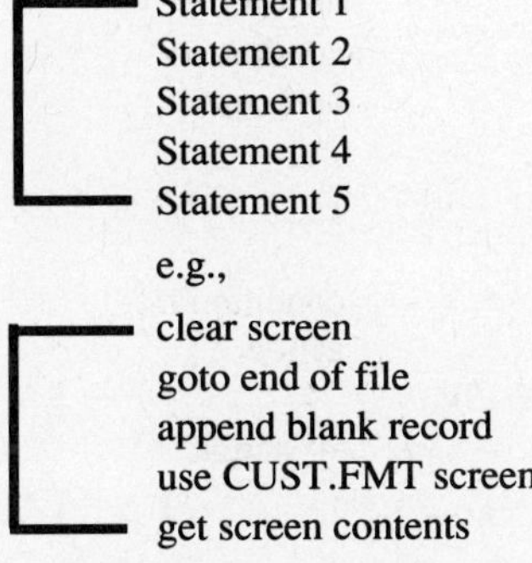

FIGURE 14-16 Sequence.

The CASE structure, illustrated in Figure 14-18, is an IF-THEN-ELSE where the condition can take on multiple values rather than just true or false. The action diagram notation is a bracket with a branch for each possible outcome. dBASE uses the same format; an example is illustrated in Figure 14-27).

The next four control structures are all variants of the *loop*—a group of statements repeated a particular number of times. What distinguishes the four variations is the condition that stops the loop. For all of these control structures, the action diagram notation is a bracket with a double top. If a language does not contain all of these control structures, the missing ones can be constructed from the DO WHILE.

DO WHILE (Figure 14-19) tests for the appropriate condition at the start of the loop. If the condition is false, the loop will never be executed. dBASE (as illustrated in Figure 14-28 implements this with `DO WHILE condition` and ends it with `ENDDO`.

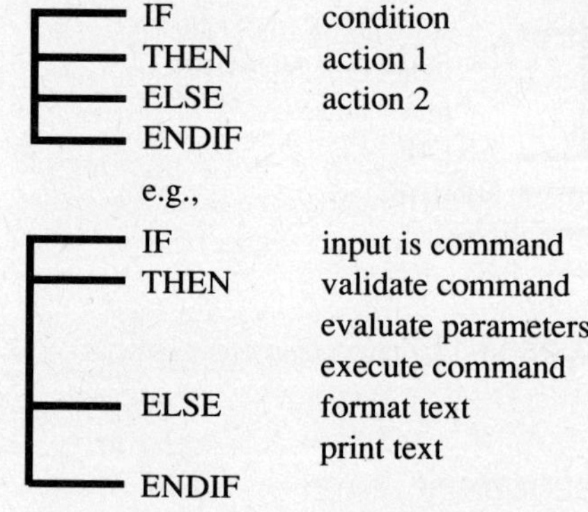

FIGURE 14-17 IF THEN ELSE.

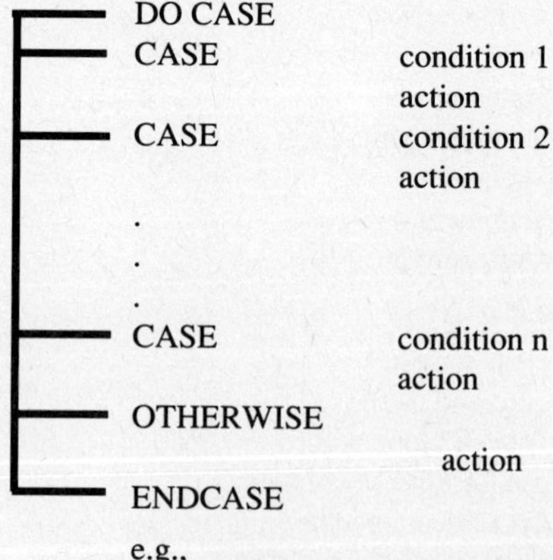

FIGURE 14-18 CASE. (continued)

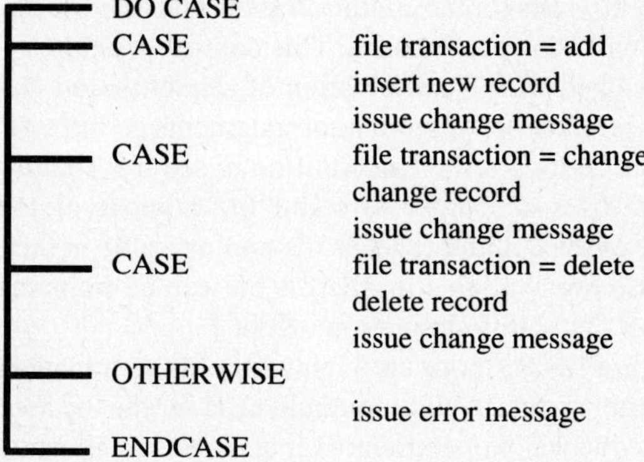

FIGURE 14-18 CASE.

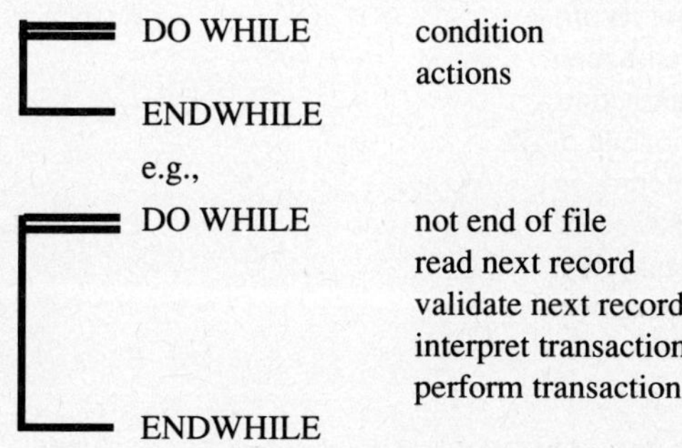

FIGURE 14-19 DO WHILE.

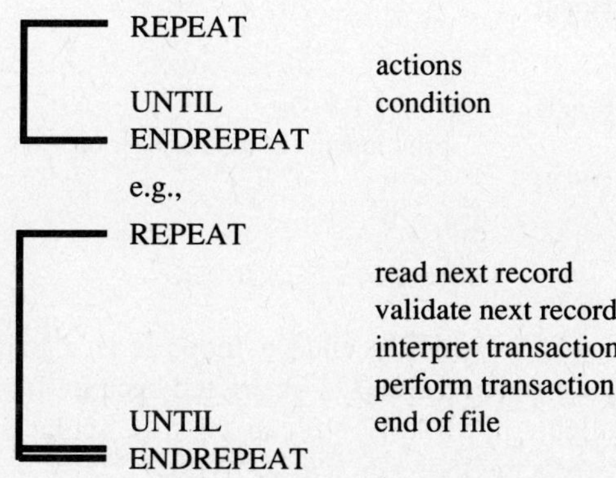

FIGURE 14-20 REPEAT UNTIL.

REPEAT (Figure 14-20) tests for the condition at the end of the loop. If the condition is not true, the statements will be executed once. This control structure is not available in dBASE, but can be synthesized with a combination of sequence and `DO WHILE`, as illustrated in Figure 14-21. Here, the set of sequential statements go through the process one time, and then the `DO WHILE` loop tests the condition to see if it should continue.

FOR (Figure 14-22) uses a counter to count the number of loop iterations. It terminates when the value of the counter reaches the ending value in the TO clause. This control structure is likewise not available in dBASE but can be implemented with a `DO WHILE`. Figure 14-23 shows how this simulation works.

DO FOREVER (Figure 14-24) loops until it is explicitly terminated (with a BREAK statement or by the end of the module). It is commonly used for the top levels of a program, which carry out the same sequence of operations over and over. As illustrated in Figure 14-26, it is implemented in dBASE with `DO WHILE .T.`

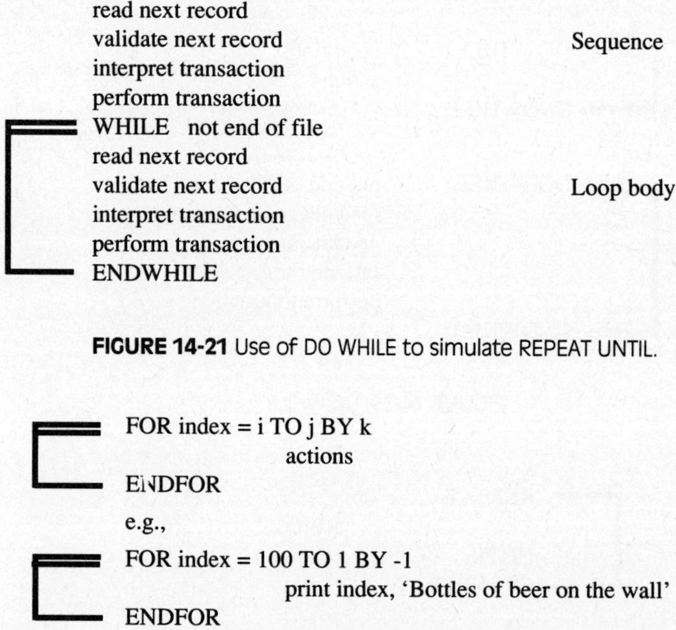

FIGURE 14-21 Use of DO WHILE to simulate REPEAT UNTIL.

FIGURE 14-22 FOR INDEX.

BREAK (Figure 14-25) explicitly ends a loop. It is usually used for unusual conditions. It is basically a restricted GOTO—restricted because it can go only to the end of the loop. It is not available in dBASE, but can often be replaced with an alternative dBASE command that breaks the loop (such as `RETURN`).

Figure 14-26 illustrates the translation of DO FOREVER (light shaded box) and IF-THEN-ELSE (darker shaded box) into dBASE III; Figure 14-27 illustrates `DO WHILE` (light shaded box) and `CASE` (darker shaded box). Note that `EOF ()` indicates the condition *end of file* and can take on the values true or false. `ACCEPT "message" TO memory variable` displays the message on the screen, and puts the next word typed on the keyboard into the memory variable. `INPUT` is used instead of `ACCEPT` if a number rather than a word is to be entered from the keyboard. The question mark (`?`) is dBASE for PRINT; it puts a message on the screen.

SUMMARY

Operations are the manipulations that can be performed on data. Control structures determine which operations get performed on which data under what conditions. In specifying the contents of a module, operations and control structures are combined to specify algorithms: the logical steps taken to perform a task. Algorithms are represented by action diagrams. A program is made up of modules; each module contains data and an algorithm, and is documented with an action diagram

It should be emphasized that you produce *a separate action diagram* for each module in a program—not a single large action diagram for the program as a whole.

```
INDEX = 100
DO WHILE index > 0
            print index, 'Bottles of beer on the wall'
            INDEX = INDEX  - 1
ENDWHILE
```

FIGURE 14-23 Use of DO WHILE to simulate FOR INDEX.

```
DO FOREVER
   clear screen
   goto end of file
   append blank record
   use CUST.FMT screen
   get screen contents
   ask for another customer? (YES or NO)
   .
   .
   .
ENDDO
```

FIGURE 14-24 DO FOREVER.

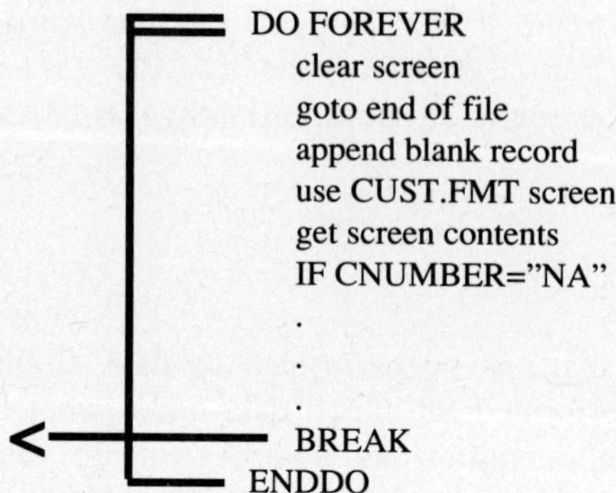

FIGURE 14-25 BREAK.

```
********************************
* Correct Inventory Items INVUP
*
********************************
USE INVENTRY
DO WHILE .T.
ACCEPT "Item number to update?" TO INB
LOCATE FOR NUMB = INB
IF EOF()
? "Can't find that number"
ELSE
SET FORMAT TO INV.FMT
CLEAR
READ
ENDIF
@ 18,5 SAY "  "
ACCEPT "Update another Item (Y or N)" TO YN
IF YN="N"
SET DEVICE TO SCREEN
RETURN
ENDIF
ENDDO
CLOSE DATA BASES
RETURN
```

FIGURE 14-26 DO-FOREVER and IF-THEN-ELSE.

```
DO WHILE .NOT. EOF()
DO CASE
CASE WOTYPE="G"
STORE IPRICE*WOQUANT+TOTALP TO TOTALP
CASE WOTYPE="E"
STORE IPRICE*WOQUANT+TOTALP TO TOTALP
CASE WOTYPE="SH"
STORE IPRICE*WOQUANT+TOTALSH TO TOTALSH
CASE WOTYPE="SB"
STORE IPRICE*WOQUANT+TOTALSB TO TOTALSB
OTHERWISE
STORE IPRICE*WOQUANT+TOTALL TO TOALL
ENDCASE
SKIP
ENDDO
.
.
.
```

FIGURE 14-27 `DO WHILE` and `CASE`.

QUESTIONS AND EXERCISES

1. Structured programming is
   a. The selection of appropriate modules for a program.
   b. The selection of appropriate data structures for a program.
   c. Programming without GOTO statements.
   d Limiting the use of GOTO statements.
2. Detailed flowcharts
   a. Hide the true structure of a program.
   b. Are an essential tool for program design.
   c. Do not match the structure of modern programming languages.
   d. Reveal the true structure of a program.
3. Structured English
   a. Is ordinary English with correct sentence structure required.
   b Is a form of pseudocode.
   c. Uses only nouns from the data dictionary.
   d. Limits the control structures that can be used.
4. Pseudocode
   a. Is program code without format statements.
   b Is another name for structured English.
   c. Uses notation from the PASCAL programming language.
   d. Limits the control structures that can be used.

5. Action diagrams are
   a. Pseudocode with a graphical overlay.
   b. A form of flowchart adapted to modern programming languages.
   c. Used in the Yourdon systems design methodology.
   d. A graphical form of structured English.
6. A DO WHILE control structure
   a. Tests a condition at the top of the loop.
   b. Tests a condition at the bottom of the loop.
   c. Continues a loop until a break statement is encountered.
   d. Will always execute at least once.
7. A REPEAT UNTIL control structure
   a. Is an essential part of modern programming languages.
   b. Will always execute at least once.
   c. Executes until a count limit is reached.
   d. Continues a loop until a BREAK statement is encountered
8. A FOR control structure
   a. Is an essential part of modern programming languages.
   b. Will always execute at least once.
   c. Executes until a count limit is reached.
   d. Continues a loop until a BREAK statement is encountered
9. Which of the following control structures is built into dBASE?
   a. REPEAT UNTIL.
   b. FOR NEXT.
   c. BREAK.
   d. DO WHILE.
10. In an IF-THEN-ELSE control structure
    a. There is a single boolean-valued condition.
    b. Both the THEN and ELSE clauses are required.
    c. Both clauses must be single lines.
    d. Compound conditions may cause neither clause to be executed.
11. A CASE control structure
    a. Guarantees that all possible conditions will have responses.
    b. Requires that there be the same number of responses as there are possible condition values.
    c. Is not provided in dBASE, but can be simulated with nested **IF** statements.
    d. Works with nonboolean variables.

DISCUSSION QUESTIONS

1. What are the possible sources and destinations for data movement? Under what circumstances would you want to use each combination?

2. What are the alternative notations for representing control structures? What are the strengths and weaknesses of each?
3. What are the three minimum control structures required for modern programming? How can all of the other control structures be created from them?
4. Should a programming language include a GOTO statement? Why or why not?

NORTHSTAR AVIATION

Part 9

In the previous section, you set up a structure chart for Northstar's new system. Two of the modules in your structure chart (hopefully) were **MAIN-MENU** and **ISSUE PURCHASE ORDER**. Decide what detailed operations need to be carried out to perform these tasks and produce action diagrams for each.

REFERENCES

GLASS, R. *The Power of Peonage*. Computing Trends Press, Seattle, WA, 1979

MARTIN, J. & C. MCCLURE. *Diagramming Techniques for Analysts and Programmers*. Prentice Hall, Englewood Cliffs, NJ, 1985.

Chapter 15

DATA STRUCTURE BASED DESIGN

CHAPTER GOALS

- **Learn how to use of the Jackson program design method for detailed design of modules.**

Data-structure based design techniques for modules were developed independently by Michael Jackson [Jackson 1975; King 1988] in England and by Jean Dominique Warnier [Warnier 1981; Orr 1977] in France. Both techniques have evolved into full-fledged commercial analysis and design methodologies. This chapter shows how to use the Jackson techniques for the design of individual modules. The presentation is unusual in that these techniques are traditionally presented as program architecture design tools rather than module design tools [Cameron 1986, 1987]. Our approach, which uses them for the module design stage, was brought about by changes in system type and in programming languages, specifically the use of fourth generation languages.

Figure 15-1 reviews the change that has occurred since interactive, screen-oriented systems replaced earlier batch- and command-oriented systems. Most modern systems are organized not as a series of small, separate programs but as an integrated, hierarchical whole. Data-structure based design was originally developed to support the design of smaller, batch-oriented programs; these programs are today's modules. Additionally, these techniques were developed for programming in second and third generation languages. When they are applied to fourth generation languages, the structure charts that they generate have modules that map into a single line of code.

In spite of these changes, data structure oriented design techniques are still among the most useful tools in a programmer's bag of tricks, since they are the most general-purpose tool that we have for the design of individual modules. They can be used in any situation in which we are converting data from one form to another. For example, the events and reports discussed in Chapter 11 all involve conversion from external nonnormalized data to internal normalized data. In most instances, actions and inquiries also involve the conversion of data from one form to another. For all of these, data-structure based design techniques can produce action diagrams to solve the problem.

The techniques are based on the observation that high level data structures are identical to modern control structures. Figure 15-2 reviews the three basic data structures in data-structure diagram form: sequence, alternation (choice), and iteration (repetition). In the data dictionary notation that we have been using in this book, the data structures illustrated in Figure 15-2 are

Name = Lastname + First name + Middle name

Third name = [Middle name | Maiden name]

Customer file = {Customer record}

These structures are identical to the three basic control structures (sequence, alternation, and iteration) that we discussed in Chapter 14. Figure 15-3 reviews these control structures in action diagram format. The additional control structures that we discussed (CASE, REPEAT-UNTIL, FOR, etc.) are all special cases of the three basic structures in Figure 15-3.

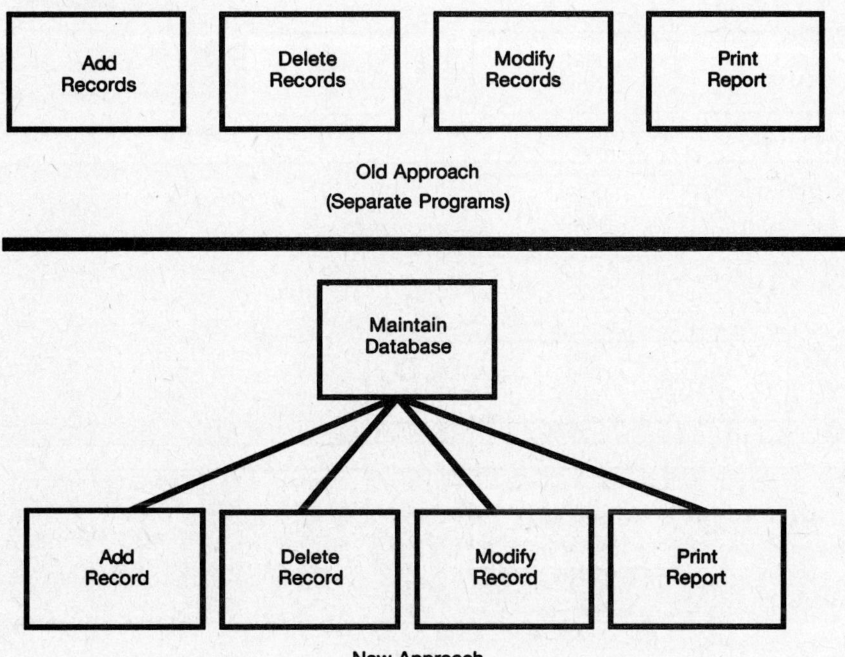

FIGURE 15-1 Expansion of system size.

Given this correspondence between data structures and control structures (Figure 15-4), you have probably already figured out the basic method: map each data structure into the corresponding control structure. In more detail,

- Define data structures for input and output data.
- Map into corresponding control structures to produce module control structures.
- Define module tasks in terms of elementary operations.
- Assign operations to the appropriate control structure.

Examples of elementary operations are MOVE, READ, and ADD, which are illustrated in Figures 14-2, 14-3 and 14-4.

This technique of mapping data structures into control structures can be used to build action diagrams for the standard programming objects such as events and reports, which were discussed in Chapter 11. The rest of this chapter shows how to do this.

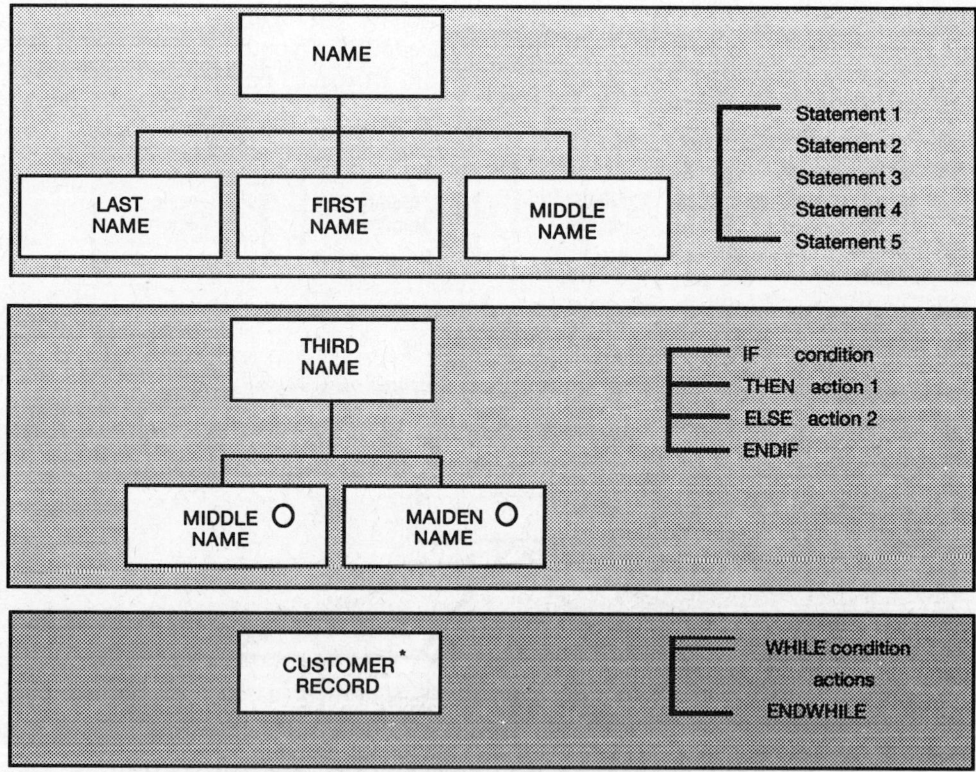

FIGURE 15-2 Basic high-level data structures.

ACTION DIAGRAMS FOR REPORTS

Figure 15-5 reviews the standard structure chart for a report from Chapter 11. Let us see how we can use data-structure based design to design the action diagram for the module **PRODUCE REPORT**. The first step in our procedure is

- Define data structures for input and output data.

The general data structure of a report is

Report = {Permanent entity data + Report header + {body line}}

In English, we have one or more pages, each page containing data on a permanent entity, data about the transaction that the report represents, and a list of detail items (usually concerning another permanent entity). The control structures derived from this data dictionary entry is illustrated in Figure 15-6, and the corresponding action diagram is illustrated in Figure 15-7.

The next step in our procedure is

- Map into corresponding control structures to produce module control structures.

The preceding eport structure can be simplified as

$$\text{Report} = \{x + y + \{z\}\}$$

Which is to say that it consists of iterations of sequential data with another nested iteration within the overall structure. This means that we will have two WHILE loops, one for each

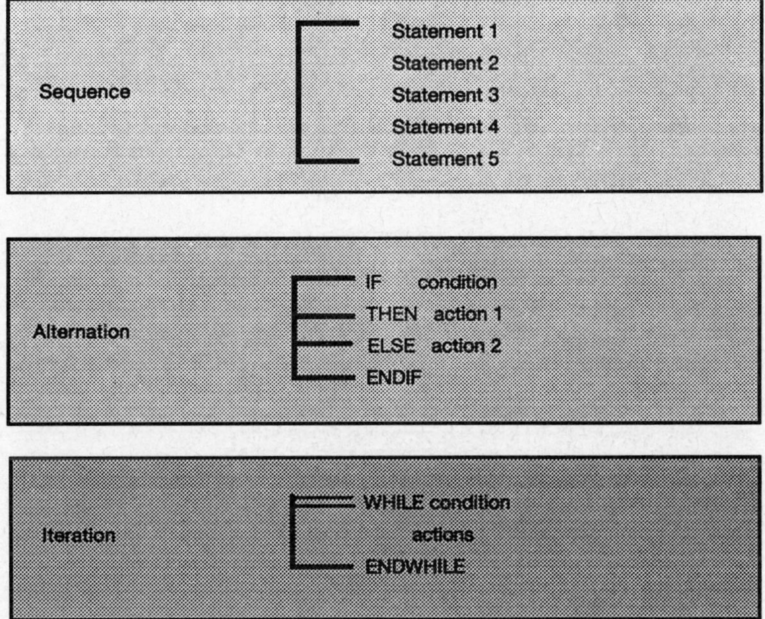

FIGURE 15-3 Basic control structures.

iteration (set of curly brackets). The overall structure of the report is as illustrated in Figure 15-6: a pair of nested WHILEs that will have sequential operations inserted in the appropriate places.

The final steps in our procedure are

- Define module tasks in terms of elementary operations.
- Assign operations to the appropriate control structure.

The basic module tasks are to get the appropriate records from each of the entities in the database and to print the contents of those records on the report. The operations in question are

- Get permanent entity record.
- Get transaction record.
- Get transaction detail.
- Print permanent entity record.
- Print transaction record.
- Print transaction detail.

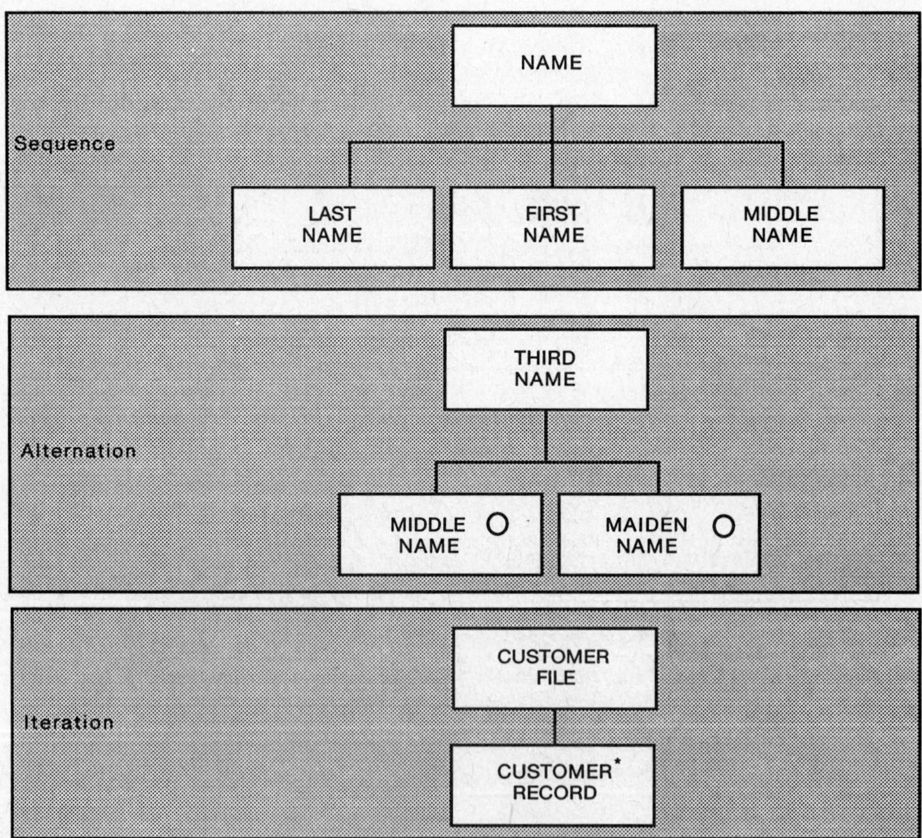

FIGURE 15-4 Correspondence.

Figure 15-7 shows these operations assigned to the appropriate control structures. Note also that we have had to decide what conditions will produce the correct results and set up beginning values for these conditions. What Figure 15-7 says in English is that when the module encounters the condition where **End of Page** is true, it prints the permanent entity and transaction header data. Otherwise, it loops through the transaction detail file until either an **End of Page** condition is true or the transaction number changes.

This example shows the four modules of Figure 15-5 condensed into one. This sort of condensation is a common minor redesign when adding structure charts to action diagrams. However, there is danger in doing this, in that the procedures **PRINT TRANSACTION DETAIL**, **PRINT PERMANENT ENTITY RECORD**, and **PRINT PURCHASE ORDER RECORD** may prove to be fairly complex because of formatting requirements. Chapter 19 shows that, especially in dBASE III+, these activities still rate a module by themselves, even though the action diagram is simple.

As a specific example, Figure 15-8 shows a purchase order with the different components shaded. Figure 15-9 shows its data structure diagram,and how the diagram is mapped into an action diagram.

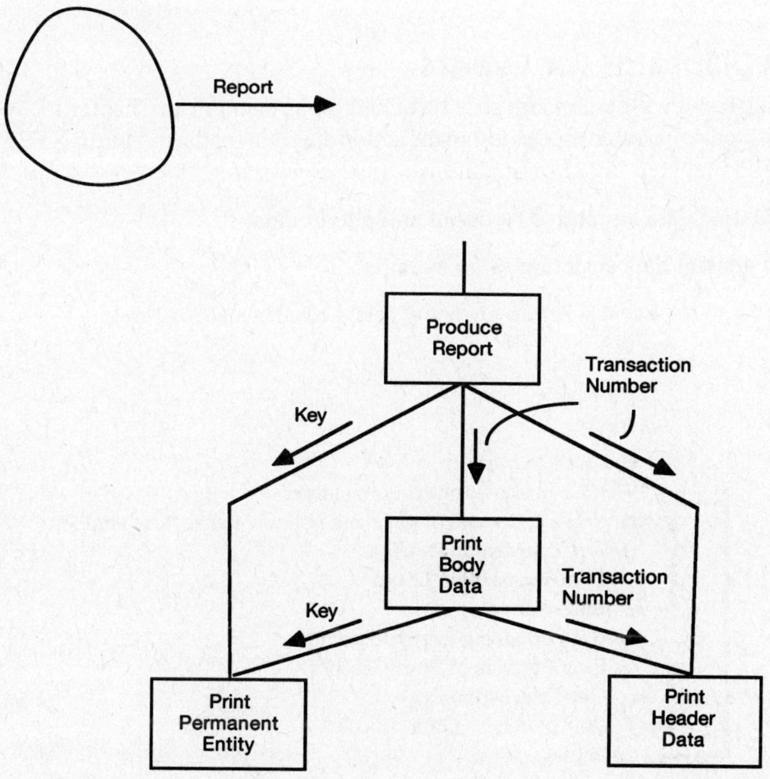

FIGURE 15-5 Structure chart ofr a report.

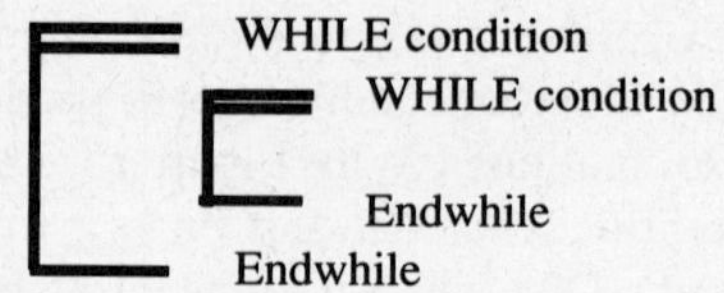

FIGURE 15-6 Control structures for a report.

To keep the example simple, we make the assumption that no purchase order will be greater than one page. Thus, the structure of a purchase order is

Purchase order = Supplier data + Purchase order data + {Purchase order detail}

As with most transaction-oriented documents, there are three parts to the purchase order: supplier data, purchase order data common to the purchase order as a whole, and detail data for the individual lines. There is a single iteration structure for the detail lines. Figure 15-9 shows how this iteration structure maps into a WHILE control structure on the action diagram.

Action Diagrams for Events

Figure 15-10 reviews the standard structure chart for an event from Chapter 11. We can also use data-structure based design to design the action diagram for the module **ENTER EVENT DATA**. The first step in our procedure is

- Define data structures for input and output data.

The general data structure of an event is

Event = Permanent entity data + Header + {body line}

FIGURE 15-7 Action diagram for a report.

In English, we have a single entry or confirmation of data on a permanent entity, data about the transaction that the report represents, and a list of detail items (usually concerning another permanent entity). The control structures and the corresponding action diagram derived from this data dictionary entry are illustrated in Figure 15-11.

The basic module tasks are to enter the appropriate records into each of the entities in the database. The operations in question are

- Enter or update permanent entity record.
- Enter transaction record (header).
- Enter transaction detail lines.

If multiple events are to be entered in at one time, we would add an additional WHILE loop around the entire action diagram. This is shown in Figure 15-12.

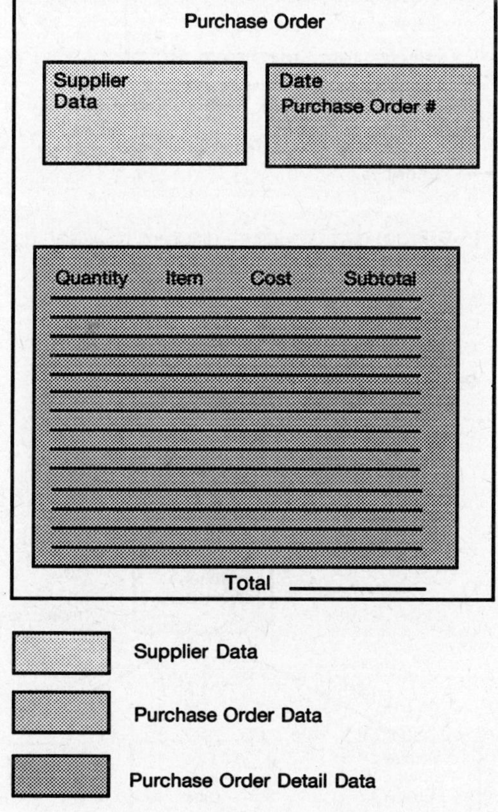

FIGURE 15-8 Purchase order.

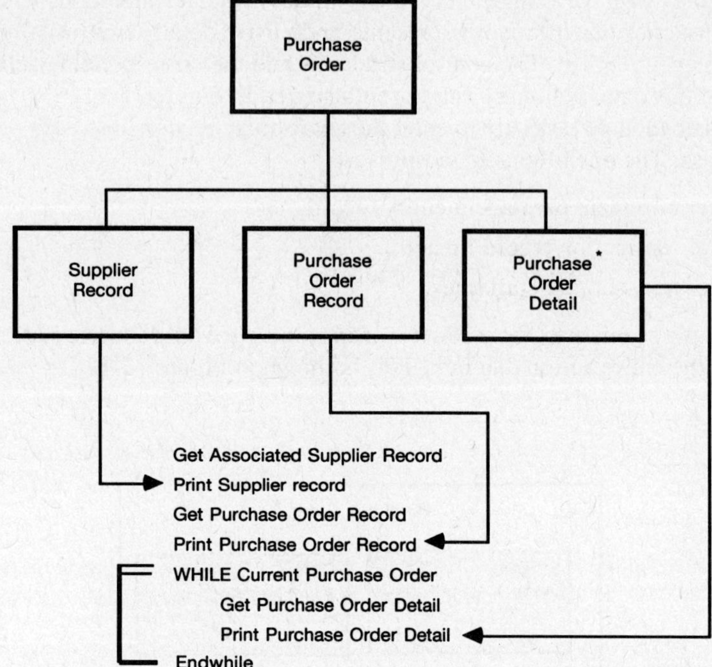

FIGURE 15-9 From data-structure diagram to action diagram.

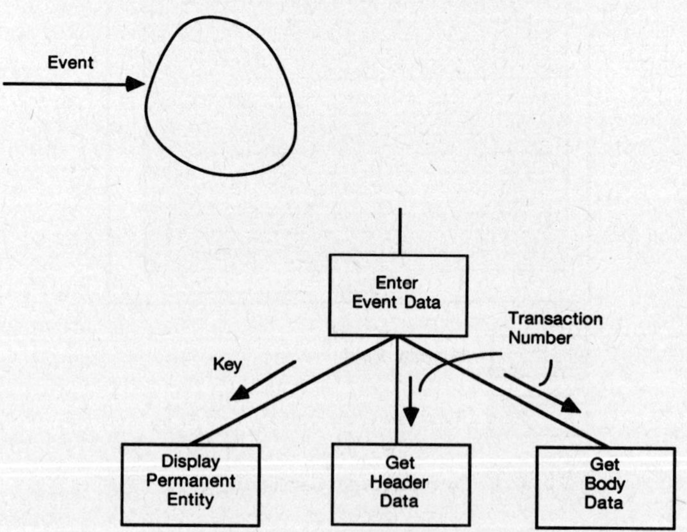

FIGURE 15-10 Structure chart for an event.

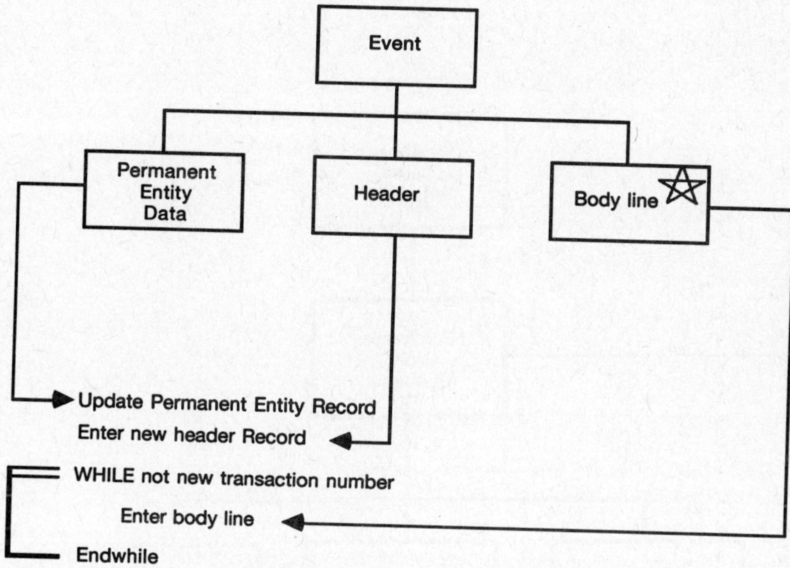

FIGURE 15-11 Action diagram for an event.

Action Diagrams for Actions

Figure 15-12 shows an example of the use of data-structure based design to design response to an action, something which we have been unable to do until now without resorting to functional decomposition. The action in question is **ENTER PURCHASE ORDER REQUESTS**, a program fragment used by an operator to enter purchase requisitions that will later be sent out as purchase orders. The format is almost the same as that for the program to print purchase orders; this is expected, since the structure of the data is the same. The major difference is that there are two iteration loops: one for the action itself, and one to repeat the action for multiple requests.

The examples thus far have assumed that the structure of the input files was normalized and the structure of the output file was a combination of input files (for a report), or vice-versa (or an event). The only problem was, what data to get and put, in what order.

Often, especially for inquiries, a problem is structured such that an output record is composed of selections from several related files rather than being a simple combination of normalized relations to reconstruct a paper form. Figure 15-13 shows a simple example, in which salary information is kept separate from the employee file and combined on a report. Data in the output is shaded according to source; dark shading for the data that comes from the first input file, and lighter shading for data that comes from the second input file.

In the module design (Figure 15-13), the program adopts the structure from the first file since it corresponds more closely to the structure of the output. The additional data (**Employee salary** in this case) is then searched for as needed. In a modern database

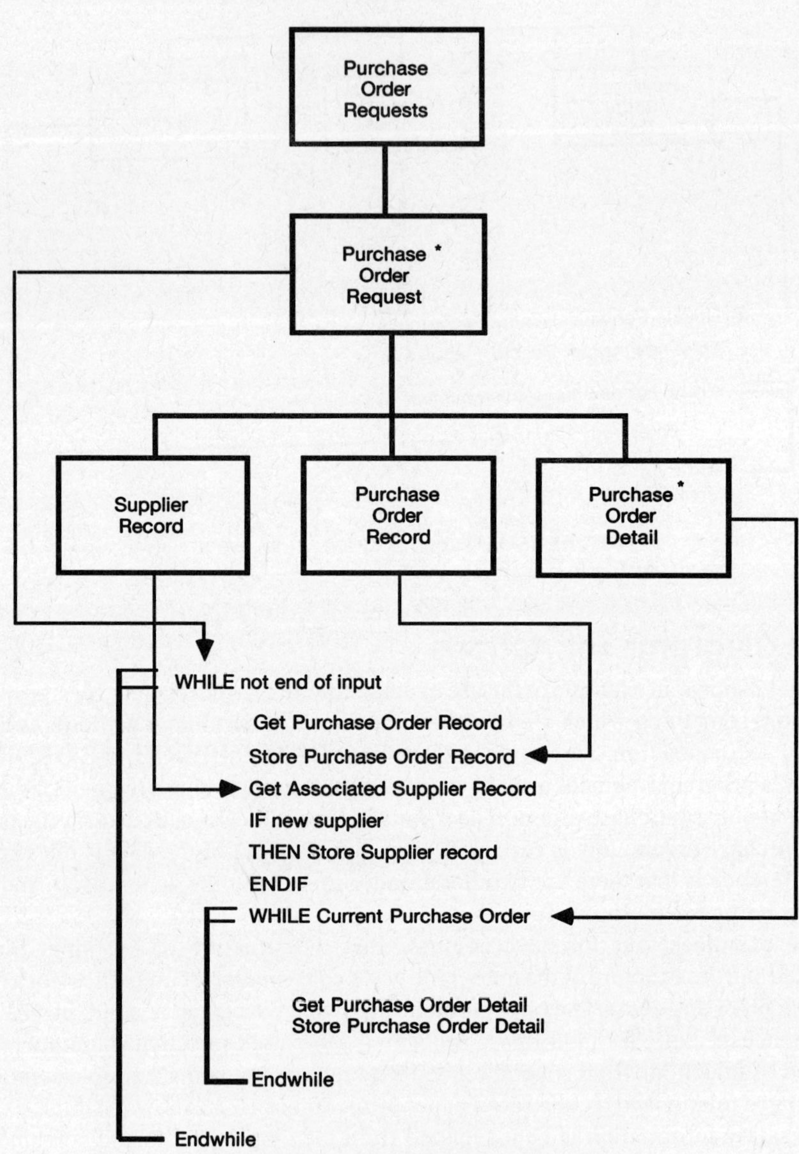

FIGURE 15-12 ENTER PURCHASE ORDER design.

```
WHILE not end of file on EMPLOYEE file
    Get EMPLOYEE ID
    Get EMPLOYEE NAME
    Get DEPARTMENT NUMBER
    Get EMPLOYEE SALARY from EMPLOYEE SALARY FILE
    Write EMPLOYEE ID, EMPLOYEE NAME, DEPARTMENT NUMBER,
    EMPLOYEE SALARY to SALARY REPORT
ENDWHILE
```

FIGURE 15-13 Action diagram for merged report in Figure 15-12.

environment this is a trivial task; in some third generation language environments it was considerably more complicated. In dBASE IV, the `SQL SELECT` operation can carry out all of Figure 15-13 in one statement.

This combining of data from two records to form a new record (technically called a **join**) is used not only for inquiries and simple reports, as illustrated in Figures 15-13 and 15-14, but also as a part of actions and reports. Figure 15-15 shows the dBASE definitions and Figure 15-16 shows the data-structure diagrams for this sort of problem. Here, work-order type is stored in the form of a two-letter code. Reasons for this might be to make clerical entry easier and also to reduce storage requirements. For example, if the average description of an action is 30 characters and there are 100,000 work order detail records, the file size would be reduced by almost 3 million bytes by storing abbreviations. Moreover, the data-entry clerk does not have to type 30 characters for each entry. On the other hand, customers will want to see on invoices the full description of work performed, so it is necessary to expand the file.

Figure 15-17 shows annotated dBASE III code for solving the problem illustrated in Figure 15-14.

An additional example of this sort of problem would be the expansion of a file in which parts were identified by number to one in which names were substituted. Where only one or two items need to be expanded, dBASE is able to perform such substitutions with a single `REPLACE` command (`REPLACE WOCODE WITH "Certify transponder" FOR WOCODE = "CT"`); where there are different alternatives available for substitution (there may be 10,000 different parts in inventory), the procedural approach illustrated above is far better.

EXERCISES

Given the illustrations of work orders and invoices in Figures 3-3 and 3-4:

1 Create a data structure diagram of each.

2. Use the data structure diagrams to generate action diagrams for the modules **ENTER WORK ORDER** and **PRINT INVOICES**.

3. Translate the data structure diagrams into dBASE files and the action diagram for **ENTER WORK ORDER** into one or more dBASE procedure(s).

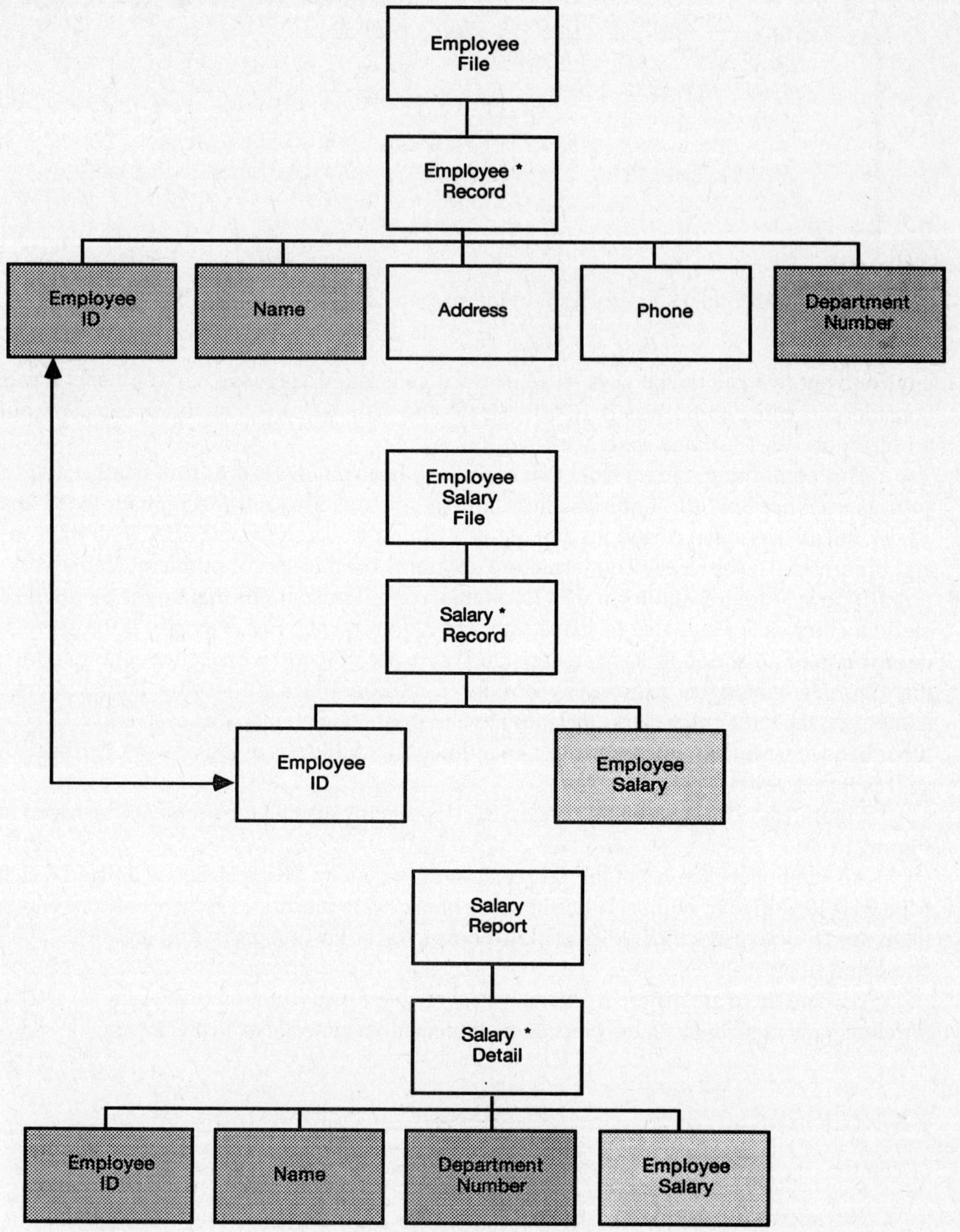

FIGURE 15-14 Select one from column A; one from column B.

```
Structure for database: C:CODES.dbf
Number of data records: 0
Date of last update   : 03/18/87
Field    Field Name      Type          Width      Dec
1        WOCODE          Character     2
2        CODENAME        Character     40
3        DRACCT          Character     4
4        CDACCT          Character     4
5        CODECOST        Numeric       6          2
** Total **                            57

Structure for database: C:WODET.dbf
Number of data records: 1
Date of last update   : 04/02/87
Field    Field Name      Type            Width    Dec
1        WONUMB          Character       6
2        WOTYPE          Character       2
3        WOQUANT         Numeric         8        2
4        INUMB           Character       40
5        IPRICE          Numeric         9        2
** Total **                              66
```

FIGURE 15-15 Data definitions for examplanded work orders.

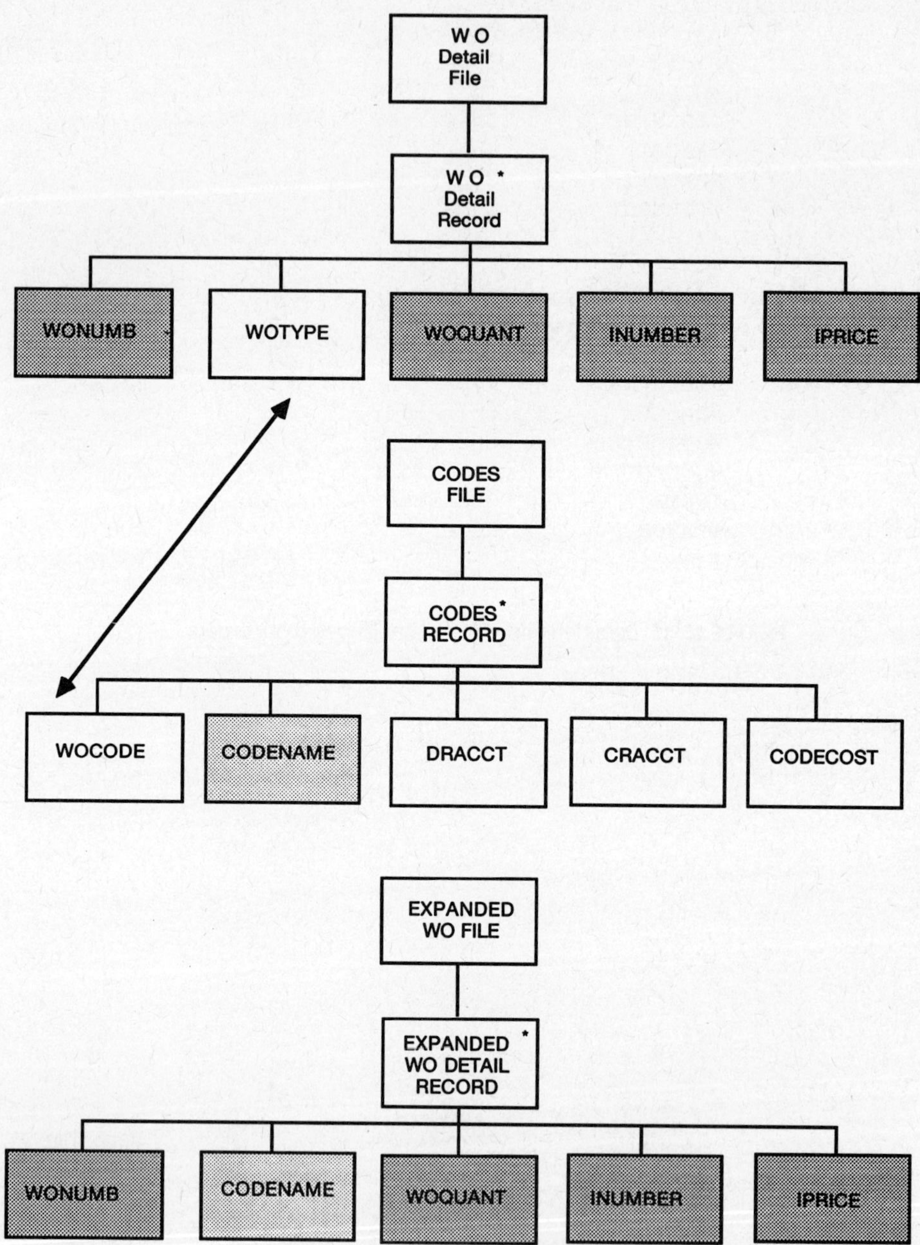

FIGURE 15-16 Expanded word-order data structure.

```
*****************************************************************
* Insert description of 2 letter Work Order Codes into EXPANDWO *
*****************************************************************
CLEAR
SELECT B
USE EXPANDWO
ZAP
                                        Empty file EXPANDWO and copy
                                        the content of WODET into it. This
                                        includes the 2 letter code WOTYPE
APPEND FROM WODET
GO TOP
SELECT A
USE WODET
SELECT C
USE CODES INDEX CODEID
SELECT A
DO WHILE .NOT. EOF()
SELECT A
STORE A->WOTYPE TO THISCODE             Get the 2 letter code WOTYPE
SELECT C
SEEK THISCODE                           Find the record with key value =
                                        THISCODE
SELECT B
REPLACE B->WOTYPE WITH C->CODENAME      Replace 2 letter code with expanded
                                        value
SELECT A
SKIP
LOOP
ENDDO
CLOSE DATABASES
RETURN
```

FIGURE 15-17 Annotated dBASE code for the problem in Figure 15-14.

REFERENCES

JACKSON, M. *Principles of Program Design*. London, Academic Press, 1975.

KING, D. *Creating Effective Software: Computer Program Design Using the Jackson Methodology*. Prentice-Hall (YourdonPress), New York, 1988

WARNIER, J. *Logical Construction of Systems*. Van Nostrand–Reinhold, Princeton, NJ, 1981.

ORR, K. *Structured Systems Development*. Prentice-Hall (Yourdon Press) New York, 1977.

CAMERON, J. An Overview of JSD. *IEEE Transactions of Software Engineering,* 21(2) 222–240, 1986.

CAMERON, J. *The Jackson Approach to Software Development,* 2nd ed. IEEE Computer Society Press, Washington, DC, 1989.

Chapter 16

CASE STUDY USING ACTION DIAGRAMS

CHAPTER GOALS

- Present an integrated example of detailed module design using action diagrams.
- Show how action diagrams are used to complete module designs using the techniques of this section.

In this chapter we illustrate the use of action diagrams in systems design by producing them for the system described in Chapter 13. Figure 16-1 lists the modules in the system in the order in which they are discussed, along with the figure numbers for each action diagram. We will need an action diagram for each module. Figures 16-2 to 16-4 review the structure chart for this system. Where possible, the action diagrams for these modules are presented top down and left to right.

The program main procedure (**INVENTORY SYSTEM**) in Figure 16-5 is a simple menu for choosing which major function is desired: **MAINTAIN ENTITIES** or **MANAGE PARTS**. There are no data flows on the structure chart, and, hence, no parameters in the action diagram. The command DISPLAY is used in this version of action diagrams to indicate output onto the screen or other device. INPUT is used to output a message and get a response.

The procedure **MAINTAIN ENTITIES** (Figure 16-6) is likewise a menu to choose which entity to maintain. The structure chart of Figure 16-3 calls for it to invoke one of two modules: **LOAD PART DATA** or **LOAD SUPPLIER DATA.** However, the procedure **LOAD PART DATA** turns out to be only three lines of pseudocode, that is,

Inventory system	Figure 5
Maintain entities	Figure 6
Load Part data	
Load Supplier data	
Maintain entity	Figure 7
Enter record	Figure 9
Update record	Figure 10
Delete record	Figure 11
List contents of entity	Figure 12
Manage transactions	
Produce report	Figure 13
Print permanent entity	Figure 17
Print header data	Figure 18
Print body data	Figure 19
Enter event data	Figure 20
Display permanent entity	
Get header data	
Get body data	

FIGURE 16-1 Modules for inventory system (Chapter 13).

```
filename="PART"
formatname="PART"
sortfield="PNUMBER"
```

Hence, it is included in **MAINTAIN ENTITIES.** Likewise, the procedure **LOAD SUPPLIER DATA** turns out to be only three lines of pseudocode, that is,

```
filename="SUPPLIER"
formatname="SUPPLIER"
sortfield="SUPPNAME"
```

Therefore, it is also included in **MAINTAIN ENTITIES**. The revised structure chart is shown in Figure 16-6. Figure 16-7 shows the complete action diagram derived from Figure 16-6.

This sort of retroactive redesign of a structure chart is common when designing detailed module content and discovering that tasks are either simpler or more complicated than they appeared during the architectural design phase.

Note that there are now data flows on the structure chart,and that these are reflected as parameters in the module calls, that is, DO x (parameter 1, parameter 2, . . .parameter n), and in the **PARAMETERS** section of the lower level modules (e.g., Figure 16-8). Note also that the action diagram shows the elements in the parameter list (e.g., file name, format

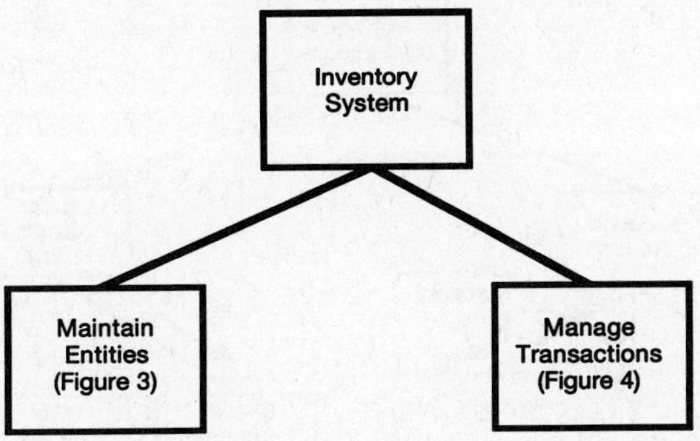

FIGURE 16-2 Overview structure chart for inventory system (Chapter 13).

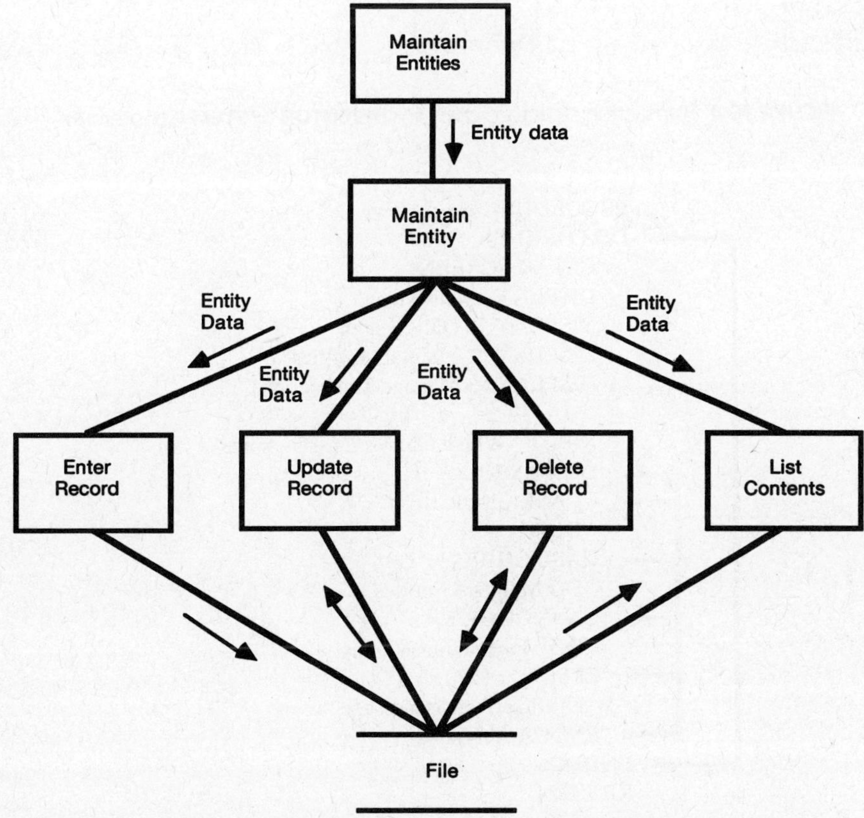

FIGURE 16-3 MAINTAIN ENTITIES structure chart for inventory system (Chapter 13).

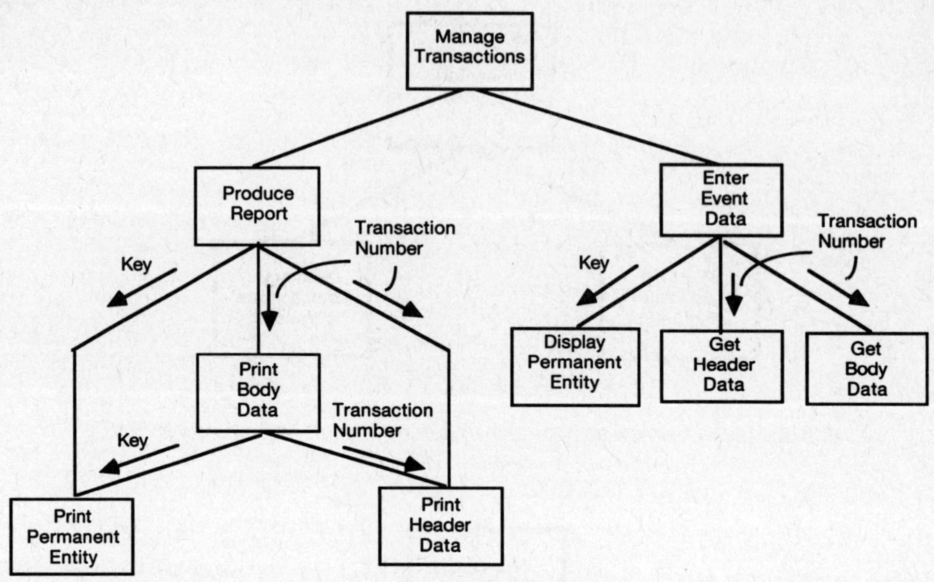

FIGURE 16-4 Transaction structure chart for **INVENTOR SYSTEM** (Chapter 13).

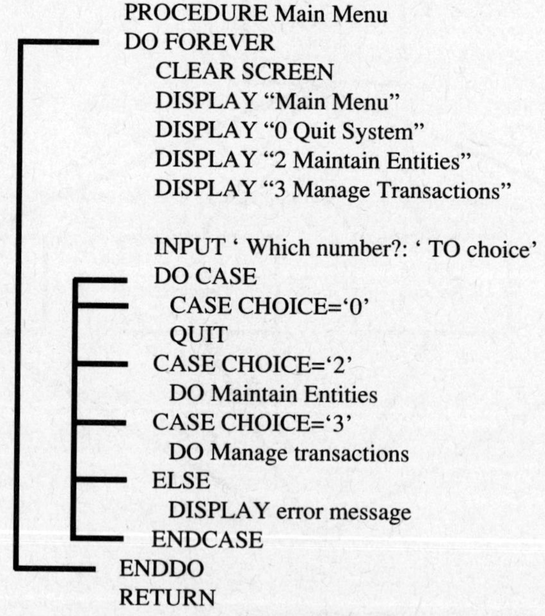

```
PROCEDURE Main Menu
DO FOREVER
   CLEAR SCREEN
   DISPLAY "Main Menu"
   DISPLAY "0 Quit System"
   DISPLAY "2 Maintain Entities"
   DISPLAY "3 Manage Transactions"

   INPUT ' Which number?: ' TO choice'
   DO CASE
     CASE CHOICE='0'
     QUIT
   CASE CHOICE='2'
     DO Maintain Entities
   CASE CHOICE='3'
     DO Manage transactions
   ELSE
     DISPLAY error message
   ENDCASE
ENDDO
RETURN
```

FIGURE 16-5 Action diagram for **INVENTORY SYSTEM MAIN MENU**.

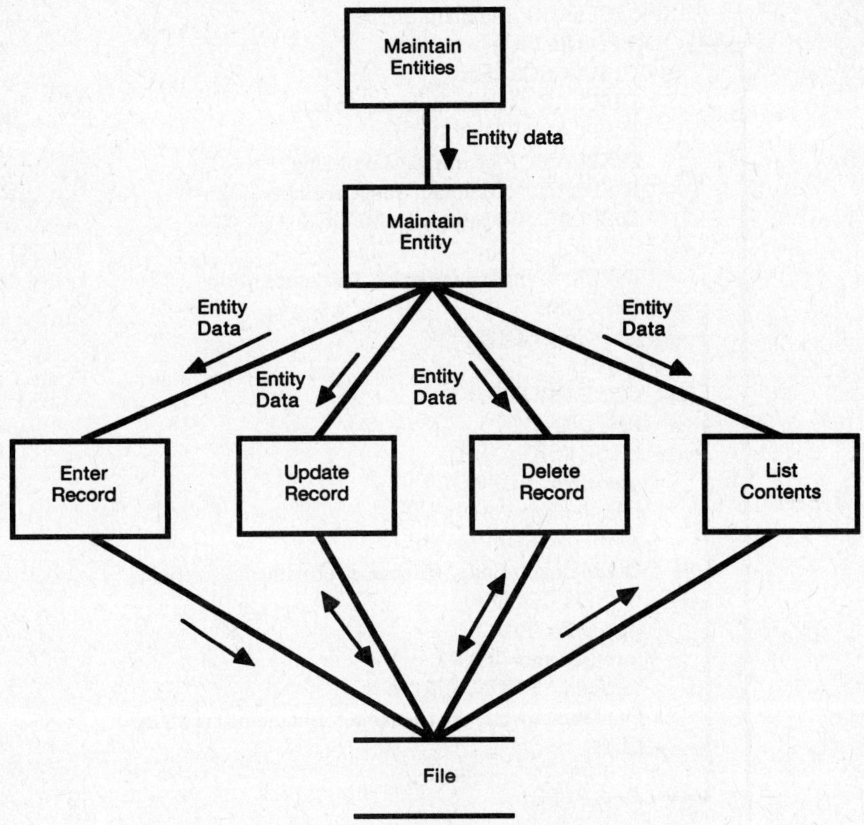

FIGURE 16-6 Revised **MAINTAIN ENTITIES** structure chart.

field, sort field), whereas the structure chart shows the name of the overall structure (e.g., part data).

The procedure **MAINTAIN ENTITY** in Figure 16-8 is likewise another menu, selecting which maintenance task to perform on the selected entity. Figures 16-9 to 16-12 illustrate the actions performed in maintaining an entity. All of these are general-purpose modules as discussed in Chapters 10 and 12, with names of files, screens, and fields passed as parameters.

Figure 16-9 (**ENTER RECORD**) shows the use of a predefined screen, the name of which is passed as a parameter. Note that as in actual program code, action diagrams do not require that the names of parameters in the lower-level records match those in upper-level records but do require that the number, position, and type of the parameter elements be the same. The reason for this looseness is to facilitate the use of general-purpose modules, which are used in many structure charts. Note also that some action diagram commands such as ASK WHETHER TO CONTINUE or IF NO, will require slight logical expansion

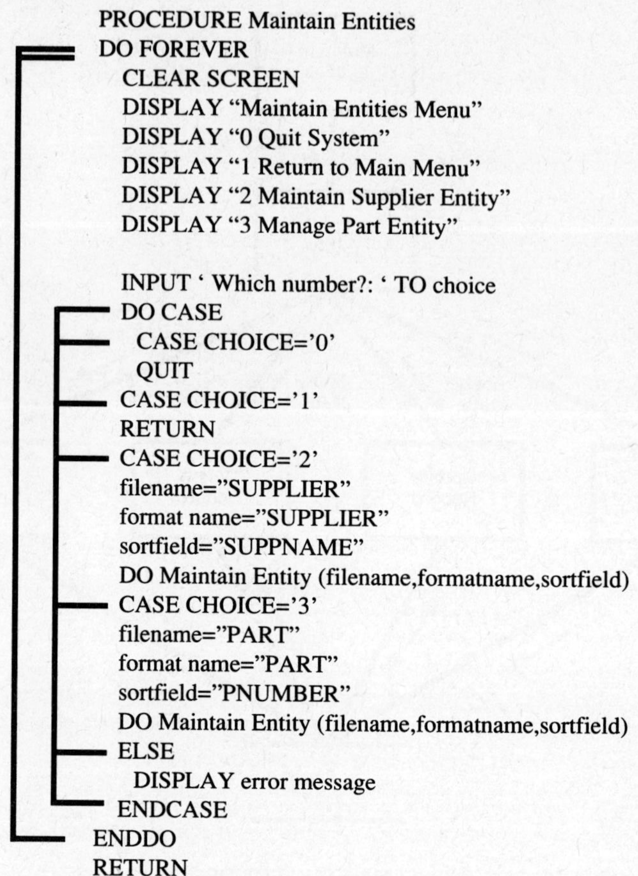

FIGURE 16-7 Action diagram for **MAINTAIN ENTITIES.**

in the actual code; something on the order of:

```
INPUT "Do you want to continue (Y or N) " TO YESNO
IF YESNO = "Y" ...
```

The same is true with statements such as Figure 16-11's ASK WHETHER TO DELETE RECORD, where the expansion into program logic is so straightforward that it does not require specification.

The procedure **LIST CONTENTS OF ENTITY** (Figure 16-2) shows the use of the LIST command, which is common to almost all fourth generation languages. A more complicated predefined report could also be specified here, using terminology such as "ACTIVATE REPORT xxx." As with all action diagrams, the exact format of the command is arbitrary, so long as it is clear.

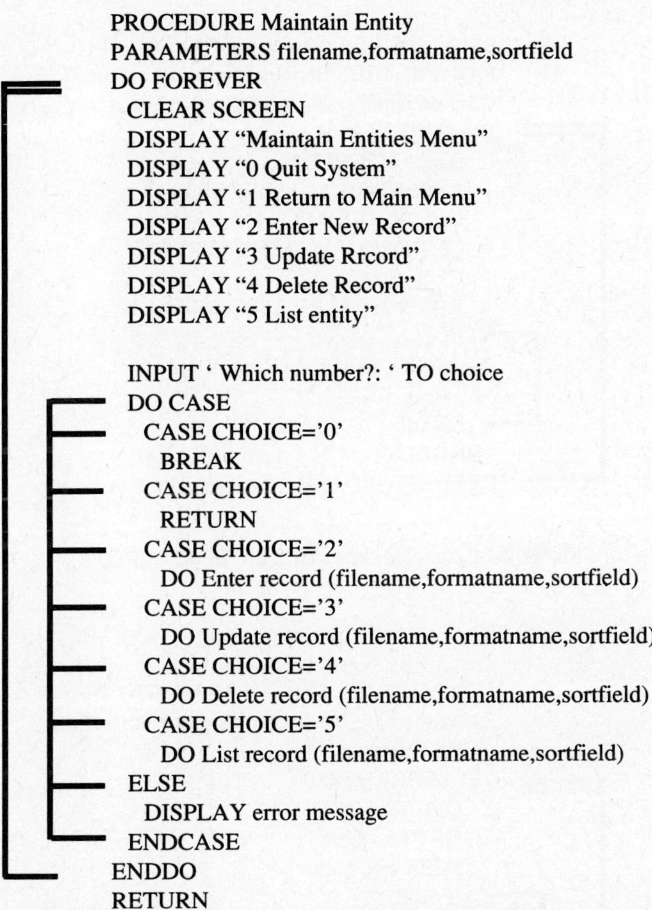

```
PROCEDURE Maintain Entity
PARAMETERS filename,formatname,sortfield
DO FOREVER
  CLEAR SCREEN
  DISPLAY "Maintain Entities Menu"
  DISPLAY "0 Quit System"
  DISPLAY "1 Return to Main Menu"
  DISPLAY "2 Enter New Record"
  DISPLAY "3 Update Rrcord"
  DISPLAY "4 Delete Record"
  DISPLAY "5 List entity"

  INPUT ' Which number?: ' TO choice
  DO CASE
    CASE CHOICE='0'
      BREAK
    CASE CHOICE='1'
      RETURN
    CASE CHOICE='2'
      DO Enter record (filename,formatname,sortfield)
    CASE CHOICE='3'
      DO Update record (filename,formatname,sortfield)
    CASE CHOICE='4'
      DO Delete record (filename,formatname,sortfield)
    CASE CHOICE='5'
      DO List record (filename,formatname,sortfield)
  ELSE
    DISPLAY error message
  ENDCASE
ENDDO
RETURN
```

FIGURE 16-8 Action diagram for **MAINTAIN ENTITY.**

The remainder of the action diagrams show the right-hand part of the structure chart under **MANAGE TRANSACTIONS.** No action diagram is show for **MANAGE TRANSACTIONS** itself, since it is just another menu similar to that of Figure 16-5.

PRODUCE REPORT

The procedure **PRODUCE REPORT** is basically the control structure for the three operations required to turn normalized relations into a three-part form. Figure 16-13 shows the action diagram for **PRODUCE REPORT**; Figures 16-14 and 16-18 show the action diagrams for the subordinate modules.

PRODUCE REPORT, along with the next three action diagrams, illustrates the use of the programming object **WINDOW**. The availability of windows as an object makes the

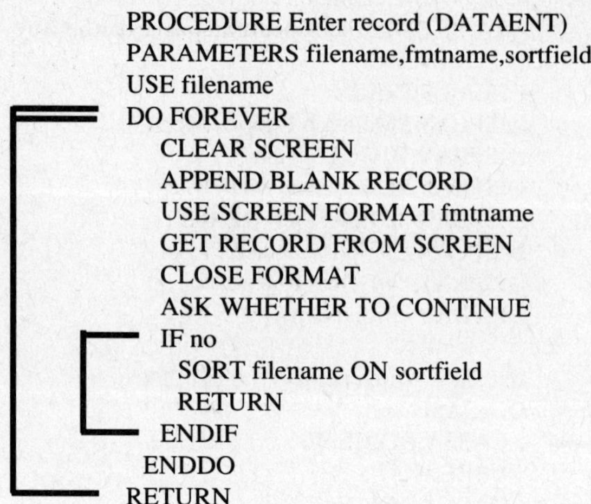

```
PROCEDURE Enter record (DATAENT)
PARAMETERS filename,fmtname,sortfield
USE filename
DO FOREVER
  CLEAR SCREEN
  APPEND BLANK RECORD
  USE SCREEN FORMAT fmtname
  GET RECORD FROM SCREEN
  CLOSE FORMAT
  ASK WHETHER TO CONTINUE
  IF no
    SORT filename ON sortfield
    RETURN
  ENDIF
 ENDDO
RETURN
```

FIGURE 16-9 Action diagram for **ENTER RECORD.**

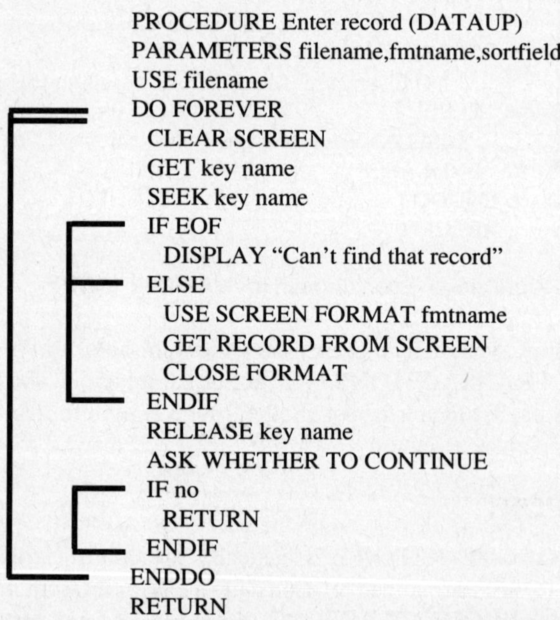

```
PROCEDURE Enter record (DATAUP)
PARAMETERS filename,fmtname,sortfield
USE filename
DO FOREVER
  CLEAR SCREEN
  GET key name
  SEEK key name
  IF EOF
    DISPLAY "Can't find that record"
  ELSE
    USE SCREEN FORMAT fmtname
    GET RECORD FROM SCREEN
    CLOSE FORMAT
  ENDIF
  RELEASE key name
  ASK WHETHER TO CONTINUE
  IF no
    RETURN
  ENDIF
ENDDO
RETURN
```

FIGURE 16-10 Action diagram for **UPDATE RECORD.**

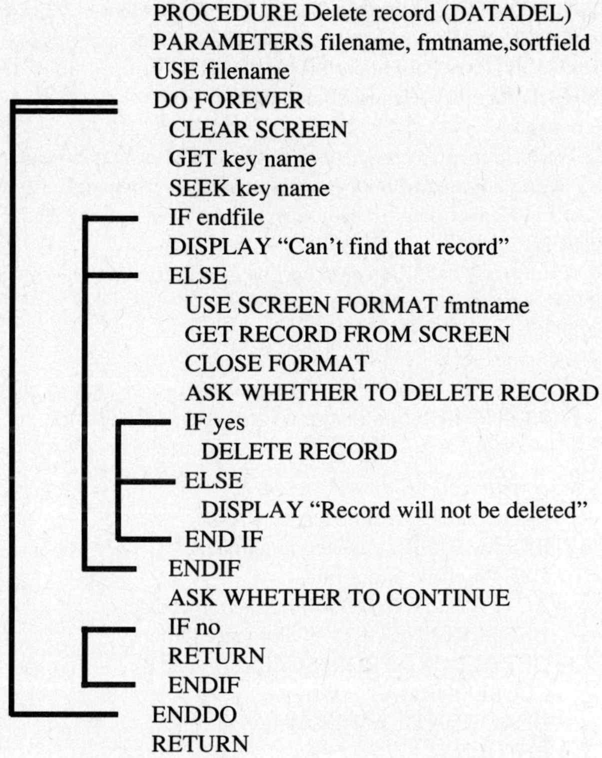

FIGURE 16-11 Action diagram for **DELETE RECORD.**

```
PROCEDURE  List Contents
PARAMETERS filename,fmtname,sortfield
USE filename
LIST filename to printer
RETURN
```

FIGURE 16-12 Action diagram for **LIST CONTENTS OF ENTITY.**

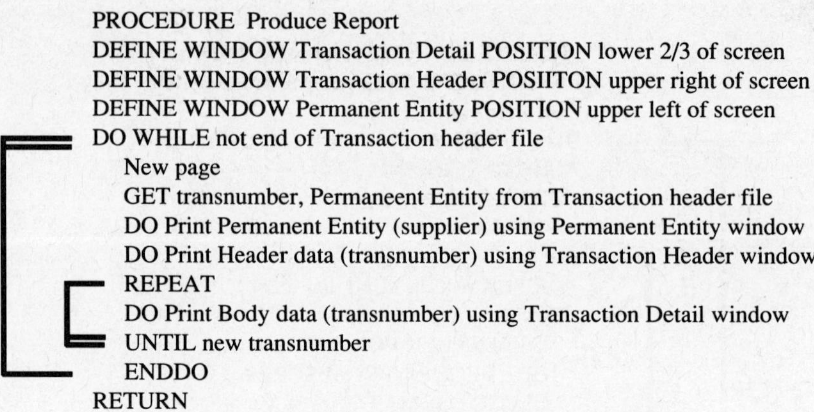

```
PROCEDURE  Produce Report
DEFINE WINDOW Transaction Detail POSITION lower 2/3 of screen
DEFINE WINDOW Transaction Header POSIITON upper right of screen
DEFINE WINDOW Permanent Entity POSITION upper left of screen
DO WHILE not end of Transaction header file
  New page
  GET transnumber, Permaneent Entity from Transaction header file
  DO Print Permanent Entity (supplier) using Permanent Entity window
  DO Print Header data (transnumber) using Transaction Header window
  REPEAT
  DO Print Body data (transnumber) using Transaction Detail window
  UNTIL new transnumber
  ENDDO
RETURN
```

FIGURE 16-13 Action diagram for **PRODUCE REPORT.**

```
PROCEDURE  Print Header DAta
PARAMETERS transaction number
USE Purchase Order File
ACTIVATE WINDOW Transaction Header
USE SCREEN FORMAT Purchase Order
GET RECORD FROM SCREEN
CLOSE FORMAT
DEACTIVATE WINDOW
RETURN
```

FIGURE 16-14 Action diagram for **PRINT HEADER DATA.**

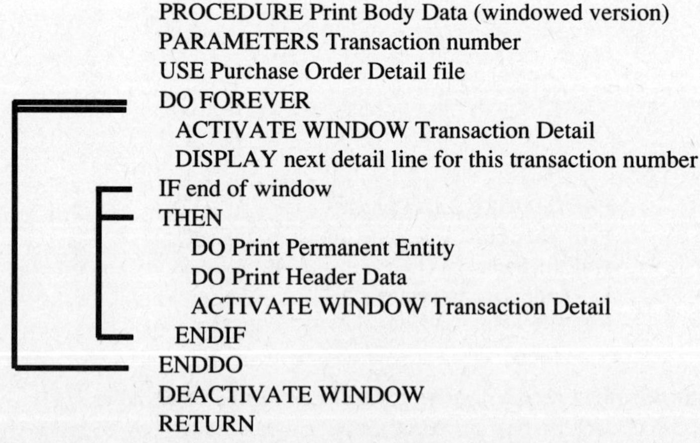

```
PROCEDURE Print Body Data (windowed version)
PARAMETERS Transaction number
USE Purchase Order Detail file
DO FOREVER
  ACTIVATE WINDOW Transaction Detail
  DISPLAY next detail line for this transaction number
IF end of window
THEN
    DO Print Permanent Entity
    DO Print Header Data
    ACTIVATE WINDOW Transaction Detail
  ENDIF
ENDDO
DEACTIVATE WINDOW
RETURN
```

FIGURE 16-15 Action diagram for **PRINT BODY DATA**. (continued)

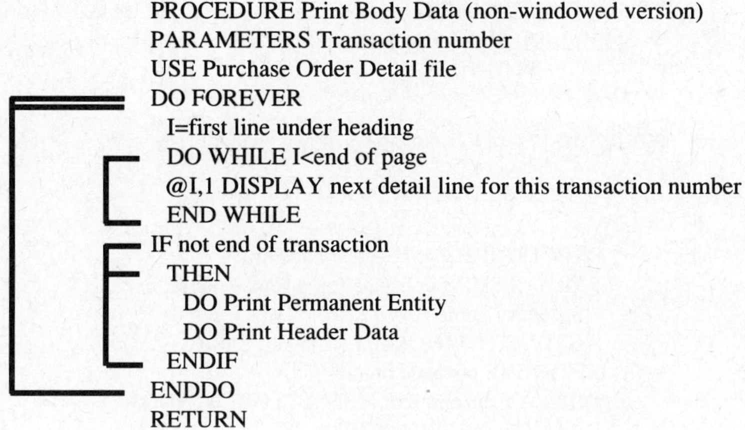

```
PROCEDURE Print Body Data (non-windowed version)
PARAMETERS Transaction number
USE Purchase Order Detail file
DO FOREVER
  I=first line under heading
  DO WHILE I<end of page
  @I,1 DISPLAY next detail line for this transaction number
  END WHILE
IF not end of transaction
  THEN
    DO Print Permanent Entity
    DO Print Header Data
  ENDIF
ENDDO
RETURN
```

FIGURE 16-15 Action diagram for **PRINT BODY DATA.**

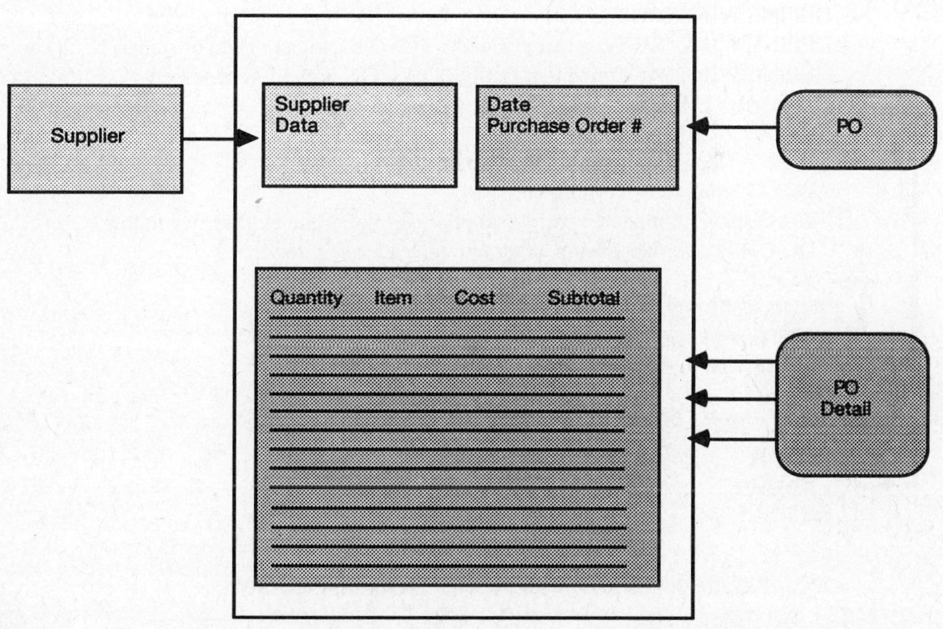

FIGURE 16-16 Three-part form implemented by windows.

```
I = 1
DO WHILE I < 15
@ I,5 SAY next detail line
END WHILE
```

FIGURE 16-17 Implementing windows procedurally.

```
PROCEDURE Print Permanent Entity
PARAMETERS entity name, instance name
USE entity name
ACTIVATE WINDOW Permanent Entity
RETRIEVE instance name
DISPLAY current record IN ACTIVE WINDOW
DEACTIVATE WINDOW
RETURN
```

FIGURE 16-18 Action diagram for **PRINT PERMANENT ENTITY.**

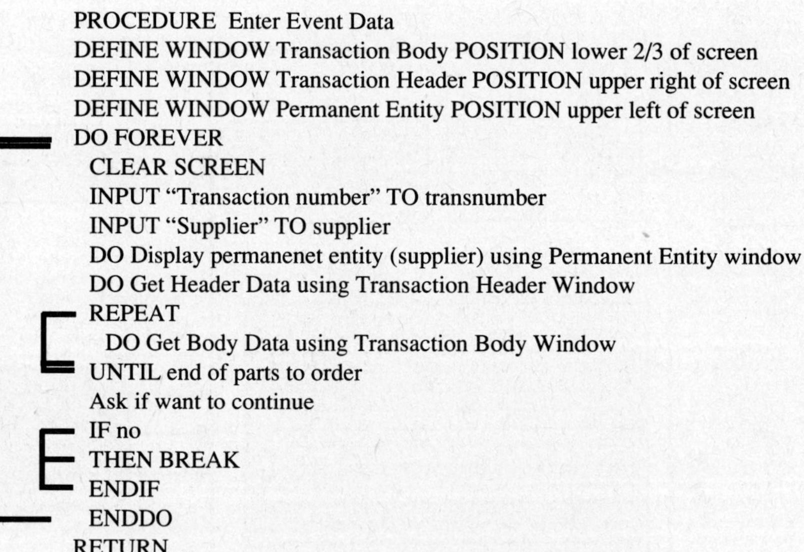

```
PROCEDURE  Enter Event Data
DEFINE WINDOW Transaction Body POSITION lower 2/3 of screen
DEFINE WINDOW Transaction Header POSITION upper right of screen
DEFINE WINDOW Permanent Entity POSITION upper left of screen
DO FOREVER
  CLEAR SCREEN
  INPUT "Transaction number" TO transnumber
  INPUT "Supplier" TO supplier
  DO Display permanenet entity (supplier) using Permanent Entity window
  DO Get Header Data using Transaction Header Window
  REPEAT
    DO Get Body Data using Transaction Body Window
  UNTIL end of parts to order
  Ask if want to continue
  IF no
  THEN BREAK
  ENDIF
  ENDDO
RETURN
```

FIGURE 16-19 Action diagram for **ENTER EVENT DATA.**

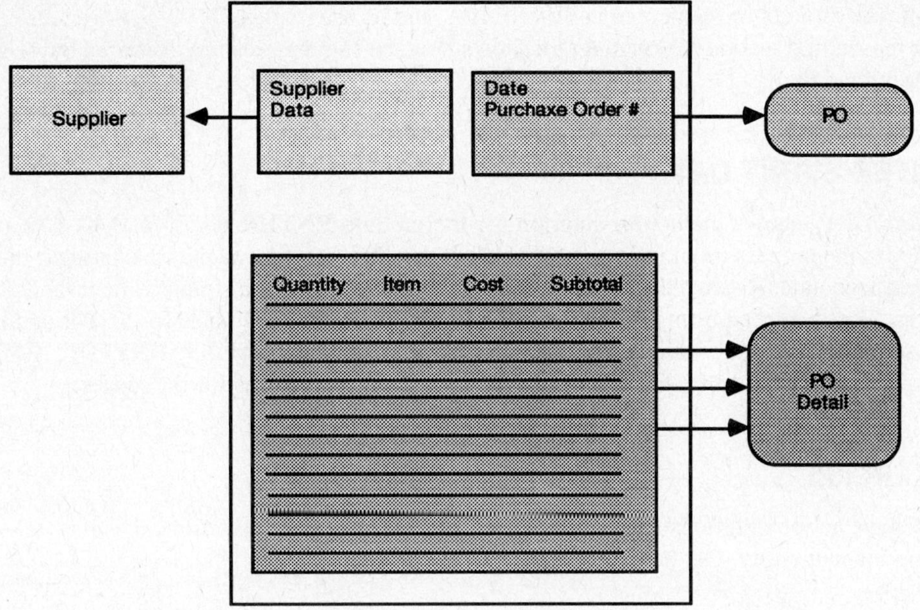

FIGURE 16-20 Translation of input forms to normalized data.

transfer of normalized relations into three-part transaction form very easy. As illustrated in Figure 16-13, the form is divided into a window for each part and then each normalized relation is displayed in its separate window (Figure 16-16). If windows are not available in the target language (e.g., if we are using dBASE III rather than dBASE IV), they have to be programmed procedurally by checking the current cursor location on the screen explicitly. Figure 16-17 shows how to do this. Note also that in the actual dBASE code, the locations and descriptions of the windows would need to be defined more exactly. In practice, this would probably be done by using computer-aided software engineering (CASE) tools, such as the facilities of the Control Center in dBASE IV.

The approach in the previous paragraph bears repeating, since it reduces a complicated problem (that of translation between normalized and nonnormalized data) to a simple one. One considers the "real-world" forms, which contain nonnormalized data, as a collection of windows into normalized relations. In translating from transactions to internal data, one identifies the windows and transfers the data from each window into the appropriate relation. In producing transactions as output, one designs the windows on the form, then transfers the appropriate data to each window. In other words, the input or output form is viewed not as a single collection of disparate data but as a paper screen containing windows into different relations.

Figure 16-15 shows two alternative action diagrams for **PRINT BODY DATA**. The first makes use of windows, which matches the structure of the problem. However, this cannot be directly implemented in dBASE III+, and its use in dBASE IV is restricted. For that reason, the second action diagram shows how the same procedure is carried out with no windowing.

ENTER EVENT DATA

Figure 16-19 shows the action diagram for the module **ENTER EVENT DATA**. It illustrates the process of taking an input event with a three-part form and translating it into normalized data. Again, the program object **WINDOW** is used to simplify the task. Data for each entity is read from its associated window as illustrated in Figure 16-20. The action diagrams for the subordinate modules (**DISPLAY PERMANENT ENTITY**, **GET HEADER DATA**, and **GET BODY DATA**) are left as exercises for the reader.

EXERCISE

1. Create action diagrams for the missing modules Manage Transactions, Display permanent entity, Get header data, and Get body data.

Section V

CODING

This section discusses how to turn the action diagrams and data dictionary that make up module designs into program code for the machine of our choice. Figure S-5-1 reviews where we are in the program development life-cycle.

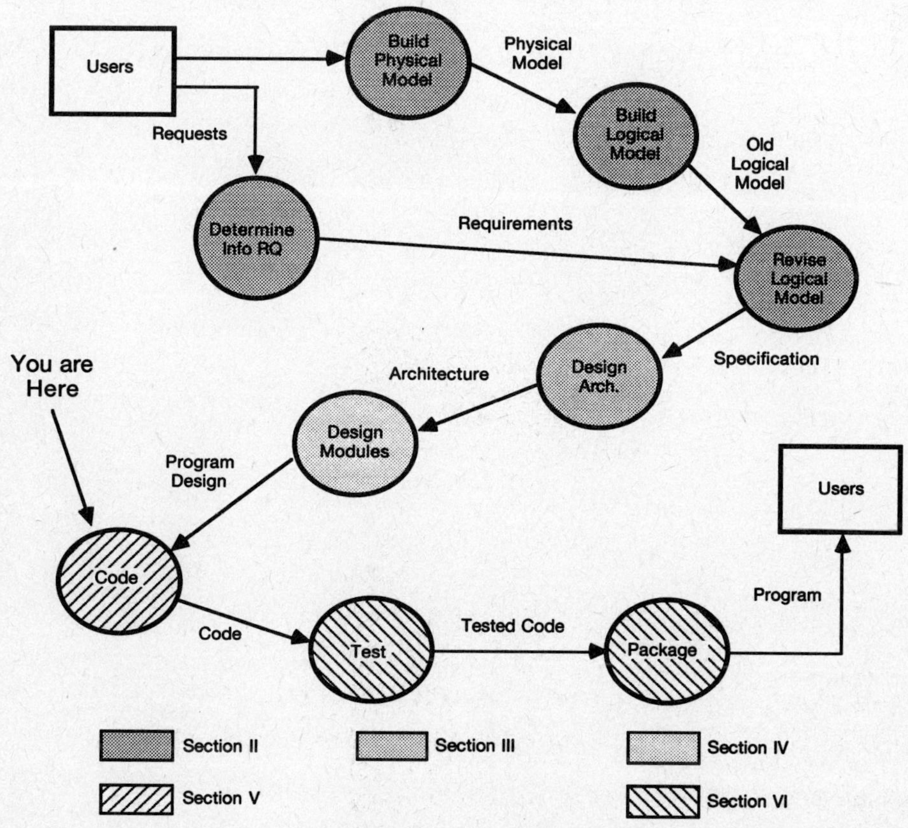

FIGURE S-5-1 Where we are.

Chapter 17 discusses aspects of dBASE III that have not already been discussed in the book. Chapter 18 extends the discussion to dBASE IV. Chapter 19 presents a case study in translating action diagrams into code. The contents of this section are what most people call "programming."

Chapter 17

DBASE III+ CODING

CHAPTER GOALS

- Introduce the basic operations and functions in dBASE III+.

Figure 17-1 reviews the generic operations found in fourth generation languages. The rest of this chapter discusses the way in which dBASE III+ implements these generic operations. The chapter is not complete, in that it makes no effort to cover all of the possible commands in the dBASE language and does not cover all of the forms in which the commands may appear. The subset of commands presented here, however, is complete enough to write programs, especially if used as a supplement to the dBASE manuals.

We shall change the order of the operations in Figure 17-1 so as to be able to build programs as we go. Figure 17-2 shows the order of discussion.

Input/Output commands in dBASE III+ may involve any combination of files and physical devices (keyboard, screen, printer, serial ports). Figure 17-3 shows some of the possible permutations.

One of the major differences between a fourth generation language such as dBASE and third generation languages like COBOL is that data definitions were part of the program in third generation languages, whereas in fourth generation languages they are part of the data. In writing a system using dBASE, therefore, one first defines the contents and the formats of all of the data files, using the `DEFINE` command either from the dot prompt or from the Assistant. Thenceforth, whenever you wish to use that data in a program, the file is attached to the program with the `USE` command.

```
USE CLIENT
```

1. MOVE
2. ARITHMETIC
   2.1. ADD
   2.2. SUBTRACT
   2.3. MULTIPLY
   2.4. DIVIDE
   2.5. FUNCTIONS
3. STRING
   3.1. EXTRACT SUBSTRING
   3.2. CONCATENATE
   3.3. COMPARE
4. LOGICAL
   4.1. AND
   4.2. OR
   4.3. NOT
   4.4. XOR
5. CONVERT DATA TYPES
6. INPUT/OUTPUT
   6.1. OPEN
   6.2. CLOSE
   6.3. READ
   6.4. WRITE
   6.5. REWRITE
7. RELATIONAL
   7.1. SELECT
   7.2. PROJECT
   7.3. JOIN
   7.4. UPDATE
   7.5. SORT
8. CONTROL
   8.1. CALL
   8.2. TEST
   8.3. BRANCH
   8.4. IF-THEN-ELSE
   8.5. DO-WHILE
   8.6 REPEAT-UNTIL
   8.7. FOR
   8.8. CASE

FIGURE 17-1 Operations at the very-high-level language level.

Input/Output
Move
Control
Logical
Sring
Convert data types
Arithmetic
Relational

FIGURE 17-2 Order of discussion.

Input from	*Output to*
Database	Database
Database	Screen (dumb terminal)
Database	Screen (full screen)
Keyboard	Database
Keyboard	Memory variable
Memory variable	Screen (full screen)
Memory variable	Screen (dumb terminal)
Memory variable	Printer
Database	Printer
Database	Text file
Text file	Database

FIGURE 17-3 Possible combinations of input./output.

All statements that perform input or output with a datafile must have that file attached with the `USE` command. The program does not contain any other data definitions for items in those files.

Moving data from one database to another is done by the `APPEND` command:

```
USE POSENT
APPEND FROM PO
```

This appends the contents of the database **PO** to the end of the database **POSENT**.

Input from a database with output to a screen in dumb terminal mode (one character at a time) is a leftover from the days when teletypes and other relatively inexpensive terminals were connected to early personal computers. In dBASE III, this is done with the `DISPLAY` command:

```
USE CLIENT
DISPLAY LNAME,FNAME,PHONE
```

Further details of the `DISPLAY` command are discussed in the section on relational commands. Another, more elegant way to perform this function is with the `REPORT FORM` command, although this is more commonly used for output to a printer.

Input from a database with output to a screen (using the full screen and defining where data is to appear) is the normal mode of use in fourth generation languages. In dBASE III, this is done with a group of `@x,y SAY` commands:

```
USE CLIENT
@ 5,5 SAY LNAME
@ 5,40 SAY FNAME
@ 6,5 SAY PHONE
```

The `@x,y` defines the row and column on the screen where the output will occur. These statements are usually contained in a separate screen definition file (with a suffix of

.FMT). They may be created from the Assistant. The data, while read, is not displayed on the screen until either a READ command or a CLEAR GETS command is executed. The latter does not work with .FMT files.

Before putting the record on the screen, the program must be using not only the correct file but also the correct record within the file. If you are working with an existing record, the program may be positioned to the correct record with any of the following commands:

GO record number

LOCATE key value

SEEK key value (works only with indexed files)

```
GO 10
LOCATE FOR LNAME = "LEHMAN"
SEEK NEWNAME
```

Once the program is positioned to the record, input and output commands will work with the record at hand.

dBASE III+ allows you to work with up to 10 files at a time. The SELECT command is used to determine which file a given operation will refer to. The name following the SELECT is the name of the work area to be used in referring to that file.

```
SELECT B
USE INVENTRY INDEX INUMBER
SELECT A
USE PODET INDEX ITEMP
```

At any one time, all dBASE III+ file commands (such as USE, LIST, READ, etc.) apply to the file defined in the current work area. If one wishes to use more than one relation (file) at a time, each is opened in a different work area. Conceptually, this is much like having each file on a separate diskette in MSDOS and switching between diskettes (A:, B:, etc.).

Input from a keyboard with output to a database is usually done in conjunction with display from a database to the screen. In dBASE III, this is done with the @GET command, followed by the READ command:

```
USE CLIENT
@ 5,20 GET LNAME
@ 5,60 GET FNAME
@ 6,20 GET PHONE
READ
```

Input from a keyboard with output to a memory variable is usually used to get answers to questions: menu selections, search values, or answers to questions like "Do you want to update another record (Y/N)?". In DBASE III, this is done with the `ACCEPT` command:

```
ACCEPT "Another Record (Y/N) " TO YN
```

In this example, `YN` is a memory variable. Related commands are those to print a longer message on the screen (`PRINT` or `?`) and those to wait for any key to be pressed before going on (`WAIT`):

```
? "Sorting and indexing supplier file: please
stand by"
? "Press any key to continue"
WAIT
```

Input from a memory variable with output to the screen in full screen mode is done with `@SAY`:

```
@23,10 SAY YN
```

Input from a memory variable with output to a screen (dumb terminal) is a variation of the above. In dBASE III, this is done with the `PRINT` or `?` command:

```
? "Your answer is ",YN
```

Input from a memory variable with output to a printer is done in the same way. The only difference is that first the printer is turned on. Anything sent to the screen in non–full screen mode after a `SET PRINT ON` command is also sent to the printer.

```
SET PRINT ON
? "Your answer is ",YN
SET PRINT OFF
```

This is often used in conjunction with predefined reports;

```
SET PRINT ON
REPORT FORM SUPPLIST
SET PRINT OFF
```

If you want to use full-screen mode, the additional command

```
SET DEVICE TO PRINT
```

will direct all output from `@SAY` and `@GET` commands to the printer. The command

```
SET DEVICE TO SCREEN
```

will redirect output to the screen.

```
SET DEVICE TO PRINT
@ 22,1 SAY "Quantity"
@ 22,10 SAY "Part Number"
@ 22,51 SAY "Description"
@ 22,96 SAY "Price"
```

Input from a database with output to a printer is done the same way as above. If the desired output is not in full-screen mode (e.g. the output from the `DISPLAY` or `REPORT` commands), use `SET PRINT ON` and `SET PRINT OFF`. If output from `@SAY` and `@GET` commands is to be sent to the printer, use

```
SET DEVICE TO PRINT
@ I,1 SAY POQUANT
@ I,10 SAY INUMB
@ I,51 SAY INAME
@ I,92 SAY IPRICE
STORE I+1 TO I
```

Note that in this example, the row number is a memory variable rather than a numeric constant.

Input from a database with output to a text file is used when you want to use the results from a dBASE III+ system with some other program, such as Lotus 123 or BPI accounting. This is done with the `COPY` command:

```
COPY TO filename
```

or

```
COPY DELIMITED
```

or

```
COPY DELIMITED WITH '
```

The first form copies the dBASE III+ file as a plain text file, rather like the output from the DISPLAY command. The second form separates variables with commas and encloses strings with double quote marks; this is the form that BASIC requires. The third form allows you to choose what will be used to separate variables; in the example it will be a single quote.

Input from a text file with output to a database is used to load information from another system into dBASE. The data must be in row and column format, one record to a line of text. The APPEND command is used:

```
APPEND FROM filename
```

or

```
APPEND DELIMITED
```

or

```
APPEND DELIMITED WITH '
```

The DELIMITED statement has the same meaning as on output, but this time it defines the format of the input file.

Move commands in dBASE III+ are used to move constant values to memory variables or to fields in the database, to move constant values from fields in the database to memory variables, or to move constant values from memory variables to fields in the data base.

A value is stored to a memory variable with the STORE command and is stored to a file in a database with the REPLACE command:

```
STORE "Y" TO YN
STORE LNAME TO LASTNAME
REPLACE LNAME WITH "LEHMAN"
REPLACE LNAME WITH LASTNAME
```

REPLACE commands apply to the current record unless otherwise specified; they can be applied either to all records or to a subset of records, for example,

```
REPLACE ACCTPAID WITH .T. ALL
REPLACE MAILED WITH .T. FOR STATE="AK"
```

CONTROL STRUCTURES

Control structures were discussed in Chapter 16. dBASE III+ provides

Sequence
IF-THEN-ELSE
CASE
WHILE

IF-THEN-ELSE is implemented in dBASE III+ with

```
IF condition
statements
ELSE statements
ENDIF
```

For example:

```
IF I > PAGEEND
SELECT B
DO POADDR
SELECT A
STORE 24 TO I
ENDIF
```

CASE is implemented in dBASE III+ with `DO CASE`, for example:

```
ACCEPT ' Which number? ' TO CHOICE
DO CASE
CASE CHOICE='0'
QUIT
CASE CHOICE='1'
RETURN
CASE CHOICE='2'
DO DATAENT WITH
FILENAME,FMTNAME,SRTFIELD,INDXFILE
CASE CHOICE='3'
DO DATAUP WITH
FILENAME,FMTNAME,SRTFIELD,INDXFILE
CASE CHOICE='4'
STORE DISPFILE TO FMTNAME
DO DATADEL WITH
FILENAME,FMTNAME,SRTFIELD,INDXFILE
CASE CHOICE='5'
USE &FILENAME
SET PRINT ON
REPORT FORM &rptname
SET PRINT OF
CASE CHOICE='6'
USE &FILENAME
ENDCASE
```

WHILE is implemented in dBASE III+ with the following:

```
DO WHILE conditions
statements
LOOP
ENDWHILE
```

For example:

```
DO WHILE .T.
CLEAR
ACCEPT "Key name " TO SN
GO TOP
SEEK S
SET FORMAT TO &FMTNAME
CLEAR
READ
CLOSE FORMAT
@ 23,5 SAY "Another record? (Y or N) "
@ 23,40 GET YN
READ
IF YN="N"
RETURN
ENDIF
ENDDO
```

A final control statement is the one used to invoke a module: DO module name or DO module name WITH parameters:

```
DO DATAENT WITH
FILENAME,FMTNAME,SRTFIELD,INDXFILE
```

```
PROCEDURE DATAENT
PARAMETERS FILENAME,FMTNAME,SRTFIELD,INDXFIL
USE &FILENAME
```

Logical operations are used with IF-THEN-ELSE and CASE statements, as well as with some of the relational statements described below, in order to deal with complex conditions. For example:

```
IF .NOT. (EOF() .OR. BOF())
```

```
IF WOTYPE <> 'S' .AND. WOTYPE <> 's' .AND. WOTYPE <> 'l'
.AND. WOTYPE <> 'L
```

String commands are used to manipulate character data types. All of them are in function form, which means that the operation name is followed by its object, in parentheses (ACTION(**object**)). In alphabetical order, the most common dBASE III+ string commands are

ISALPHA(**string**) is true if **string** begins with a letter.

ISLOWER(**string**) is true if **string** begins with a lower case letter.

ISUPPER(**string**) is true if **string** begins with an upper case letter.

LEFT(**string,number**) extracts a substring starting from the left, and of the length specified by **number**.

LEN(**string**) is the length of the specified string.

LOWER(**string**) converts its object from upper to lower case.

LTRIM(**string**) removes leading blanks from its object.

RIGHT(**string,number**) extracts a substring starting from the right, and of the length specified by **number**.

SUBSTR(**string,start,number**) extracts a substring starting from the number of positions from the left specified by **start**, and of the length specified by **number**.

```
STORE SUBSTR(INDATE,1,2) TO MM
STORE SUBSTR(INDATE,4,2) TO DD
STORE SUBSTR(INDATE,7,2) TO YY
```

UPPER(**string**) converts its object from lower to upper case.

Conversion of data types is used when data is stored or input as one data type, but is needed in another format. For example, a data field may need to be inserted into a character field in another file, or a number may need to be stored as part of a character field. The most commonly used data conversion functions in dBASE III+ are

CTOD(string) converts character data to date data. For example:

```
STORE CTOD('02/14/88') TO THISDATE
```

DTOC(date) converts a date type to character type. For example:

```
STORE DTOC(DATE()) TO DATECHAR
```

STR(number,length,decimal) converts a number to a character string with the given length and number of decimal places. For example:

```
STORE STR(INTEREST,8,2) TO ACCTNOTE
```

VAL(character) converts a character representation of a number to numeric form. For example:

```
STORE BALANCE*VAL('1.05') TO ACCRUED
```

```
STORE DAYTOT + VAL(DD) TO DAYTOT
```

Arithmetic operations are addition, subtraction, multiplication, and division. They are represented conventionally as

+ addition, e.g., x + y
- subtraction, e.g., x - y
* multiplication, e.g., x*y
/ division, e.g., x/y

For example:

```
REPLACE AMOUNT WITH A->IPRICE*WOQUANT
```

```
STORE (TOTALDAYS*INTRATE*BALANCE)+INTEREST TO INTEREST
```

Additional functions are

ABS(x) Absolute value of **x**
EXP(x) e^x
MOD(x,y) The remainder of **x** divided by **y**
ROUND(x,y) **x** rounded to **y** decimal places
SQRT(x) The square root of **x**

Relational operations are single operations which apply to two or more files at once. The most common relational operations in dBASE III+ are DISPLAY, which extracts all or a subset of elements and records from a file; JOIN, which combines two files; and UPDATE, which updates the records in a master file with transactions. Related commands are SORT, which sorts a file, and INDEX, which indexes a file.

DISPLAY displays the contents of all or part of a file. The FOR clause is used to define the subset of records displayed. It is intended to display data on the screen and pauses every 20 lines. The LIST command is similar except that it does not pause every 20 lines; it can also be used to print file contents, although REPORT is a better way to do this.

```
DISPLAY WONUMB,WODATE FOR WOCUST = "10234"
LIST WONUMB,WODATE FOR WOCUST = "10234"
LIST WONUMB,WODATE FOR WOCUST = "10234" TO PRINT
```

`REPORT` is similar to `LIST TO PRINT` except that it provides headings, page breaks, labels, totals, and subtotals if desired. A report form is created with the command `CREATE REPORT`. The report can then be used in a program with the `REPORT FORM` command. For example:

```
SET PRINT ON
REPORT FORM SUPPRPT
SET PRINT OFF
```

or

```
SET PRINT ON
REPORT FORM PBLRPT FOR POPAID="N"
SET PRINT OFF
```

`JOIN` combines two files; it unnormalizes. The files in question are identified with the `SELECT` and `USE` commands, then combined based on a common key value. For example, the following `JOIN` statement uses two files defined as follows:

WO = WONUMB + WODATE + WOCUST + WOTAX

WODET = WONUMB + WOTYPE + WOQUANT + INUMB + IPRICE

and produces

TEMP = WONUMB + WODATE + WOCUST + WOTAX+ WOTYPE + WOQUANT + INUMB + IPRICE

```
SELECT B
USE WO
SELECT A
USE WODET
JOIN WITH WO TO TEMP FOR WONUMB=B->WONUMB
```

`UPDATE` is used to modify all of the values in a file based on those in another. The example below inserts into **PODET** the current values of partname (**Iname**) and price (**Iprice**) from the inventory file.

```
USE PODET
INDEX ON INUMB TO ITEMP
SELECT B
USE INVENTRY INDEX INUMBER
SELECT A
USE PODET INDEX ITEM
UPDATE ON INUMB FROM INVENTRY REPLACE IPRICE WITH B->NPRICE
RANDOM
UPDATE ON INUMB FROM INVENTRY REPLACE INAME WITH B->INAME
RANDOM
```

SORT is used to sort records into order.

```
SORT ON PONUMB TO TEMP1
```

INDEX is used to build indices on file keys. A file may have as many indices as it has separate keys. The format of the command is

INDEX ON sortfield TO indexfile.

The following fragment deletes an existing index file whose name is contained in the variable **Indexfile** and builds a new index by that name on the field contained in the variable **Sortfield**.

```
USE &FILENAME
DELETE FILE &INDXFILE
INDEX ON &SRTFIELD TO &INDXFILE
```

Chapter 18

ADDITIONAL FEATURES OF dBASE IV

CHAPTER GOALS

- Introduce SQL model.
- Discuss new operations and functions not in dBASE III.
- Discuss new program objects available in dBASE IV.

In terms of packaging, dBASE IV provides both a new user interface (discussed in Chapter 4) and a series of program development tools. As a programming language, dBASE IV introduces the following improvements over dBASE III:

- It introduces additional data structures for memory variables (Chapter 7).
- It makes index use and manipulation (Chapter 7) easier.
- It adds a floating point data type (Chapter 7).
- It expands the relational operations and allows SQL syntax.
- It adds additional commands and functions.
- It provides direct support for the following user interface objects:
  Windows (Chapter 9)
  Menus (Chapter 9)

This chapter discusses the improvements that have not already been discussed in Chapters 7 and 9.

SQL

SQL (Structured Query Language) is a set of relational commands that is standardized for all sizes and makes of computers. It was originally developed by IBM for use with the mainframe DB2 database management system. SQL is not a complete language; it contains operations and relational data definitions but no memory data definitions (or operations) or control structures. It was intended for stand-alone use for simple queries or for use embedded in existing programming languages. Mainframe systems often embed SQL commands in existing third generation languages such as COBOL, PL/1, and BASIC. dBASE IV embeds SQL commands in the dBASE language.

SQL versus dBASE Mode

Because the structure of SQL database is very different from that of dBASE files and because some of the standard SQL commands have the same names as some dBASE commands but different formats or results, one has to tell the dBASE system whether commands and data are to be interpreted as traditional dBASE or as SQL. To switch from dBASE mode to SQL mode, one uses the command `SET SQL ON`. `SET SQL OFF` switches back from SQL to dBASE mode.

Generally, dBASE control structures, program-oriented objects, and input/output manipulation statements are available in SQL mode. dBASE statements that manipulate relations (e.g., `USE`, `SELECT`, `LIST`, `BROWSE`, `JOIN`, `UPDATE`) are not available in SQL mode; SQL provides replacements for these operations.

SQL Data Definition

SQL stores all of the information related to a given application in a single database file. This includes tables, views, and indices. By contrast, in dBASE, each table is stored as a separate file, as are indices, views, and other objects related to the tables.

An SQL database is created with the command

```
CREATE DATABASE (application name);
```

```
CREATE TABLE supplier
ID_number     CHAR (6),
Lastname      CHAR (12),
Firstname     CHAR (10),
Address       CHAR (32)
City          CHAR (32)
State         CHAR (2),
ZIPcode       CHAR (5),
Phone         CHAR (14);
```

FIGURE 18-1 Creating a table in SQL.

Note that all SQL commands end with a semicolon (;). In following examples, note also that the list of objects in a command are enclosed in parentheses. A database is activated with the command

```
START DATABASE (application name);
```

Tables within a database are created with the command `CREATE TABLE`. An example is shown in Figure 18-1.

Data is inserted into a table directly by using the `INSERT INTO` command:

```
INSERT INTO supplier
VALUES ("110024","Lehman","John","118 Bunnell",
"Fairbanks","AK","99775","(907) 474-7266");
```

It can be inserted from another table by using a `SELECT` clause instead of a `VALUE` clause as above.

```
INSERT INTO supplier
SELECT *
FROM Customer
WHERE Lastname = "Lehman";
```

The `SELECT` clause is discussed at length in the next section entitled SQL Queries.

Tables may be updated with the `UPDATE` command, and items may be deleted with the `DELETE FROM` command:

```
UPDATE supplier
SET Phone =("(907) 474-7266")
WHERE Lastname="Lehman";
```

```
DELETE FROM supplier
WHERE Lastname = "Lehman";
```

New columns may be added to existing tables using the `ALTER TABLE` command:

```
ALTER TABLE supplier
ADD (Discount NUMERIC(3,3);
```

```
Structure for database: D:po.dbf
Number of data records: 0
Date of last update        : 10/28/87
Field      Field Name         Type        Width    Dec
1          PONUMB             Character   6
2          PODATE             Character   8
3          POSUPP             Character   40
4          POPAID             Character   1
** Total **                               56
```

```
Structure for database: D:supplier.dbf
Number of data records: 13
Date of last update        : 01/22/88
Field      Field Name         Type        Width    Dec
1          SNAME                          Character      32
2          SNUMBER            Character   4
3          SALESMN            Character   32
4          SADDR1             Character   32
5          SADDR2             Character   32
6          SADDR3             Character   32
7          SPHONE             Character   20
8          DUEDAYS            Numeric     2
9          DISCOUNT           Numeric     4        2
10         DISCDAYS           Numeric     2
11         SNOTES             Character   32
** Total **                               225
```

FIGURE 18-2 Input data structures.

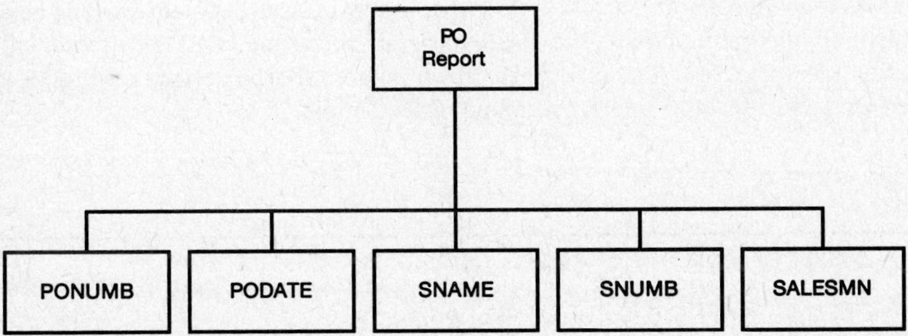

FIGURE 18-3 Output data structures.

```
SELECT B
USE SUPPLIER
SELECT A
USE PO
JOIN WITH SUPPLIER TO TEMP FOR POSUPP=SUPPLIER->SNUMB
USE TEMP
LIST PONUMN, PODATE, SNAME, POSUPP, SALESMN
```

FIGURE 18-4 dBASE code.

SQL Queries

Technically, the major difference between native dBASE mode and SQL mode is that dBASE formulates queries by using "relational algebra" whereas SQL formulates queries by using "relational calculus." What this means in English is that in dBASE, you need to tell the system *how* you want to combine two or more tables (relations), whereas in SQL you specify the *result* of that combination. dBASE provides a very limited version of relational calculus with the `SET RELATION TO` command; in SQL, this is the normal way of doing things.

Specifically, SQL does not require the use of work areas (e.g., `SELECT A`) and explicit `JOIN` commands. Rather, in SQL, a query may make use of several data relations at once.

Let us assume that we want a report on purchase orders and their suppliers. The relations (`.DBF` files in dBASE) are **PO** and **SUPPLIER** as illustrated in Figure 18-2. The result is to look like the data structure diagram of Figure 18-3.

In dBASE III, we would have to write code such as that in Figure 18-4. This involves first joining the two files and then listing the results. In SQL, we would write a `SELECT` request as illustrated in Figure 18-5.

SQL Views

Views in SQL, as in dBASE, are virtual tables; a view may be a subset of an existing table or a combination of existing tables. Views are basically predefined `SELECT` statements and are defined with the `SELECT` clause which would produce the desired results. They are defined with the `CREATE VIEW` command. For example:

```
SELECT PONUMB, PODATE, SNAME, SNUMB, SALESMN
FROM PO, SUPPLIER
WHERE PO.POSUPP=SUPPLIER.SNUMB;
```

FIGURE 18-5 SQL code.

```
CREATE VIEW PO_header
(POdate, POnumb, supplier)
AS SELECT POdate, POnumb, sname
FROM PO, SUPPLIER
WHERE PO.POSUPP=SUPPLIER.SNUMB;
```

Views are deleted with the `DROP VIEW` command. They are activated by the statement `SELECT * FROM` viewname; (the * means all rows).

The availability and unlimited nature of views in SQL means that the program object inquiry (Chapter 11) will usually be defined directly as a view, and, therefore, will not be designed with a structure chart and action diagram for implementation in code.

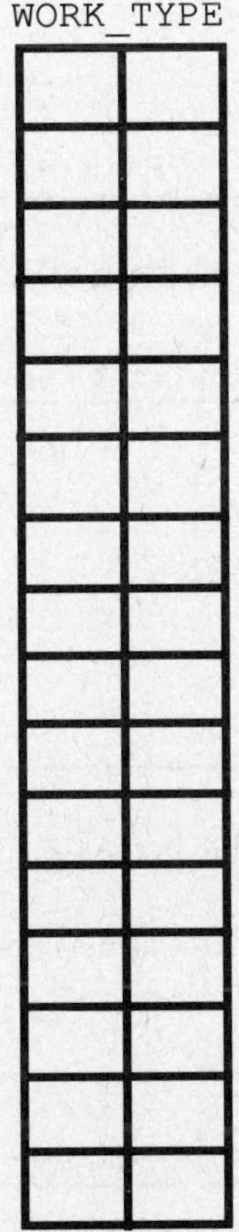

FIGURE 18-6 The `DECLARE` command creates an array of length 16 with 2 columns.

dBASE NATIVE MODE

Manipulation of Arrays

Arrays, by way of review from Chapter 7, are groups of identical elements or structures. The array can be referenced as a group, or the individual items in an array can be referenced independently. Arrays are commonly used to implement mathematical vectors and matrices as well as in-memory tables. Arrays in dBASE IV are created with the DECLARE command:

```
DECLARE work_type[16,2]
```

This creates an array of length 16 with 2 columns as illustrated in Figure 18-6 where one might store the key for work type in column one and the value in column 2. Values are assigned with normal assignment statements. For example:

```
work_type[1,1] = "G"
      work_type[1,2] = "SALES"
      work_type[2,1] = "R"
      work_type[2,2] = "REPAIR"
```

Use of array variables often takes the form of selection via an index variable. For example:

```
I = 1
DO WHILE I <= 16
 IF work_type[I,1] = thistype
   ? work_type[I,2]
 ELSE
   I = I + 1
 ENDIF
ENDDO
```

This cycles through the array until the value in the first column of the table is equal to that of the variable thistype.

The command APPEND FROM ARRAY allows one to append data stored in an array to a relation. For example:

```
USE parts
APPEND FROM ARRAY new_parts
```

Conversely, the command COPY TO ARRAY allows one to append data stored in a relation to an array. For example:

```
USE parts
COPY TO ARRAY new_parts
```

Other Changes

Character variables can now be used directly as objects of commands; the & operator is no longer needed to specify that the value of the variable is being used. Thus, given the command

```
STORE "CLIENT.DBF" TO workfile
```

one need not say

```
USE &workfile
```

but can now say

```
USE workfile
```

Variables of type Date are now delimited with { }:

```
STORE {10/11/1974} TO ADATE
```

New Control Structure

SCAN/ENDSCAN is a new control structure similar to DO WHILE except that it scans the entire file rather than forcing the programmer to step through record by record. Often it is used to get all occurrences of a given condition in an indexed file. For example, in dBASE III, to print all of the customers who own a Cessna, one would write

```
USE planes INDEX type
DO WHILE .NOT. EOF()
      IF type = "CESSNA"
            ? cust_name
      ENDIF
      SKIP
ENDDO
```

Using the scan control structure one would write:

```
USE planes INDEX type
SEEK "CESSNA"
SCAN WHILE type = "CESSNA"
     ? cust_name
ENDSCAN
```

Window Support

Windows were introduced in Chapter 9, and their use was illustrated in the extended case study of Chapter 16. Explicit support for windows is one of the major advantages of dBASE IV. Windows may be any portion of the screen; while a window is active it forms a virtual screen to which all output is sent. Row and column numbers in SAY and GET commands refer to coordinates within the window relative to its boundaries. I.e., in Figure 18-7, if window C is active, the command

```
@ 1,1 SAY "Here I am"
```

will appear at the upper left-hand corner of window C about one third of the way down the screen rather than in the upper left-hand corner of the screen, as would be true if no window were active.

In using windows, a window must first be defined, giving its position on the screen in terms of upper left corner and lower right corner. For example, the command

```
DEFINE WINDOW poheader FROM 2,33 TO 10,70
```

defines a window named poheader located with its upper left corner in row 2 column 33 and its lower right corner in row 10 column 70 (about the location of window B in Figure 18-7). The command

```
DEFINE WINDOW supplier FROM 2,2 TO 10,32 DOUBLE
```

defines a window named supplier located with its upper left corner in row 2 column 2 and its lower right corner in row 10 column 32 (about the location of window A in Figure 18-7). Once a window is defined, it exists as a potential object until deleted with a RELEASE WINDOW windowname command (to erase a specific window) or a CLEAR WINDOWS command (to erase all windows). It does not, however, take effect until it is activated.

A window is activated with the ACTIVATE WINDOW command. Once this command is issued, all subsequent screen operations refer to the window until such time as it is deactivated. In the following example, the three SAY commands output to the window called poheader (upper right hand corner of the screen). Windows are deactivated with

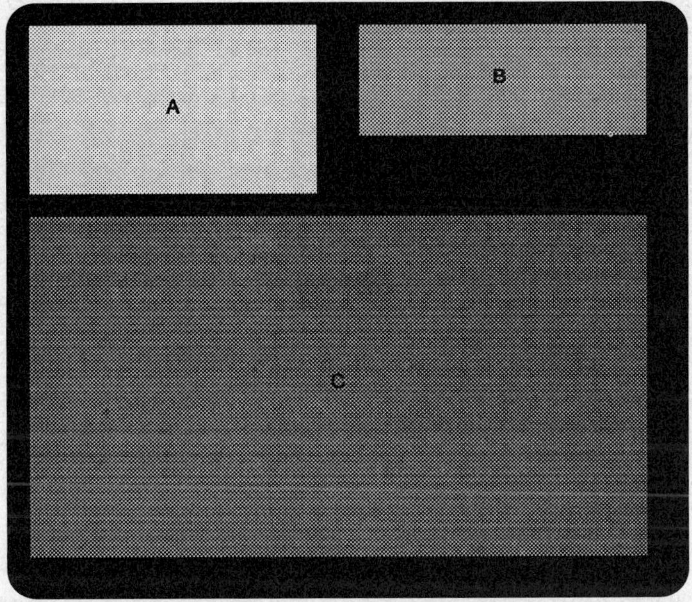

FIGURE 18-7 Windows.

the DEACTIVATE WINDOW command. Alternatively, the command ACTIVATE SCREEN may be used; this is especially useful when one wants to keep a window (or a pop-up menu) on the screen for reference but not use it.

```
ACTIVATE WINDOW poheader
@ 0,0 SAY ponumb
@ 2,1 SAY podate
@ 3,1 SAY posupp
DEACTIVATE WINDOW poheader
```

Window definitions may be saved to a file with the SAVE WINDOW command and restored with the RESTORE WINDOW command. This is useful when defining standard windows for use throughout a large system.

Menu Support

There are two forms of predefined menu-types available in dBASE IV. Pop-ups are special windows that contain menus. Like other menus, they are defined, activated, and cleared. When a pop-up menu is defined, each of the lines (bars) in the menu must also be defined. The syntax is as follows:

```
DEFINE POPUP <popup name> FROM <row> <column>
DEFINE BAR <line number> OF <popup name> PROMPT <message>
```

For example:

```
DEFINE POPUP main FROM 10,2 TO 20,70;
MESSAGE "Press first letter of MENU choice; or highlight,
then press <Enter>"
DEFINE BAR 1 OF main PROMPT "MAIN MENU " SKIP
DEFINE BAR 2 OF main PROMPT " RETURN TO dBASE"
DEFINE BAR 3 OF main PROMPT " QUIT TO DOS"
DEFINE BAR 4 OF main PROMPT " CUSTOMERS"
DEFINE BAR 5 OF main PROMPT " SUPPLIERS"
DEFINE BAR 6 OF main PROMPT " INVENTORY"
DEFINE BAR 7 OF main PROMPT "PURCHASE ORDERS"
DEFINE BAR 8 OF main PROMPT "PACKING LIST"
ON SELECTION POPUP main DO Main
```

See Figure 18-8 for the results.

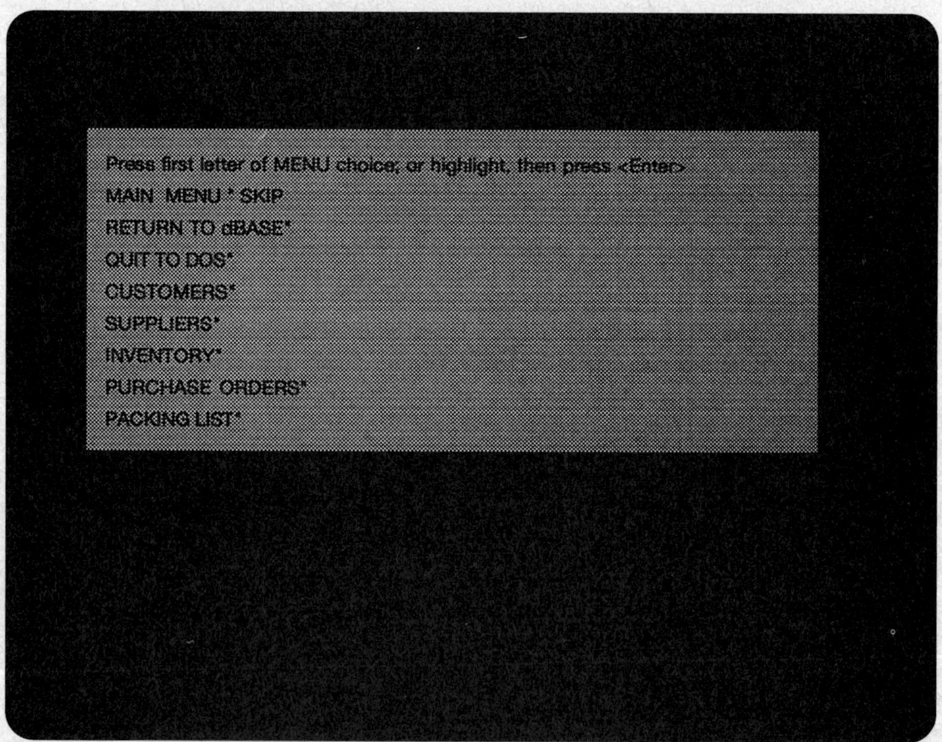

FIGURE 18-8 Pop-up menu.

FIGURE 18-9 Pop-up menu as part of bar menu.

Pop-up menus, like windows, are not active when first defined. To activate a pop-up menu, one uses the command: ACTIVATE POPUP <popup name>. For example:

```
ACTIVATE POPUP main
```

Pop-up menus are deactivated with the command DEACTIVATE POPUP. They are erased from memory with the command CLEAR POPUPS.

The other sort of predefined menu in dBASE IV is a bar menu (similar to those in Windows, in the Presentation Manager, or on an Apple Macintosh. As expected, the appropriate commands are DEFINE MENU, ACTIVATE MENU, DEACTIVATE MENU, and CLEAR MENU. In addition, one has to define the "pads" on each bar—the selections. This is done with the DEFINE PAD command. Actions to be taken if a pad is selected are defined with the ON PAD command. Syntax is as follows:

```
DEFINE MENU <menu name>
DEFINE PAD <pad name> OF <menu name> PROMPT <message>
ACTIVATE MENU <menu name> [PAD <pad name>]
DEACTIVATE MENU
CLEAR MENUS
RELEASE MENUS <menu name list>
ON PAD <pad name> OF <menu name> <action>
```

Often bar menus are combined with pop-up menus, as illustrated in Figure 18-9.

```
ON PAD exit OF pomenu ACTIVATE POPUP exit
```

dBASE IV has a large number of additional commands, some of which are cosmetic (such as the ability to work in multiple colors) and many of which allow great flexibility in file and data transfer. Since this is a book on program design rather than on dBASE IV, interested readers are referred either to the dBASE manuals or to books specifically on dBASE coding. The command set discussed here is sufficient for our purposes (and for most actual programming).

Chapter 19

CASE STUDY IN CODING

CHAPTER GOALS

- **Present an integrated example of translation of the action diagrams of Chapter 16 into dBASE code.**

In this chapter, we take the action diagrams from the case study in Chapter 16 and turn them into dBASE code. Figures 19-1 to 19-3 reviews the structure of the resulting system (from Chapter 13).

Figure 19-4 reviews the action diagram for the main (top level) module referred to as "Inventory System" in the structure chart of Figure 19-1. Figure 19-5 shows the dBASE code to implement this action diagram. Translation from action diagram to code is fairly straightforward. The major changes are in the DO FOREVER control structure and the statements to display data on the screen.

dBASE does not have a DO FOREVER command, so we simulate it with a `DO WHILE` command. In this case, we store the logical value .T. (true) in the logical variable `RUN`, and use `RUN` as the condition of the `WHILE`. This is a common technique in dBASE (and in most other procedural languages) because it gives us an infinite loop that can, if necessary, be stopped by changing the value of `RUN` from within the loop.

In displaying the menu on the screen, we use a set of `@ row,column SAY` statements. We could also use the print command (`?`) here to translate the action diagram's "DISPLAY." (This is illustrated in the `ELSE` clause of the `CASE` statement in Figure 19-5.) Very often we will have the choice of a number of dBASE statements (often with subtle differences) which can implement a given statement in an action diagram; in such cases we can either choose the most appropriate dBASE statements or simply standardize on a single translation. As has been mentioned in previous chapters, it is possible to write working dBASE programs using only a small fraction of the commands available in the dBASE language.

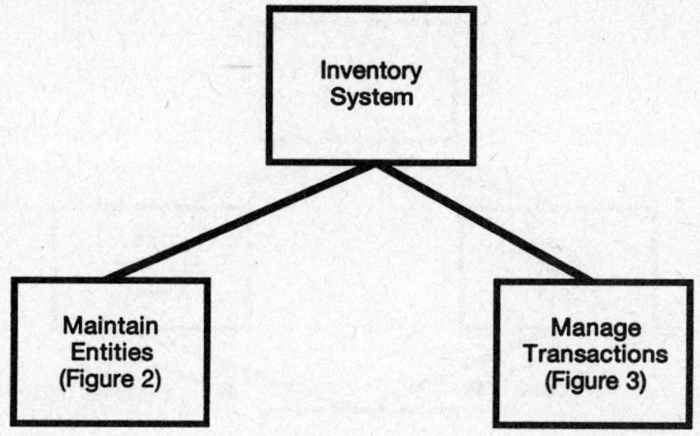

FIGURE 19-1 Overview structure chart for inventory system (Chapter 13).

Figure 19-6 shows the action diagram for the module **MAINTAIN ENTITIES**; Figure 19-7 shows the translation into dBASE. Note that the structure of this module is almost identical with that of the module in Figure 19-5; it is normal to keep a single **MENU** module which a programmer modifies to produce each new menu. Alternatively, dBASE will create menus using the program generating tools in the package. Either way, the amount of new code that has to be written is minimized, thus productivity is increased.

The only new (actually review) feature of this code is the passing of data to lower-level modules via the `DO procedure WITH parameters` statement.

Figure 19-8 shows the action diagram for **MAINTAIN ENTITY**; Figure 19-9 shows the dBASE III code, and Figure 19-10 shows the dBASE IV code. Both of these are menus similar in structure to those above. The difference between the dBASE III and the dBASE IV versions is that the former uses the `&` macro expander to indicate that the program should use the value of the memory variable. In dBASE IV, this is not necessary. Also, the dBASE III version requires an additional parameter to hold the name of the index file; dBASE IV takes care of the index file without the programmer having to specify it.

Figure 19-11 shows the action diagram for **ENTER RECORD**; Figure 19-12 shows the code. This is the first non-menu module that we have encountered. This is a general-purpose module that can be used to enter data into any entity for which we have an associated screen format defined. The code differs from the action diagram in the addition of a parameter for index file name. This is required for dBASE III but not for dBASE IV, which maintains the indices automatically. Note also that the use of the `&` operator would not be required under dBASE IV.

An additional difference from the action diagram is the paragraph added to sort and index the file. This is used because even though logically we are sorting a particular file, dBASE requires that a file be sorted to another file with a different name and that indices be written to specific files. The sequence of code in the sort and index section uses temporary files for this to create the illusion that the existing datafile is sorted directly.

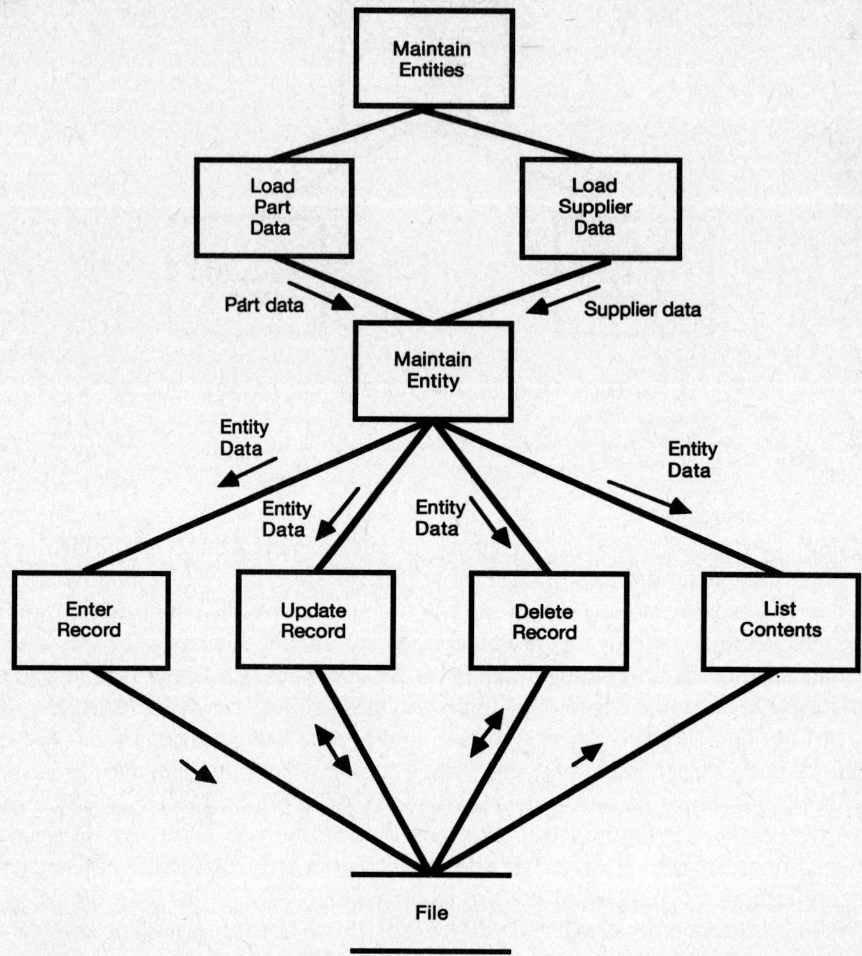

FIGURE 19-2 MAINTAIN ENTITIES structure chart for inventory system (Chapter 13).

Figure 19-13 shows the action diagram for **UPDATE RECORD**; Figure 19-14 shows the code. Like Figures 19-11 and 19-12, this is a general-purpose module that can be used to update data for any entity for which we have an associated screen format defined. As is true for data entry, the code differs from the action diagram in the addition of a parameter for index file name.

Figure 19-15 shows the action diagram for **DELETE RECORD**; Figure 19-16 shows the code. This is another general-purpose module. The major differences in the code arise from the fact that in dBASE records are marked for deletion by the `DELETE` command but are not actually deleted until the `PACK` command is given.

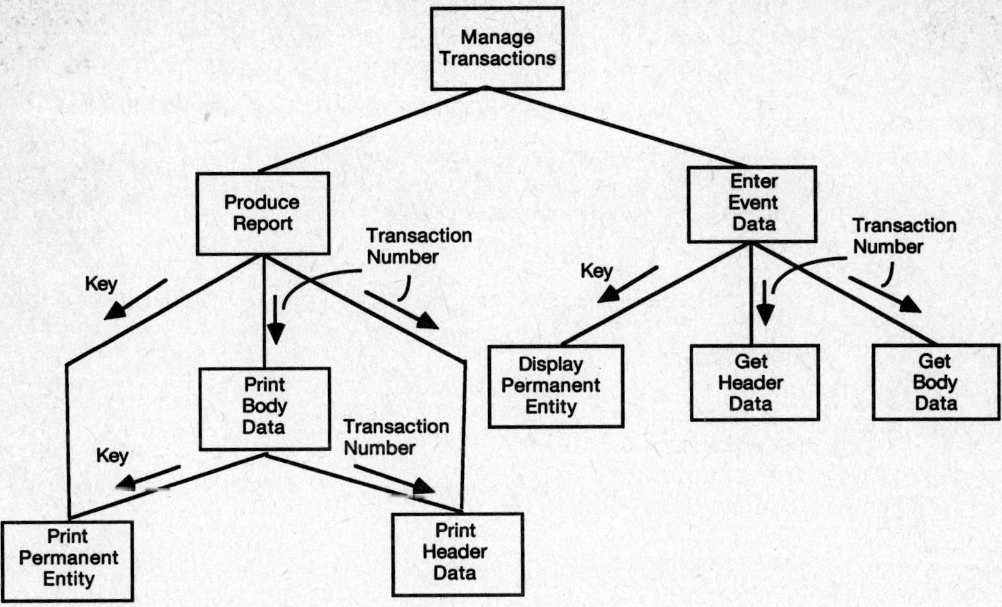

FIGURE 19-3 Transaction structure chart for inventory system (Chapter 13).

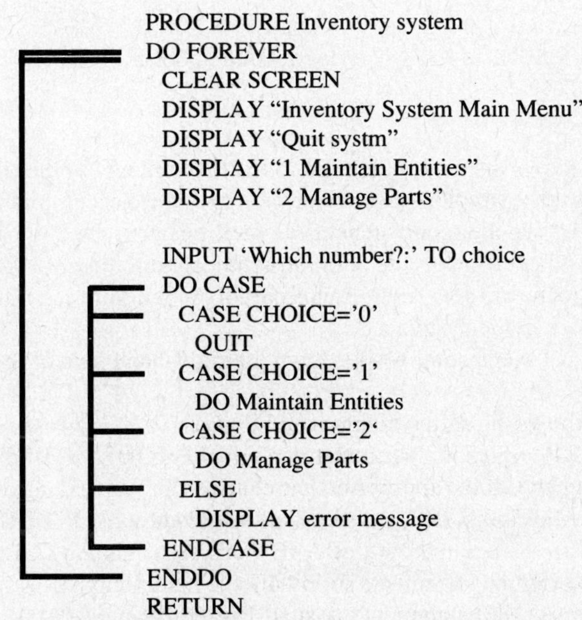

```
PROCEDURE Inventory system
DO FOREVER
  CLEAR SCREEN
  DISPLAY "Inventory System Main Menu"
  DISPLAY "Quit systm"
  DISPLAY "1 Maintain Entities"
  DISPLAY "2 Manage Parts"

  INPUT 'Which number?:' TO choice
  DO CASE
    CASE CHOICE='0'
      QUIT
    CASE CHOICE='1'
      DO Maintain Entities
    CASE CHOICE='2'
      DO Manage Parts
    ELSE
      DISPLAY error message
  ENDCASE
ENDDO
RETURN
```

FIGURE 19-4 Action diagram for **MAIN** module.

```
PROCEDURE Main
STORE .T. TO RUN
DO WHILE RUN
 CLEAR
 @ 2,15 SAY "Inventory System Main Menu"
 @5,10 SAY ") Quit system"
 @6,10 SAY "1 Maintain Entitites"
 @7,10 SAY "2 Manage Parts"
 ?
 ACCEPT 'Which number?' TO CHOICE
 DO CASE
  CASE CHOICE='0'
   QUIT
  CASE CHOICE='1'
   DO MAINTAIN
  CASE CHOICE='2'
   DO PARTS
  ELSE
 ?"Invalid choice - please enter one of the above"
 ENDCASE
LOOP
ENDDO

RETURN
```

FIGURE 19-5 dBASE code for **MAIN** module.

Figure 19-17 shows the action diagram to list the contents of the file; Figure 19-18 shows the code. This is the simplest possible version of code to accomplish the task; a more elegant version would use the report-generating facilities described in Chapter 9.

This completes the left-hand side of the structure chart in Figure 19-2. Note that with very minor changes to the top-level menus, this part of the program can be used to maintain any permanent entities in the system.

The remainder of the chapter works down the right-hand side of the structure chart in Figure 19-3.

Figure 19-19 shows the action diagram and Figure 19-20 shows the code for **ISSUE PURCHASE ORDER**, which is a particular version of **PRODUCE REPORT**. The code in Figure 19-20 assumes that the appropriate purchase order files exist and outputs only to the printer. The code in Figure 19-20 works with three relations: **PO DETAIL**, **PO**, and **SUPPLIER**. These are associated with dBASE work areas named C, B, and A, respectively. Thus, all file-oriented statements following the command `SELECT A` refer to the **PO** file until another `SELECT` statement is issued. The command `SET PRINT ON` directs all non–full-screen output to the printer. The command `SET DEVICE TO PRINT` directs all full-screen output (such as the object of a `SAY` statement) to the printer.

The next three modules get data from the appropriate tables and print it in the proper order. The use of windows is simulated with position statements in the dBASE code for these routines to allow maximum design flexibility for the outputs. The action diagrams for the procedure **PRODUCE SUPPLIER** is shown in Figure 19-21. **PRODUCE PURCHASE ORDER HEADER** is shown in Figure 19-23, and **PRODUCE PURCHASE ORDER BODY** is shown in Figure 19-25. These action diagrams are simply specific versions of the ones presented in Chapter 16.

The dBASE modules to implement these action diagrams are shown in Figures 19-22, 19-24, and 19-26.. The locations on the screen are hard-coded in Figures 19-22 and 19-24; in Figure 19-26, row locations are determined by the value of the variable I, which is set between 24 and 53.

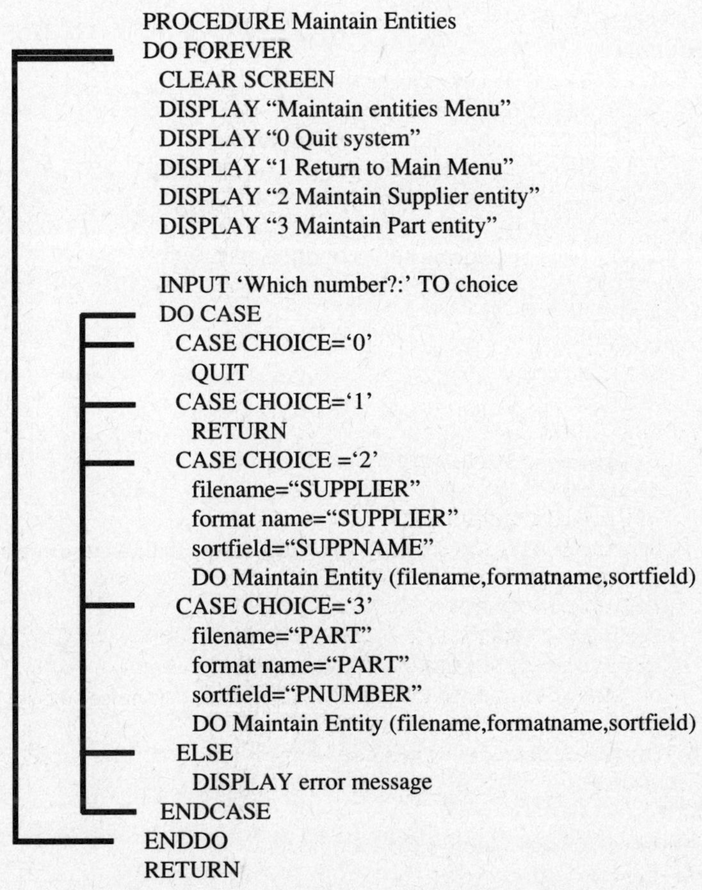

FIGURE 19-6 Action diagram for **MAINTAIN ENTITIES**.

Figure 19-27 shows an alternative implementation of **PRINT PURCHASE ORDER** as a single module. The code in Figure 19-27 is a direct translation of the action diagram presented as Figure 15-9; the major differences are the addition of printer formatting commands and the specification of page layouts with `@ SAY` statements.

Whether it is better to implement the activity as four modules, as in Figures 19-19 to 19-26, or as a single module, as in Figure 19-27 is a matter to be decided by applying the measurement tools of Chapter 12. Here, there can be no single correct conclusion, because issues such as size and coupling conflict with others such as generality (the module **PRODUCE SUPPLIER**, for example, may be used in several places throughout the system).

```
PROCEDURE MAINTAIN
STORE .T. TO RUN
DO WHILE RUN
 CLEAR
 @ 2,15 SAY "Maintain Entities Menu"
 @ 5,10 SAY "0 Quit system"
 @ 5,10 SAT "1 Return to Main Menu"
 @ 7,10 SAY "2 Maintain Supplier Entity"
 @ 8,10 SAY "3 Maintain Part Entity"
 ?
 ACCEPT 'Which number?' TO CHOICE
 DO CASE
  CASE CHOICE='0'
   QUIT
  CASE CHOICE='1'
   RETURN
  CASE CHOICE='2'
   filename="SUPPLIER"
   fmtname="SUPPLIER"
   srtfield="SUPPNAME"
   DO Maintain Entity WITH filename,fmtname,srtfield
  CASE CHOICE='3'
   filename="PART"
   fmtname="PART"
   srtfield="PNUMBER"
   DO Maintain Entity WITH filename,fmtname,srtfield
  ELSE
 ?"Invalid choice - please enter one of the above"
  ENDCASE
LOOP
ENDDO
RETURN
```

FIGURE 19-7 dBASE code for **MAINTAIN ENTITIES**.

EXERCISE

1. Code the action diagrams that you developed for the exercise in Chapter 16.

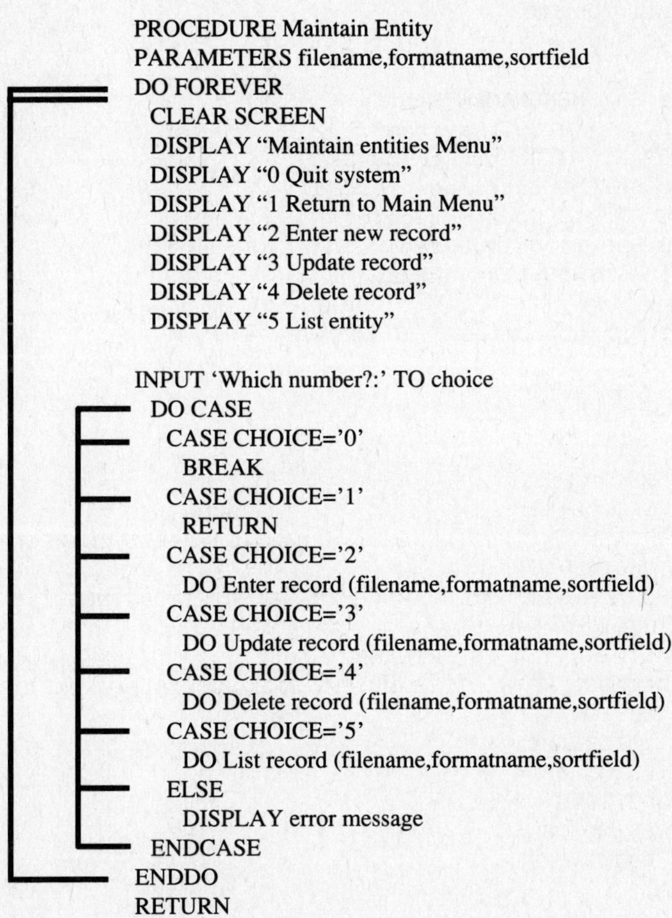

```
PROCEDURE Maintain Entity
PARAMETERS filename,formatname,sortfield
DO FOREVER
  CLEAR SCREEN
  DISPLAY "Maintain entities Menu"
  DISPLAY "0 Quit system"
  DISPLAY "1 Return to Main Menu"
  DISPLAY "2 Enter new record"
  DISPLAY "3 Update record"
  DISPLAY "4 Delete record"
  DISPLAY "5 List entity"

INPUT 'Which number?:' TO choice
  DO CASE
    CASE CHOICE='0'
      BREAK
    CASE CHOICE='1'
      RETURN
    CASE CHOICE='2'
      DO Enter record (filename,formatname,sortfield)
    CASE CHOICE='3'
      DO Update record (filename,formatname,sortfield)
    CASE CHOICE='4'
      DO Delete record (filename,formatname,sortfield)
    CASE CHOICE='5'
      DO List record (filename,formatname,sortfield)
    ELSE
      DISPLAY error message
  ENDCASE
ENDDO
RETURN
```

FIGURE 19-8 Action diagram for MAINTAIN ENTITY.

```
PROCEDURE MAINTENT
* DBASE III Version
PARAMETERS
MENUNAME,FILENAME,FMTNAME,SRTFIELD,INDXFILE,DISPFILE,RPTNAME
STORE "Y" TO YN
STORE .T. TO RUN
DO WHILE RUN
 CLEAR
 @ 2,15 SAY MENUNAME+"Menu"
 @ 5,10 SAY "0 Quit system"
 @ 5,10 SAT "1 Return to dBASE"
 @ 7,10 SAY "2 Enter new record"
 @ 8,10 SAY "3 Update record"
 @ 9,10 SAY "4 Delete record"
 @ 10,10 SAY "5 List entity"
 ?
 ACCEPT 'Which number?' TO CHOICE
 DO CASE
  CASE CHOICE='0'
   QUIT
  CASE CHOICE='1'
   RETURN
  CASE CHOICE='2'
   DO DATAENT WITH FILENAME,FMTNAME,SRTFIELD,INDXFILE
  CASE CHOICE='3'
   DO DATAUP WITH FILENAME,FMTNAME,SRTFIELD,INDXFILE
  CASE CHOICE ='4'
   STORE DISPFILE TO FMTNAME
   DO DATADEL WITH FILENAME,FMTNAME,SRTFIELD,INDXFILE
  CASE CHOICE='5'
   USE &FILENAME
   SET PRINT ON
   REPORT FORM &rptname
   SET PRINT ON
   SET PRINT OFF
 ENDCASE
LOOP
ENDDO
RETURN
```

FIGURE 19-9 dBASE III code for **MAINTAIN ENTITY.**

```
PROCEDURE MAINTENT
* DBASE IV Version
PARAMETERS
MENUNAME,FILENAME,FMTNAME,SRTFIELD,DISPFILE,RPTNAME
STORE "Y" TO YN
STORE .T. TO RUN
DO WHILE RUN
 CLEAR
 @ 2,15 SAY MENUNAME+"Menu"
 @ 5,10 SAY "0 Quit system"
 @ 6,10 SAT "1 Return to dBASE"
 @ 7,10 SAY "2 Enter new record"
 @ 8,10 SAY "3 Update record"
 @ 9,10 SAY "4 Delete record"
 @ 10,10 SAY "5 List entity"
 ?
 ACCEPT 'Which number?' TO CHOICE
 DO CASE
  CASE CHOICE='0'
   QUIT
  CASE CHOICE='1'
   RETURN
  CASE CHOICE='2'
   DO DATAENT WITH FILENAME,FMTNAME,SRTFIELD
  CASE CHOICE='3'
   DO DATAUP WITH FILENAME,FMTNAME,SRTFIELD
  CASE CHOICE ='4'
   STORE DISPFILE TO FMTNAME
   DO DATADEL WITH FILENAME,FMTNAME,SRTFIELD
  CASE CHOICE='5'
   USE FILENAME
   SET PRINT ON
   REPORT FORM rptname
   SET PRINT OFF
 ENDCASE
LOOP
ENDDO
RETURN
```

FIGURE 19-10 dBASE IV code for **MAINTAIN ENTITY**.

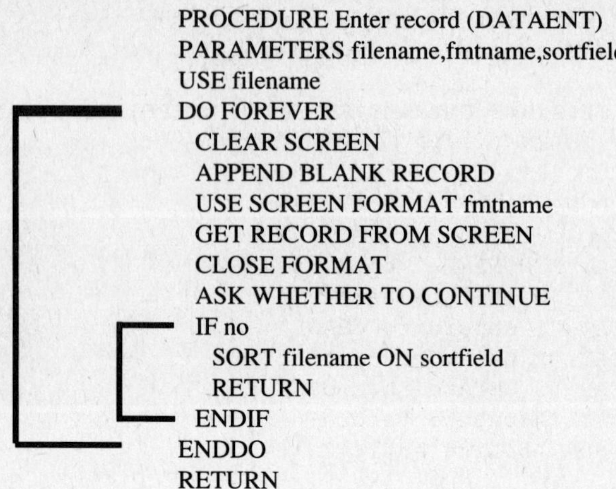

FIGURE 19-11 Action diagram for **ENTER RECORD**.

```
PROCEDURE(DATAENT)
PARAMETERS FILENAME,FMTNAME,SRTFIELD, INDXFILE
USE &FILENAME
DO WHILE .T.
  CLEAR
  APPEND BLANK
  GO BOTTOM
  SET FORMAT TO &FMTNAME
  READ
  CLOSE FORMAT
  @ 23,5 SAY "Another? (Y or N)"
  @ 23,40 GET YN
  READ
* Sort and index
  IF YN="N"
  SORT ON &SRTFIELD TO SXXX
  USE
  RENAME &FILENAME TO SYYY.DBF
  DELETE FILE SYYY.DBF
  USE &FILENAME
  DELETE FILE &INDXFILE
  INDEX ON &SRTFIELD TO &INDXFILE
  ENDIF
 ENDDO
RETURN
```

FIGURE 19-12 Code for **ENTER RECORD.**

```
PROCEDURE Update record (DATAUP)
PARAMETERS filename,fmtname,sortfield
USE filename
DO FOREVER
  CLEAR SCRREN
  GET key anme
  SEEK keyname
  IF EOF
    DISPLAY "Can't find that record"
  ELSE
    USE SCREEN FORMAT fmtname
    GET RECORD FROM SCREEN
    CLOSE FORMAT
  ENDIF
    RELEASE keyname
    ASK WHETHER TO CONTINUE
  IF no
    RETURN
  ENDIF
ENDDO
RETURN
```

FIGURE 19-13 Action diagram for **UPDATE RECORD**.

```
PROCEDURE DATAUP
PARAMETERS FILENAME,FMTNAME,SRTFIELD,INDXFILE
USE &FILENAME INDEX &INDXFILE
DO WHILE .T.
 CLEAR
 ACCEPT "Key name" TO SN
 GO TOP
 SEEK SN
 IF EOF()
 ?"Can't find that record"
 ELSE
  SET FORMAT TO &FMTNAME
  CLEAR
  READ
  CLOSE FORMAT
 ENDIF
 RELEASE SN
 @ 23,5 SAY "Another record? (Y or N)"
 @ 23,40 GET YN
 READ
 IF YN="N"
 RETURN
 ENDIF
ENDDO
RETURN
```

FIGURE 19-14 Code for **UPDATE RECORD**.

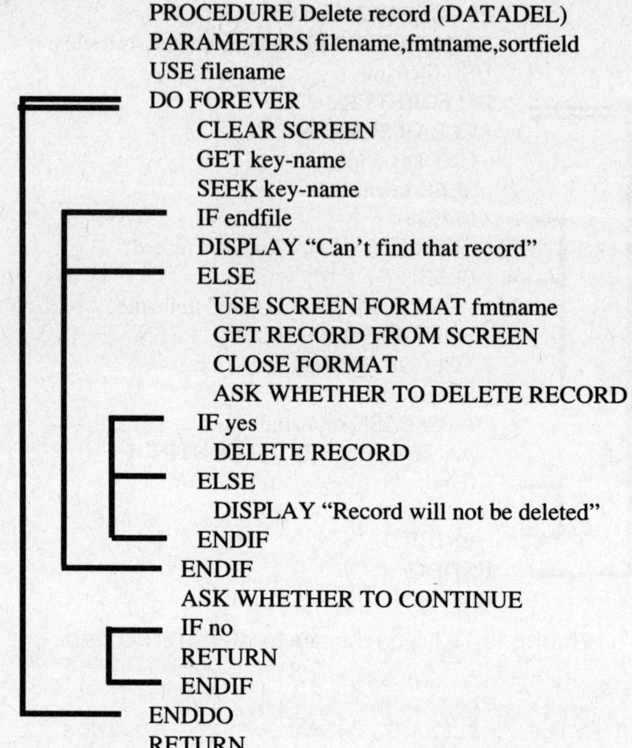

FIGURE 19-15 Action diagram for **DELETE RECORD.**

```
PROCEDURE DATADEL
PARAMETERS FILENAME,FMTNAME,SRTFIELD,INDXFILE
USE &FILENAME INDEX &INDXFILE
 DO WHILE .T.
 CLEAR
 ACCEPT "Key name" TO SN
 GO TOP
 SEEK SN
 IF EOF()
 ? "Can't find that record"
 ELSE
  SET FORMAT TO &FMTNAME
  READ
  CLOSE FORMAT
  @21,5 SAY "Delete this record? (Y or N)"
  @ 21,40 GET TN
```

FIGURE 19-16 Action diagram for **DELETE RECORD**. (continued)

```
   READ
   IF YN="Y"
    DELETE
   ELSE
    @22,5 SAY "Record will not be deleted"
   ENDIF
  ENDIF
  @ 23,5 SAY "Another record? (Y or N)"
  @ 23,40 GET TN
  READ
  IF YN="N"
  PACK
  RETURN
  ENDIF
 ENDDO
 RETURN
```

FIGURE 19-16 Action diagram for **DELETE RECORD.**

```
PROCEDURE List Contents
PARAMETERS filename,fmtname,sortfield
USE filename
LIST filename to printer
RETURN
```

FIGURE 19-17 Action diagram for **LIST CONTENTS**.

```
PROCEDURE LISTDATA
PARAMETERS FILENAME,FMTNAME,SRTFIELD,INDXFILE
USE &FILENAME INDEX &INDXFILE
SET PRINT ON
LIST
SET PRINT OFF
RETURN
```

FIGURE 19-18 Code for **LIST CONTENTS**.

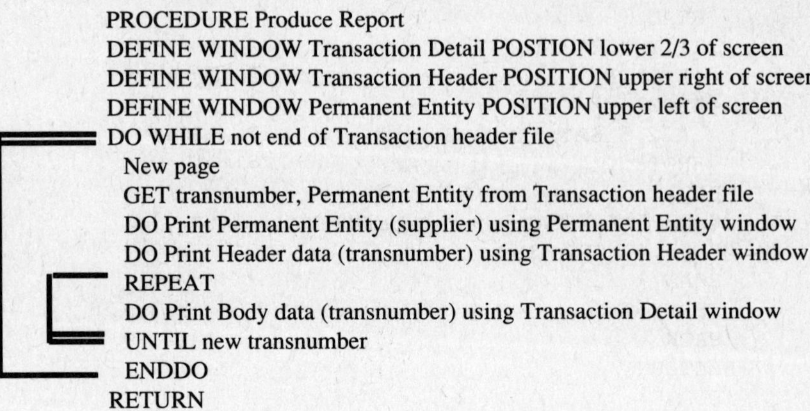

```
PROCEDURE Produce Report
DEFINE WINDOW Transaction Detail POSTION lower 2/3 of screen
DEFINE WINDOW Transaction Header POSITION upper right of screen
DEFINE WINDOW Permanent Entity POSITION upper left of screen
DO WHILE not end of Transaction header file
  New page
  GET transnumber, Permanent Entity from Transaction header file
  DO Print Permanent Entity (supplier) using Permanent Entity window
  DO Print Header data (transnumber) using Transaction Header window
  REPEAT
  DO Print Body data (transnumber) using Transaction Detail window
  UNTIL new transnumber
  ENDDO
RETURN
```

FIGURE 19-19 Action diagram for **PRODUCE REPORTS**.

```
PROCEDURE PRINTPO
SELECT C
USE PODET
SELECT B
USE SUPPLIER INDEX SUPPLID
SELECT A
USE PO
SET PRINT ON
SET DEVICE TO PRINT
DO WHILE .NOT. EOF()
 SELECT A
 STORE PONUMB TO PON
 DO POSUPP
 DO POHEADER
 DO POBODY
 LOOP
ENDDO
SET PRINT OFF
SET DEVICE TO SCREEN
RETURN
```

FIGURE 19-20 dBASE III+ code for **PRINT PURCHASE ORDER**.

```
PROCEDURE Produce Supplier
PARAMETERS supplier name
USE supplier
ACTIVATE WINDOW supplier
RETRIEVE supplier name
DISPLAY current record IN ACTIVE WINDOW
DEACTIVATE WINDOW
RETURN
```

FIGURE 19-21 Action diagram for **PRODUCE SUPPLIER**.

```
PROCEDURE POSUPP
*
* DBASE III version
*
 SELECT B
 SEEK SUPPNAME
@ 2,5 SAY SNAME
@ 3,5 SAY SADDR1
@ 4,5 SAY SADDR2
@ 5,5 SAY SADDR3
RETURN
```

FIGURE 19-22 dBASE III code for **PRODUCE SUPPLIER**.

```
PROCEDURE Produce Purchase Order Header
PARAMETERS PO number
USE Purchase Order File
ACTIVATE WINDOW Purchase Order
APPEND BLANK RECORD
USE SCREEN FORMAT Purchase Order
GET RECORD FROM SCREEN
CLOSE FORMAT
DEACTIVATE WINDOW
RETURN
```

FIGURE 19-23 Action diagram for **PRODUCE PURCHASE ORDER HEADER**.

```
PROCEDURE POHEADER
@ 7,1 SAY "Purchase Order Date:"
@ 7,15 SAY PODATE
@ 7,25 SAY "Purchase Order Number:"
@ 7,47 SAY PONUMB
@ 7,57 SAY "Today's date:"
@ 7,70 SAY MDATE
RETURN
```

FIGURE 19-24 dBASE III code for **PRODUCE PURCHASE ORDER HEADER**.

```
PROCEDURE Produce Purchase Order Body
PARAMETERS PO number
USE Purchase Order Detail file
DO FOREVER
  ACTIVATE WINDOW Purchase Order Detail
  DISPLAY next detail line for this PO number
  IF end of window
  THEN
    DO Produce PO Supplier
    DO Produce PO Header
    ACTIVATE WINDOW Purchase Order Detail
  ENDIF
END DO
DEACTIVATE WINDOW
RETURN
```

FIGURE 19-25 Action diagram for **PRODUCE PURCHASE ORDER BODY**.

```
PROCEDURE POBODY
*
* DBASE III VERSION
*
SELECT C
STORE 53 TO PAGEEND
STORE 24 TO I
STORE 0 TO TOTAL
STORE PONUMB TO PON
@ 22,1 SAY "Quantity"
@ 22,10 SAY "Part Number"
@ 22,51 SAY "Description"
@ 22,96 SAY "Price"
DO WHILE PON=PONUMB .AND. .NOT. EOF ()
```

FIGURE 19-26 dBASE III code for **PRODUCE PURCHASE ORDER BODY**. (continued)

```
 @ I,1 SAY POQUANT
 @ I,10 SAY INUMB
 @ I,51 SAY INAME
 @ I,92 SAY IPRICE
 STORE I+1 TO I
 IF I > PAGEEND
  DO POSUPP
  DO POHEADER
  SELECT C
  STORE 24 TO I
 ENDIF
 SKIP
ENDDO
RETURN
```

FIGURE 19-26 dBASE III code for **PRODUCE PURCHASE ORDER BODY**.

```
PARAMETERS PON
SET PRINT ON
SET DEVICE TO PRINT
SELECT C
USE PODET
SELECT B
USE SUPPLIER INDEX SUPPLID
SELECT A
USE POFILE
GO PON
STORE POSUPP TO SUPPNAME
STORE 24 TO 8
@ 5,30 SAY "Purchase Order"
************************
* PRINT ADDRESS FOR PO *
************************
SELECT B
SEEK SUPPNAME
@ 12,5 SAY SNAME
@ 13,5 SAY SADDR1
@ 14,5 SAY SADDR2
@ 15,5 SAY SADDR3
***********************
* PRINT HEADER FOR PO *
***********************
SELECT A
@ 19,1 SAY "Purchase Order Date:"
```

FIGURE 19-27 dBASE code for **PUCHASE ORDER**. (continued)

```
@ 19,22 SAY PODATE
@ 19,40 SAY "purchase Order number:"
@ 19,65 SAY PON
@ 19,80 SAY "Today's date:"
@ 19,95 SAY MDATE
*********************************
* write body for purchase order *
*********************************
SELECT C
@ 22,1 SAY "Quantity"
@ 22,10 SAY "Part Number"
@ 22,51 SAY "Description"
@ 22,96 SAY "PRICE"
@ 23,1 SAY " "
DO WHILE PON=PONUMB .AND. .NOT. EOF()
  @ I,1 SAY POQUNT
  @ I,10 SAY INUMB
  @ I,51 SAY IPRICE
  STORE I+1 TO I
SKIP
ENDDO
SET PRINT OFF
SET DEVICE TO SCREEN
RETURN
```

FIGURE 19-27 dBASE code for **PURCHASE ORDER**.

Section VI

LATER STAGES IN THE LIFE-CYCLE

This section describes what needs to be done with a system after it is coded. Figure S-6-1 reviews where we are in the program development life-cycle. Chapter 20 describes how to test and debug programs. Chapter 21 describes how to package parts of a system into memory and how to make sure that the program runs fast enough.

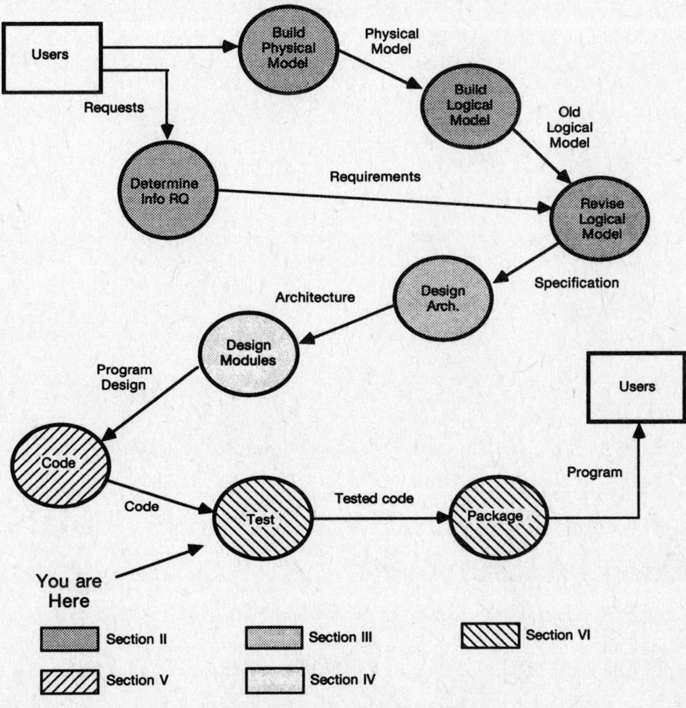

FIGURE S-6-1 Where we are.

Chapter 20

PROGRAM TESTING

CHAPTER GOALS

- Learn the different types of testing available.
- Learn the position of testing in the life-cycle.
- Learn to select a testing strategy appropriate to the problem.
- Learn principles of debugging.

Ideally, a well-designed program would work as intended the first time it ran. In practice, anyone who has done programming knows that this is unlikely. There are five sorts of common errors (Figure 20-1). The most trivial are language syntax errors—writing a statement in the language incorrectly. These are trivial, because the language interpreter or compiler will find them! In dBASE III, a syntax error results in the message like the following:

```
Unrecognized command verb.
?
Do you want some help (Y/N)?
```

The exact content of the first line will vary depending on what mistake you have made; mistyping a variable name, for example, results in a variable not found message. The system provides an on-line reference manual with which to look up statement format.

The second form of error (semantic error), somewhat less trivial, involves writing syntactically correct statement in the language that does not do what you had intended it to do. For example, in dBASE III, a `CLEAR GETS` command will not display a record on the screen if the screen format is defined in a format file. dBASE II programmers upgrading to

1. Syntax errors
2. Semantic errors
3. Interfacing errors
4. Misspecifying module design
5. Design errors

FIGURE 20-1 Types of programming errors.

dBASE III often found this a surprise (I certainly did). Here, the problem is simply one of determining what language statements will produce the expected results.

The third form of error is one of interfacing between modules. This results from communicating the wrong data (via `PARAMETER` and `DO WITH` statements). Close attention to and checking of the structure chart should catch most of these problems.

The fourth form of error, much more serious that the others, involves misspecifying the module design. In such a situation, either the action diagram is incomplete or it is incorrect. Such a module may execute perfectly, but it will do the wrong thing.

The most serious error is a higher-level design error. This may be either a problem with the program architecture or a misinterpretation of user requirements. Fixing such an error is like redoing the foundation of a house—it is expensive, and often requires that a great deal of lower-level work be thrown away.

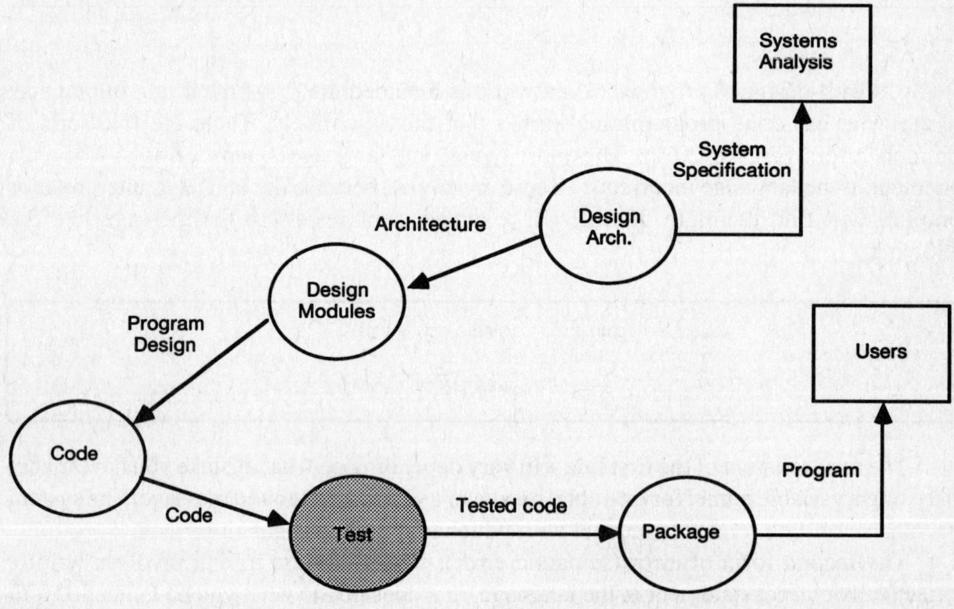

FIGURE 20-2 Testing in the program development life-cycle.

In the best of all possible worlds, program design methodologies would ensure that only errors of the first sort ever occurred; while we are in a fantasy world, we might as well also ask that such methods do the translation into code automatically and prevent all errors. There are various techniques to produce "provably correct" programs; these use propositional calculus to guarantee that the translation from action diagram into code is done correctly. They do not help with design errors [Linger et al. 1979; Mills et al. 1986]. Other methodologies have been advertised as providing provably correct programs throughout the lifcycle [Martin 1985]; these work by redefining the systems analysis task as what we have called module design. In short, all of these techniques work only at the module level, and all require considerably more mathematical sophistication than most programmers have.

This means that the rest of us must find errors in our programs by testing. Figure 20-2 shows the traditional position of testing in the program development life-cycle; in practice, it should occur at all stages. For example, in a description of the system design methodology used by the accounting firm of Touche Ross [Biggs et al. 1980], almost 25% of the activities involve testing or other forms of quality control.

Testing is a form of statistical sampling. Since the number of possible states of a complex program is, for all practical purposes, infinite, it is impossible to perform the programming equivalent of a census; any test will be a sample from a population. This sample can never demonstrate that the program is error free. In fact, it is doubtful that any very large program is error free. What testing can do is provide a desired confidence level in the operation of the program.

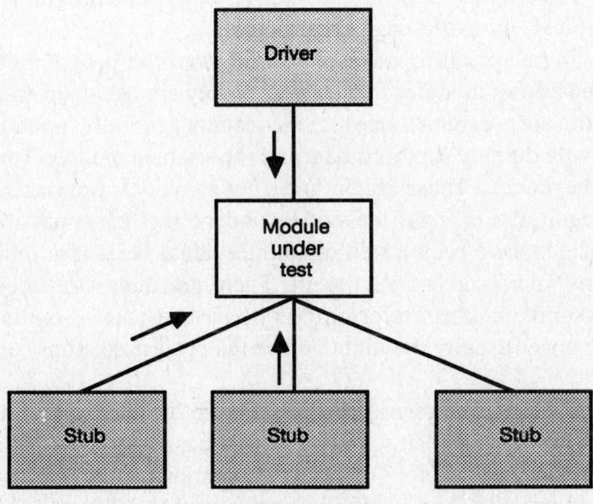

FIGURE 20-3 Driver and stubs.

DEFINITIONS

The classic work on program testing is *The Art of Software Testing* [Myers 1979], from which the following definitions are drawn:

> **Testing**: executing a program with the intent of finding errors.
> **Debugging**: diagnosing and correcting known errors.
> **Module testing:** verifying single modules out of context.
> **Integration testing**: verifying the interfaces among modules.
> **Function testing**: verifying that the system meets specifications.
> **System testing**: verifying that the system meets user needs.
> **Acceptance testing:** the users' system test.

The definition of testing as executing a program with the intent of finding errors is based on psychological factors; it means that a successful test is one that finds errors. Most programmers who test their own programs have (consciously or not) a rather different goal—demonstrating that there are no errors. Therefore, a programming group that wishes to sample test its programs most effectively should not have the original programmer test his or her own work. Indeed, many organizations have separate development and quality assurance groups for this very reason.

The definition of debugging as diagnosing and correcting known errors, and the differentiation of debugging from testing, is consistent with the decomposition of tasks that we have been using throughout this book. One of the major reasons for having programmers test their own code is the argument that no one else will know how it works. That, however, is the very reason why someone else should test the code while the programmer debugs it (removes the errors that are identified). Incidentally, "bugs" in a program are referred to as "undocumented features" by marketing departments.

Consistent with the spreading of testing throughout the program development life-cycle, module testing allows modules to be tested as they are designed and built but before they are integrated into the program. Since modules cannot generally function by themselves, they must be tested with dummy superordinate and subordinate modules (drivers and stubs). Figure 20-3 shows the process. These drivers and stubs are very simple modules that perform only the functions required to exercise the module under test (such as passing constant data).

Once the modules have been tested on an individual basis it is time for integration testing; verifying the interfaces between them. There are three strategies for integration testing. The first has sometimes been referred to as "shake and bake"—putting all of the tested modules together at once (usually the night before the project deadline) and seeing if they work. They won't.

The second approach is top-down integration (Figure 20-4). This should be distinguished from the sort of top-down design that we have been discussing to date—it assumes that the design and construction are complete! Top-down integration means first testing the modules at the top of the structure chart, and working down from there. Tested modules are used as drivers for modules under test, so the system grows downward. This has the major advantage that it produces an up-and-limping version of the program at an early stage. Much of the

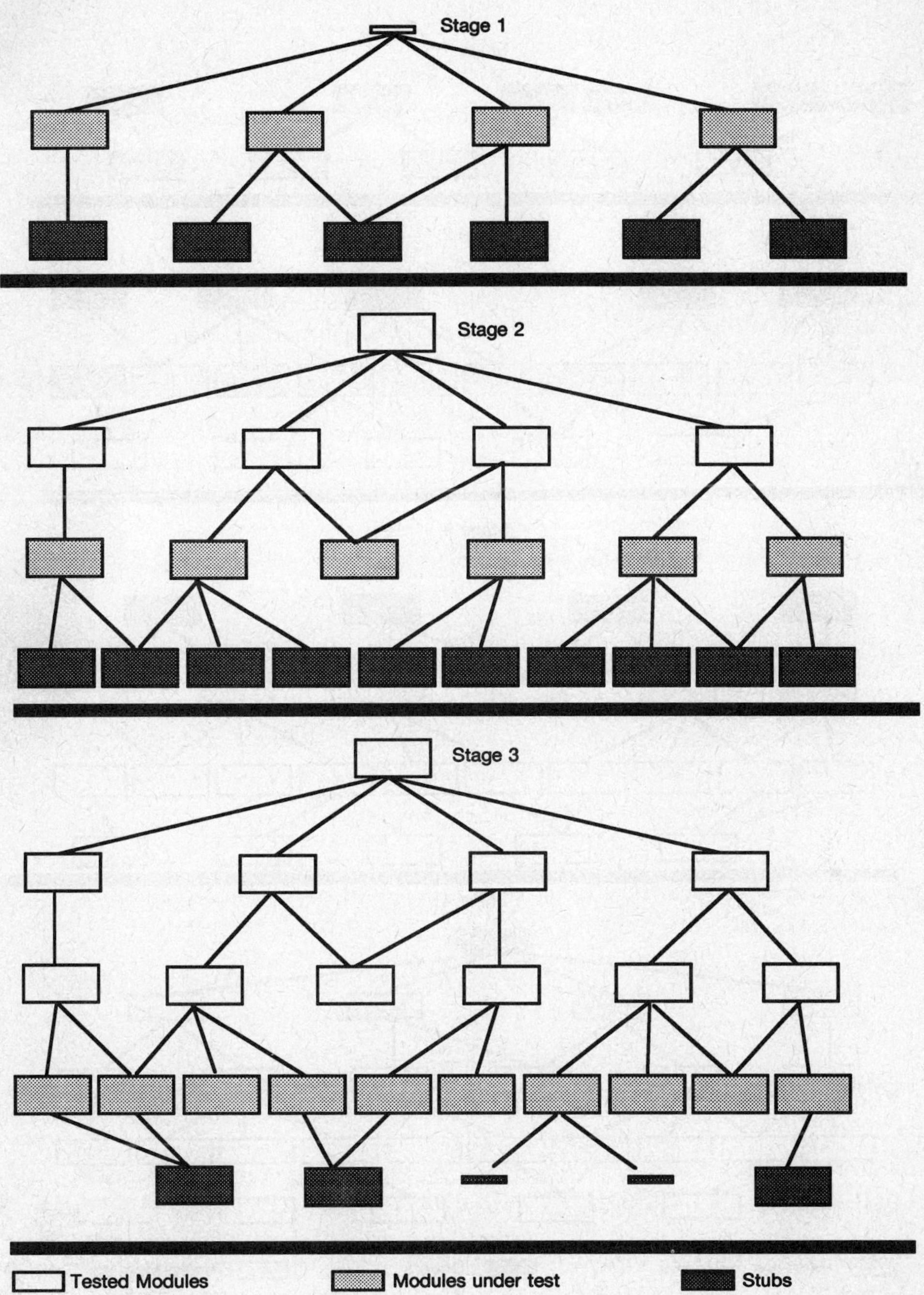

FIGURE 20-4 Top-down integration.

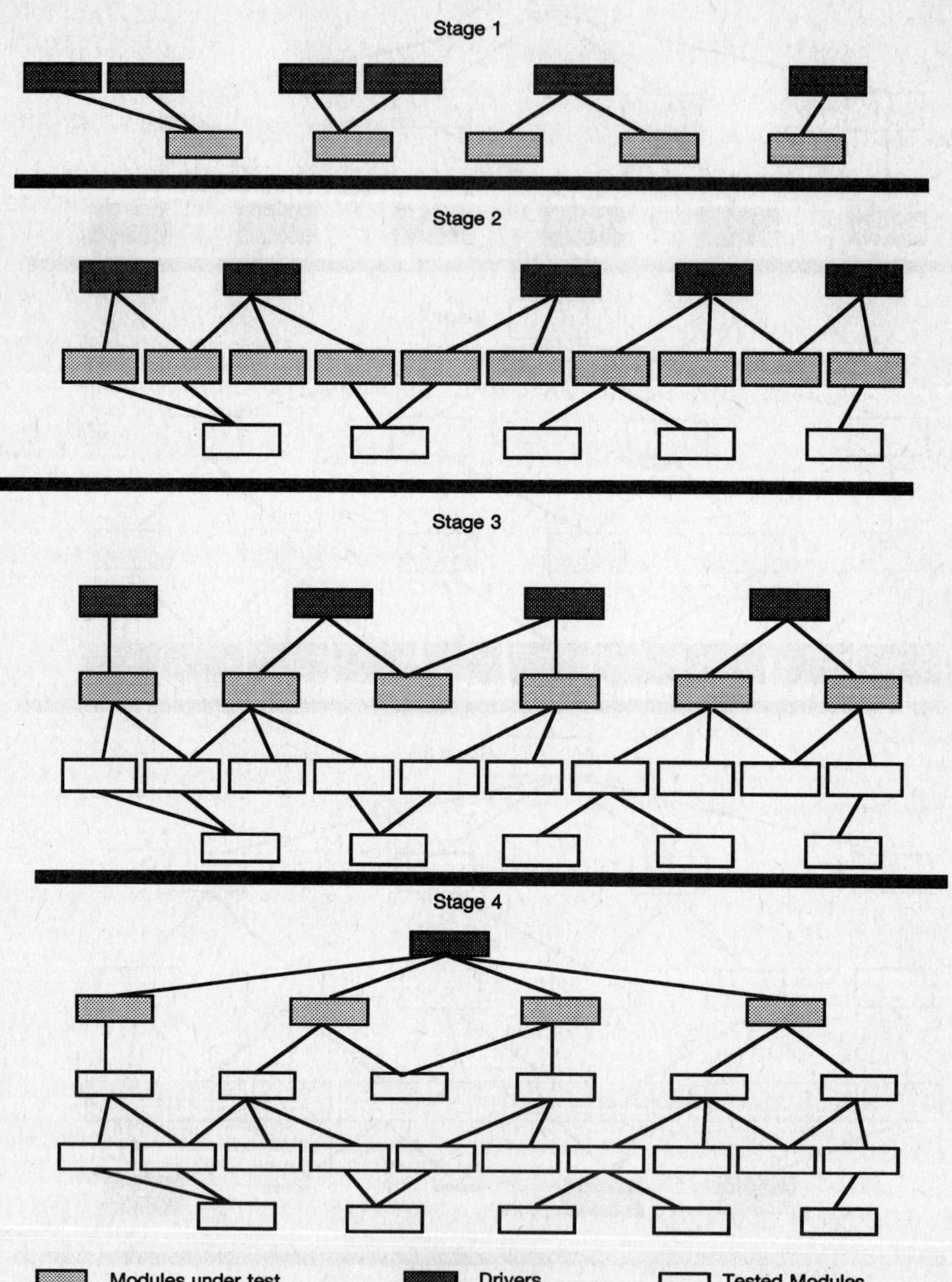

FIGURE 20-5 Bottom-up integration.

functionality is missing, but the user interface and the overall logic can be examined, verified, and demonstrated. This not only allows early feedback but also has obvious political advantages. The major disadvantages are that there are quite a few stub modules to be created, and that test conditions involving input and output (which are usually at the bottom of the structure chart) may be impossible to create.

The third approach is bottom-up integration (Figure 20-5); starting with the lowest level modules and building upwards. In this approach, tested modules serve as stubs for testing of higher-level modules. It is a useful approach if there are complicated test conditions, especially involving input and output. Bottom-up testing is almost required for real-time systems (although such systems are not built in dBASE). Results are also easier to observe. On the negative side, many driver modules necessary, and these usually involve some sort of input and output in order to create test conditions and to observe the results. Finally, the system as a whole does not exist until the last module is tested.

Yet another approach is sometimes known as middle-out. It usually involves a combination of top-down and bottom-up testing and integration as appropriate.

Once the pieces have been put together and made to fit, the next step is function testing: verifying that the system meets specifications. Part of the program specifications coming out of the systems analysis phase should be criteria for functional verification.

Unfortunately, just because the system meets its functional specifications does not mean that it meets user needs; this is verified as part of system testing. Obviously, the contents of this stage depend on whether the software is being developed on contract for a specific user, or whether it is marketed as a product. In the latter case, system testing means test marketing. This is usually combined with *beta testing,* which is the release of the software to a limited test market before it is released to the public. The motivation for beta testing on the part of the vendor is clear. The motivation on the part of the user is to get an early start on evaluation and adaptation of an attractive product.

This advantage for the user is offset by the fact that beta-test software is generally too buggy for production use. It is fine for experimentation and evaluation, but one does not want to trust it for any important systems or projects. Part of the reason for this is that specifications are subject to change. The major reason is that the software (or hardware) is not likely to work reliably at this stage (this advice comes from 12 years personal experience in beta testing software!).

Acceptance testing is the users' system test. For off-the-shelf software, this is the purchase decision. For custom software, it is usually provided as part of the development contract.

Figure 20-6 illustrates the testing cycle.

SAMPLING STRATEGIES FOR TESTING

Figure 20-7 shows the methods for testing a program. There are two basic approaches to testing a module: white box and black box. White-box testing is "playing computer"—executing the statements in a program one at a time. Black-box testing assumes no knowledge of the contents of a module but, instead, tests its functional performance.

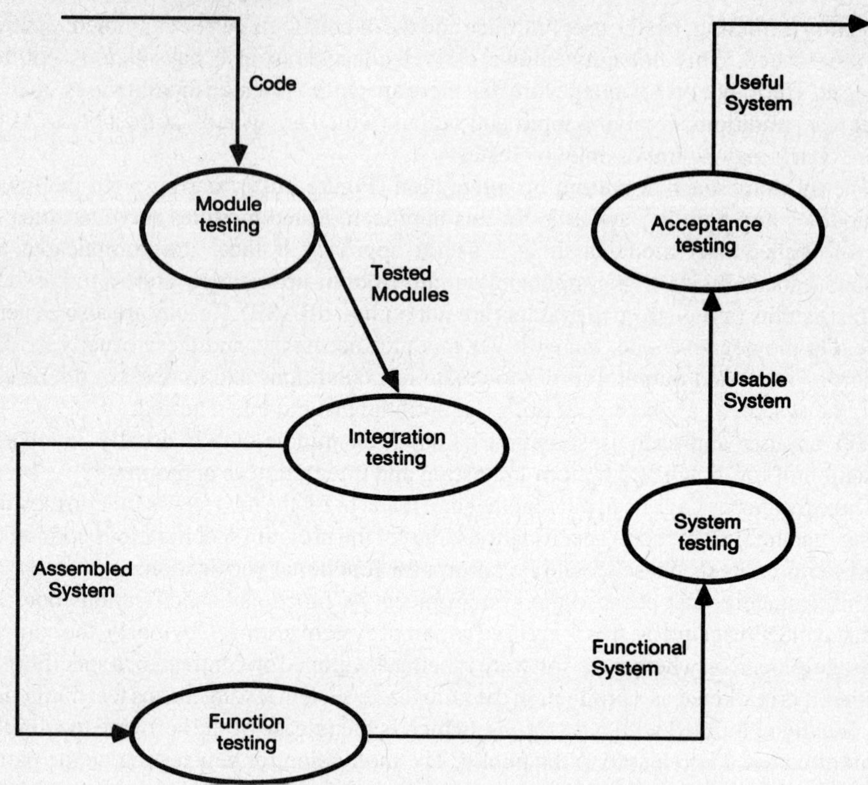

FIGURE 20-6 Testing life-cycle.

White box testing is divided into statement-coverage and logic-coverage techniques. Statement coverage means that each statement in the module is executed at least once. This tests for type one and type two errors (syntax and semantic errors) (see Figure 20-1). Logic-coverage testing not only tests the statements themselves, but also tests that the statements work correctly under different conditions (e.g., that WHILE works both when the condition is true and when it is false). This is especially important for programs that have complex conditions using AND and OR. Logic-coverage testing identifies errors of misspecified module design as well as syntax and semantic errors.

Black-box testing is a form of statistical sampling applied to programming. Its goal is to find the subset of test conditions that has the highest probability of detecting the most errors. The program tester's problem is very similar to that faced by an auditor: certifying the functioning of a system from a limited sample. More details may be found in textbooks covering either auditing or sampling [e.g., Kish 1965]. The basic strategies, as in any sampling problem, are random, stratified, and cluster sampling.

Random sampling is the easiest of the three strategies and the least powerful. The difficulty is in creating a random sample of the program; the tester must ensure that a representative sample of all possible input conditions is present.

Stratified sampling is the most widely used. Here, possible inputs are grouped into classes, and each class is sampled. Possible classes might include

A range of valid values.

A set of valid values.

A set of invalid value.

A single required value.

Proper identification of strata is important because it can vastly decrease the number of test cases required. For example, in the module of Figure 20-8, the range of valid values is all real positive numbers and the range of invalid values is all negative numbers. Testing all real numbers is obviously infeasible. Testing a few positive and a few negative values will probably be sufficient to determine whether the system works. There are two basic approaches to more sophisticated stratified testing: boundary testing and the use of decision tables.

Stratified sampling on the boundary between valid and invalid cases is a fruitful way to turn up errors. In the case of our **CALCULATE SQUARE ROOT** module above, this

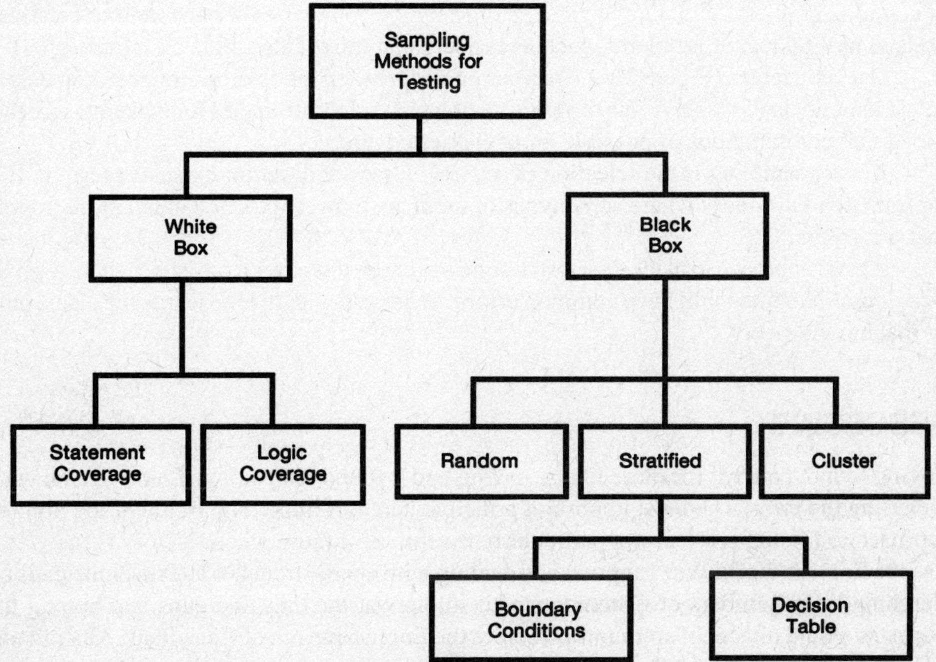

FIGURE 20-7 Testing methods.

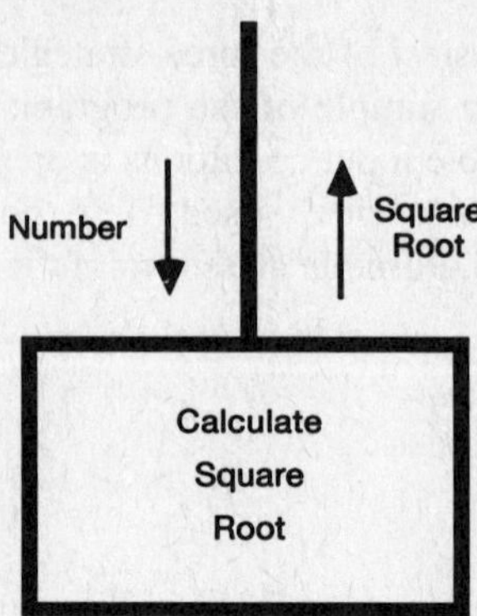

FIGURE 20-8 Modeule for black-box testing.

could include numbers close to zero on both sides and numbers that are close to perfect squares (e.g., 4.00001). It might also include numbers that are even powers of 2 plus or minus 1 (e.g., $2^{15}+1$) in order to check for machine representation problems. For file processing, checking a program using an empty file or a file with only one record is a good way to turn up common problems with loop logic. Testing near the boundaries of pages and screens also tends to turn up lots of problems, such as headers that move lines of data up or down.

Decision tables (Figure 20-9) are a common approach for determining requirements at the systems analysis stage. At the program testing phasc they are useful for makeing sure that one has all combinations of possible input classes covered.

Cluster sampling is the selection of several classes of input for extensive testing. It is appropriate in instances where some types of input are expected to give much more trouble than are others.

A final approach to black-box test design is to chose test cases from experience. A given type of problem often will have common errors associated with it. One learns this, alas, only by making the errors.

DEBUGGING

Having found the error (or more likely, having had it found for you), you have to find what is causing the error. The most important principle here is **Think!** The Battle of the Somme approach to finding errors is not particularly fruitful. (For those whose history is rusty, this was the English World War I approach to dealing with enemy trenches and machine guns by marching large numbers of Commonwealth soldiers at the machine guns and hoping the Germans would run out of ammunition before the English ran out of Canadians, Australians, and Scots. It didn't work.) So, do not start inserting print statements or using an automated debugger without first applying a little logic.

Degree Program	Undergrad	Y	Y	Y	Y	N	N	N	N
	In State	Y	Y	N	N	Y	Y	N	N
	Professional	Y	N	Y	N	Y	N	Y	N
Tuition Rate	Low		X						
	Moderate	X			X		X		
	High			X		X			X
	Outrageous							X	

FIGURE 20-9 Decision table for tuition charges.

The logic is: identify a probable cause and identify the evidence that you need to determine whether your hypothesized cause is the real one. Do what needs to be done to gather the evidence. If you got it right, move on to the next bug (there is seldom a "last bug" in spite of the contrary arguments of generations of programming students). If you got it wrong, go back to the beginning of the paragraph and try another hypothesis.

If you get stuck while debugging, explain the problem to someone else. Often you will realize the solution yourself as you explain it; otherwise, your audience will often spot something that you have overlooked. If this does not work and if you have time, sleep on the problem (most employers frown on your doing this at work, so it will probably have to be done on your own time). Warning: If you do sleep on the problem, be sure to keep a pad of paper and a pen near the bed. The only thing worse than not thinking of the answer is thinking of it, going back to sleep, and being unable to remember it in the morning. Awakening your spouse and telling her or him the answer is not a workable alternative. It also may help contribute to the fact that people in data processing have the second highest divorce rate of any profession (air traffic controllers are number one).

One final bit of advice: Test your fix.

QUESTIONS AND EXERCISES

1 The most serious form of error in a program is a

a. Syntax error.
b Interfacing error.
c. Semantic error.
d. Design error.

2. At what stage of the system development life-cycle testing should begin?

a. After coding.
b. After packaging.
c. During design.
d. During analysis.

3. Testing is the execution of a program

a. To find errors.
b. To determine whether or not there are errors.
c. To demonstrate that there are no errors.
d To diagnose errors.

4. Module testing is

a. Testing groups of modules.
b. Testing single modules.
c. White-box examination of a module.
d. Black-box testing of a module.

5. Acceptance testing is

a. Testing to see if the system meets specifications.
b. Testing to see if the system can handle real-world volumes.
c. Testing to see if the system meets user needs.
d. Testing to see if the user thinks the system meets user needs.

6. Top-down integration testing is best when

a. One is working with a menu-driven system.
b. One wants to test the user interface early in the process.
c. There are major input/output difficulties anticipated.
d. Major problems are expected to be toward the bottom of the structure chart.

7. Bottom-up testing is best when

a. One is working with a menu-driven system.
b. One wants to test the user interface early in the process.
c. There are major input/output difficulties anticipated.
d. An "up-and-limping" system is important for political reasons.

8. Black-box testing

a. Should exhaustively test possible inputs.
b. Can demonstrate that a system always produces the correct results.
c. Should be based on stratified sampling strategies.
d. Should be used only when access to source code for white-box testing is not possible.

9. White-box testing
   a. Can test every possible path through a small program.
   b Can test every possible path through a large program.
   c. Is more difficult than black-box testing.
   d. Finds most data specification errors.
10. Debugging
   a. Can be automated with program tools.
   b Is the process of finding errors.
   c. Involves finding the reasons for errors.
   d. Is a form of testing.

DISCUSSION QUESTIONS

1. What is testing? Where does each form of testing fit in the life-cycle?
2. Discuss the differences between testing and debugging.
3. What are appropriate organizational strategies for testing?
4. Discuss the relationship of testing and sampling.

REFERENCES

LINGER, R., H. MILLS, and B. WITT. *Structured Programming: Theory and Practice.* Addison-Wesley, Reading, MA, 1979.

MILLS, H., R. LINGER, and A. HEVNER. *Principles of Information Systems Analysis and Design.* Academic Press, New York, 1986.

MARTIN, J. *System Design from Provably Correct Constructs.* Prentice-Hall, Englewood Cliffs, NJ, 1985.

BIGGS, C., E. BIRKS, and W. ATKINS. *Managing the Systems Development Process.* Touche Ross & Co., Prentice-Hall, Englewood Cliffs, NJ, 1980

MYERS, G. *The Art of Software Testing.* Wiley, New York, 1979.

KISH, L. *Survey Sampling*, Wiley, New York, 1965.

Chapter 21

PHYSICAL PACKAGING

CHAPTER GOALS

- Learn how to make a program work in the amount of memory available.
- Learn how to make programs run faster.

To those raised on traditional program design, it probably seems strange that the discussion of efficiency issues like how to make a program fit into memory and how to make it run fast enough has been postponed until almost the end of the book. This is deliberate, partly because of the position of these issues in the program development life-cycle (Figure 21-1) and partly because they are not very important in the overall scheme of things.

The reason for postponing physical issues until the end is simple; they have nothing to do with solving the right problem (which is what design is all about). The strategy is similar to the classic one for successful marriage—make sure the important things are going to work together before committing yourself physically. Historically, program design ignored this strategy with the silicon equivalent of sex on the first date. The reason has to do with the history of technology. Let us first look at memory, and then at speed.

INTERNAL MEMORY

Early computers had, by modern standards, ludicrously small amounts of internal memory. For example, in 1961 the popular IBM 1401 provided between 8 and 16K of core memory (the equivalent of today's RAM). This was for a computer intended to serve the needs of a large organization. By 1977, the IBM 370/168 provided between 256 and 512K of memory—again, to serve the needs of perhaps 10,000 users. Today, we grumble because our MSDOS personal computers can only use 640K of memory; machines running Unix

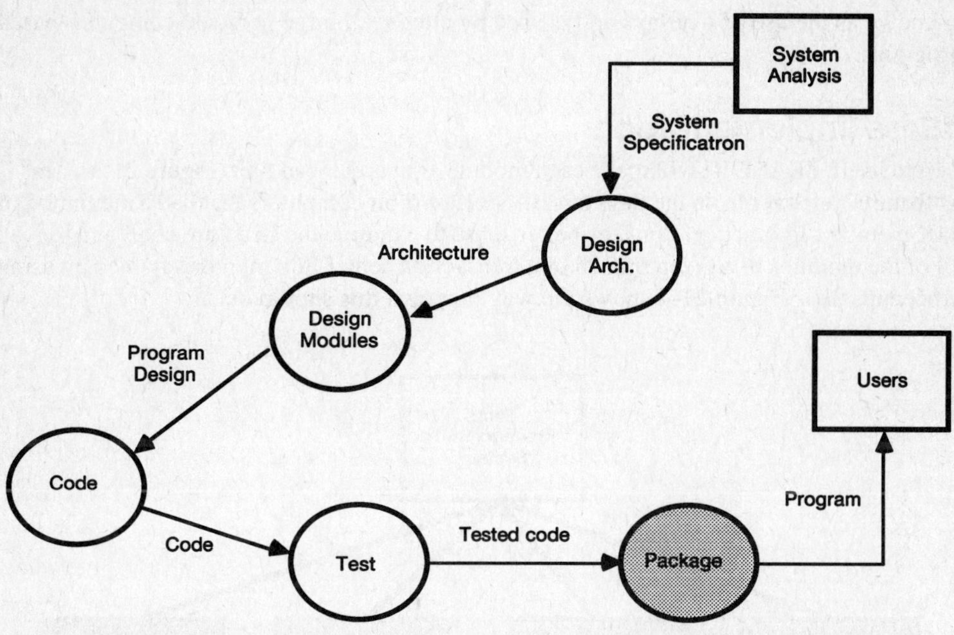

FIGURE 21-1 Physical considerations in the program development life-cycle.

or OS-2 and Apple Macintoshes may have two to eight megabytes, and mainframes such as the IBM 3098 use more than 24 megabytes.

In the "old days," programmers were obviously very concerned about whether their programs would fit into memory. Today, especially on mainframes and minicomputers with virtual memory, this is no longer a major consideration. However, one of the laws of computing seems to be that programs will require more memory than is available. As a result, we still run out on a routine basis (I crashed my two megabyte Macintosh a few minutes ago when I tried to run four programs simultaneously. Time to upgrade to eight megabytes).

Program complexity is one reason we still have to worry about memory space—our modern graphics-oriented programs require much more memory. Another reason we might be concerned is geographic isolation—programs are often run on networks of computers, each of which must have the appropriate part of the program loaded. A third reason is the existence of control and audit requirements—it may be unacceptable to have the accounts receivable module running on the same computer as the cash disbursement module. The answer to all of these problems is a concept called a load unit.

A load unit is a chunk of code and/or data that can be loaded into memory and run independently of the rest of the program. Figure 21-2 shows an example with five load units (shown shaded in the structure chart, and as they would be loaded into memory).

In this example, only one of the five subsystems will be run at a given time; therefore, only the one being run need occupy memory. This strategy for dealing with scarce memory is known as the use of overlays and is used by almost all large personal computer–based programs.

dBase Implementation

Left to itself, dBASE III will make each module a separate load unit (Figure 21-3). This is a "feature" left over from the days of dBASE II on 8 bit computers that had a maximum of 64K memory. In practice, it makes better sense to examine the structure chart and to load all of the modules in a given branch of a transaction center into memory at once by using procedure files. Figure 21-4 shows the way in which this should occur.

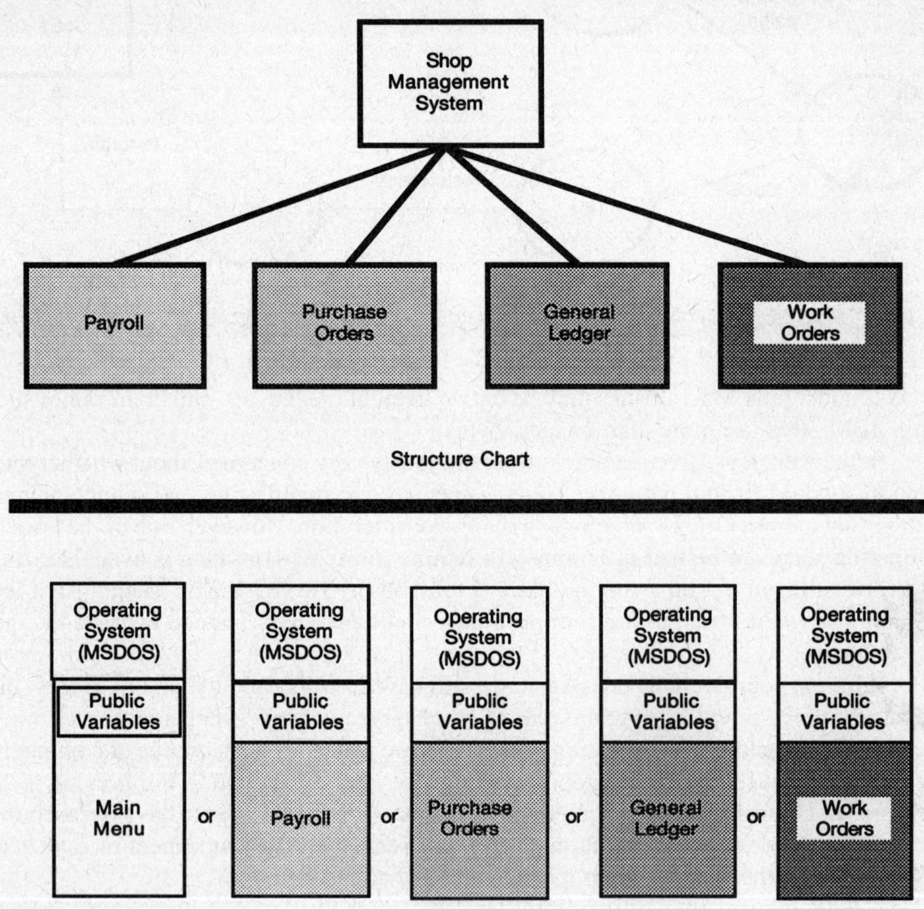

FIGURE 21-2 Load units.

The structure of Figure 21-4 is better than that of Figure 21-3 because all of the modules in the **MAINTAIN SUPPLIER FILE** branch of the structure chart are likely to be used at the same time. In Figure 21-3, each time the user goes from entering a new item to updating an old one, the **ENTER DATA** module must be unloaded and the **UPDATE DATA** module brought in from disk. Because disk access is mechanical rather than electronic, it takes several thousand times longer than does referencing the module in memory as in Figure 21- 4.

The general rule for packaging in overlays is to make the overlay structure hierarchical and problem related. The problem relationship should be focused on time; the point is that those modules that will be used at the same time should be loaded at the same time. This usually means packaging branches of a structure chart together. For example, in Figure 21-5, some or all of the modules will be used every time a purchase order is entered, and purchase orders are likely to be entered continuously in batches. It therefore makes sense that all of the modules in Figure 21-5 should be loaded into memory at the same time.

We are trying to maximize cohesion within a load unit and to minimize coupling between load units. One way to do this is to package modules that are part of a given

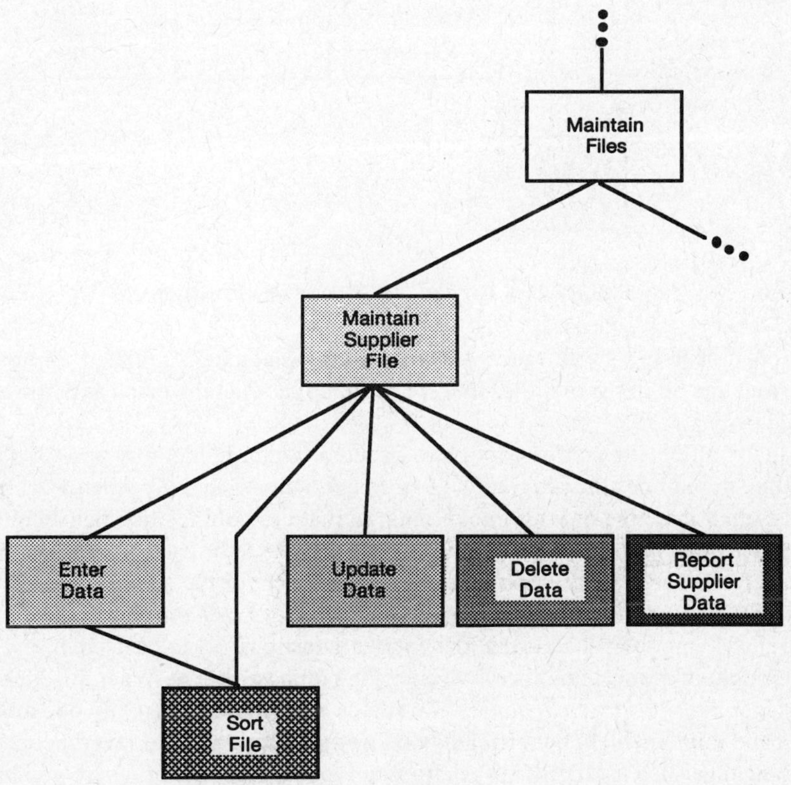

FIGURE 21-3 Default dBASE III overlay structure.

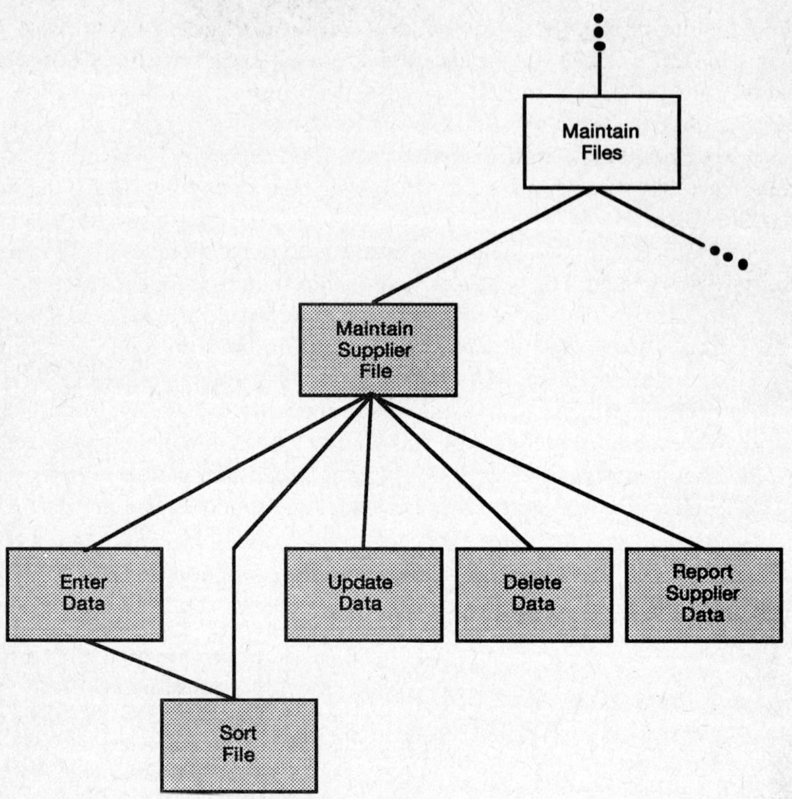

FIGURE 21-4 Desired dBASE III overlay structure.

transaction processing cycle (such as purchasing) together. A related approach is to package together all of the modules that are run at a specific time (such as at the end of the month).

Usually all of this will be enough to fit the program in memory and to reduce disk access time. Sometimes the program will still be too big, especially when working with a relatively small machine or with lots of data. In that case, things like help screens, error handling, and other parts of the program that are not likely to be used on a regular basis may be packaged separately. This should free up more space for the operating code.

Figure 21-5 points out another issue with overlays—dealing with fan-in (Chapter 12). The shaded modules that deal with supplier data are likely to be used in several other places throughout the system other than entering purchase orders. What this means is that one packages *multiple physical copies* of routines with high fan-in. Only one module was designed and implemented, but efficiency in operation may require several copies. When using a language such as dBASE, it is important to keep records of where you have done this so that the modules can all be updated if needed. Mainframe systems usually have this record keeping built in.

To create the sort of hierarchical load unit illustrated in Figure 21-4, dBASE uses `PROCEDURE`s. A procedure file is a file that contains code for all of the modules in the desired load unit and that has the standard dBASE `.PRG` suffix. Rather than having the modules identified by their file names (e.g., `Dataent.PRG`), they are identified by a `PROCEDURE` statement in the file (e.g., `PROCEDURE DATAENT`). The load unit is loaded by the statement `SET PROCEDURE TO <filename>`. Figure 21-6 illustrates the format.

EXTERNAL MEMORY

Another set of packaging problems arises not because we do not have enough RAM available but because of a lack of disk space. Again, this is partly a historical problem. For example, in 1961 the IBM 1405 disk drive had a capacity of only 400K. Early 1970s

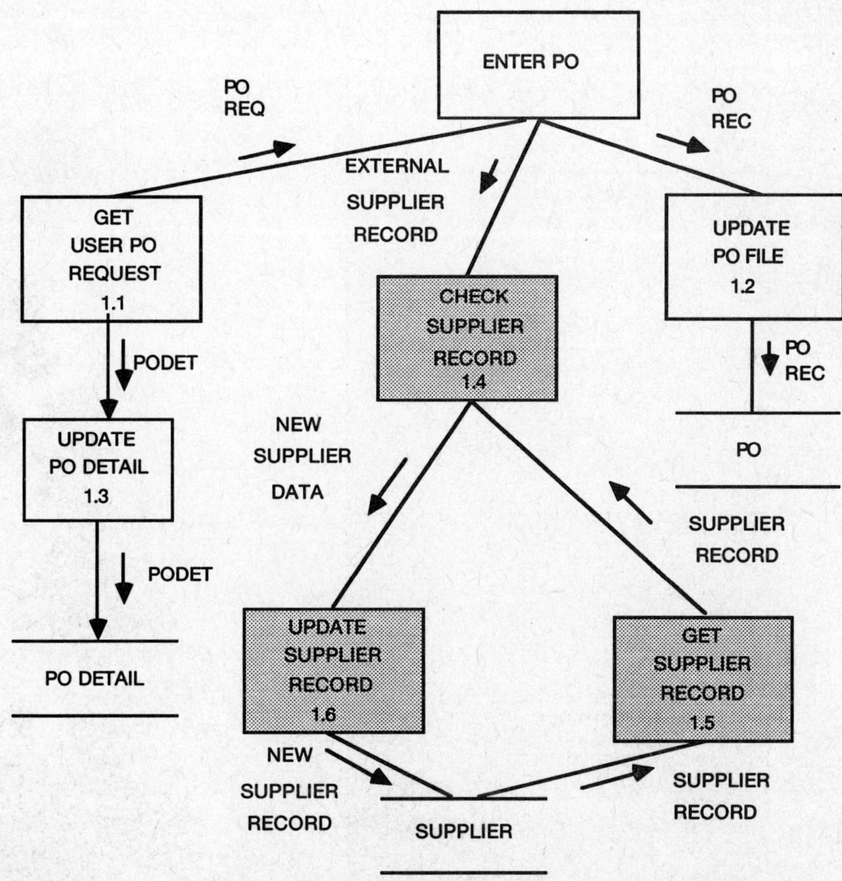

FIGURE 21-5 Structure chart for **ENTER PURCHASE ORDER**.

vintage hard disk drives for the DEC PDP-8 had capacities of only 32K: one-tenth the capacity of a low-density floppy disk! In 1977, an IBM 370/168 computer serving an entire organization had a capacity of only 32 megabytes on a disk—precisely the software design limit on disk capacity under MSDOS. Today an IBM 3098 will have more than 2000 megabytes.

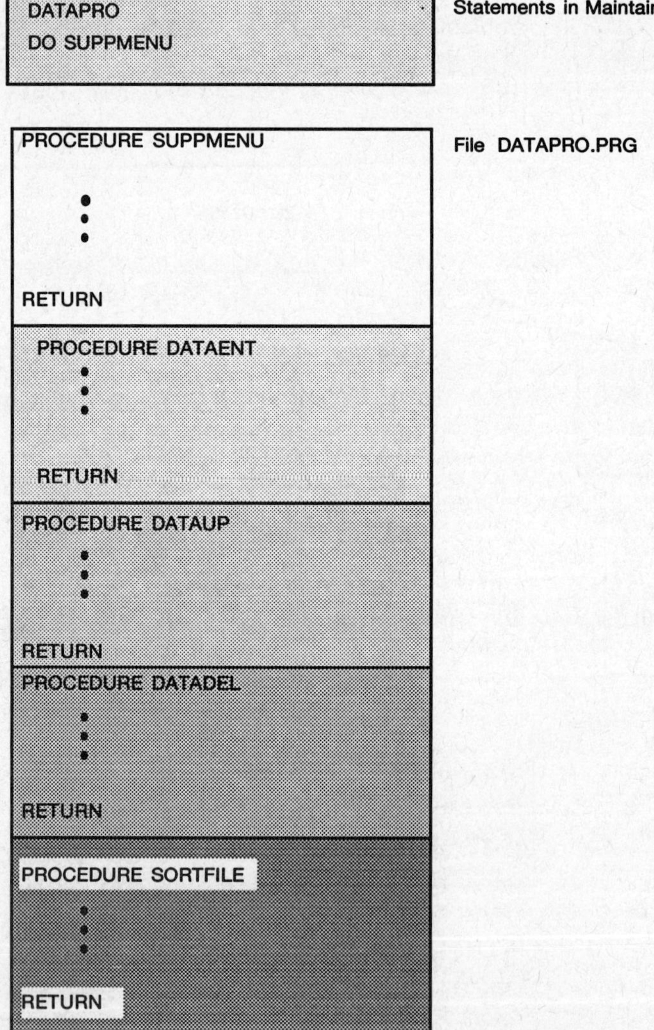

FIGURE 21-6 Format for dBASE III overlays.

In the personal computer world, most disk size limitations came from the use of floppy disks. Early Apples had less that 100K available per diskette, and early CP/M machines could hold about 250K on one of their 8-inch floppy disks. Hard disks were unavailable or cost more than the rest of the computer put together. Today, no serious personal computer users should be without a hard disk.

Current problems with disk capacity come from poor management of hard disks and from the 32-megabyte limit that is built into MSDOS versions previous to 4.0. Larger disks can be divided into several virtual (imaginary) smaller disks called partitions, but this is very inefficient. A better approach is to use several hard disks. Because the read/write heads can move independently, this allows far faster file access than the use of a single disk (something mainframe programmers have been taking advantage of for decades). dBASE allows the use of databases spread over several disk drives (just specify which drive each relation is on, for example, **`D:Supplier.DBF`**).

One problem that is very much with us today, especially for systems like dBASE, is disk access speed (or the lack thereof). There are two partial solutions—speed up the hardware or speed up the operating system access.

Speeding up the hardware may mean going to a faster processor or to a faster disk. Neither is likely to have much of an impact alone. For example, doubling the speed of the processor will mean that much of its time is spent waiting for the disk drive; getting a faster disk drive means that it will deliver data faster than the processor can receive it. Hence, putting a 80386 accelerator card into your XT chassis will not help a great deal, since the XT disk drive is so slow. Hardware upgrades should involve matching the processor speed with the disk speed, or they are likely to be wasted.

There are two approaches to speeding up file processing via software. The easiest is to increase the amount of RAM that your system uses to buffer files (Figure 21-7). With buffering, each disk access reads more data in than is needed and stores the excess in memory. Subsequent access to the data in memory is thousands of times faster than going out to the disk again. dBASE III will work with the default level of two buffers (dBASE IV will not), but 20 (the DOS command **BUFFERS=20** in your **CONFIG.SYS** file) work much better. The more memory you have, the more memory space you can afford to allocate to buffers; two buffers cost about 1K of memory.

An even better approach if you have enough memory is to use a disk caching extension to MSDOS. Such systems are basically super buffers; they take 64K or more of memory and use it to buffer disk activities. Especially if you have a machine with more than 640K of memory, it will help considerably to devote the excess (which MSDOS cannot use with dBASE anyway) to disk caching.

MACHINE SPEED

The above discussion about increasing disk speed is a subset of the overall problem of increasing program speed. Programs have never run fast enough. Historically, things were much worse; in 1961 the IBM 1401 mentioned above had a 1150-ns clock cycle time (about a 0.9 mHz clock speed). In 1977, the IBM 370/168 had a 150-ns cycle time (somewhat over a 6-mHz clock rate). Today, a high-end MSDOS machine based on the Intel 80386 chip has a 33 mHz clock rate, which is equivalent to a mainframe of a few years ago.

Today we need more speed because of the widespread use of graphics (which require far more processing and memory than do text-oriented interfaces), because of the use of much more user-friendly software, and because we tend to work with much larger amounts of data and do much more with that data. Equally important, current users are far less patient than they used to be and are not willing to wait until tomorrow for a sort to finish.

So, the $64K question is: How does one make sure that a program runs fast enough? The first part of the response is, make certain it works correctly first. It doesn't matter how fast it runs if it doesn't do the right thing! Thus, the reason for all of the design material presented thus far in the book.

The next question is, does the program need to run faster? In many instances, the answer is no. Always get the program running, make sure it works, and try it out first. Programmers tend to expect much more of their programs than do end users; often the user will be happy with an unoptimized program right out of the box.

Let us assume that the program **is** too slow. It is unlikely that the entire program is too slow; most likely only a few functions are dragging their feet. As a general rule, 20% of the code in any program accounts for 80% of the execution time. Only those functions that are too slow need to be speeded up.

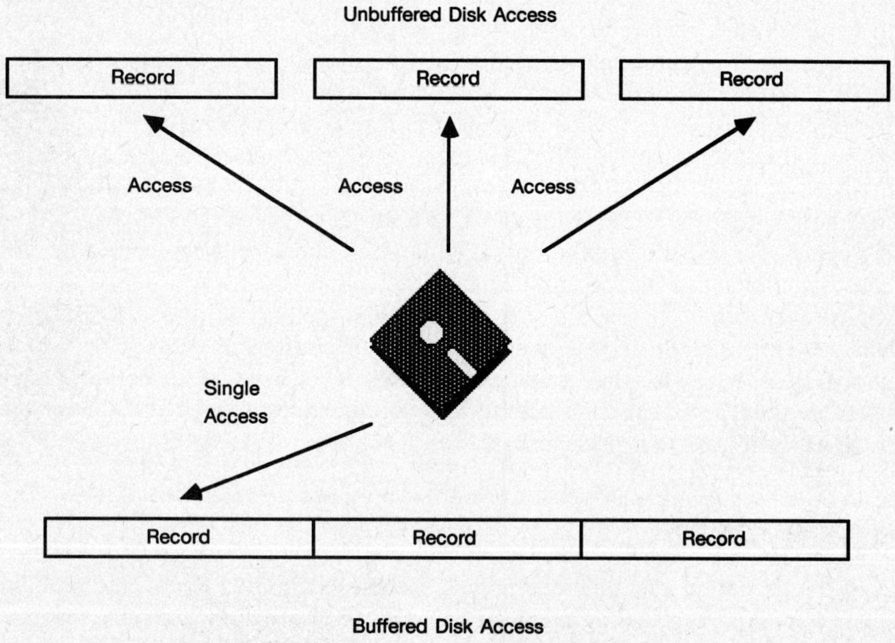

FIGURE 21-7 Disk buffering.

```
While not end of file
Do accrue interest
Endwhile

vs.

While not end of file
.
.
.
Statements to accrue interest
.
.
.
Endwhile
```

FIGURE 21-8 Unfactoring.

In applications using dBASE, most speed problems will be due to the disk speed limitations discussed in the preceding paragraphs. The first step is thus to package modules correctly and to make sure that file buffers are adequate. Often this will cure the problem. If not, more drastic measures may be needed.

With modular code, it is obvious which sections of the code are not executing rapidly enough because user functions correspond to modules. If it is not obvious, wait until the program is stuck in the slow function and hit the **Esc** key; dBASE will halt and tell you the name of the offending module. This means that usually you can speed up the program by dealing only with the few slowest modules. Some of the techniques you can use include (in approximate order of effort):

Unfactoring

Changing file access

Repackaging small files in memory

Performing high level operations procedurally

Changing languages

Changing hardware

Unfactoring means putting two or more modules into one. If procedure files are used, this does not help a great deal. However, if one of the modules is the body of a loop (Figure 21-8), unfactoring may improve performance substantially.

Changing file access is often a way to speed up performance dramatically. If you are using sequential file access (`LOCATE`), going to indexed access (`SEEK`) will often be all the modification needed to obtain adequate speed.

Repackaging small files in memory works, since many of the speed problems with dBASE III arise from the slowness of disk access. MSDOS allows one to set up a virtual disk drive using part of memory as an imaginary disk (the **VDISK** program in version 3 and higher of MSDOS; earlier versions can use various non-Microsoft virtual disk programs). Even a small virtual disk (64 to 128K) will allow you to store small files in memory, speeding up access to them dramatically. Remember, however, to save the contents to a real disk when you finish, since the contents of virtual disks vanish when the power is turned off or the machine is reset.

Performing high-level operations procedurally means writing code to do things like `UPDATE` and `JOIN`. Since the built-in dBASE III routines are intended to be general purpose, they are often slower than are custom programmed versions that do only what a particular problem requires.

Changing languages can be done at several levels. A good systems programmer can interface modules written in compiled third (or second) generation languages to dBASE programs. This is not a trivial task; if you know 8086 assembly language, the documentation for the `LOAD` command in the dBASE III manual will get you started. If you do not know assembly language, forget it.

More practical in most situations is using a compiler for the entire program. dBASE III is an interpreter, meaning that each statement is deciphered and executed as it is encountered. A compiler, which translates the entire program into machine code, is much faster. At the moment, Nantucket Software's Clipper and Wordtech's Quicksilver are products that produce machine code (the popular Foxbase+ produces an intermediate code that is faster than interpreted dBASE III, but not as fast as machine code. On the other hand, when disk access times are taken into account, it is often faster than its competitors). In addition, there are several products that convert dBASE III code into C, which can then be compiled into machine code. Current offerings tend to be advertised in *Dr. Dobb's Journal of Software Tools.*

Changing hardware is always a final (and expensive) option. Going to a faster machine is the bulldozer approach to speeding up one's programs!

SUMMARY

First, do it right. Optimization should not be part of the design task. Once the program is designed and coded, packaging and selective optimization of any modules that are too slow should get things up to speed.

QUESTIONS AND EXERCISES

1. Modern programmers worry about memory constraints because
   a. Personal computers are limited to very little memory by historical standards.
   b. Graphical user interfaces consume a great deal of memory.
   c. Modern computer architectures are less efficient than older ones.
   d. Modern languages like C are less memory efficient than was assembly language.

2. A load unit is
   a. A program segment loaded into memory and run separately from the rest of the program.
   b. A 64K segment of program in Intel machine architecture.
   c. A part of a program loaded into a memory page with virtual storage.
   d. The part of a program that is loaded into RAM by the loader.
3. An overlay is
   a. A section of a program loaded into memory and run separately from the rest of the program.
   b. The portion of a program loaded into virtual storage.
   c. The data segment of a program (as opposed to the code segment in Intel architectures).
   d. The way in which Unix provides multitasking on the same machines that can only do single tasking under MSDOS.
4. Overlays should be packages based on
   a. Structure charts.
   b. Entity-relationship diagrams.
   c. Action diagrams.
   d. Memory segments.
5. Overlays should maximize
   a. Coupling
   b. Cohesion.
   c. Fan-in.
   d. Fan-out.
6. A given overlay should contain modules that relate to a given
   a. Entity.
   b. Diagram.
   c. Transaction cycle.
   d. Control structure.
7. Which form of cohesion is appropriate for overlays but not for system designs?
   a. Sequential.
   b. Communicational.
   c. Procedural.
   d. Temporal.
8. dBASE programs can be made to run faster by
   a. Interpreting each module
   b. Predefining execution paths
   c. Packaging each module in a separate `.PRG` file.
   d. Packaging all modules from a load unit into a single procedure file.
9. dBASE programs can be made to run faster by storing
   a. All files in a single disk partition.
   b. Program files in one disk partition and data files in another.
   c. Related data files in different disk partitions.
   d. Related data files on different disks.

10. A virtual disk is
    a. RAM.
    b. A faster disk reassigned with the MSDOS ASSIGN command.
    c. A diskette remapped to a hard disk.
    d. Created with the FILES=x command in **CONFIG.SYS**.

DISCUSSION QUESTIONS

1. What techniques are available for making dBASE programs run faster?
2. Explain the difference between compilers and interpreters.
3. How does buffering speed up file processing?
4. Compare access speeds for sequential and indexed sequential file processing. Under what circumstances is each preferred?

EXERCISE

Attached are structure charts for a transaction processing system. Assume that the system uses dBASE III packaging rules by default (one module in memory at a time). Design a better system of load units. For each load unit, list the modules that are included, either textually or in structure chart format.

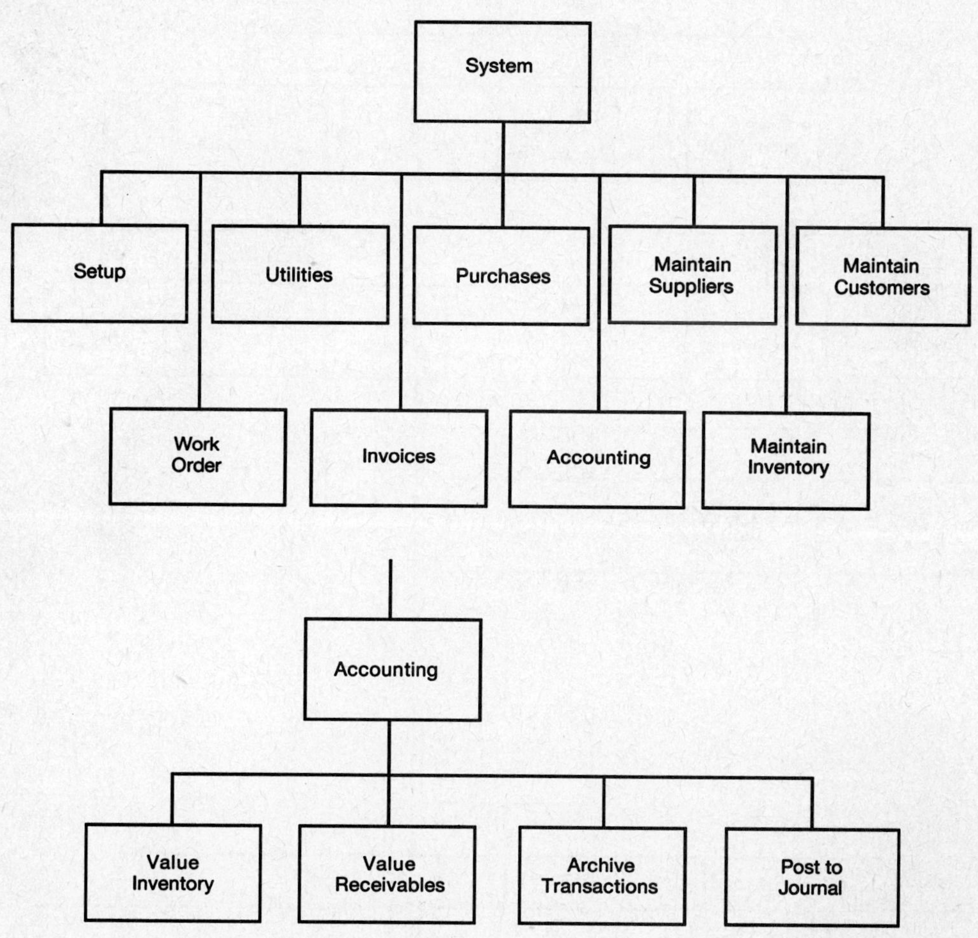
System
Setup
Utilities
Purchases
Maintain Suppliers
Maintain Customers
Work Order
Invoices
Accounting
Maintain Inventory
Accounting
Value Inventory
Value Receivables
Archive Transactions
Post to Journal

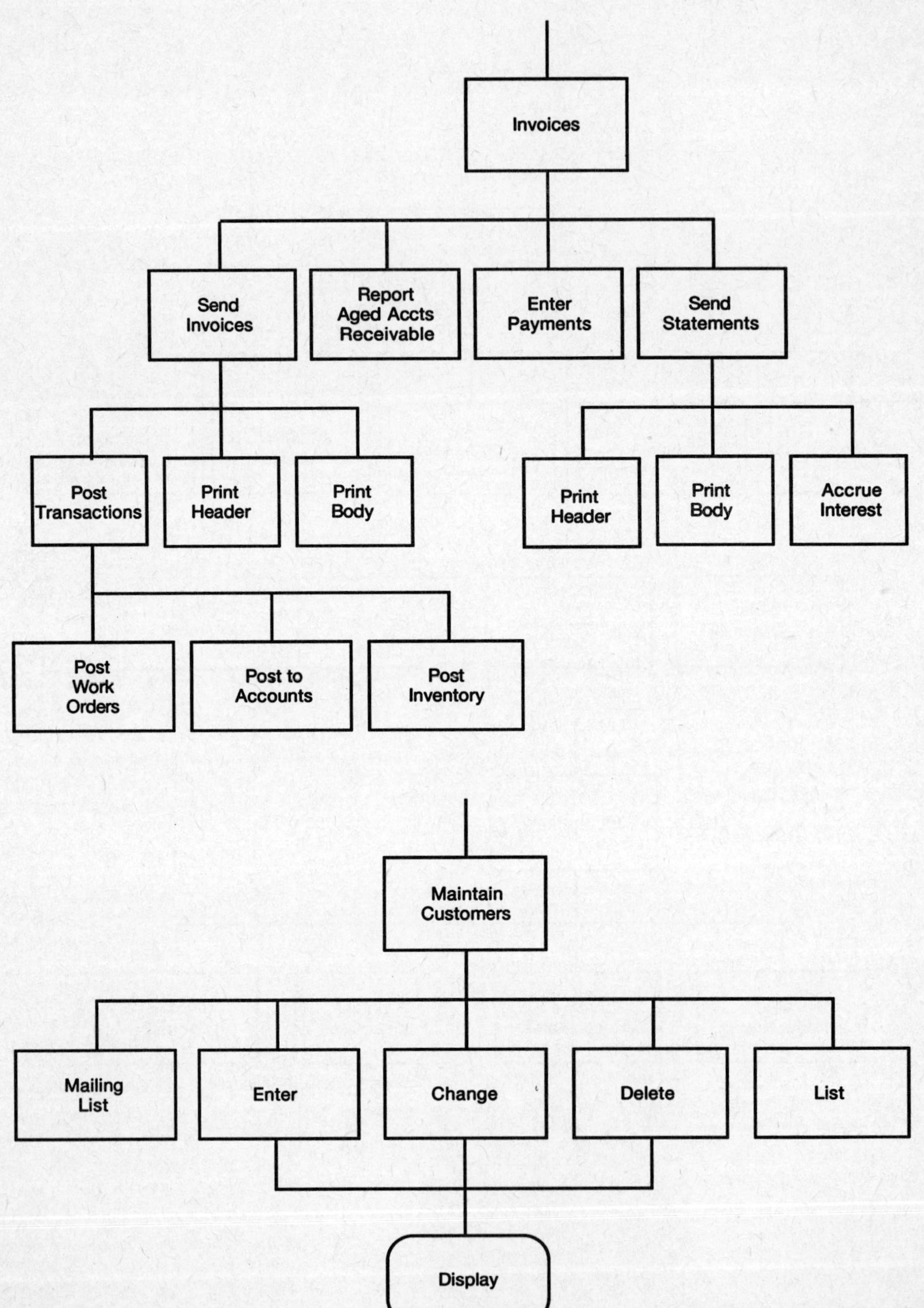

Invoices
Send Invoices
Report Aged Accts Receivable
Enter Payments
Send Statements
Post Transactions
Print Header
Print Body
Print Header
Print Body
Accrue Interest
Post Work Orders
Post to Accounts
Post Inventory
Maintain Customers
Mailing List
Enter
Change
Delete
List
Display

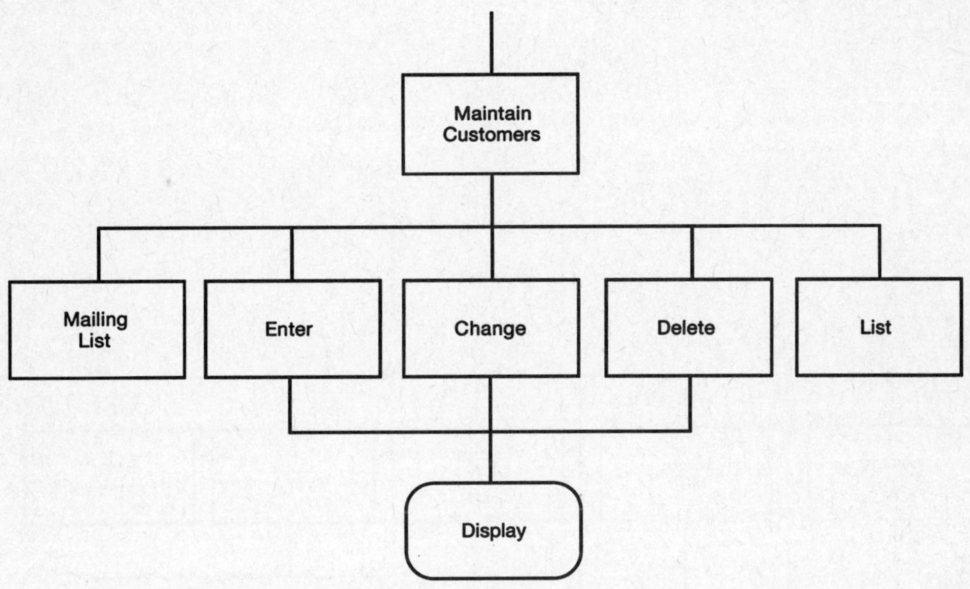
Maintain
Customers
Mailing
List
Enter
Change
Delete
List
Display

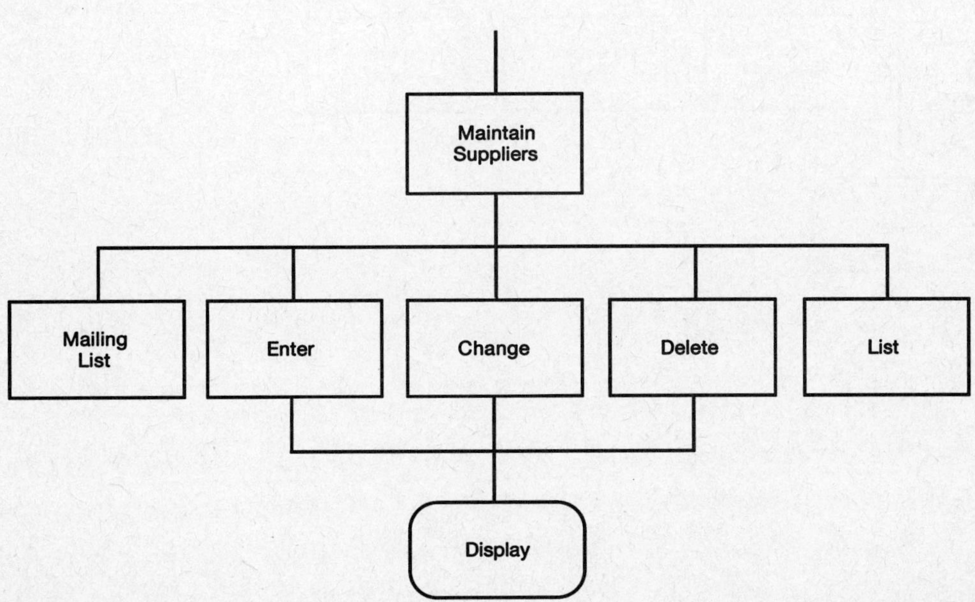
Maintain
Suppliers
Mailing
List
Enter
Change
Delete
List
Display

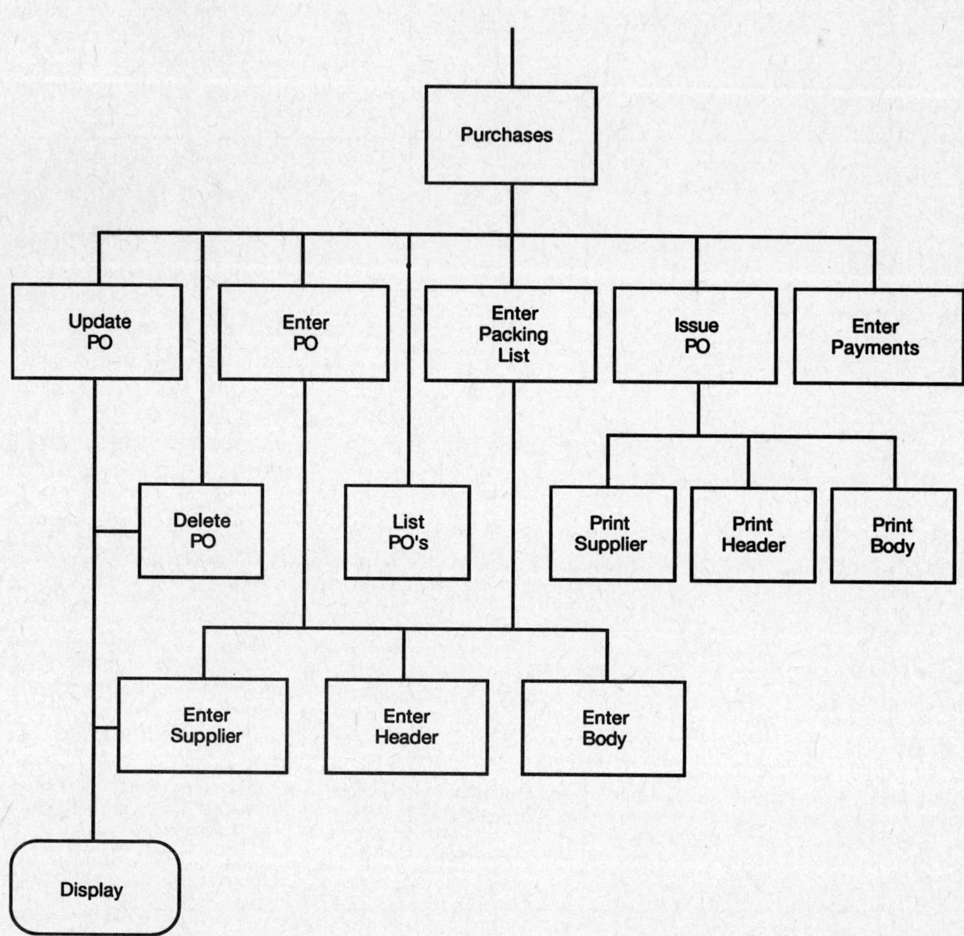
Purchases
Update PO
Enter PO
Enter Packing List
Issue PO
Enter Payments
Delete PO
List PO's
Print Supplier
Print Header
Print Body
Enter Supplier
Enter Header
Enter Body
Display

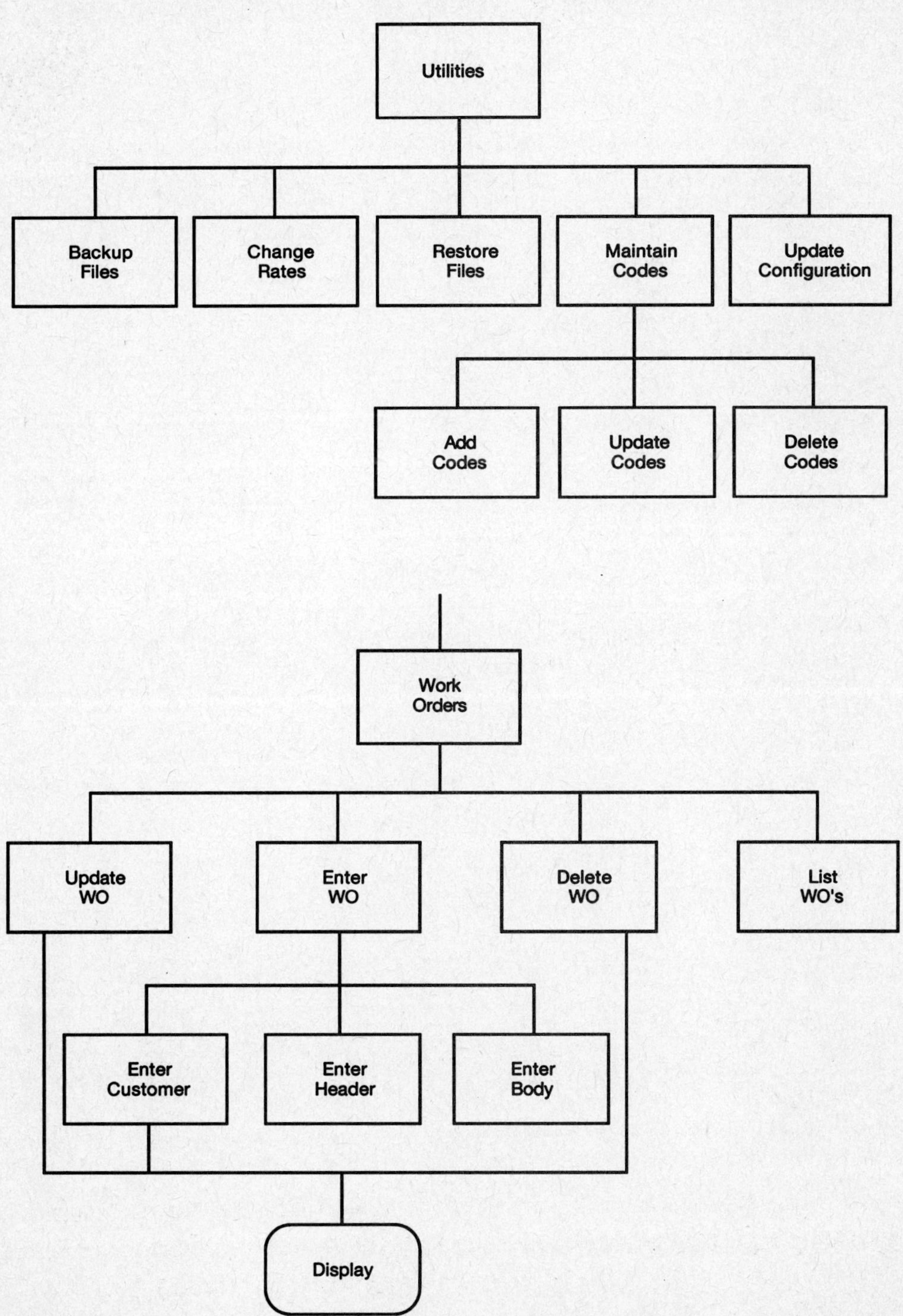
Utilities
Backup Files
Change Rates
Restore Files
Maintain Codes
Update Configuration
Add Codes
Update Codes
Delete Codes
Work Orders
Update WO
Enter WO
Delete WO
List WO's
Enter Customer
Enter Header
Enter Body
Display

EPILOGUE

In the last 21 chapters we have covered how to design computer-based systems, how to design the associated programs, how to code those programs, and how to put the parts of the programs together into working systems. The book has been, in fact, a whirlwind tour through the systems development life-cycle with brief stops at tools and techniques that are most useful to programmers using a fourth generation language for business programming in a database environment.

On the top shelf of a bookcase in my office is a 1957 text by Daniel McCracken entitled *Digital Computer Programming (Wiley 1957).* This book covered in 216 pages everything a graduate student or a practitioner needed to know about computer programming at the time. For anyone to even pretend to write such a comprehensive book today would be ludicrous.

There have been thousands of books written on computer programming in the last 35 years, and this one is built on its predecessors. Much history and controversy in the programming field has been hidden within these pages; careers both in academia and in industry have been built on issues to which this text devotes at best a page or two. Part of this is due to breadth of coverage; part of it is due to our exclusive focus on what techniques are most useful to programmers using a fourth generation language for business programming in a database environment. There is no question but that this treatment has been intensive.

Between 1983 and 1989, I taught program design in the American Assembly of Collegiate Schools of Business summer MIS Faculty Development Institute, which was an intensive training program for college-level faculty at smaller schools. These professors-turned-students covered three semester-length courses in five weeks. We even held class on the Fourth of July! Professor Gary Dickson, the director of the Institute, used to describe it as “drinking through a fire hose.”

This book preserves a bit of that “drinking through a fire hose.” Many universities take five semesters to cover the material that you have just studied (the courses have titles such as Cognitive Psychology, Accounting Systems, Database Management Systems, Program Design, and Fourth Generation Programming). Indeed, over the past 10 years, I have taught semester-length courses in all but the first topic (that of Chapter 2). Moreover, almost every chapter in this book is the subject of several book-length treatments by other authors. You have covered the material in significantly less depth than would be the case had you taken five courses and read 25 books, but I hope you have been able to integrate the material much better, so that in the future as you work more intensively with database management systems or programming you can fit your new knowledge into what you know already. There is never any shortage of details in the data processing field. The difficult thing is to know what details to pay attention to and how to integrate them with what you already know.

Your learning must continue, because although there is no question that the computer field is one of the most exciting places to be, one must run fast to keep up with the great rate of change. Most of the dBASE material in this text will be obsolete in five years; the principles of program design that you have been learning have a much longer life-cycle.

As this manuscript goes to the publisher, it is the beginning of a new decade and just before the vernal equinox, which the Romans, wiser than we, decided was the beginning of the new year. In central Alaska, site of the world's farthest north MIS program, we have left the arctic winter darkness behind and now have more daylight than anywhere to the south. By the time the book goes to press, we will have 24 hours of daylight each day. I hope some of that light gets passed on to the readers of this book.

John Lehman
College, Alaska
March, 1990

Appendix A

dBASE III PROGRAMMING CASE STUDY

Figure A-1 shows the structure chart for this case study. It maintains a supplier file using general-purpose modules. The top-level module **SUPPMENU** is a special-purpose module in that it identifies:

- the file to be maintained (SUPPLIER)
- the screen definition for file display and manipulation (**`supp.fmt`**, and **`suppdisp.fmt`**),
- the key field for sorting, searching, and indexing (SNAME)
- the index file (SUPPID).

All of these specifications are included in the supplier specification record in Figure A-1 and are implemented by assigning fixed values to memory variables at the beginning of **SUPPMENU**.

The next level of modules (**DATAENT, DATAUP**, and **DATADEL**) and the lower-level **SORTFILE** are general purpose—they will work with any relation (entity) that is specified in their parameters. The screen formats **`supp.fmt`**, and **`suppdisp.fmt`**, and the file SUPPLIER are, of course, specific to the maintain supplier file application.

In Figure A-2, the highlighted code shows where values are assigned to parameters in order to make the general purpose modules work with this specific application. Note in the middle of the `CASE` statement that the `DO` statements are coded to match their corresponding modules in Figures A-2 to A-6.

In Figures A-2 to A-6 the statements that work with values passed via parameters are highlighted. The "`&`" function in dBASE III tells the system to interpret the value of the variable rather than trying to use it directly as a file or field name. Thus, dBASE III would interpret `USE filename` to mean "open the file named **`filename.dbf`**." `USE & filename` means "open the file whose name is contained as the value of **`filename`**."

In Figure A-5, the format definition **`suppdisp.fmt`** is used rather than **`supp.fmt`** is because there is no data to be entered (no `GET` statements)—only data to be displayed (`SAY` statements).

By way of reminder, the code listed in Figures A-2 to A-6 will work with any dBASE III+ file provided that

- the file is defined and contains data
- display definitions have been defined both to get and to display data
- an index file has been set up
- the correct parameters are used in the calling program

The program will also work in dBASE IV; a dBASE IV program would usually use the dBASE IV built-in menu objects rather than creating a menu procedurally as in Figure A_2.

EXERCISE

Convert SUPPMENU into a general-purpose menu program. It should be driven by a higher-level, application-specific module as illustrated in Figure A-7.

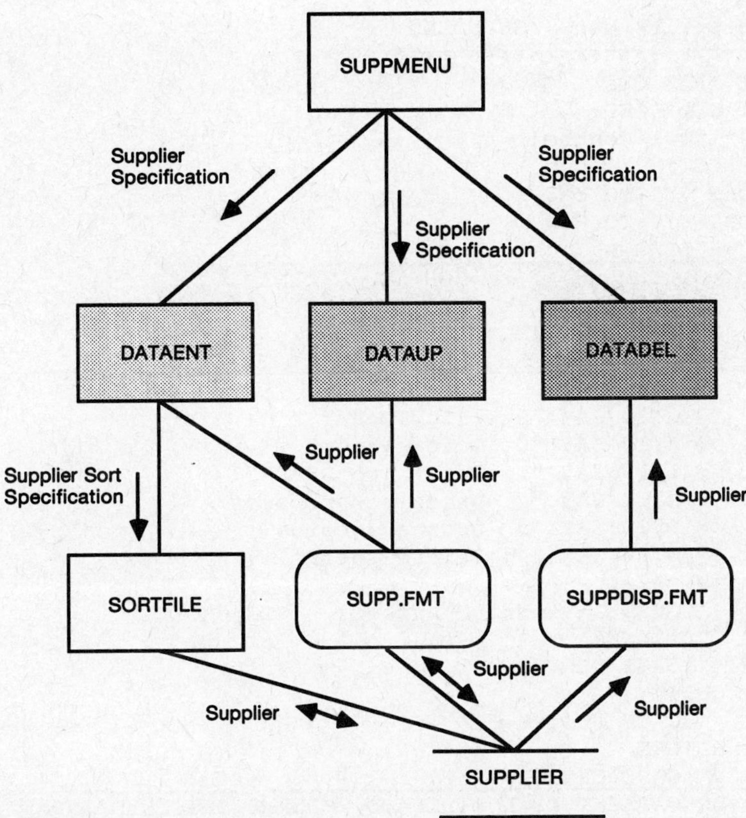

Supplier Specification = Filename + Format name + sort field + index file

Supplier Sort Specification = Filename + sort field + index file

FIGUREA_1 Structure chart for dBASE III example

```
****************************
* Supplier Menu  SUPPMENU  *
****************************
SET TALK OFF
SET BELL OFF
* Printer control
PUBLIC YN
STORE "Y" TO YN
STORE .T. TO RUN
DO WHILE RUN
    STORE "SUPPLIER.DBF" TO FILENAME
    STORE "SUPP.FMT" TO FMTNAME
    STORE "SNAME" TO SRTFIELD
    STORE "SUPPID.NDX" TO INDXFILE
    CLEAR
    @ 2,15 SAY "Supplier Menu"
    @ 5,10 SAY "0  Quit system"
    @ 6,10 SAY "1  Return to DBASE"
    @ 7,10 SAY "2  Enter new records"
    @ 8,10 SAY "3  Update record"
    @ 9,10 SAY "4  Delete record"
    ?
    ACCEPT '    Which number?  ' TO CHOICE
    DO CASE
      CASE CHOICE='0'
   QUIT
      CASE CHOICE='1'
   RETURN
      CASE CHOICE='2'
   DO DATAENT WITH FILENAME,FMTNAME,SRTFIELD,INDXFILE
      CASE CHOICE='3'
   DO DATAUP WITH FILENAME,FMTNAME,SRTFIELD,INDXFILE
      CASE CHOICE='4'
   STORE "SUPPDISP.FMT" TO FMTNAME
   DO DATADEL WITH FILENAME,FMTNAME,SRTFIELD,INDXFILE
    ENDCASE
LOOP
ENDDO
RETURN
```

FIGURE A_2 Code for supplier menu.

```
************************
*  Enter data DATAENT *
************************
PARAMETERS FILENAME,FMTNAME,SRTFIELD,INDXFILE
USE &FILENAME
DO WHILE .T.
     CLEAR
     APPEND BLANK
     SET FORMAT TO &FMTNAME
     READ
     CLOSE FORMAT
     @ 23,5 SAY  "Another? (Y or N) "
     @ 23,40 GET YN
     READ
     IF YN="N"
 DO SORTFILE WITH FILENAME,FMTNAME,SRTFIELD,INDXFILE
 RETURN
     ENDIF
  ENDDO T
RETURN
```

FIGURE A-3 Code for general purpose data entry (**DATAENT**).

```
*************************
*  Correct data  DATAUP *
*************************
PARAMETERS FILENAME,FMTNAME,SRTFIELD,INDXFILE
USE &FILENAME INDEX &INDXFILE
DO WHILE .T.
     CLEAR
     ACCEPT "Key name " TO SN
     GO TOP
     SEEK SN
     IF EOF()
        ? "Can't find that record"
     ELSE
         SET FORMAT TO &FMTNAME
         CLEAR
         READ
         CLOSE FORMAT
     ENDIF
     RELEASE SN
     @ 23,5 SAY  "Another record? (Y or N) "
     @ 23,40 GET YN
     READ
     IF YN="N"
        RETURN
     ENDIF


ENDDO T
RETURN
```

FIGURE A-4 Code for general purpose data update (**DATAUP**).

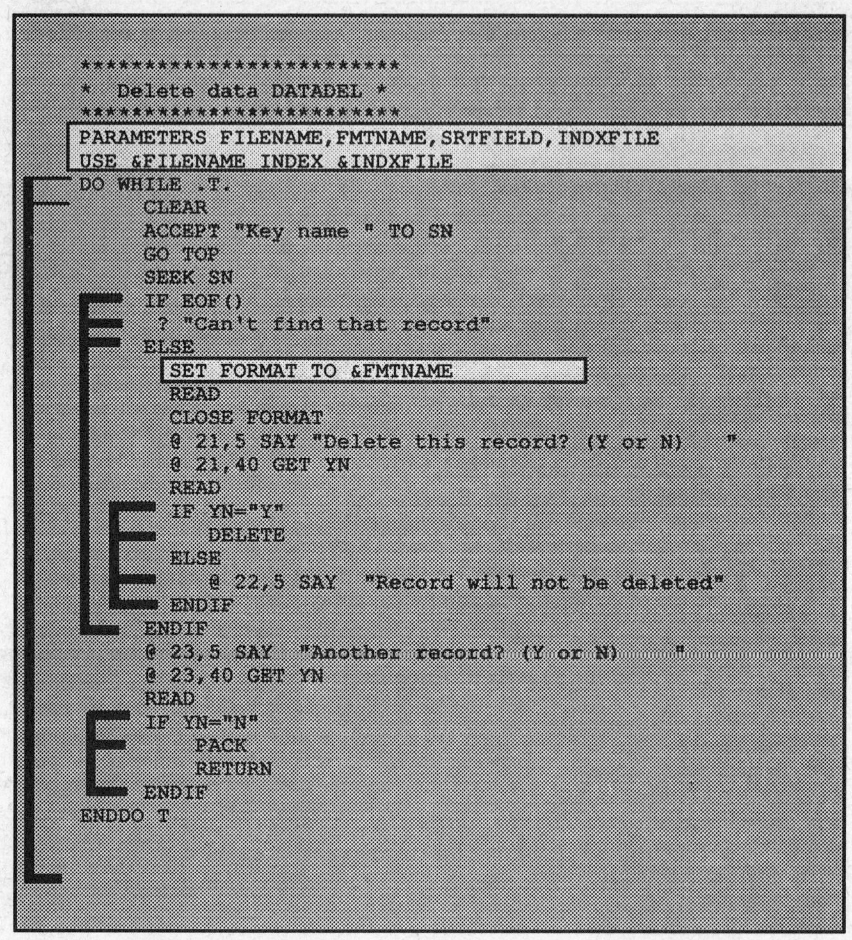

```
*************************
*  Delete data DATADEL *
*************************
PARAMETERS FILENAME,FMTNAME,SRTFIELD,INDXFILE
USE &FILENAME INDEX &INDXFILE
DO WHILE .T.
     CLEAR
     ACCEPT "Key name " TO SN
     GO TOP
     SEEK SN
     IF EOF()
      ? "Can't find that record"
     ELSE
       SET FORMAT TO &FMTNAME
       READ
       CLOSE FORMAT
       @ 21,5 SAY "Delete this record? (Y or N)    "
       @ 21,40 GET YN
       READ
       IF YN="Y"
          DELETE
       ELSE
          @ 22,5 SAY  "Record will not be deleted"
       ENDIF
     ENDIF
     @ 23,5 SAY  "Another record? (Y or N)      "
     @ 23,40 GET YN
     READ
     IF YN="N"
         PACK
         RETURN
     ENDIF
ENDDO T
```

FIGURE A-5 Code for general-purpose date deletion (**DATADEL**).

```
***********************
*  Sort file SORTFILE *
***********************
PARAMETERS FILENAME,FMTNAME,SRTFIELD,INDXFILE
USE &FILENAME
  STORE "Y" TO YN
  ACCEPT "Sort file? (Y or N) " TO YN
  IF YN="Y"
     SORT ON &SRTFIELD TO SXXX
     USE
     RENAME &FILENAME TO SYYY.DBF
     RENAME SXXX.DBF TO &FILENAME
     DELETE FILE SYYY.DBF
     USE &FILENAME
     DELETE FILE &INDXFILE
     INDEX ON &SRTFIELD TO &INDXFILE
  ENDIF
RETURN
```

FIGURE A-6 Code for general purpose sort and index (**SORTFILE**).

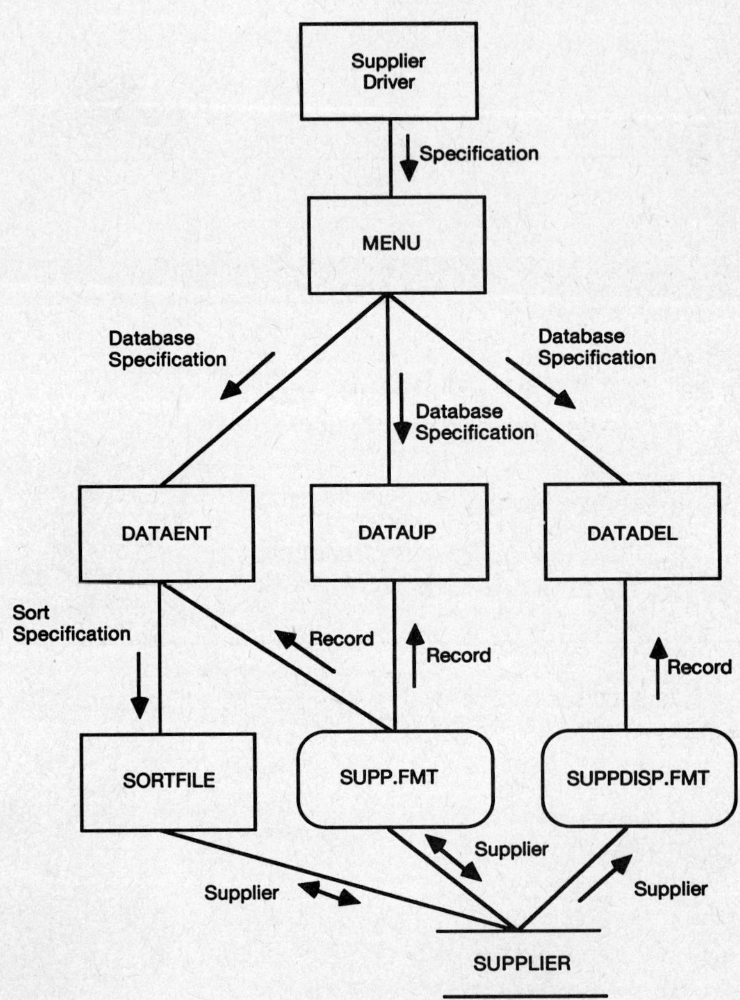

Specification = Filename + Format name + sort field + index file + Menu name

Sort Specification = Filename + sort field + index file

FIGURE A-7 Structure chart for general purpose menu-driven system.

SUBJECT INDEX